Handbook on Brand and Experience Management

Handbook on Brand and Experience Management

Edited by

Bernd H. Schmitt

Center on Global Brand Leadership, Columbia Business School, USA

and

David L. Rogers

Center on Global Brand Leadership, Columbia Business School, USA

Edward Elgar

Cheltenham, UK • Northampton, MA, USA

Published by
Edward Elgar Publishing Limited
The Lypiatts
15 Lansdown Road
Cheltenham
Glos GL50 2JA
UK

Edward Elgar Publishing, Inc.
William Pratt House
9 Dewey Court
Northampton
Massachusetts 01060
USA

A catalogue record for this book
is available from the British Library

Library of Congress Control Number: 2008937107

PEFC
PEFC/16-33-111
CATG-PEFC-052
www.pefc.org

ISBN 978 1 84720 007 5

Printed and bound in Great Britain by MPG Books Ltd, Bodmin, Cornwall

Contents

Contributors

Christian Blümelhuber is Associate Director of The Center on Global Brand Leadership, Munich, Germany

J. Joško Brakus is Assistant Professor of Marketing at the William E. Simon Graduate School of Business Administration of the University of Rochester, USA

Benjamin Brudler is Research Coordinator at The Center on Global Brand Leadership, Munich, Germany

Dae Ryun Chang is Professor of Marketing and Associate Dean at the Graduate School of Business, Yonsei University in Seoul, Korea

Tanya L. Chartrand is Assistant Professor of Marketing and Psychology at The Fuqua School of Business at Duke University, USA

Ravi Dhar is George Rogers Clark Professor of Management and Marketing and Director of the Center for Customer Insights at the Yale School of Management, USA

Basil G. Englis is a Richard Edgerton Professor of Business Administration and Chair of the Department of Marketing at the Campbell School of Business at Berry College in Rome, Georgia, USA

Franz-Rudolf Esch is University Professor for Business Management and Head of Marketing at the Justus-Liebig-University in Gießen, Germany, Director of the Institute of Brand and Communication Research, vice-president of the German Marketing Association and Founder of the Consultancy firm ESCH. The Brand Consultants

Rosellina Ferraro is an Assistant Professor of Marketing at the Robert H. Smith School of Business at the University of Maryland, USA

Gavan J. Fitzsimons is an Associate Professor of Marketing at The Fuqua School of Business at Duke University, USA

Susan Fournier is Associate Professor of Marketing at Boston University School of Management, USA

Francisco Guzmán is Professor of Marketing at ESADE Business School in Barcelona, Spain

Deborah J. MacInnis is Charles and Ramona I. Hilliard Professor of Marketing at the University of Southern California, USA

Anton Meyer is Chair of Marketing at Munich University, Germany

Tom Meyvis is Associate Professor of Marketing at Stern School of Business of New York University, USA

Isa Moll is a Ph.D. candidate in the Department of Marketing Management at ESADE Business School in Barcelona, Spain

Jordi Montaña is a lecturer in the Department of Marketing Management at ESADE Business School in Barcelona, Spain

Noriyuki Nakai is the Deputy General Manager of International Account Management for ADK Inc, Japan

C. Whan Park is Joseph A. DeBell Professor of Marketing at the University of Southern California, USA

Joseph Priester is Assistant Professor of Marketing at the University of Southern California, USA

Rajagopal Raghunathan is Assistant Professor of Marketing at McCombs School of Business at the University of Texas at Austin, USA

David L. Rogers is the Director of the Center on Global Brand Leadership at Columbia Business School, USA

Hayes Roth is the Chief Marketing Officer of Landor Associates, USA

Bernd H. Schmitt is Robert D. Calkins Professor of International Business at Columbia Business School in New York, USA and the Executive Director of the Center on Global Brand Leadership

Joanna Seddon is the Executive Vice President of Millward Brown Optimor, USA

Donald Sexton is Professor of Marketing at Columbia University Business School and President of the Arrow Group, Ltd.®, USA

Michael R. Solomon is a Human Sciences Professor of Consumer Behavior in the Department of Consumer Affairs, College of Human Sciences, at Auburn University and the Director of Mind/Share®, USA

Sanjay Sood is an Assistant Professor of Marketing at the John E. Anderson Graduate School of Management at University of California, Los Angeles, USA

Lia Zarantonello is a Post Doctoral Research Fellow at Università L. Bocconi, Milano, Italy

Shi Zhang is an Associate Professor of Marketing at the John E. Anderson Graduate School of Management at University of California, Los Angeles, USA

Preface

Since the literature on brand management first arose in the 1990s, a set of conceptual frameworks and concepts have developed that have permeated academic research as well as brand management across industries. These include: the concept of brand equity, brand associations, brand personality, brand extensions, brand valuation, and the like.

The purpose of this handbook is not to retread these paths, but rather to explore new and emerging directions in both research and practice. While the reader will find discourse and critique of the basic frameworks and concepts, the focus will be on exploring new concepts such as brand attachment, brand permission and brand meaning; new contextual factors such as digital convergence, target group multiplicity, and the rise of experience economies; and new research domains such as empirical tests of consumer experiences, incidental brand exposure, and brand naming.

In particular, the last 10 years have seen the rise of new concepts around the paradigm of brand and customer experiences, as evidenced by a variety of academic and trade publications on the subject. These concepts are being utilized within the branding and marketing functions of many companies and agencies and are now entering the academic field as well.

The focus on customer experience has led a shift away from an analytical and largely cognitive view of branding that views customers as information-processors towards a more holistic view of customer value that encompasses rational and emotional benefits. Obviously, this shift in perspective has had a profound impact on the practice and meaning of branding. In some cases, experience is framed in relation to a new, broader vision of branding – for example that the customer experience is what shapes all perceptions and value of the brand. In other cases, experience is used as its own paradigm, with branding (traditionally defined more narrowly as visual identity, advertising and communications) being one domain of the customer experience, along with other domains such as innovation and service interactions.

We therefore chose to focus this handbook on perspectives on brand management, on experience management, and perspectives that combine the two.

The handbook encompasses a diverse set of approaches in its five parts:

- Part I, 'Concepts and frameworks of brand management', presents the latest academic research offering new frameworks for understanding brand management
- Part II, 'Managerial concepts', brings to bear the researcher's perspective on current tools in practice by brand managers today, linking theory and practice
- Part III, 'Concepts and frameworks of experience management', presents new research and conceptual frameworks for understanding and managing customer experiences
- Part IV, 'Empirical studies and scales for brand and experience management', presents recent empirical research and scale development in both brand and experience management

- Part V, 'Practitioner perspectives', presents articles by practitioners involved in brand and experience management, focusing on practical, managerial and organizational best practices

We hope the reader will find the breadth of these contributions useful in gathering new theoretical concepts to test, new methodologies to put to use, and new questions to stimulate further research.

PART I

Concepts and frameworks of brand management

In this part, the authors present a variety of new concepts and frameworks of brand management. Based on recent academic research, these concepts and frameworks address a variety of branding issues and can be applied directly to practitioners' branding challenges. In addition, they identify and describe new areas for continued research to further our understanding of brand management.

Park, MacInnis and Priester present the concept of 'brand attachment'. They examine how brand attachment can be used to develop and establish strong brand relationships, and offer the 'strategic brand exemplar' as a management tool.

Meyvis and Dhar examine how 'brand permission' determines whether new initiatives – from line extensions, to new communications strategies, to changes of target segments – are viewed as appropriate by consumers.

Fournier, Solomon and Englis address the role of 'brand meaning' (the collection of associations and beliefs that a consumer has about the brand) in the creation of brand equity via brand strength, focusing on three types of brand resonance and a variety of facets which create these types.

Esch analyzes how brand identity is used to guide successful branding, and presents the 'brand steering wheel' to navigate brand benefits, tonalities, iconography and attributes.

1. Brand attachment and a strategic brand exemplar

C. Whan Park, Deborah J. MacInnis and Joseph Priester

BRAND ATTACHMENT AND MANAGEMENT OF A STRATEGIC BRAND EXEMPLAR

Despite years of research, debate still rages over the meaning, boundaries and measures of brand equity. This lack of consensus is reflected in the numerous measures and theoretical perspectives (for example, customer-based, product market-based, and financial marketplace-based) that underlie the brand equity construct (see, for example, Ailawadi et al., 2003). For example, a consensus has not emerged on whether brand equity refers to the value of a brand name or the value of a brand which is denoted by a brand name. Such lack of definitional clarity has serious measurement implications as different definitions of the term 'brand equity' would clearly imply different measures. For example, the net difference approach between a target brand and a fictitious/generic/private label brand reflects the value of a brand name, not the value of a brand.

Lack of clarity notwithstanding, a consensus does seem to emerge regarding the notion that strong brand equity is contingent on a powerful relationship between the customer and the brand. In the context described here, the term 'brand' is used broadly to refer to a branded product (for example, Diet Coke), service (for example, UPS), retailer (for example, Gap Kids), company (for example, IBM), person (for example, a politician, celebrity), organization (for example, the Boy Scouts), group (for example, a sports team), or place (for example, a city brand). As Figure 1.1 shows, brand–customer relationships vary on a strength dimension, from weaker forms involving simple liking and purchase to stronger forms involving customers' desire to stay in brand relationships (for example repeat purchase, resisting negative brand information or advances of competitors), actively promoting the brand (for example, through positive word-of-mouth), sacrificing their own resources for the brand (paying a price premium), and/or postponing purchase when the brand is unavailable. Given this hierarchy of behaviors, brand managers face a critical task of attempting to move a brand–customer relationship strength hierarchy so as to foster strong brand equity.

Unfortunately, little is known about the factors that underlie strong brand relationships. This chapter attempts to glean insight into such factors by using the theoretical construct of brand attachment. Below, we define the construct of brand attachment. While other constructs may prove relevant as well, we believe they pose some inherent problems given state-of-the-art knowledge. For example, we ignore the construct of attitude valence, given the limited empirical support for the attitude–behavior relationship (Eagly

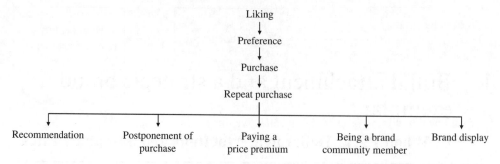

Figure 1.1   Consumers' behavioral hierarchy

and Chaiken, 1993). We avoid the term 'attitude strength' given the divergent views about the concept and how it should be measured (Converse, 1995; Fazio, 1989; Wegener et al., 1995). We also avoid a focus on the construct of commitment, regarding it as an outcome of a strong customer–brand relationship as opposed to a construct that describes the relationship itself.

Given a lack of focus on the brand attachment construct, it comes as no surprise that little research has examined the antecedents of strong brand attachments. We suggest that such attachments are contingent on the kind of customer goals enabled through brand–customer interactions and the kinds of marketing activities that link customers' goals to the brand. As Figure 1.2 shows, we posit that strong brand–customer attachments derive from the brand's success in creating strong brand self-connections by pleasing, enriching, and/or enabling the self. These successes are themselves contingent on the effectiveness of marketing activities that use affect, typicality, vividness and rich information to foster a strong brand–self connection.

The remaining sections of the chapter describe the attachment construct, its relationship to brand equity, the nature of brand–self connections, and the role of strategic brand exemplars on these connections. Theoretical and managerial issues follow in the discussion section.

THE ATTACHMENT CONSTRUCT

What is Attachment?

Bowlby's (1982) pioneering work on attachment in the realm of parent–infant relationships proposed that human infants are born with a repertoire of behaviors (attachment behaviors) designed by evolution to assure proximity to supportive others (attachment figures) so as to secure protection from physical and psychological threats, promote affect regulation, and foster healthy exploration (see also Mikulincer and Shaver (2005) and Berman and Sperling (1994) for the discussion).

Bowlby's efforts sought to understand the adverse influences of inadequate maternal care during early childhood on personality development (Bowlby, 1988). He related attachment to individual differences (that is, attachment style) that are derived from the interaction between the self and others (Bowlby, 1973, 1988). He defined an attachment

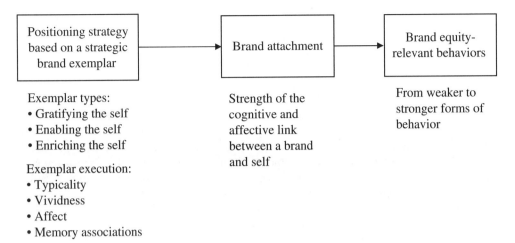

Figure 1.2   A schematic representation of the determinants and effects of brand attachment

as an *emotion-laden target-specific bond* between a person and a specific object that varies in strength. Some individuals exhibit a weak bond with a given object; others exhibit a strong bond.

Brand Attachment

While research in psychology has tended to concentrate on people's attachments to other individuals (for example infants, mothers, romantic mates – see Weiss, 1988), extant research in marketing (Belk, 1988; Kleine et al., 1993; Mehta and Belk, 1991) suggests that such attachments can extend beyond the person–person relationship context. That research shows that consumers can develop attachments to gifts (Mick and DeMoss, 1990), collectibles (Slater, 2001), places of residence (Hill and Stamey, 1990), brands (Schouten and McAlexander, 1995), other types of special or favorite objects (Ball and Tasaki, 1992; Kleine et al., 1995; Richins, 1994; Wallendorf and Arnould, 1988), or sports teams. For example, sports fans – or rather sports fanatics – have been shown to bet against all odds on their favorite teams, which is not rational behavior (Babad, 1987).

Moreover, while the attachment concept has been studied in numerous contexts (romantic relationship, kinship, friendship, and so on) and from varying perspectives (for example, individual difference vs. relationship perspectives) (see Baldwin et al., 1996, for more discussion), we approach attachment from the perspective of an individual's *relationship* with the brand as the attachment object. In this context, we define attachment as *the strength of the cognitive and affective link between a consumer and a brand*. It denotes a psychological *state* of mind in which a strong cognitive and affective bond connects a brand to an individual in such a way that the brand is an extension of the self. This relationship perspective differs sharply from a trait perspective in which attachment reflects an individual difference variable characterizing one's systematic style of connection across relationships (that is, secure, anxious-ambivalent, and avoidant styles).

Consistent with some prior literature, brand attachment is characterized by a strong linkage or connectedness between the brand and the self (cf. Kleine et al., 1993; Schultz et al., 1989). Evidence of the connection is revealed by indexical (personalized) and affect-based representations of the brand as part of the consumer's self-concept. Such representations are highly salient and are automatically retrieved when activating self-concept of the consumer (Greenwald and Pratkanis, 1984).

Consumer behavior researchers have recognized the importance of the consumer's self-concept and its relationship to brands and marketable entities. For example, Belk (1988) reveals the extension of the self into things such as people, places, experiences, ideas, beliefs and material possession objects. Kleine and Baker (2004) suggest that self-extension processes decommodify, singularize and personalize particular material objects symbolizing autobiographical meanings: adult possessions may become 'contaminated' through constant or habitual use and dependency (for example, one's 'faithful' wristwatch or constantly worn piece of jewelry), endowing it with personal meaning connecting self and object (Belk, 1988). Statements like 'mine', 'part of me', 'reflecting me', 'expressing me', 'an extension of myself', 'aesthetically appealing to me', or 'emotionally relating to me' all reflect different aspects of a brand–self connection.

A person or an object, including a brand, becomes connected to the self when it is included in one's self memory. The interesting question is why some objects and persons become part of one's self memory. Aron et al. (2005) offer a motivational view toward the inclusion of others in the self memory: the main benefit of including another in the self would be the resources aspect. As the relationship is forming, the other person makes his or her resources (social, knowledge, material, and so on) readily available to the self. This in turn leads to a cognitive organization that makes that other's resources seem as if they were one's own, and thus coming to take on the other's perspectives and identities as one's own.

Prior research on brand relationships has indirectly touched on the construct of brand attachment. For example, Fournier (1998) identified 15 types of consumer–brand relationships. While these relationships are described along several dimensions including love, commitment, intimacy and passion, feelings of attachment lie at the 'core of all strong brand relationships' (Fournier, 1998, p. 363). Hence, one can ascertain that strong consumer–brand (and consumer–consumer) relationships, such as committed partnerships, best friendships and secret affairs, are likely to be characterized by strong degrees of attachment. Others, such as enslavements, arranged marriages and marriages of convenience are likely to be characterized by low levels of attachment. The attachment construct may thus serve as a useful higher order construct that discriminates among the relationships identified by Fournier.

Importantly, attachments differ from evaluation-based responses like brand attitudes and have effects that are more powerfully related to sustained, cross-time consumer brand behaviors and exchanges (Thomson et al., 2005). While consumers who are strongly attached to a brand undoubtedly have strong and positive attitudes toward it, not all strong and positive brand attitudes are indicative of strong customer–brand relationships. As we describe later, past research in human–human attachment shows that the attachment construct accounts for higher-order behaviors associated with commitment to a relationship. We therefore speculate that the attachment construct may offer a new theoretical perspective toward consumer behavior that goes beyond the traditional attitude construct and that accounts for the higher order consumer behaviors in the exchange context (between a firm and consumers).

Furthermore, while attachment bears some similarity to the commitment construct, we regard commitment and attachment as separate constructs. While attachment describes the strength of the cognitive and affective bond linking an individual with an entity, we view commitment in a manner analogous to Dwyer et al. (1987), who define it as an implicit or explicit pledge to remain in a relationship in the future. Such pledges can be based on attachment. But they may also be driven by other factors associated with the costs of leaving a relationship. For example, one may be committed to a partner or an organization simply because of a lack of other alternatives or because severing the relationship would prove too costly. In this circumstance, commitment is not driven by attachment. Strong attachment, however, should predict a pledge to continue with a relationship and bring with that pledge the emotional energy that creates a satisfying long-term relationship, including stronger forms of brand equity-relevant behaviors (see Figure 1.2).

Why is Attachment Important to Brand Equity Management?

Though space limitations preclude a complete detailing of our logic, we posit that attachment is a critical driver of the financial value of the brand to the firm – 'brand equity.' According to various brand metrics (Ailawadi et al., 2003; Interbrand model), such value is typically affected by the brand's (a) unit price (P_t), (b) unit marketing costs (MC_t) and (c) the number of units sold (Q). These three components are directly tied to and reflect the nature and intensity of customers' attachment and commitment to a brand.

The stronger the customers' attachment to the brand, the higher the unit price that the brand can bear – that is, attachment is related to customers' willingness to pay a price premium (Thomson et al., 2005; van Lange et al., 1997). Strong attachments also induce a devaluation of competing alternatives (Johnson and Rusbult, 1989), a willingness to forgive its mishaps (McCullough et al., 1998), a willingness to inhibit impulses to react destructively when being confronted with a partner's potentially destructive act (Rusbult et al., 1991), and willingness to stay in the relationship (Drigotas and Rusbult, 1992). These intentions and behaviors all influence the stability of the Q component and reduce the costs of customer retention. Finally, strong attachments toward brands or individuals impact trust of a partner, willingness to promote positive word-of-mouth, and a relative insensitivity to the reciprocity by one's partner (for example, active marketing effort by a brand to reinforce or appreciate its customers' loyalty) (Thomson, et al., 2005; Wieselquist et al., 1999). Such outcomes should both impact the Q component and make the MC component more cost efficient.

WHAT CAUSES ATTACHMENT?

Bases for Attachment

Prior research suggests that the desire to make strong attachments to particular human others serves a basic human need (Ainsworth et al., 1978; Bowlby, 1973; Reis and Patrick,

1996), beginning from a child's attachment to his/her mother (Bowlby, 1982) and continuing through the adult stage with romantic relationships (Hazan and Shaver, 1994), kinships and friendships (Trinke and Bartholomew, 1997). In the human infant, attachment forms when a primary caregiver is responsive to the needs of the infant on a continuing and consistent basis. For an infant, such needs include comfort, sustenance (derived from food), sleep, sensory gratification (oral, gustatory, tactile auditory, visual), and the lack of sensory and biological discomforts. They also include security derived from knowing who is and is not part of one's group and who can be relied on for care. As an infant grows, attachments enable the infant to differentiate the self from the primary care-giver, engage in exploration, and master independent experiences.

In an analogous way, we propose (see Figure 1.2) that brand attachments form when brands satisfy key aspects of the self: (a) pleasing and comforting the self, (b) enriching the self, and (c) enabling the self. Thus, a consumer perceives a brand as being personally significant and connects the brand to the self when it (a) *pleases and comforts* the self by providing sensory, hedonic or aesthetic pleasure, or removing such dimensions of pain or (b) psychologically *comforts* the self by offering relief and security (Mikulincer and Shaver, 2005). They become attached when the brand *enriches* the self by representing, defining or expressing the actual or desired self (Kleine and Baker, 2004). And they become attached when the brand enables mastery experiences that help the individual achieve other goals relevant to the self.

Creating Strong Attachments in Marketing

Brand marketing activities can foster attachment and create strong self–brand connections to the extent that such activities can additively and jointly foster the three self-related associations. The stronger each of the self–brand connections, the stronger the consumer's attachment to the brand.

Gratifying the Self through Aesthetic/Hedonic Experience

Aesthetics portrayed through various brand elements are important elements in creating the brand–self connection. Here, the brand–self connection is based on one's appreciation of a brand's aesthetic qualities and attractiveness. A brand, through these aesthetic qualities, offers important resources such as pleasing the consumers' selves, with which they can maintain an optimistic and hopeful stance regarding daily distress management, keep emotional stability, and cope with life problems (Mikulincer and Shaver, 2005). For example, people's fascination and obsession with Leonard da Vinci's Mona Lisa, Van Gogh's sunflower painting, or even with that adorable Hello Kitty logo fit with the brand–self connection through the perceptual-sensory aesthetics. The so-called environmental branding through a combination of mood, look and sensory perception created by the environment and the front-line personnel can literally delight the five senses and provide memorable brand experiences. This was demonstrated by the Disney Store, which displays a full-scale Mickey Mouse and other magical characters to bring the Disney brand to life. Music with a nostalgic appeal elicits memories about gratifying aspects of adolescence that bring back the aura of happy past days, old neighborhoods, former love relationships, and sporting events (Kaplan, 1987). The coordination of the sensory elements of a brand is particularly important for eliciting the emotional connection between self and a brand. *Perceptual-sensory aesthetics thus gratify the self.*

Enriching the Self through Brand Concept Internalization

A brand can enrich the self by offering consumers core ideology or values. Enrichment can also occur thorough the symbolic representation of a brand. Some brands take on symbolic meaning, representing who one is or wants to be, and perhaps communicating some aspect of self to others. Other brands also offer consumers identities through their affiliation with a group or an entity (for example, alumni, brand community). Identification is a key process for this enrichment. A person derives *meaning* from close relationships and other life goals that reflect his or her core beliefs, values and role identities (Lydon et al., 2005; Shavitt and Nelson, 2000).

For example, many owners of Harley-Davidson motorcycles report being deeply attached to their bikes since the values of freedom and machismo, values that are intrinsic parts of the owners' desired selves, resonate through the Harley brand. Many lifestyle brands transcend the product-only customer relationship and have developed emotional and long-term bonds with a target market. Ralph Lauren's customers strongly believe that the legendary RL brand accurately symbolizes a posh and upscale lifestyle. These loyal customers purchase active lifestyle brands not for what they are (their function utility), but rather for what they represent. Starbucks promotes freedom and self-expression. By wearing Nike shoes, some consumers form a personal link to the best athletes in the world by believing that they are the best they can be when they 'Just Do It', although they know that they are not Lance Armstrong or Michael Jordan. With Body Shop, some consumers define themselves in terms of the concerned citizen of the environment and nature.

A brand can also enrich the self by referencing idiosyncratic or individual events that consumers want to share and internalize for their self reinforcement. Place brands, like a geographic location (for example, a birthplace) that emotionally binds a person to that place, are related to self-identity and the maintenance of a coherent sense of self over time. They keep one's past alive and thus relate to the later-life tasks of maintaining a sense of continuity, fostering identity, protecting the self against deleterious change, strengthening the self, and retaining a positive self-image (Rubinstein and Parmelee, 1992). These brands are significantly connected to consumers' mental representation of the self. Finally, enrichment may also occur through nostalgia, connecting the self and the brand to bittersweet feelings and memories about the past (Kaplan, 1987; Snyder, 1991). Many brands related to music, sport halls of fame, athletes, celebrities, museums, and so on create strong connections with consumers through nostalgia (Snyder, 1991).

In short, a brand becomes connected to one's self when (1) a brand provides an identity to a consumer through its ideology or principles (reflecting who I am and what I believe; for example, Body Shop, Red Cross, Amnesty International), (2) a brand serves a consumer as a means to express himself/herself symbolically, thus offering self pride and self worth (expressing me and myself; for example, Hummer, Harley Owners Group (HOG), Rolex), or (3) a brand elicits nostalgic feelings. *The brand concept internalization thus enriches the self.*

Enabling the Self through Product Performance

Finally, strong attachments can occur when a brand creates a sense of an efficacious and capable self, enabling the consumer to pursue his or her own goals and tasks. Creating a sense of efficacy is in turn contingent on product performance attributes that consistently and reliably enable task performance. If and when a brand is not able to serve consumers' needs effectively through reliable functional performance, the basic assumption behind the attachment would be violated. Consumers' trust with a brand's competence is therefore critical for the attachment formation and its sustainability. For example, FedEx's overnight delivery assurance and a Swiss Army Knife's versatile applications must have contributed to the consumers' attachment to these so-called functional brands (by fostering mastery of the environment). *Product performance enables the self.*

MENTAL REPRESENTATION OF BRAND MEMORY

Mental representations, including representations of the self and the brand, can include semantic or abstract representations such as category characteristics, beliefs, values and abstract affect, as well as episodic memories linked to specific experiences with the object (Sia et al., 1999). Such episodic experiences are concrete and vivid specific instantiations as opposed to their more abstract semantic-based counterparts (Carlson and Smith, 1996). Episodic representation may be constructed on the basis of actually perceiving the stimulus object, imagining it, being told about it second-hand, and so on (Smith, 1998, p. 411).

To illustrate, based on an encounter with an individual who acts inappropriately, one may store a complex memory trace of that person (for example, inferences about their hostile nature), as well as episodic and contextual information about the situation or context in which the information was processed. If the memory is cued by an object and contextual information, traces of episodes in which those attributes were present together will be retrieved. The retrieved traces will include information about other attributes that were encoded in the same trace or traces. In this way, processing episodes resemble the effects of schemas (Carlson and Smith, 1996).

Based on a number of theorists' views, Sia et al. (1999) noted that people make judgments about abstract concepts by using specific remembered instances. They also note that people find it easier to reason with concrete examples than with semantic abstractions, especially when they are familiar with a particular judgment task. Because it is often impossible to engage in an exhaustive search of all relevant information stored in memory when making a judgment, the outcome of a search will be influenced by the relative accessibility of the relevant information. Based on the ready accessibility of episodic memory, they demonstrated the powerful role of episodes on attitude formation, attitude change, and attitude–behavior consistency.

Episodic memory is often visually represented (Brewer, 1988). Moreover, a given brand category may include numerous episodic memory links. The fact that they are episodic in nature means that such associations are idiosyncratic to the individual and the specific brand. In this way, specific episodes become like instances or exemplars of the brand–self interaction.

Assuming that multiple types of exemplars may exist as members of a brand, the next task is to address the kind of exemplar that is most effective for the development of brand attachment. One may find many brands with uniquely distinctive characteristics that may possibly be called exemplars. For example, one may associate brands such as Elvis Presley, Hello Kitty, Marlboro, Harley-Davidson, Tiffany and Godiva with their vivid prototypic exemplars such as the handsome man with a guitar in a gyrating body gesture, the cute and appealing cat, the rugged-looking western cowboy, a freedom-loving and tough-looking man with sunglasses on a motorcycle, the elegant robin's-egg blue package, and the high status chocolate wrapped in a precious-looking package, respectively.

It should be noted that not all episodes or exemplars are equally effective at cuing or representing the brand category as such episodic associations vary in their typicality, vividness, affect intensity and information richness. For example, consider the earlier mentioned possible exemplar of the Hello Kitty brand category and the smiling grandfather, Colonel Sanders, of the KFC brand category. The two seem to be quite different from each other in the level of vividness, affect intensity, the degree of their exclusive association with a main product, and the amount of information related to them. In fact, Hello Kitty's ability to extend its name to a variety of products (more than 63 product categories) without suffering its identity and KFC's limited ability to extend its name to other product categories may have something to do with the way these exemplars are communicated to and understood by consumers.

A STRATEGIC BRAND EXEMPLAR

Exemplars in psychology have been examined primarily in the naturally or socially agreed categories (for example, oak tree as a member of the tree category, Bill Clinton as a member of the politician category). Exemplars may also be understood in terms of a person's trait-relevant behaviors or episodes when determining his/her traits (Klein et al., 1992). In these categories, one can readily find many specific instances as their members. In contrast, the category of a brand does not have readily agreeable members that define the category itself. While instances of a brand category have been typically identified in terms of the specific product categories a brand is associated with (Loken, Barsalou and Joiner, in press; Loken, Joiner and Peck, 2002; Mao and Krishnan, in press; Ng and Houston, 2006), brand categories do not have to be limited to the product categories.

Since a brand category does not have naturally defined category members in the first place, it resembles more the ad hoc category (Barsalou, 1983). What serves as the likely members of a brand category depends primarily on a firm's marketing strategy for a brand.

As alluded to above with the Hello Kitty and KFC brands, some brand exemplars may contain only a limited degree of information and the associated affect may be weak, while other exemplars may contain a rich set of self-relevant information with strong built-in affect. An exemplar that is rich in self-relevant information and strongly affective in character is more likely to be highly accessible and easily retrieved and hence enable a brand–self connection. So, too, is one that is vivid and highly typical of the brand category (Barsalou, 1983).

A strategic brand exemplar is defined as the self-associated symbol (for example, person, animal or object) that represents the core benefits of a brand described in terms of 'when' (time of usage), 'where' (place of usage), 'how' (the manner in which a brand is used), 'why' (reason for its use), and/or 'whom' (target customers). This symbol should not only trigger thoughts about the brand's benefits but also elicits strong self-implications with affect. It is a specific episode or instance with which (1) consumers identify themselves as well as the brand category and (2) the core benefits of a brand are recognized and appreciated in specific usage contexts by customers. When exemplars satisfy these two criteria, they may be called *strategic brand exemplars*. Such exemplars are salient and readily accessible in memory. As such, they often serve as the processing and retrieval unit, fostering elaboration and inducing greater linkages to the self. As they become more elaborate, they also induce positive predispositions and brand–customer linkages through strong built-in affect (Bodenhausen et al., 1995).

Therefore, a strategic brand exemplar is not simply a logo or a symbol. It is not merely any association customers have with a brand, either. For example, there are many symbols consumers can easily associate brands with. They include the Morton Salt Girl, Aunt Jemima lady, Tony the Tiger, the Energizer Bunny, Morris the Cat and the Jolly Green Giant, among others. While these symbols as 'spokes-characters' may serve as the effective identification feature of a brand, they may not be called strategic brand exemplars in the sense that they are more likely to remain just as symbols only without going beyond the identification role.

The most critical issue in developing brand attachment through *strategic brand exemplars* with the above desirable characteristics is to decide (1) what type of exemplar to create and (2) how to make it salient and readily accessible. The previous discussion of attachment determinants helps to identify the most effective *strategic brand exemplars*. It was noted earlier that three possible self-related associations may be created through marketing activities of a brand. They are the gratifying type, the enriching type and the enabling type. Specifically, the strategic brand exemplar may help to create a strong connection with consumers through its ability to create sensory gratification and/or aesthetic attractiveness (for example, Hello Kitty, Mickey Mouse, Tiffany). The strategic brand exemplar may also help to create a strong connection with consumers through its ability to perform the product functions that induce a sense of efficacy at attaining functional performance goals (for example, Maytag, Michelin, Swiss Army Knife). Finally, it may help to create a strong connection through its ability to provide self identity and self definitional values to consumers (for example, Harley-Davidson, Body Shop, Steinway, Rolex).

Which exemplar type to adopt in order to develop a specific brand–self connection relates to a positioning decision, while how to make the *strategic exemplar* readily accessible pertains to an execution issue. In order to make the exemplar highly accessible, it needs to be presented and communicated in such a way that it becomes vivid, typical, affective, and rich in memory associations. This is because when the exemplar is highly vivid, typical of a brand category, and possesses richer memory associations and stronger affective links, it becomes highly accessible in memory, being automatically retrieved whenever exposed to the appropriate cues. These two tasks are inseparable though and must be coordinated. If these strategic and execution-related activities are performed successfully, they foster a competitive advantage, enable efficient growth through line and brand extensions, and hence enhance the equity of the brand. Specifically, when a brand creates a strong connection with consumers through the category-representing vivid exemplar, it becomes highly salient, facilitates many stronger forms of behaviors and induces top-of-mind retrieval.

Such exemplars also support flexible extension boundaries through an exemplar-based *fit* judgment (exemplar matching), as opposed to the feature-based *similarity* judgment. The exemplar-based fit judgment tends to be more holistic and more inclusive in a way similar to the configural model-based judgment (see Fiske and Pavelchak, 1986, for the discussion). For example, by bringing two products (the parent product and the extension product) under the same exemplar (for example, the same lonely repairman touting the functional performance of his product), the new extension product may be categorized as belonging to the parent brand category, being thus able to overcome the potential problems associated with dissimilar extensions. Although it may not be called a strategic brand exemplar in the strictest sense, the Hello Kitty exemplar (the cute-looking cat with other related associations) seems to allow many seemingly dissimilar product categories together (for example, babies' and children's furniture, women's camisoles, video games, coffee makers, body jewelry, cookbooks, automotive accessories, clocks, bracelets, bath linens, camping and hiking gear, bowling equipment, women's underwear, toasters, hair care, and so on). In this case, the Hello Kitty exemplar appears to serve as an organizing category under which seemingly dissimilar products are all housed without diluting its core meaning.

Alternatively, because of their rich memory associations, exemplars may allow consumers to find a fit between a parent brand and a brand extension. To illustrate, some consumers may have highly sophisticated knowledge associated with the Hello Kitty exemplar. They may thus be able to retrieve whatever information is contained in the exemplar to make sense in light of the extension product category. In this way, rather than examining the similarity between the parent product and its extension product, consumers may create a meaning from the exemplar that fits the extension product category. Relating to the explanation of the richer memory associations, one may also understand why symbolic brands with highly vivid exemplars can extend to seemingly dissimilar product categories (Park et al., 1991). Consumers may be able either to identify or to create the basis to connect the two together based on the rich set of associations linked to the exemplar.

Finally, strategic brand exemplars may also enhance the parent brand. Specifically, the exemplar-based line and brand extensions may strengthen the salience, vividness and the memory association of the strategic brand exemplar itself. Going back to the Hello Kitty brand, the more extensions it makes, the more vivid and meaningful its exemplar may become. Its application to a variety of usages appears to make its exemplar more interesting and less boring through the exemplar variety. Also, the extensions of symbolic brands with strong exemplars to many dissimilar products may make the exemplars more *complete* (for example, a tough freedom-seeking man not only rides a Harley-Davidson motorcycle but also drinks coffee with a Harley-Davidson mug). Increasing the extension boundary of a brand through the strategic brand exemplar will increase the consumer's exposure to and use of the exemplar. To the extent that consumers are exposed to and use these exemplars often and recently, their accessibility will be greatly facilitated. This increased accessibility makes them highly salient in memory, affecting consumers' judgment. Reyes et al. (1980) showed that the accessible information was more vivid, better recalled, and had a greater influence on juror verdicts. Thus, it appears to be quite possible that strategic brand exemplars not only facilitate dissimilar brand extensions (positive extension effects) but also strengthen the parent brand through such extensions (positive feedback effects).

It should be noted that not all products can create strong attachments with their customers due to the difficulty in creating self-connecting strategic brand exemplars. It may be extremely difficult to create a strong brand attachment to a brand that involves limited self-interaction. For example, while Drano solves clogging problems, it does not involve any direct interface with the customer's self at the sensory, physiological, or even psychological level. On the other hand, Tums offers very tangible benefits to customers with its ability to handle stomach acid. There is a direct interface between the brand Tums and customers with respect to what it does to their selves (for example, offering comfort and security). To the extent that a brand does not involve any direct interface with its customers, it may be difficult for it to create the strategic brand exemplar and to develop the meaningful relationship with its consumers.

DISCUSSION

This chapter has examined three key issues in developing and establishing strong brand relationships with customers. The first issue addressed the concept of attachment as a distinctive higher order construct that bears critical implications for the enhancement of brand equity. The second key issue addressed how a brand may be able to create a meaningful personal connection with its customers in order to create and establish brand attachment. Here, three different brand–self associations were introduced. The third and final issue addressed the importance of the strategic brand exemplar as the most fundamental tool that offers a firm valuable opportunity for a brand's sustainable competitive advantages and growth. The essential requirement for this opportunity to be realized is the firm's strategic choice of a brand's exemplar and the carefully executed strategy to manage the exemplar over time so as to nurture and accumulate its effects.

Specifically, a firm may pay particular attention to two tasks. The first task is to ensure that the strategic brand exemplar serves as the prototypic member of the brand category, being also vivid. To make the strategic brand exemplar most typical of the brand category perhaps requires the creative linkage between a brand and its exemplar as the category member right from the introduction stage of the brand to the market. For example, the female silhouette accompanied with iPod may be identified as its key differentiating feature. How to make it the most typical instance of the iPod brand category and how to make it most vivid would require the ongoing management attention and the creative nurturing process from a firm. Equally important is the second task of associating the exemplar with a richer set of coherent meanings and strong built-in affect. For example, to convey a rich set of meanings about iPod and to elicit strong emotions from iPod through the female silhouette would require carefully developed communication strategies that should be accumulative in nature over time.

Going back to many decades, one can identify many successful brands that have been defying the decline stage of the product life cycle. Despite the enormous competitive pressure and the absence of any industry-wide technological breakthrough, they have been nevertheless successful in maintaining their strong relationships with customers. They include Morton Salt, Planter's peanuts, Aunt Jemima syrup, Green Giant vegetables, Barbie doll, and the Swiss Army Knife. One wonders whether these visual symbols or images are simply one of many differentiating features associated with these brands or whether they are more likely to serve as strategic brand exemplars that were discussed earlier. Moreover, it is also an interesting issue to examine whether brands in the high technology category or in business-to-business markets are so different from these consumer market brands that strategic brand exemplars are not relevant concepts to them. As long as there is a direct interface between customers and a brand at the sensory, physiological or psychological level, it seems that the strategic brand exemplar is a worthy idea for securing sustainable competitive advantages and future growth. For example, many successful brands such as Toyota, Samsung, Honda, Sony, IBM, Microsoft and Intel have been doing well without any readily accessible and meaningful strategic brand exemplars. This does not, however, mean that they can become even more successful and sustain their competitive advantages with the help of strategic brand exemplars. They may pay very hefty opportunity costs by not taking advantage of their benefits.

REFERENCES

Ailawadi, K.L., D.R. Lehmann and S.A. Neslin (2003), 'Revenue premium as an outcome measure of brand equity', *Journal of Marketing*, **67**, 1–17.

Ainsworth, M.D.S., M.C. Blehar, E. Waters and S. Wall (1978), *Patterns of Attachment: A Psychological Study of the Strange Situation*, Hillsdale, NJ: Erlbaum.

Aron, A., D. Mashek, T. McLaughlin-Volpe, S. Wright, G. Lewandowski and E.N. Aron (2005), 'Including close others in the cognitive structure of the self', in M.W. Baldwin (ed.), *Interpersonal Cognition*, New York: Guilford Press, pp. 206–32.

Babad, E. (1987), 'Wishful thinking and objectivity among sports fans', *Social Behavior*, **2**, 231–40.

Baldwin, M.W., J.P.R. Keelan, B. Fehr, V. Enns and E. Koh-Rangarajoo (1996), 'Social-cognitive conceptualization of attachment working models: availability and accessibility effects', *Journal of Personality and Social Psychology*, **71**, 94–109.

Ball, A.D. and L.H. Tasaki (1992), 'The role and measurement of attachment in consumer behavior', *Journal of Consumer Psychology*, **1**, 155–72.

Barsalou, L. (1983), 'Ad hoc categories', *Memory & Cognition*, **11**, 211–27.

Belk, R.W. (1988), 'Possessions and the extended self', *Journal of Consumer Research*, **15**, 139–68.

Berman, W.H. and M.B. Sperling (1994), 'The structure and function of adult attachment', in M.B. Sperling and W.H. Berman (eds), *Attachment in Adults: Clinical and Developmental Perspectives*, New York: Guilford Press, pp. 3–28.

Bodenhausen, G.V., N. Schwarz, H. Bless and M. Wanke (1995), 'Effects of atypical exemplars on racial beliefs: enlightened racism or generalized appraisals?', *Journal of Experimental and Social Psychology*, **31**, 48–63.

Bowlby, J. (1973), *Attachment and Loss: Vol. 2. Separation: Anxiety and Anger*, New York: Basic Books.

Bowlby, J. (1982), *Attachment and Loss: Vol. 3. Loss*, New York: Basic Books.

Bowlby, J. (1988), *A Secure Base: Clinical Applications of Attachment Theory*, London: Routledge.

Brewer, M.B. (1988), 'A dual process model of impression formation', in T. Srull and R. Wyer (eds), *Advances in Social Cognition, Vol. 1*, Hillsdale, NJ: Erlbaum, pp. 177–83.

Carlson, D.E. and E.R. Smith (1996), 'Principles of mental representation', in E.T. Higgins and A.W. Kruglanski (eds), *Social Psychology: Handbook of Basic Principles*, New York: Guilford Press, pp. 184–210.

Converse, P.E. (1995), 'Foreword', in R.E. Petty and J.A. Krosnick (eds), *Attitude Strength: Antecedents and Consequences*, Hillsdale, NJ: Erlbaum, pp. xi–xvii.

Drigotas, S.M. and C.E. Rusbult (1992), 'Should I stay or should I go? A dependence model of breakups', *Journal of Personality and Social Psychology*, **62**, 62–87.

Dwyer, F.R., P.H. Schurr and S. Oh (1987), 'Developing buyer–seller relationships', *Journal of Marketing*, **51**, 11–27.

Eagly, A.H. and S. Chaiken (1993), *The Psychology of Attitudes*, New York: Harcourt Brace Jovanovich.

Fazio, R.H. (1989), 'On the power and functionality of attitudes: the role of attitude accessibility', in A.R. Pratkanis, S.J. Breckler and A.G. Greenwald (eds), *Attitude Structure and Function*, Hillsdale, NJ: Erlbaum, pp. 153–79.

Fiske, S.T. and M.A. Pavelchak (1986), 'Category-based versus piecemeal-based affective responses: developments in schema-triggered affect', in R.M. Sorrentino and E.T. Higgins (eds), *Handbook of Motivation and Cognition: Foundations of Social Behavior*, New York: Guilford Press, pp. 167–203.

Fournier, S. (1998), 'Consumers and their brands: developing relationship theory in consumer research', *Journal of Consumer Research*, **24**, 343–73.

Greenwald, A.G. and A.R. Pratkanis (1984), 'The self', in R.S. Wyer and T.K. Srull (eds), *Handbook of Social Cognition*, Hillsdale, NJ: Erlbaum, pp. 129–78.

Hazan, C. and P.R. Shaver (1994), 'Attachment as an organizational framework for research on close relationships', *Psychological Inquiry*, **5**, 1–22.

Hill, R.P. and M. Stamey (1990), 'The homeless in America: an examination of possessions and consumption behaviors', *Journal of Consumer Research*, **17**, 303–21.

Johnson, D. and C.E. Rusbult (1989), 'Resisting temptation: devaluation of alternative partners as a means of maintaining commitment in close relationships', *Journal of Personality and Social Psychology*, **57**, 967.

Kaplan, H.A. (1987), 'The psychopathology of nostalgia', *Psychoanalytic Review*, **74**, 465–86.

Klein, S.B., J. Loftus, J.G. Trafton and R.W. Furhman (1992), 'Use of exemplars and abstractions in trait judgments: a model of trait knowledge about the self and others', *Journal of Personality and Social Psychology*, **63**, 739–53.

Kleine, R.E., III, S.S. Kleine and J.B. Kernan (1993), 'Mundane consumption and the self: a social identity perspective', *Journal of Consumer Psychology*, **2**, 209–35.

Kleine, S.S. and S.M. Baker (2004), 'An integrative review of material possession attachment', *Academy of Marketing Science Review*, **1**, retrieved 14 March 2006, from www.amsreview.org/articles/kleine01-2004.pdf.

Kleine, S.S., R.E. Kleine, III and C.T. Allen (1995), 'How is a possession "me" or "not me": characterizing types and an antecedent of material possession attachment', *Journal of Consumer Research*, **22**, 327–43.

Loken, B., L.W. Barsalou and C. Joiner (in press), 'Categorization theory and research in consumer psychology: category representation and category-based inference', in C.P. Haugtvedt, F. Kardes and P.M. Herr (eds), *The Handbook of Consumer Psychology*, Hillsdale, NJ: Erlbaum.

Loken, B., C. Joiner and J. Peck (2002), 'Category attitude measures: exemplars as inputs', *Journal of Consumer Psychology*, **12**, 149–61.

Lydon, J.E., K. Burton and D. Menzies-Toman (2005), 'Commitment calibration with the relationship cognition toolbox', in M.W. Baldwin (ed.), *Interpersonal Cognition*, New York: Guilford Press, pp. 126–52.

Mao, H. and H.S. Krishnan (in press), 'Effects of prototype and exemplar fit on brand extension evaluations: a two-process contingency model', *Journal of Consumer Research*.

McCullough, M.E., K.C. Rachal, S.J. Sandage, E.L. Worthington, Jr., S.W. Brown and T.L. Hight (1998), 'Interpersonal forgiving in close relationships: II. Theoretical elaboration and measurement', *Journal of Personality and Social Psychology*, **75**, 1586–603.

Mehta, R. and R.W. Belk (1991), 'Artifacts, identity, and transition: favorite possessions of Indians and Indian immigrants to the US', *Journal of Consumer Research*, **17**, 398–411.

Mick, D.G. and M. DeMoss (1990), 'Self-gifts: phenomenological insights from four contexts', *Journal of Consumer Research*, **17**, 322–32.

Mikulincer, M. and P.R. Shaver (2005), 'Mental representations of attachment security: theoretical foundation for a positive social psychology', in M.W. Baldwin (ed.), *Interpersonal Cognition*, New York: Guilford Press, pp. 233–66.

Ng, S. and M.J. Houston (2006), 'Exemplars or beliefs? The impact of self-view on the nature and relative influence of brand associations', *Journal of Consumer Research*, **32**, 519–29.

Park, C.W., S. Milberg and R. Lawson (1991), 'Evaluation of brand extensions: the role of product feature similarity and brand concept consistency', *Journal of Consumer Research*, **18**, 185–93.

Reis, H.T. and B.C. Patrick (1996), 'Attachment and intimacy: component processes', in E.T. Higgins and A.W. Kruglanski (eds), *Social Psychology: Handbook of Basic Principles*, New York: Guilford Press, pp. 523–63.

Reyes, R.M., W.C. Thompson and G.H. Bower (1980), 'Judgmental bases resulting from differing availabilities of arguments', *Journal of Personality and Social Psychology*, **39**, 2–12.

Richins, M.L. (1994), 'Special possessions and the expression of material values', *Journal of Consumer Research*, **21**, 522–33.

Rubinstein, R.L. and P.A. Parmelee (1992), 'Attachment to place and the representation of the life course by the elderly', in I. Altman and S.M. Low (eds), *Place Attachment*, New York: Plenum Press, pp. 139–63.

Rusbult, C.E., J. Verette, G.A. Whitney, L.F. Slovik and I. Lipkus (1991), 'Accommodation processes in close relationships: theory and preliminary empirical evidence', *Journal of Personality and Social Psychology*, **60**, 53–78.

Schouten, J.W. and J.H. McAlexander (1995), 'Subcultures of consumption: an ethnography of the new bikers', *Journal of Consumer Research*, **22**, 43–61.

Schultz, S.E., R.E. Kleine and J.B. Kernan (1989), 'These are a few of my favorite things: toward an explication of attachment as a consumer behavior construct', *Advances in Consumer Research*, **16**, 359–66.

Shavitt, S. and M.R. Nelson (2000), 'The social-identity function in person perception: communicated meanings of product preferences', in G. Maio and J.M. Olson (eds), *Why we Evaluate: Functions of Attitudes*, Mahwah, NJ: Erlbaum, pp. 37–57.

Sia, T.L., C.G. Lord, M.R. Lepper, K.A. Blessum and J.C. Thomas (1999), 'Activation of exemplars in the process of assessing social category attitudes', *Journal of Personality and Social Psychology*, **76**, 517–32.

Slater, J.S. (2001), 'Collecting brand loyalty: a comparative analysis of how Coca-Cola and Hallmark use collecting behavior to enhance brand loyalty', *Advances in Consumer Research*, **28**, 362–9.

Smith, E.R. (1998), 'Mental representation and memory', in D.T. Gilbert, S.T. Fiske and G. Lindzey (eds) *Handbook of Social Psychology, Vol. 1*, New York: McGraw-Hill, pp. 391–445.

Snyder, E.E. (1991), 'Sociology of nostalgia: sport halls of fame and museums in America', *Sociology of Sport Journal*, **8**, 228–38.

Thomson, M., D.J. MacInnis and C.W. Park (2005), 'The ties that bind: measuring the strength of consumers' emotional attachments to brands', *Journal of Consumer Psychology*, **15**, 77–91.

Trinke, S.J. and K. Bartholomew (1997), 'Hierarchies of attachment relationships in young adulthood', *Journal of Social and Personal Relationships*, **15**, 603–25.

Van Lange, P.A.M., C.E. Rusbult, S.M. Drigotas, X.B. Arriaga, B.S. Witcher and C.L. Cox (1997), 'Willingness to sacrifice in close relationships', *Journal of Personality and Social Psychology*, **72**, 1373–96.

Wallendorf, M. and E.J. Arnould (1988), 'My favorite things: a cross-cultural inquiry into object attachment, possessiveness and social linkage', *Journal of Consumer Research*, **14**, 531–47.

Wegener, D.T., J. Downing, J. Krosnick and R.E. Petty (1995), 'Measures and manipulations of strength-related properties of attitudes: current practice and future directions', in R.E. Petty and J.A. Krosnick (eds), *Attitude Strength: Antecedents and Consequences*, Hillsdale, NJ: Erlbaum, pp. 455–88.

Weiss, R.S. (1988), 'Loss and recovery', *Journal of Social Issues*, **44**, 37–52.

Wieselquist, J., C.E. Rusbult, C.A. Foster and C.R. Agnew (1999), 'Commitment, pro-relationship behavior, and trust in close relationships', *Journal of Personality and Social Psychology*, **77**, 942–66.

2. Brand permission: a conceptual and managerial framework

Tom Meyvis and Ravi Dhar

It is by now widely accepted by managers and academics alike that brand names can be highly valuable assets. Just how valuable is demonstrated by Ford's willingness to pay over $1.4 billion to purchase Jaguar's intangible assets. Aside from being defined in such financial terms, brand equity can also be examined from a consumer perspective, as the effect of brand knowledge on consumers' response to a marketing action by that brand (Keller, 1993). For instance, although Toyota Corolla and GM's Prizm are based on identical platforms and sold at almost identical prices, Toyota Corolla was in substantially higher demand, resulting in an annual revenue premium of close to $500 million (Srinivasan, 2006). Companies do not just value brand names because they can produce more favorable consumer reactions to their *existing* products and marketing strategies, but also because they have the potential to add value to *new* products and *novel* marketing actions. However, there may be limits to customers' willingness to accept a familiar brand name in new roles and situations. Consider for example how consumers would react to an announcement that the Altria group (marketers of Marlboro cigarettes) plans to leverage its insights into people's health and open Marlboro-branded research and treatment centers that specialize in lung cancer. Alternatively, consider the decision of a major technology company to market its existing products to line-of-business executives rather than to IT managers, based on research findings that choices about technology products are increasingly being made jointly by both types of executives. The technology company may find it very difficult to gain access to the line-of-business managers even though there is high awareness of the brand and no new product is involved.

As these two very different examples illustrate, brands may not always have consumers' permission to engage in a novel strategy or to offer certain new products or services. In this chapter, we introduce the concept of *brand permission* to capture an essential part of consumers' reaction to any new brand initiative. These initiatives can be viewed as varying along the elements of the marketing mix, be it introducing a new brand extension, reaching out to a different customer segment, or changing its pricing or its communication strategy. The concept of brand permission provides a parsimonious tool for addressing a variety of issues, ranging from Coca-Cola receiving permission to change its original formula to Mattel receiving permission to launch a Barbie Luxe clothing line for adults. In addition, it also provides more insight into the process that underlies consumers' reactions to these new initiatives by specifying a preliminary stage that is a prerequisite for a favorable consumer response. Finally, and perhaps most important, brand permission highlights a normative component to consumers' reactions that has not been fully captured by prior brand extension research, which has mostly focused on quality perceptions and inferred benefits.

In the remainder of this chapter, we will first review the existing research on consumer reactions to brand extensions, the most extensively studied type of new brand initiative. We will argue that the concept of brand fit, which is the basis of most theorizing in this area, does not fully capture consumers' response to new brand extensions or other changes in brand strategy. We will then define the concept of brand permission and explain how it can help us understand consumers' reactions to novel brand actions, such as the two examples discussed above or, more generally, to changes in any element of a brand's marketing mix. Finally, we will propose a framework describing how brand permission may operate and we will suggest guidelines for measuring and managing brand permission.

CONSUMER REACTIONS TO BRAND EXTENSIONS

Companies invest substantial resources to build strong brands, and they do so with good reason. Strong brands result in more favorable consumer responses to a wide variety of firm activities, including price increases, advertising appeals, and product modifications. Moreover, one of the most important strategic benefits of owning a strong brand is that this strength can be leveraged into new categories. This insight has resulted in a proliferation of brand extensions in many industries, ranging from packaged food products (for example, Heinz baby food) to consumer electronics (for example, the Apple iPod) and commercial airlines (for example, Virgin airlines). The popularity of the brand extension strategy has resulted in a large body of research aimed at understanding how consumers react to such a new brand initiative.

A common finding in empirical studies of consumers' response to brand extensions is that consumers evaluate extensions more favorably when there is a better fit between the parent brand and the extension category. The concept of fit (or similarity) has surfaced as a critical factor early on in the literature on brand extension evaluations (Fry, 1967; Neuhaus and Taylor, 1972; Tauber, 1988), but it was first rigorously defined by Aaker and Keller (1990), who focused on the fit between the host category and the extension category. Two product categories are said to have a higher fit when the product classes are viewed as complements or substitutes and when the two products are perceived as requiring similar manufacturing abilities. Whereas some later studies similarly focused on the fit between product categories (for example, Boush and Loken, 1991), others have illustrated that extension evaluations also depend on the consistency of the extension category with the brand concept (Park et al., 1991) or, more generally, the fit between the extension category and any type of brand-specific association (Broniarczyk and Alba, 1994).

For instance, Tide's recent extension to stain removal pens (Tide to Go) fits the Tide brand because producing an effective stain removal pen requires similar abilities to those required when producing an effective laundry detergent. Likewise, Mr Clean Windshield Wash is a good fit with the Mr Clean brand given the similarity between wiper fluid and all-purpose cleaner. In contrast, Iams pet insurance may seem like quite a stretch given the difference in capabilities required for providing insurance versus producing food. However, pet insurance is very consistent with Iams' brand-specific association of caring about pets' health, and therefore fits the brand reasonably well. Conversely, some examples of recent extensions that are a poor fit with the parent brand image include

Harley-Davidson cake decoration kits and the failed extensions of Hooters Air and Reebok Fitness Water.

The manner in which perceived fit influences consumers' extension evaluations has been the topic of considerable debate. Boush and Loken (1991) distinguish between two processes. On the one hand, extensions that either fit very well or very poorly are evaluated using a categorization-based affect transfer mechanism (Fiske and Pavelchak, 1986); the positive attitude associated with the parent brand will transfer to the brand extension when the extension is very typical for the brand, but not when the extension is clearly atypical. Thus, the Tide to Go pen benefits from consumers' positive attitude towards Tide because of its high fit. In contrast, the positive attitude towards Reebok does not transfer to Reebok Fitness Water due to the atypicality of the extension, resulting in negative evaluations of this extension.

On the other hand, extensions that fit moderately well are evaluated using a piecemeal, analytical assessment process (Fishbein and Ajzen, 1975); the attitude towards the extension is computed as a weighted combination of attribute values. Broniarczyk and Alba (1994) formulate a specific version of this latter process. They argue that consumers simply use the brand's benefit associations to infer whether the brand extension will deliver the critical benefit that is typically sought in the extension category. By producing healthy pet food, Iams has demonstrated that it cares about pets' health and it can therefore be expected to show the same concern in its pet insurance business.

This conceptualization of two separate routes to brand extension evaluations (affect transfer versus piecemeal processing) can indeed account for many findings in the brand extension literature. However, this framework is overly restrictive in its consideration of possible evaluation processes and, furthermore, at odds with our current understanding of judgment and decision making. In particular, in recent decision research, effortless processes such as affect transfer are usually conceptualized as a necessary precursor for the more effortful, analytical decision processes. We therefore propose a slightly altered conceptual framework based on Kahneman and Frederick's (2002) distinction between automatic, effortless *System I* cognitive processes and conscious, more effortful *System II* processes. As illustrated in Figure 2.1, we propose that consumers first generate an initial, intuitive response to the new brand extension using automatic, effortless System I processes. Consumers could engage in categorization-based affect transfer, as proposed by Boush and Loken (1991), but they could also rely on other automatic processes, such as inferring their liking of the extension from the ease with which they can process the extension (for example, Winkielman and Cacioppo, 2001). Consumers next assess their intuitive confidence in this initial response to the brand extension (Simmons and Nelson, 2006). If their intuitive confidence is high, as would be the case when the extension fits the brand very well or very poorly, consumers will be satisfied with this initial response and not engage in any additional, more effortful processing. However, if their intuitive confidence in this response is low, they will engage in additional, System II processing to arrive at a more reliable evaluation of the extension – provided they have the motivation and ability to do so. This additional, effortful processing could consist of the piecemeal construction of an attitude towards the extension or a conscious assessment of the likelihood that this extension will deliver a specific desired benefit.

For instance, when presented with a Tide to Go stain removal pen, consumers may automatically generate a confident, positive response that does not trigger any additional

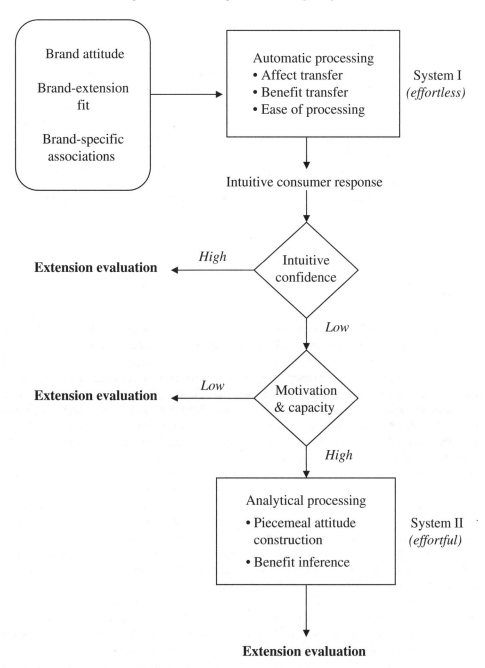

Figure 2.1   A two-system model of brand extension evaluations

processing. Conversely, being informed about Hooters Air may automatically elicit a confident, negative response that similarly precludes additional processing (and hence any opportunity for this enterprise to redeem itself with favorable attribute information). In contrast, Iams pet insurance will also automatically trigger an intuitive response, but because of the modest fit of this extension, the initial response will be rather ambiguous and not inspire much confidence. Consequently, consumers will feel the need to activate the effortful System II processes, which may result in the conscious inference that Iams may provide good pet insurance since this is a company that has clearly demonstrated that it cares about pets' health.

SHORTCOMINGS OF THE BRAND EXTENSION CONCEPT

Yet in spite of the many empirical studies and conceptual frameworks, prior research on consumers' response to brand extensions still falls short in a number of ways. First, by restricting the scope of their studies to the domain of brand extensions, researchers have focused on factors that are specific to extensions (for example, category fit, breadth of the brand's product portfolio), while ignoring general issues that are common to any type of new brand initiative. By broadening the scope of the inquiry, we hope to develop new insights about consumer reactions to other novel brand initiatives as well as brand extensions. Indeed, companies not only build strong brands to leverage this strength in new categories, they also count on strong brands to produce more favorable consumer responses to strategic changes in existing categories, including price changes, changes in brand positioning, changes in brand communication strategies, and so on. For instance, while brand extension research informs us about how consumers may react to a Coca-Cola sports drink, it does not address whether consumers give Coca-Cola permission to alter its formula (New Coke), nor does it tell us whether IBM is allowed to communicate with LOB managers directly or whether Marlboro can sponsor lung cancer treatments.

Second, although researchers have formulated multiple processes for brand extension evaluations, each of these mechanisms is focused on the final stage: the actual evaluation of the extension. This approach ignores those consumer decisions that precede final evaluations, such as the decision to seek out more information about a product or, more generally, to try to assess the quality of the product. We will argue that before consumers evaluate a new extension, they need to consider and accept it. Accordingly, we will propose an additional, preceding stage that needs to be favorably concluded to make a positive evaluation possible. For instance, consumers may not have an unfavorable evaluation of Reebok Fitness Water, but may instead not even want to consider a beverage produced by a shoe brand. As a result, they will not be interested in evaluating it and hence ignore any additional information they may encounter. Similarly, if consumers had really considered and evaluated New Coke, they may have evaluated it favorably (as the taste tests prior to its launch suggested). However, given that consumers felt that Coca-Cola was not allowed to tinker with its original formula, they may have refused to even consider (and evaluate) any modification of the original.

Finally, the existing brand extension research is overly focused on the perceived quality of the extension, while ignoring other issues, such as the perceived appropriateness of the extension. As we will argue, it is possible that a high quality extension that obviously delivers the key benefit of the product category, may still be rejected by consumers because of lack of appropriateness. Consider, for instance, a respected not-for-profit organization that introduces a regular, branded packaged good to generate revenue for its operations, for example, Red Cross adhesive bandages. While most consumers may assume these bandages to be of the highest quality given Red Cross's solid reputation in emergency health care, they may still be reluctant to accept that a non-profit organization markets a regular drugstore product. Similarly, even though Altria's corporate expertise may guarantee an efficient and reliable lung cancer treatment center, consumers may still find it unseemly for a major cigarette producer to become involved in this industry.

Given these various limitations of the existing brand extension literature, we propose a new concept that captures consumers' concerns about the appropriateness of the extension, is applicable to a type of new brand initiative, and specifies a necessary stage that precedes the extension evaluation process.

DEFINING BRAND PERMISSION

To better address situations such as those described in the examples, we introduce the concept of *brand permission*. Brand permission is defined as *consumers' openness to considering a new brand initiative* (including, but not limited to, using the brand name in a different product category). This definition carries several important implications. First and foremost, brand permission has to be granted by consumers. It is not something that a brand can claim based on its quality or accomplishments. It depends on consumers' subjective judgments and will therefore differ across consumers. Some consumers may give the Red Cross permission to market adhesive bandages whereas others may not.

Second, brand permission concerns new brand initiatives. We conceptualize these initiatives very generally as any type of adjustment of the marketing mix. It could concern Coca-Cola's decision to alter its original formula (permission to alter the product), to sell Coke through vending machines in schools (permission to distribute in schools), to raise its price when the temperature rises (permission to vary price in response to fluctuations in demand), or to use shocking images in its advertising (permission to radically change the brand image).

Finally, the third implication of the definition is that brand permission is about being open to considering, not about favorable evaluations or ready acceptance. As such, brand permission resides at the consideration stage in the classic consumer purchase cycle (see Figure 2.2). *Awareness* of the novel brand action is an essential requirement for brand permission to be granted, which, in turn, is a necessary antecedent for a favorable *evaluation*. Even when consumers can be confident that a brand's strategic change will deliver high quality results, consumers will only evaluate the change favorably if the brand is also perceived to have permission to make this change. The pleasant taste of New Coke is rendered irrelevant by consumers' refusal to grant Coke permission to tinker with its formula. Similarly, even if consumers are convinced that Disney has sufficient talent and creativity at its disposal to produce entertaining movies for adults, they will never use this information if they feel the Disney brand lacks permission to produce grown-up entertainment. However, while brand permission is a necessary antecedent for favorable evaluations, it is not sufficient. It cannot compensate for low quality products or poorly fitting extensions.

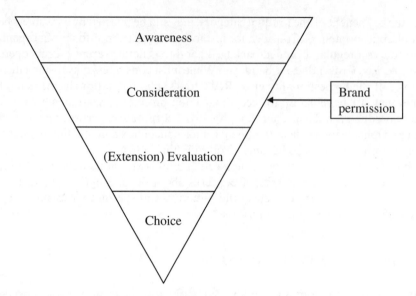

Figure 2.2   Position of brand permission in the consumer purchase cycle

Even if a consumer doesn't mind seeing the Disney brand name on movies for adults, she may still not like this new strategy if she's not convinced that Disney has the necessary know-how to produce high quality entertainment for this different audience. For a new brand strategy to be favorably received by consumers, brand permission is necessary, but not sufficient. In the domain of brand extensions, this implies that a brand can be said to have consumers' permission to extend into a new product category if consumers favorably evaluate the new product *provided that it delivers high quality and desirable benefits.*

GRANTING BRAND PERMISSION

We propose that the granting of brand permission is usually an effortless and unconscious process. In particular, consumers may never notice the granting of permission, but may only notice when norms have been violated and permission cannot be granted (in which case quality does not matter). When Coca-Cola introduced Vanilla Coke, no norms were violated and consumers simply wondered whether this would be a flavorful beverage that they should try out. There was no active, conscious granting of permission. In contrast, when Coca-Cola changed its Classic Coke formula, consumers felt that this violated their expectations based on Coke's image of being the original, classic soda. This feeling of violation resulted in an active, conscious denial of permission. However, this does not imply that granting permission is always unconscious, whereas refusing permission is not. For instance, when a pet owner shopping for insurance is confronted with 'Iams pet insurance', permission may be not be granted automatically. Instead, she may consciously ponder whether it is appropriate for a pet food brand to provide pet insurance. If she ends up deciding that it is appropriate, she will move on to the next step: evaluating whether Iams can provide high quality pet insurance.

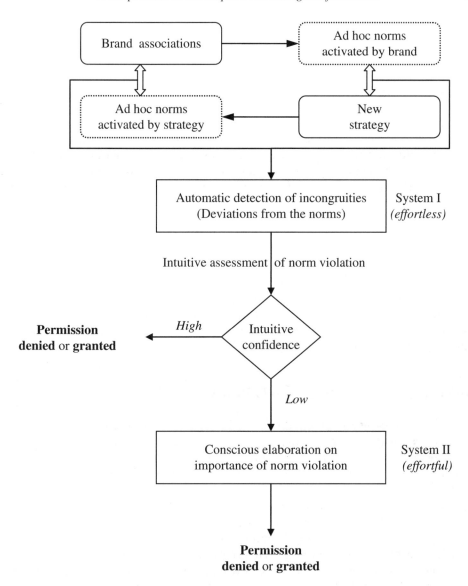

Figure 2.3   The process of granting brand permission

We can again conceptualize this using Kahneman and Frederick's (2002) System I/
System II terminology. When consumers encounter a novel brand initiative, they will initially process it automatically and unconsciously using an effortless System I process that
scans for major incongruities (see Figure 2.3). This scanning process consists of a quick
and unconscious comparison of the brand's action to automatically activated comparison standards. These comparison standards are in essence specific norms that are constructed ad hoc and activated based on the distinguishing elements of both the brand and
the novel strategy (Kahneman and Miller, 1986). These *ad hoc norms* can be thought of

as a list of strategies that are permissible for a brand and a list of brand characteristics that are perceived as congruent with the novel strategy. It is important to note that the ad hoc norms that are activated by a given brand initiative are not the same for each consumer, but instead depend on the more permanent, general norms that are being held by that consumer. These general norms reflect the consumer's knowledge of the brand and his relationship to the brand as well as his social environment. We will discuss the nature and influence of these norms in more detail in the next section.

If the new brand initiative does not clearly deviate from the activated norms, consumers will simply proceed to assessing the expected performance of the new product or strategy (still relying on System I processes, as explained in Figure 2.1). Alternatively, if this initial process detects a strong incongruity between the new brand initiative and the activated norms, consumers will deny permission and refuse to consider the new initiative without giving it any further (conscious) thought. However, if the incongruity detected by the System I processes is only moderate, consumers will not be very confident of their initial assessment and activate more conscious and effortful System II processes. The goal of these System II processes is to determine whether the observed incongruities reflect an important norm violation. If consumers decide that an important norm has been violated, they will deny permission and will refuse to consider the new brand initiative. Alternatively, if they decide that no important norms have been violated, they will consciously grant permission and proceed to assess the expected performance of the new initiative using conscious System II processes.

DETERMINANTS OF BRAND PERMISSION

Which factors determine if a brand will receive permission for a new branding strategy? We have argued that obtaining brand permission is distinct from obtaining favorable extension evaluations. Yet, this distinction is only relevant if brand permission has its own, unique set of antecedents – and if these antecedents can be identified and brought under managerial control. Figure 2.4 provides a schematic overview of the different factors that are believed to influence brand permission.

First, it is worth noting which factors are *absent* from this framework. In contrast to brand extension evaluations, brand permission is not directly dependent on consumers' attitude towards the brand, the perceived fit between the brand and the new strategy, the brand's perceived resources, or the brand's existing benefit associations. Stated differently, brand permission is not directly influenced by factors that determine the expected *quality* of the outcome of the strategy change.

Instead, we propose that brand permission primarily depends on consumers' perceptions of norm violations. Consumers will grant a brand permission if the novel strategy is deemed normatively appropriate. This illustrates a unique, essential aspect of brand permission. Whereas brand extension evaluations are essentially individualist in nature ('What will this new extension do for me?'), brand permission is a more social construct ('Should we, consumers, allow the brand to make this change?'). As a result, social norms, such as cultural norms and marketplace conventions, play an important role in determining brand permission. In addition, norms can originate from brand-specific associations or from the nature of the relationship between the brand and the consumer. Finally, individual consumer

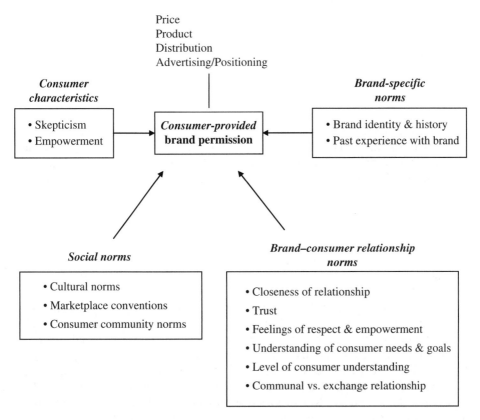

Figure 2.4   Determinants of brand permission

characteristics, such as dispositional skepticism and feelings of empowerment, will influence consumers' tolerance for norm violations and thus their general tendency to grant brand permission. In the remainder of this section, we will separately discuss each of these four determining factors (see Figure 2.4 for a schematic overview).

Brand-Specific Norms

Consumers will only grant a brand permission to launch a new initiative if the initiative is not incongruent with the associations that consumers have with the brand. While this is somewhat reminiscent of the 'fit' concept in the brand extension literature, a low fit between the brand and the extension category does not necessarily imply a violation of brand-specific norms (although the reverse does hold). For instance, the introduction of a soft drink (for example, Virgin Cola) is a poor fit with the Virgin brand since Virgin does not produce any other food-related products, nor is cola a category that is particularly trendy, glamorous, or entertaining – typical associations with the Virgin brand name. However, Virgin does have permission to introduce Virgin Cola since the brand does have a history of implausible extensions and consumers may therefore be willing to consider another poorly fitting extension.

The brand-specific norms can be based on the brand's history and identity (as in the Virgin Cola example), but also on consumers' personal experience with the brand. For instance, consumers may be generally reluctant to give Disney permission to attach its brand name to violent grown-up movies (because of its child-focused brand identity), but this may be especially true for parents of toddlers who watch many animated Disney movies (because of their personal experience with the brand). Furthermore, the effect of a brand's history and identity on its ability to obtain permission depends on the type of initiative it wants to launch; the same brand characteristic can facilitate some requests for permission, but frustrate others. For instance, the non-profit nature of the Red Cross may make people more accepting of the variety of methods it employs to generate funds, but it may also make it harder to gain acceptance on drugstore shelves (for example, selling Red Cross branded adhesive bandages).

Social Norms

Whether brand permission is granted not only depends on characteristics of the brand, but also on the expectations that consumers hold, independent of those specific brand characteristics. We already mentioned consumers' personal experience with the brand as one factor that determines consumers' expectations about the brand and, thus, their willingness to grant permission. In addition, consumers' expectations are also influenced by social norms: general cultural norms, marketplace conventions, and norms that are prevalent in a given consumer community. Cultural differences can influence the granting of brand permission through differences in consumers' perceptions of the brand. For instance, since Stella Artois beer has a more upscale positioning in the US and the UK than in Belgium, American and British consumers are more likely to accept Stella's sponsorship of a classical opera performance than are Belgian consumers. Furthermore, even if a brand is perceived similarly in different cultures, these cultures may still differ in the type of activities that a brand in that product category is allowed to engage in. For instance, a beer brand sponsoring a college event is probably less permissible to American consumers than it is to the average Belgian consumer.

Similarly, a brand's ability to generate permission also depends on the conventions that are prevalent in the marketplace that the brand operates in. For instance, consumers hold different expectations for online retailers than for bricks-and-mortar retailers and will grant permission accordingly. One implication is that consumers may more readily accept extensive customization and storage of purchase preferences from online retailers than from traditional retailers. Marketplace conventions also refer to specific actions undertaken by competitors. If the introduction of Reebok Fitness Water had been successful, people would probably be more willing to consider a Nike sports drink in the future.

Finally, the norms that a brand is supposed to adhere to can also originate in specific consumer communities. The rise of the Internet has led to a marked increase in the popularity of virtual consumer communities. One particularly relevant type of consumer community is the online brand community, such as groups of diehard Harley Davidson fans and Apple aficionados who exchange suggestions, opinions, and the latest brand rumors through emails and in online chat rooms. Furthermore, other virtual communities that are not focused on a particular brand, such as communities organized around specific product categories (for example, cars or electronics), demographics (for example, single mothers), or interests and behaviors (for example, long-distance running) are also relevant since they exchange opinions and information about brands that relate to their interests. Through the exchange of information about brands and product categories, these communities create normative guidelines that their members expect brands to adhere to.

Consumer–Brand Relationship Norms

In line with this last observation, the relationship between the brand and the consumer also influences a brand's ability to obtain permission for changes in its strategy, often in ways that are not intuitive. Consider, for instance, the closeness of consumers' perceived relationship with the brand. A consumer who feels that she has a close connection with the brand will probably have a very favorable opinion of the brand and, compared to the average consumer, be more likely to believe that any new initiative by this brand will be successful (for example, that a new product carrying the brand name will be of high quality). Yet if a brand is central to a consumer's lifestyle, then this consumer is also bound to be more vigilant and concerned about any novel brand actions. In other words, consumers who feel personally connected to a brand will be more likely to think that a new brand initiative will be of high quality, yet will be less likely to give the brand permission to engage in this new initiative. For instance, the aforementioned Apple aficionados may be convinced that the Apple iPhone will deliver great reception, sleek design, and a user-friendly interface, yet may still balk at the idea of the Apple brand being associated with a phone. This apparent paradox also highlights another distinction between extension evaluations and brand permission; whereas consumers focus on the extension product when evaluating an extension, the granting of permission is partially dependent on concerns about the *parent brand* itself.

Of course, a positive relationship with consumers does not necessarily make it harder for brands to gain permission. If consumers generally trust a brand and feel as if the brand respects them and understands their needs and goals, they will be more likely to suspend skepticism and consider a new brand initiative that they would have otherwise dismissed as inconsistent with their expectations. For instance, a dog owner who feels that Iams shares his concerns and trusts Iams to do what's right for his dog, is more likely to consider Iams pet insurance than a dog owner who does not feel any special attachment to Iams.

Aside from the strength of the brand–consumer relationship, the nature of that relationship matters as well. While consumers who feel that the brand understands their needs may be more likely to grant the brand permission, the *level* of understanding may limit the types of initiatives for which the brand will receive permission. For instance, even though a corporate customer may feel that IBM has a great understanding of its technology needs, they may still be reluctant to accept strategic consulting services from a technology company. Similarly, the type of activities that a brand is allowed to engage in depends on whether consumers perceive their relationship with the brand as an exchange relationship or a communal relationship. Whereas unilateral decisions based on an asymmetric power distribution are acceptable in an exchange relationship, they are generally frowned upon in a communal relationship. This is quite relevant for a lot of firms that have positioned themselves as collaborative, democratic partners of their customers.

While this friendly, egalitarian image may result in more favorable attitudes towards the company, it also carries with it the obligation to be consistent with this image and thus limits the range of actions the firm can take. For instance, eBay has promoted itself as a democratic marketplace, which sharply contrasts with its recent, unanticipated decision to greatly increase the fees for sellers on its web space. Not surprisingly, many sellers refused to grant eBay permission for such an unexpected and unilaterally decided price change and, as a result, abandoned eBay under loud protest.

Consumer Characteristics

Brand-specific associations, social conventions, and the relationship between consumers and the brand all determine the norms that brands are expected to abide by. Whether consumers will refuse to grant permission to new initiatives that fail to meet these norms depends not only on the magnitude of the violation and the importance of the norm, but also on consumers' dispositional skepticism and feelings of empowerment. To the extent that consumers are more skeptical of firms' actions and feel more empowered to decide what the marketplace should look like, they will also be more sensitive to deviations from their expectations and, thus, more likely to refuse permission for those brand initiatives that do violate these expectations.

MEASURING BRAND PERMISSION

Of course, brand permission can only be a managerially actionable construct if it can be measured and manipulated. Let us first address how it could be measured. Brand permission can *not* be measured by assessing the expected performance of the new initiative, since brand permission is independent from expected quality. For instance, asking consumers whether they liked the taste of New Coke did not reveal that consumers considered it inappropriate for Coca-Cola to change its classic formula. Alternatively, one could directly measure consumers' purchase intentions. However, this will also yield imperfect information since brand permission is necessary, but not sufficient for favorable purchase intentions. If consumers appear to be willing to purchase Iams pet insurance, that would indeed indicate that Iams has permission to introduce pet insurance. However, if consumers indicate little interest in purchasing Iams pet insurance, this does not imply that they deny Iams permission to offer this service. Indeed, consumers may consider it completely appropriate for Iams to offer insurance, but simply do not expect that it will be of high quality.

Instead of measuring whether consumers like the new brand initiative, we propose that brand permission can be assessed by measuring whether consumers would *consider* the new initiative *provided it performs well*. For instance, would pet owners consider Iams as a legitimate provider of pet insurance if Iams were to offer high quality pet insurance? Likelihood of consideration can be assessed directly by asking consumers if they would include it in their consideration set, but it can also be measured indirectly by gauging consumers' willingness to search for more information about this new initiative: to what extent are consumers willing to find out more about Iams pet insurance? Similarly, IBM could measure its brand's permission to provide strategic management advice by measuring whether managers would be willing to listen to IBM advisers provided they were sufficiently competent at this task.

Thus, brand permission (that is, consumers' openness to a brand initiative) can be generally operationalized as consumers' willingness to consider the new initiative if it provides an acceptable level of quality. More concretely, brand permission can be measured by first assuring respondents of the quality of the new initiative and then asking them to indicate whether they are open to the initiative, whether they find it appropriate for the brand to launch this new initiative, whether they would consider it, and whether they would be willing to find out more information about it. For instance, Reebok could ask amateur athletes if they would be willing to consider a Reebok sports drink if it tasted similar to the drinks they are currently consuming.

MANAGING BRAND PERMISSION

Companies can manage brand permission effectively by taking it into account when deciding on new initiatives, by presenting new initiatives in a way that is less likely to elicit incongruent expectations, and by managing their long-term ability to generate permission. The first point is rather straightforward. Brands should refrain from launching initiatives for which they are unlikely to receive permission and should instead try to tailor their strategies to consumers' expectations. However, to implement this recommendation successfully, managers not only need to be able to measure brand permission (see the preceding section), but also need to be aware of consumers' expectations. This implies a thorough understanding of the determinants of brand permission we discussed earlier, ranging from consumers' brand perceptions and their personal relationship with the brand to expectations created in consumer communities and general cultural norms.

Second, firms can also increase the likelihood that a given initiative will receive permission by carefully managing how the initiative is presented in order to avoid activating incongruent expectations. While it is often not feasible to change consumers' norms and expectations, it is usually possible to influence which norms consumers activate when considering a specific brand initiative. Managers should attempt to emphasize those norms that favor permission and avoid activating those that do not. For instance, when advertising its pet insurance, Iams could emphasize its understanding of pet owners' needs and customers' favorable past experiences with Iams pet food, yet should avoid drawing attention to marketplace conventions. Furthermore, managers can also increase the likelihood of gaining permission for a given initiative by changing the way in which the initiative is launched, in particular by emphasizing consumers' involvement in the development of the initiative. For instance, when Home Depot started selling potato chips and soda in some of its stores, they emphasized that they started this initiative at the request of their customers. However, one could even go further and first seek consumers' permission for the new initiative before actually launching it, and, at the time of the launch, point out that permission had already been sought and obtained. Given the social and normative nature of brand permission, information about the prior acceptance of the new brand initiative by a sizeable number of consumers should substantially increase the likelihood of gaining permission. Consider, for instance, a 2005 Procter & Gamble advertising campaign in which consumers were asked to vote online for their favorite flavor for a new Crest toothpaste line. If sufficiently publicized, the fact that a majority of consumers supported a particular product modification may facilitate other consumers' acceptance of this change in Crest's offering.

Finally, firms should also manage the brand's long-term ability to generate permission. This is no easy task since, as we pointed out earlier, the same brand characteristic (for example, a communal relationship with consumers) can facilitate gaining permission for one action but make it harder to gain permission for another. However, we contend that there are a few strategies that should increase the general likelihood of gaining permission, regardless of the nature of the initiative. First, it is essential that consumers *trust* the brand to do what is good for them. Genuine trustworthiness is not domain-specific (as is, for instance, expertise), and is instead seen as a dispositional trait of the brand. Brands that can instill this trust in consumers are more likely to receive the benefit of the doubt when proposing unorthodox changes in their strategies. As such, trust is the antidote to consumer skepticism and reduces consumers' sensitivity to norm violations. Second, managers should be careful not to *typecast* brands. Consumers should feel that the brand understands their needs and goals, but consumers' favorable impression of the brand should not be completely tied to the brand's specific area of expertise. For instance, IBM's historic background and its communication focus on IT managers has allowed the firm to (successfully) typecast itself as a technology company, but this now makes it harder for them to gain access to other executives and to provide strategic consulting services.

CONCLUSION

In this chapter we have proposed a new construct, brand permission, as a way to better understand consumers' reactions to new brand initiatives. We have defined brand permission as consumers' openness to considering a new brand initiative. Unlike extension evaluation, brand permission applies to changes in every aspect of the marketing mix and does not depend on the perceived quality of the initiative, but rather on its perceived appropriateness. We have proposed a multi-stage model in which consumers who encounter a new brand initiative first decide whether to grant the brand permission (that is, whether to consider the initiative) and, if this stage is concluded favorably, then proceed to assess the perceived quality of the initiative (for example, evaluate the brand extension).

In our proposed model, consumers first decide whether to grant the brand permission through an effortless, unconscious process. Only if that fails to produce a confident conclusion, will consumers consciously debate whether it is appropriate for the brand to launch this new initiative. Consumers assess the appropriateness of the initiative by comparing it to automatically activated norms. These norms could originate from the social environment (such as cultural norms and marketplace conventions), from the strength and nature of the brand–consumer relationship, or from consumers' brand-specific associations. If the new brand initiative significantly deviates from these norms, consumers are less likely to give the brand permission for the initiative. We have argued that firms can increase the likelihood of gaining brand permission in several ways. They can do so by selectively launching initiatives that are consistent with these norms, by selectively emphasizing norms that are consistent with a new initiative, by emphasizing consumers' input in the generation of the initiative, and by instilling trust in the brand and avoiding typecasting.

We hope that this new conceptualization will contribute to existing branding research and practice by providing a general framework that captures consumers' initial reaction to any type of new brand initiative, and by emphasizing the distinction between this initial consideration decision and the subsequent quality assessment. Most important, however, we want to draw attention to the *normative* component of consumer reactions, which we feel has thus far been ignored due to an almost exclusive focus on perceived quality and performance. Even if consumers believe that a new brand initiative will deliver superior performance, they may still be unwilling to consider that initiative because they do not deem it appropriate. This distinction between quality and normative appropriateness has important implications, which we will briefly discuss in conclusion. A first implication concerns the effect of emotional attachment to the brand. Compared to the average consumer, consumers who have a very close relationship with a brand are more likely to believe that anything the brand engages in will be done well, yet they are less likely to grant the brand permission for any action that may make the brand different from the brand they are attached to. Therefore, while emotional attachment to the brand tends to lead to more favorable quality judgments, it also leads to less favorable permission judgments. A second implication is that, unlike extension evaluations, which are exclusively driven by consumers' concern about the extension, the granting of brand permission is also driven by concern about the brand itself. Consumers who find it inappropriate for the Red Cross to sell Red Cross branded bandages in drugstores, are not concerned about the quality of the bandages, but are concerned about what this says about the Red Cross. This suggests that the launch of a high quality initiative for which the brand does not have permission may cause greater brand dilution than the launch of a low quality initiative for which the brand did have permission. By this reasoning, the Coke brand would have been hurt less by the launch of an unappetizing new flavor than by the unacceptable improvement of the original formula. Indeed, if consumers are disappointed by the quality of a new initiative, this will mainly affect the success of the initiative. However, if consumers perceive that the new initiative is something the brand *did not have permission for*, then this reflects poorly on the brand itself.

REFERENCES

Aaker, David A. and Kevin Lane Keller (1990), 'Consumer evaluations of brand extensions', *Journal of Marketing*, **54** (January), 27–41.

Boush, David M. and Barbara Loken (1991), 'A process-tracing study of brand extension evaluation', *Journal of Marketing Research*, **28** (February), 16–28.

Broniarczyk, Susan M. and Joseph W. Alba (1994), 'The importance of the brand in brand extension', *Journal of Marketing Research*, **31**(2), 214–28.

Fishbein, Martin and Icek Ajzen (1975), *Belief, Attitude, Intention, and Behavior*, Reading, MA: Addison-Wesley Publishing Company.

Fiske, Susan T. and Mark A. Pavelchak (1986), 'Category-based versus piecemeal-based affective responses: developments in schema-triggered affect', in Richard M. Sorrentino and Edward Tory Higgins (eds), *Handbook of Motivation and Cognition: Foundations of Social Behavior*, New York: Guilford Press, pp. 167–203.

Fry, Joseph N. (1967), 'Family branding and consumer brand choice', *Journal of Marketing Research*, **4** (August), 237–47.

Kahneman, Daniel and Dale T. Miller (1986), 'Norm theory: comparing reality to its alternatives', *Psychological Review*, **93**(2), 136–53.

Kahneman, Daniel and Shane Frederick (2002), 'Representativeness revisited: attribute substitution in intuitive judgment', in Thomas Gilovich, Dale Griffin and Daniel Kahneman (eds), *Heuristics and Biases: The Psychology of Intuitive Judgment*, New York: Cambridge University Press, pp. 49–81.

Keller, Kevin Lane (1993), 'Conceptualizing, measuring, and managing customer-based brand equity', *Journal of Marketing*, **57**(1), 1–22.

Neuhaus, Colin F. and James R. Taylor (1972), 'Variables affecting sales of family-branded products', *Journal of Marketing Research*, **14** (November), 419–22.

Park, C. Whan, Sandra Milberg and Robert Lawson (1991), 'Evaluation of brand extensions: the role of product feature similarity and brand concept consistency', *Journal of Consumer Research*, **18** (September), 185–93.

Simmons, Joseph P. and Leif D. Nelson (2006), 'Intuitive confidence: choosing between intuitive and nonintuitive alternatives', *Journal of Experimental Psychology: General*, **135**(3), 409–28.

Srinivasan, Shuba (2006), 'How do marketing investments benefit brand revenue premiums?', Working Paper, The A. Gary Anderson Graduate School of Management, University of California, Riverside.

Tauber, Edward M. (1988), 'Brand leverage: strategy for growth in a cost-controlled world', *Journal of Advertising Research*, **28** (August/September), 26–30.

Winkielman, Piotr and John T. Cacioppo (2001), 'Mind at ease puts a smile on the face: psychophysiological evidence that processing facilitation elicits positive affect', *Journal of Personality and Social Psychology*, **81**(6), 989–1000.

3. When brands resonate

Susan Fournier, Michael R. Solomon and Basil G. Englis

INTRODUCTION

Managing brands is, in essence, about managing brand meanings (Allen et al., 2008; McCracken, 2005; Sherry, 2005). Brand managers craft meanings for their brands, attend to their articulation through product design and 4Ps specification, leverage claimed brand meanings through line and product extensions, refine meanings through product innovations and repositioning strategies, and organize meanings across product offerings into brand architectures that can guide brand strategies over time. Advertising agencies, package designers, naming consultants, identity firms, logo developers, brand licensing brokers, placement agencies, and public relations firms are just some of the collaborators in a global industry devoted to the task of brand meaning management. This complex and synergistic services network is based upon one simple but critical truth: strong brands are built upon strong meanings. The corollary is a straightforward one: brands die when their meanings lose significance in consumers' lives.

Feldwick (2002) formalized this implied value creation mechanism in his decompositional model of consumer-based brand equity (see Figure 3.1). Feldwick proposes a causal relationship between the various components of brand equity such that brand meanings (that is, 'the collective associations and beliefs the consumer has about the brand') drive brand strength (that is, 'a measure of the strength of consumers' attachments to a brand'), which in turn generates monetary value from the brand as a separable asset (that is, brand value) (2002, p. 11).

Despite the centrality of brand meaning to brand equity formulations, consumer research that is focused upon this crucial construct or its foundational relationship to brand equity creation is lacking. While brand practitioners pay much attention to what brands mean in the sense of their marketplace positioning, surprisingly little theorizing has occurred regarding the notion of brand meaning. In particular, researchers have paid limited theoretical attention to understanding how, why, or when a brand's particular meanings come to matter in the marketplace and in consumers' minds. Keller recently echoed these shortcomings when he noted: 'there are multiple dimensions of brand knowledge. It is essential that this multidimensionality be fully addressed in developing consumer behavior theory to explain branding phenomena. A potential danger with consumer research into branding is to adopt too narrow a perspective' (Keller, 2003, pp.595–6).

This chapter provides a conceptual framework to better understand the role of brand meaning in the creation of brand equity. Drawing upon research in a branding paradigm that emphasizes the co-creation of brands by consumers, cultures and firms (Allen et al.,

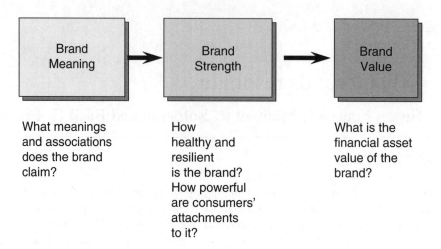

Source: Adapted from Feldwick (2002).

Figure 3.1   Feldwick's model of consumer-based brand equity

2008), we offer *brand meaning resonance* as a construct specifying the meaning-based sources from which brand strength and brand value accrue. Brand meaning resonance is the factor that helps explain the realization of a brand's claimed meaning portfolio to the brand's meaning makers. It is the quality that drives 'engagement', a popular buzzword characterizing the marketing paradigm today (McClelland, 2006; McClelland and Consoli, 2006).

In the sections below, we offer three forms or types of resonance as process moderators within the brand equity chain. Two moderators, *personal resonance* and *cultural resonance*, provide insight into the question of how brand meaning translates into and drives brand strength: that is, the brand meaning→brand strength connection. We also address the brand strength→brand value linkage in the brand equity chain, and offer *organizational resonance* as the process mechanism driving the successful capture of value from strength created in the brand. By accounting for the resonant qualities of claimed brand meanings to consumers, cultures and firms, we intend for the proposed framework to provide managers with metrics that allow sharpened insight into the creation of strong brands, and the processes that sustain brand value over the long run. This objective is in keeping with a research thrust toward greater accountability for marketing (Marketing Science Institute, 2002). It also responds to calls for more customer-centricity in our branding theories (Arnould and Thompson, 2005), and marketing that attends to broader organizational issues overall (Doyle, 2000).

Below we review literature in support of our three proposed resonance forms. With this as background, we dimensionalize each form of resonance, and provide a propositional inventory to illustrate the different routes and mechanisms through which brands can attain stronger resonance in the marketplace and consumers' lives.

SYSTEMS FOR UNDERSTANDING THE BRAND MEANING→ BRAND STRENGTH CONNECTION

After decades of brand equity research, only three evaluative meaning qualities – favorability, top-of-mind salience and uniqueness – are repeatedly recognized as important precursors of brand strength in the marketplace (cf., Keller, 1993). Farquhar et al. (1992) add dominance as an evaluative property of specific brand associations that is related to brand strength, as defined specifically within the context of brand extensions. It is interesting to note that these four meaning qualifiers all derive from the cognitive psychological paradigm that shaped them, and the experimental research traditions by which they have been advanced. There is a notable absence of an examination of brand meanings in their cultural context, as these are leveraged in the construction of personal and social lives.

It is clearly useful to understand which brand associations are top-of-mind, which are tied most closely with the brand, and which are unique vis-à-vis competitive offerings. However, these qualities are by no means exhaustive in their consideration of meaning-based routes to brand strength. Research in what some refer to as the *alternative branding paradigm* (Allen et al., 2008) suggests that a brand obtains marketplace significance through venues beyond the ownership of isolated and unique category associations. A brand can align with cultural tensions and against prevailing ideologies (Holt, 2005). It can embed itself in the fabric of popular culture and hitch itself to evocative celebrities (McCracken, 1989). It can become entrenched in household habits and rituals (Chang Coupland, 2005). It can deliver against pressing identity tasks and concerns (Fournier, 1998). Moreover, as Keller (1993) has noted, the strategy of claiming unique and favorable meanings can prove questionable when these associations have little perceived value in consumers' worlds. Nowhere in the dominant paradigm are the mechanisms through which meanings become salient or favorable specified: the *how* in addition to the *what*. Extant approaches to brand meaning qualification therefore limit managerial applicability by constraining the routes to brand strength development, or worse still, implying routes that may not translate to value capture in the end.

The alternative strength routes listed above derive from basic insights into the co-created aspects of the brand (for a detailed account of brand co-creation, see Allen et al., 2008). Departing significantly from firm-centric models that posit marketers as the brand's sole creator, the co-creation paradigm accepts two additional authors for the brand: cultures and consumers. Cultural arbiters in the process of brand meaning making – including brand communities and sub-cultures, lifestyle and interest groups, media pundits, journalists, social critics, Hollywood producers, information gatekeepers and more – craft, clarify and sort meanings for the brand, sometimes swamping marketer-controlled messages (Fournier and Herman, 2006; Holt, 2002; Kozinets, 2001; McCracken, 1986, 2005; Muniz and O'Guinn, 2001, 2005; Muniz and Schau, 2005; Solomon, 1989; Thompson and Haytko, 1997).

Holt (2004) offers perhaps the most comprehensive cultural account for the ascendancy of strong iconic brands like Volkswagen and Nike. According to Holt, a strong brand is a story that circulates in culture, a story that somehow satisfies the cultural hungers of the day. His is a top-down process model through which brands become strong by capturing the deep-seated cultural zeitgeist of the moment – a zeitgeist aligned squarely against the prevailing cultural ideology and its moral imperatives, and the anxieties and tensions that aspiration to this general national vision can create. Iconic brands deliver mythic meanings that can 'repair the culture when and where it is in particular need of mending' (Holt, 2003, p. 48). Thus, times of cultural anxiety and crisis provide windows of opportunity for laying claim to the resonant meanings capable of birthing iconic brands.

A second system for brand meaning making involves the transfer of the culturally-shared meanings resident in products and brands into the lives of the consumers that buy and use them. In the process of consumer co-creation, the person reworks the brand's shared meanings to adapt to his or her unique circumstances for purposes of individual communication and categorization (Fournier, 1998). As observed in a classic branding article, 'the power of a brand resides in the minds of customers' (Keller, 2001, p. 3) and it is in this sense that consumers are said to form relationships with brands: 'Consumers are not just buying brands because they like them or because they work well; they are involved in a myriad of different relationships with a collectivity of brands so as to benefit from the meanings they add to their lives' (Fournier, 1998, p. 361). As the meanings consumers seek are many and varied, so too are the brand relationships formed.

Through the processes of co-creation, consumers and cultures interpret brands differently, add localized meanings to them, and sometimes redirect them in unexpected ways (Fournier, 1998; Holt, 2002; Kozinets, 2001; Thompson and Haytko, 1997). Co-creation thus serves as the meta-process whereby meanings obtain relevance and significance by resonating with the hungers of broader cultures as these collide with the identity requirements of individuals' constructed lives. Put differently, strong brands 'matter' somehow to their users and the worlds in which they reside; they provide meanings that people need to make sense of and live their lives (Fournier, 1998). Knowledge-based qualifiers of the meaning→strength connection under-appreciate the brand as a contextualized psycho-cultural entity, and fail to specify the deep psycho-socio-cultural routes through which brand meanings come to matter in our individual and collective lives.

UNDERSTANDING THE BRAND STRENGTH→BRAND VALUE CONNECTION

Knowledge-based meaning qualifiers such as favorability, salience and uniqueness also miss an important part of the brand success equation. While they may help to specify the meaning→strength connection, they do not delineate the link from the creation of brand strength in the market to value capture by the firm. In fact, there is no empirical or theoretical research into processes driving the brand strength→brand value connection. To date we have simply confirmed that a strong brand delivers shareholder value or, put differently, that captured meanings translate into captured value for the firm (Aaker and Jacobson, 1994; Madden et al., 2006).

Recent work at the intersection of organizational behavior research and branding suggests that this simplistic assumption is not always true. Strong brands also require strong internal processes, structures and systems such that fulfillment of the brand promise in the marketplace is guaranteed. Brands and business models, for example, must be aligned (Aaker and Joachimsthaler, 2000). Starbucks stands here as a classic example (Bedbury and Fenichell, 2002), and has aligned its finance, human resources, real estate and supply chain strategies with its customer experience-centric definition of the brand.

Moreover, for a brand to capture value from the marketplace, all employees, from the receptionist to the CEO, must understand the brand intimately (Aurand et al., 2005) and embrace its values as their own (Van Auken, 2000). Extraction of value from the brand also requires that all employees 'live the brand', and reflect the external brand promise through the behaviors they enact on the brand's behalf (Richardson, 2000). Again, Starbucks can point to numerous human resource strategies dedicated to these exact goals. Such internal alignment on the brand has been shown to distinguish strong and weak market performers, as defined by the financial value of the brand (Davis and Dunn, 2002).

Collectively, this research suggests that a brand management function oriented solely to the external market is no longer a viable entity. As Davis and Dunn (2002) put it, strong brands have to start from the inside and then work their way out. While brand strategy research stresses the criticality of the internal story of the brand for marketplace performance, our brand equity systems and diagnostics remain silent on the internal organizational meaning-making activities required to capture value from the brand. Brand equity theory must embrace organizational theory if we are to truly understand how the corporation captures value from its brand.

A POINT OF DEPARTURE: BRAND MEANING RESONANCE

We add to the literature on salience, uniqueness, favorability and dominance and highlight a different quality of meanings that matter in the creation and capture of value through branding. Borrowing from research in psychology, literature studies, anthropology and communications (Larsen and Laszlo, 1990; McQuarrie and Mick, 1992; Mick and Buhl, 1992; Pinkett, 2002; St. Clair, 1998), we call this quality *brand meaning resonance*. Resonance refers to the reverberation of a brand's meanings within the contexts of the organization, the broader culture and the person's life. It is the echoing, playback, and refiguring of meanings that render them significant and relevant for purposes of communication, categorization and understanding. We distinguish resonance – a quality and characteristic of *meaning* – from perceived relevance, an accepted evaluative judgment of a given *brand* (Agres and Dubitsky, 1996). We offer resonance as the underspecified process mechanism that creates brand strength and brand value, which, as defined in popular brand strength models such as the Y&R AssetValuator (Agres and Dubitsky, 1996), may include perceived relevance for the brand.

Our preceding discussion leads us to argue that in order to truly gauge a brand's equity value, managers need to answer three fundamental questions concerning the resonant quality of their brands:

1. 'How and to what extent does my brand resonate with the consumers that buy and use our brand?'
2. 'How and to what extent does my brand resonate with the broader cultural worlds in which our consumers reside?'
3. 'How well does the external expression of the brand resonate internally? Does the external brand align with the brand as its stewards understand and enact it?'

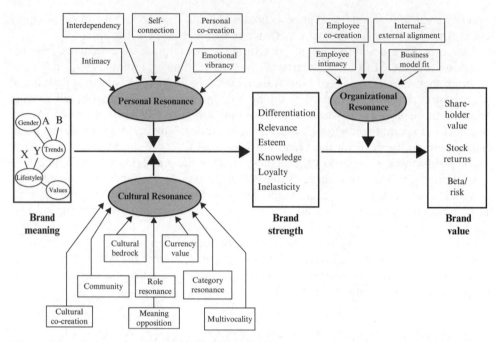

Figure 3.2   A meaning-based model of brand equity

Thus we offer three levels of analysis by which we can profitably analyze brand meaning resonance: the personal, the cultural and the organizational. We define *personal resonance* as the goodness-of-fit between a brand's architecture of claimed meanings and the meanings the consumer seeks in his/her personal life. *Cultural resonance*, in contrast, reflects the degree to which claimed brand meanings reflect, reinforce and shape meanings from the collective social space that links consumers to others in a shared language and interpretation of experience. Finally, *organizational resonance* concerns the goodness-of-fit between the brand's claimed meanings and the internal structures and processes of the firm: its operative business model, its values and goals, the behaviors of employees charged with delivering the face of the brand.

The alignment of a brand's claimed meanings with consumers, cultures and the broader organization provides the mechanism by which the firm can build powerful brands and capture the value therein created, thereby delivering shareholder wealth through the brand. As much as meanings possessing resonant characteristics will engender brand strength and value in the marketplace, brands that do not claim at least some resonance will fail to thrive, and eventually die. Figure 3.2 provides our basic conceptual model, illustrating the process roles our three resonance forms play.

Building from published research in consumer behavior, brand strategy and beyond, we further dimensionalize personal, cultural and organizational resonance by recognizing the different properties and mechanisms that give rise to these different resonance forms (see Figure 3.2). We identify a total of seventeen resonance facets below: five for personal resonance, eight for cultural resonance, and four for organizational resonance. For clarity, we offer propositions that capture anticipated relationships between each resonance dimension and the strength or value of the brand. In scrutinizing the proposed facets, it is interesting to note that while some resonance properties characterize select meaning categories or brand associations, most apply more generally to the brand's claimed meaning portfolio as a whole. This is a consideration not accommodated in extant operational models, which consider individual brand attributes or select attribute–benefit chains as opposed to holistic qualities of the meaning web claimed and captured by the brand.

UNDERSTANDING PERSONAL RESONANCE

Personal resonance is the fit between a brand's claimed meaning portfolio and the consumer's broader life context, and in this sense concerns the extent to which the meanings of the brand reverberate through the consumer's life to become personally relevant and useful (cf. Larsen and Laszlo, 1990). As the facets below detail, a brand meaning portfolio with personal resonance evokes emotions and hedonic sensations, connects at a deeper level via multiple points of contact in the person's life, becomes customized through personal embellishment, and intertwines with daily rituals and operative identity themes. Such brands garner great strength in the marketplace. More generally:

P1: A brand whose meaning portfolio is high in personal resonance will be stronger than a brand whose meaning portfolio is low in personal resonance.

Building from research on the nature and drivers of strong consumer–brand relationships, we identify five facets of personal resonance. The facets reflect different routes, in a sense, through which a brand attains and demonstrates personal resonance in a given consumer's life.

Personal Facet 1: Self-connection

A given brand resonates with a particular consumer to the extent that it establishes a self-connection and provides meanings that are purposive and useful to the living of that consumer's life (Fournier, 1998). Self-connection is revealed through brand meanings that the consumer sees as relevant, important and useful. It forms on the basis of meanings that aid in the attainment and expression of important current concerns, life goals and tasks, or long-standing life themes and identity paradoxes. Self-connecting meanings are powerful in that they help consumers find voice for operative identity and personality themes in their lives. For example, an individual negotiating the conundrums of a mid-life crisis may find increased value in the BMW Z3 brand, which signifies virility, versus the Lincoln brand, whose meanings are tied to a particular generational (and aging) cohort. More generally:

P1.1: A brand with meanings that help consumers resolve important identity issues and concerns is stronger than a brand that does not deliver against identity goals.

Personal Facet 2: Interdependency

A brand can resonate for a given individual to the extent that it engenders habits, rituals and routines that serve to entwine the brand's meanings seamlessly into the person's everyday life, thus granting them regular and reliable access (Chang Coupland, 2005; Fournier, 1998). Starbucks, for example, has perfected a product and retail strategy that encourages ritualized and frequent interaction with its brand, thus increasing consumers' interdependency levels, and hence the strength of its brand. The Harley-Davidson Owners Group works similarly to encourage regular product-centered inter-action among riders (Fournier et al., 2001a). Brand meanings that are accessed regularly and rhythmically through ritual and habit possess strength characteristics that other brands do not.

P1.2: A brand whose meanings an individual accesses on a regular or patterned basis is stronger than a brand whose meanings are tapped serendipitously or infrequently over time.

Personal Facet 3: Intimacy

The strength of the relationship between people (and thereby, the degree to which the rela-tionship reverberates in each partner's life) is often defined in terms of closeness levels (Hinde, 1979). And, closeness, in the interpersonal paradigm, is most commonly concep-tualized in terms of the intimate knowledge surrounding the relationship that a given partner can claim (Altman and Taylor, 1973). Direct corollaries in the branding world are obvious. Cult followers of brands such as Harley-Davidson and Apple Newton know details of their brand's history, including significant product development particulars, myths about product creators, and obscure 'brand trivia' or facts (Muniz and Schau, 2005; Muniz and O'Guinn, 2001; Schouten and McAlexander, 1994). This intimate knowledge is not shared by 'outsiders', and serves as a hallmark for community membership with the brand. Traces of intimate bits of knowledge signify resonant brand relationships and, hence, a stronger stature for the brand.

P1.3: Brand meaning portfolios that include intimate information not likely to be shared by 'outsiders' are stronger than portfolios that do not possess this intimacy trait.

Personal Facet 4: Personal Co-Creation

As we observed previously, we can code brand meanings according to the sources of their creation, highlighting a distinction between public (shared) and private (personally con-structed) meanings for the brand (Richins, 1994). Consumer-generated meanings are con-sidered more innately powerful (Arvidsson, 2005; Mick and Buhl, 1992), and provide the mechanisms through which consumers can establish deep personal relationships with a brand (Elliott and Wattanasuwan, 1998; Fournier, 1998). Consumers are known to create complex brand stories that sometimes include significant people and places, and this elab-oration serves to strengthen brand ties in memory (Escalas and Bettman, 2000; Ritson, 2003). A brand portfolio laden with personally-created (versus marketer-generated) meanings offers routes for enhanced personal connections and hence greater strength in the brand:

P1.4: Brand meaning portfolios with evidence of personal, co-created meanings are stronger than brand meaning portfolios without evidence of such meanings.

Personal Facet 5: Emotional Vibrancy

Some meanings are related distinctly to the worlds of emotion, feeling and hedonic experience, and these emotional meanings may become firmly attached to a given brand. Disney's meanings, for example, are tied to the emotions of happiness and joy; reflection on the handling benefits of BMW provides a pleasurable hedonic experience characteristic of the brand. Emotional and hedonic meanings add spark, vitality and engagement to an individual's lived brand experience (Hirschman and Holbrook, 1982; Schmitt and Simonson, 1997). In fact, Thompson et al. (2006) define resonance specifically in terms of the emotional connections a brand can engage. An emotionally vibrant meaning web deepens the strength of the brand overall:

P1.5: A brand whose meaning portfolio is charged with emotion and hedonic sensation is stronger than a brand whose meanings lack emotion.

UNDERSTANDING CULTURAL RESONANCE

Cultural resonance concerns the degree to which a brand's claimed meanings reflect, echo, reinforce and reshape the meanings from the collective social space that consumers access in defining and shaping their lives. Cultural resonance in a brand concerns a manifestation of meanings from the shared, symbolic language system that allows communication and understanding among members of interpretive communities. Culturally resonant brands are fixed in the social experience and fundamentally embedded in the fabrics of cultural life. The accessibility and interpretive power of the culturally resonant brand engenders brand strength:

P2: A brand whose meaning portfolio is high in cultural resonance is stronger than a brand with a portfolio that is low in cultural resonance.

Building from consumer and cultural research, we identify eight facets by which a brand can engender cultural resonance. These facets reflect the different ways in which a given brand can become embedded in culture, and the evidence that can be assembled in support of shared communicative functions for the brand.

Cultural Facet 1: Cultural Bedrock

While all meanings are constantly in motion (McCracken, 1997), some are more durable and persistent over time. McCracken (1997) calls this 'cultural bedrock' to represent the solid foundations that such meanings can reliably provide. Freedom and independence, for example, have long been noted as enduring American values, while belonging is cited as a core value in Eastern cultures (Reisman, 1969). Traditions and rituals also have cultural significance in large part because of the reliable communication value they provide (Goffman, 1959; Turner, 1969). General cultural categories such as gender also provide fundamental interpretive boundaries across time (McCracken, 2005; Holt and Thompson, 2004). Pivotal historical moments can also function as enduring cultural foundations. Decades are labeled (for example, the 1960s counter-revolution or the 1980s boom years) and specific dates (for example, September 11, D-Day) become forever emblematic of specific meanings to which they became attached. Archetypes (for example, the 'old wise man' and the 'earth mother') also function as enduring cultural meaning-making systems that appear frequently in myths, stories and dreams (Jung, 1959). Indeed, Young & Rubicam's BrandAsset Valuator® brand equity measurement system includes a typology of archetypes to sort various claimed meanings of the brand (cf. Solomon, 2007).

A brand can insinuate itself into the cultural bedrock through any number of strategies: through alignment with core values (for example, Apple represents individual freedom of expression), cultural archetypes (for example, the hero in Nike; the outlaw in Harley), pivotal historical moments (for example, Coca-Cola and World War II), or time/decade meanings (for example, Levi's jeans and the 1960s). A brand that claims meanings that are somehow embedded in the bedrock of culture exhibits sustained strength and endurance across time (Aaker, 1996).

P2.1: A brand whose portfolio of meanings includes one or more connections to enduring and characteristic cultural meaning categories will evidence greater marketplace strength than one without connections to enduring cultural meanings.

Cultural Facet 2: Currency Value

Some cultural meanings are 'hotter' than others in the sense that they play a critical role in defining the character of contemporary life. Hot meanings capture operative fads and trends, or reflect fashions of the moment (McCracken, 2005; Studeman et al., 2000). Brands often align themselves with currency meanings as a path to the creation of brand strength. Absolut has relied on a strategy of cultural currency for building its brand of vodka for over 25 years, providing a steady stream of iconic print advertisements that essentially play back the meanings-of-the-moment that defined the character of the day (for example, 'Absolut Release' ran in 1986; 'Absolut Stardom' ran in the celebrity-crazed 1990s). Some brand theorists claim that meanings with currency value are innately more powerful, especially in cultures characterized by increasing rates of change (Gladwell, 1997; McCracken, 2002). On the flip side, Thompson et al. (2006) posit lost currency value, in the form of a reduced fit of the brand with the times, as a primary metric for diagnosing brand demise. Currency value has in fact been included in select brand strength conceptualizations (for example, Landor's heat factor, Studeman et al., 2000) in light of the power that contemporary connections can weigh.

P2.2: Brands that lay claim to meanings-of-the-moment benefit from enhanced cultural resonance, and are stronger than brands that do not claim meanings-of-the-moment and lack the currency value obtained by capturing meanings-of-the-day.

Cultural Facet 3: Meaning Opposition

Prior research on the meaning of products and brands recognizes the significant semiotic properties of paradox and antithesis often operative in the meaning web (Mick and Buhl,

1992; Mick and Fournier, 1998; Zaltman, 2003). Brand meaning portfolios that naturally house oppositional meanings include, for example, the conflicting concepts of solitude and camaraderie for Starbucks and BMX mountain bikes (Christensen and Olson, 2002), or, for Martha Stewart, perfection and homemaking rolled into one (Fournier and Herman, 2006). The presence of opposing meanings in the portfolio creates energies and tensions around the brand and hence increased opportunities for processing and relating (McQuarrie and Mick, 1992, 1999; Mick and Fournier, 1998). Meaning contradictions can also manifest through juxtaposition against the prevailing ideology and in service of cultural revolution and change (Holt, 2004). Mountain Dew, for example, aligned with the emergent Slacker mentality in the early 1990s and thus gathered momentum against the goal-driven, free-agent ethos that was popular during this time of materialism and economic advance. The Martha Stewart brand also gained traction by pitting itself against the popular ethos; in this case, the feminist mystique and the rejection of traditional female roles that this characteristically entailed. More generally:

P2.3: A brand whose meaning portfolio contains oppositional meanings or offers potent juxtapositions against prevailing ideologies and tensions is stronger than a brand that does not reflect meaning contradiction in its portfolio.

Cultural Facet 4: Role Resonance and Portfolio Effects

Another way a brand can connect to culture is to become emblematic of acknowledged social roles. Research has revealed the presence of consumption constellations: collections of (functionally unrelated) brands a consumer displays across different product categories that are intricately linked to expression of a particular social role (Solomon and Assael, 1987). Consumers associate certain brands because they jointly denote Yuppies, experienced mothers, or savvy businesspersons, for example (Englis and Solomon, 1996). Research by Lowry et al. (2001) supports the cross-category consideration of brands and the holistic processing of role-related brand information, and the choice advantages of select brands in this regard. More generally:

P2.4: Brands whose meanings indicate that they are considered emblematic of a particular social role are stronger than brands that do not benefit from this meaning association.

Cultural Facet 5: Category Resonance

Brands can also become part of culture by becoming emblematic of the consumption-based meanings the product category itself conveys. These 'category meanings' are important because they provide a context in which specific brands are constructed and defined; category meanings serve as the standards against which consumers judge all brands (Carpenter and Nakamoto, 1989). Category resonance is revealed by comparing the meaning portfolio for a given brand versus salient category-level meanings to gauge the relative alignment or disconnect therein. Harley-Davidson, for example, has great category resonance. It has come to stand for all the meanings that define the essence of motorcycling, including freedom, adventure and escape (Schouten and McAlexander, 1994). In a similar sense, Porsche is the quintessential sports car (Avery, 2006). Brands that lay claim to fundamental category meanings possess advantages of saliency and consideration that can drive brand penetration and usage and hence brand strength overall.

P2.5: A brand whose meaning portfolio includes associations that quintessentially define the category is stronger than a brand that does not capture the category meanings in its set.

Cultural Facet 6: Cultural Co-Creation

As we have discussed, cultural production systems can serve as significant sources for brand meaning creation. Harley-Davidson, for example, benefited tremendously from the famed riots in Hollister, California in 1957, which were later codified in Marlon Brando's rebel role in *The Wild One*. Aston-Martin grew in stature through Q's innovative product developments in a series of James Bond films. Since culturally-generated meanings are innately more authentic and powerful (Holt, 2002, 2004), cultural meaning-making activity adds strength and stature to a brand. In the ultimate testament to this dynamic, co-created brand meanings fold back into the culture and themselves become part of the social discourse, thus contributing to cultural evolution over time. Budweiser's 'Whassup?' campaign provides a well-known example of this phenomenon. Recognition of the benefits of cultural co-creation has sparked a powerful marketing trend (Wasserman, 2006). Jones soda, for example, enlists its brand community to determine brand packages and flavors (*Business Week*, 2005); Firefox and Apple host websites for the cultural construction of advertising messages (Wasserman, 2006). While some cultural branding theorists suggest brand demise in the case of negatively-toned co-created brand messages (Thompson et al., 2006), others embrace cultural co-creation unequivocally for its ability to lend currency and clarity and hence strength to the brand (Fournier and Herman, 2006; McCracken, 2006).

P2.6: Brands whose meaning portfolios contain culturally co-created meanings are stronger than brands whose meaning portfolios do not contain evidence of cultural co-creation.

Cultural Facet 7: Multivocality

Multivocality concerns the range and diversity of meanings comprising the brand's portfolio of associations, as defined across consumers. It reflects the fact that a given brand (concept) may exhibit varied interpretations according to the unique meaning-seeking needs and demands of particular sub-groups (Elliott, 1994; Elliott and Wattanasuwan, 1998; Thompson and Haytko, 1997). A multivocal brand arguably possesses the power to attract broader and more diverse groups of meaning seekers, thus growing brand strength through numbers. Martha Stewart, for example, embodies an aspirational WASP lifestyle for certain women, legitimization of the homemaker role for some, and status education for others (Fournier et al., 2001b). Snapple's founders followed a similar meaning-making philosophy (Deighton, 2002), and supported a celebrity spokesperson list that included such diverse endorsers as Rush Limbaugh (a staunch conservative Republican) and Howard Stern (a radical, often off-color news commentator). The multivocal brand invites participation and co-creation since it is not constrained by a tight and closed meaning system around the brand.

The multivocal brand also enjoys strength advantages in the form of increased 'legs' for usage and brand extension, since multiple meaning platforms provide a range of product occasions and offerings that can legitimately be defined. Starbucks, for example, evokes meanings related to the taste of coffee, the sensory pleasures of coffee drinking, and the solitude, escapism and energy benefits that accrue. The brand can therefore serve as either a morning wake-up beverage or a social enhancement, and can legitimately support coffee-flavored ice cream, blues music, and energy drinks as attractive brand extensions. Among branding theorists (Court et al., 1997), leverageable brands are inherently stronger than brands with a more restrictive meaning base.

P2.7: A brand that sources its meanings from multiple cultural categories, or captures multiple meaning interpretations within a given cultural category, is stronger than a brand that captures a more focused and restricted meaning base.

Cultural Facet 8: Community

A final route by which a brand can attain socio-cultural resonance presents itself in the form of a community organized around the brand. Muniz and O'Guinn (2001) define brand community as 'a specialized, non-geographically bound collective based on a structural set of social relations among admirers of a brand' (p. 412). These researchers emphasize three defining characteristics of brand community: (1) a consciousness of kind and sense of belonging to an in-group through shared product consumption; (2) rituals, mythologies and traditions that reify the community and brand culture and help it to stay vital over time; and (3) a shared sense of obligation to other community members. Derivative aspects of communities involve oppositional loyalties or strong attitudes against competitive alternatives, and desired marginality whereby community members maintain cache by keeping 'true' membership restricted and small. Community allows users to connect with each other, thereby building the brand by facilitating and deepening connections between brand admirers. Empirical research supports the idea that community drives loyalty and other behavioral indicators of brand strength (Algesheimer et al., 2005; McAlexander et al., 2002).

P2.8: A brand with a meaning portfolio indicating operation of a community (through, for example, in-group versus out-group thinking, oppositional loyalties, and marginality; community rites and rituals; or normative obligations) will be stronger than a brand that has not established community connections.

ORGANIZATIONAL RESONANCE AS A DRIVER OF THE BRAND STRENGTH→BRAND VALUE CONNECTION

Our third resonance form concerns alignment of the brand's claimed meanings with the broader systems, structures and behaviors of the firm. Empirical research has shown that a brand whose claimed meanings resonate inside the company can capture more value than a brand without alignment between the internal and external faces of the brand (Davis and Dunn, 2002; Farquhar, 2005; Harris and de Chernatony, 2001). It is in this sense that *organizational resonance* governs the brand strength→brand value connection and delivers shareholder value to the firm.

P3: A brand whose claimed meaning portfolio is high in organizational resonance is more valuable than a brand with a meaning portfolio that does not resonate inside the firm.

Organizational Facet 1: Fit with the Business Model

Organizational resonance can be reflected at a very strategic level when we examine how a brand fits with the company's broader business model. The business press is filled with examples that demonstrate shareholder value creation only when the company's business model allows it to deliver the desired meanings of the brand successfully. Starbucks' business model, for example, evinces alignment across the strategic areas of finance, real estate development, supply chain, human resources, and all marketing functions to enable the multi-sensory experience that defines the Starbucks brand (Fournier, 2006). In contrast, many 'sensible' brand extensions – that is, extensions that prove logical from a meanings-fit point-of-view – have failed because of insufficient adaptations of the company business model. It made sense to extend Europe's Easy Jet brand into Easy Cafe and Easy Rental Cars, for example, but the firm lacked the core competencies and business systems to enable this brand positioning change (Kumar and Rogers, 2000). Similarly, McDonalds' Golden Arch Hotel confronts significant barriers to successful marketplace performance (Michel, 2005).

P3.1: A brand whose claimed meaning portfolio is aligned with, enabled through, and delivered by the company's business model will capture more value from the marketplace than a brand that does not benefit from synergies between its brand and business model.

Organizational Facet 2: Intimacy and Shared Understanding among Employees

A brand may successfully create meanings that resonate with consumers and the cultures in which they live, but if the firm's employees cannot accurately and consistently execute the brand, this consumer-based brand strength will not translate into captured shareholder value (Van Auken, 2000). As in all classic hierarchy-of-effects models, a first step in delivering the brand promise through brand behavior involves helping employees to develop an intimate understanding of the intended, external brand. An example of this philosophy in action concerns Nike's practice of routinely designating senior executives as 'corporate storytellers' who explain the company's heritage to other employees, from senior hires to the hourly workers at Nike's retail stores (Bedbury and Fenichell, 2002). These brand historians tell stories about the founders of Nike, including the one about the coach of the Oregon track team who poured rubber into his family waffle iron to make better shoes for his team – the origin of the Nike waffle sole. Nike's stories reinforce and reflect core brand values. They emphasize the dedication of runners and coaches involved with the company to reinforce the importance of teamwork. Nike indocrinates new employees into this legend by taking them on a pilgrimage to the track where the coach worked (Ransdell, 2000).

As Davis and Dunn (2002) observe, employees must not simply understand the brand, they must internalize it enough to make it their own. They should care sincerely about what the brand stands for and exhibit alignment between the brand's values and their own (Van Auken, 2000). This philosophy is behind the user-centric hiring programs of many firms including Harley-Davidson, which boasts a majority percentage of motorcyle riders and former Harley Owner's Group (HOG) leaders in its staff and management ranks.

P3.2: A brand that enjoys deep, shared understanding and acceptance among employees concerning the brand's claimed meanings will be able to capture more value from the marketplace than one that does not enjoy deep, shared knowledge and acceptance among employees of the firm.

Organizational Facet 3: Living the Brand through Employee Co-creation

As noted above, the capture of value from the brand requires not only that employees understand and internalize the brand's values and promise, but also that they possess the ability to accurately and consistently execute the brand promise each and every day (Davis and Dunn, 2002). To use the language of the postmodern branding paradigm, the brand is in part a co-creation of the firm's employees, and all employees – from the CEO to the desk clerks – must evince behaviors that reveal and reinforce the intended meanings of the brand. Davis and Dunn (2002) refer to this process of on-brand behaviors and interactions as 'brand assimilation'. Recent empirical research demonstrates how the extent to which employees integrate brand meanings into their own daily work activities drives the success of the company's branding efforts (Aurand et al., 2005; Boyd and Sutherland, 2006). According to Richardson (2000), employees must have accountability for behaviors that are on- versus off-brand. Many firms have incorporated this philosophy in their human resource performance programs. BP Helios, for example, rewards on-brand behavior and regularly tracks what they call 'employee engagement' along with traditional customer-based strength measures for the brand.

P3.3: A brand whose meaning portfolio is enabled directly through meaning-making activities of all employees of the firm will be able to capture more value from the marketplace than a brand that does not benefit from internal brand co-creation activities.

Organizational Facet 4: Alignment of the Internal–External Promise

A final aspect of organizational resonance concerns the degree to which the operative consumer and cultural brand meanings are consistent with the brand meaning as employees of the firm create, understand and enact them (Mitchell, 2002). Research has revealed an alarming disconnect between managers' impressions of a brand's meanings or target segments and the actual meanings and segments the brand delivers (Aaker, 1991; Hoch, 1988).

Worse still, companies sometimes exhibit conflicting internal and external brand messaging. As Mitchell (2002) reports, one health insurance company advertised that the welfare of its patients was the brand's number one priority while at the same time it circulated internal messages stressing cost reductions to drive the value of stock option shares. IBM's repositioning as an e-business specialist in the late 1990s (which led to its renaissance) provides a counter-example of the power of alignment between the internal and external brand meaning spheres. In this case IBM's consumer advertising was accompanied by an elaborate internal branding campaign aimed at convincing employees of the company's credentials as a potent player in cutting-edge technology (Mitchell, 2002).

As previously discussed, the forces of consumer and cultural co-creation can often serve to misalign the brand vis-à-vis managers' intended meanings. Consumer-created ads for the Chevy Tahoe, for example, were for the most part counterposed to the brand's intended positioning (Elliott, 2006). In one video, a shiny Tahoe motors down a country road lined with sunflower fields, jaunty music playing in the background. White lettering appears on the screen: '$70 to fill up the tank, which will last less than 400 miles. Chevy Tahoe.' Another submission asks: 'Like this snowy wilderness? Better get your fill of it now. Say hello to global warming. Brought to you in part by Chevy Tahoe.' Thompson et al.'s (2006) analysis of Starbucks' brand meaning illustrates how hijacked brand meanings and brand-focused parodies can eventually coalesce into a strong and provocative set of anti-meanings for the brand. The authors refer to this unintended consequence as the 'Doppelgänger brand image', and cite the circulation of hijacked, anti-brand messages as a warning sign for the demise for the brand.

P3.4: A brand with internal and external alignment of brand meanings – that is, a brand for which the positioning as understood by management and the positioning as interpreted by consumers are aligned and consistent – will capture more value from the marketplace than will a brand whose internal and external brand meaning portfolios are misaligned.

CONCLUSIONS AND CONTRIBUTIONS

Building from research in the cultural branding paradigm, we have provided a framework to improve our understanding of the role of brand meaning in the creation of brand equity. To this end we have offered the construct of meaning resonance as a moderating process along the brand equity chain, and we proposed seventeen facets dimensionalizing the mechanisms of personal, cultural and organizational meaning resonance that determine brand strength and value capture from the brand. Table 3.1 summarizes these types of brand meaning resonance and the various routes and processes that give rise to our three resonance forms.

It is interesting to consider how our framework and propositions compare with accepted perspectives on branding. Traditional theorists, for example, interpret multi-vocal meaning systems as 'confused brands' with mixed messages and a characteristically weaker asset base (Aaker, 1991; Keller et al., 2002; Reeves, 1961). Many argue against category-level positions for fear of easy competitive reproducibility (Ries and Trout, 2001). Others consider brands that align themselves with trends as fleeting and fundamentally compromised (Aaker, 1995). The meaning-based perspective we develop rejects these accepted 'truths' and instead considers them as potential routes for creating brand resonance. Our perspective also allows us to consider qualities such as role resonance, co-creation and brand-business model alignment – all factors not yet incorporated in equity management systems for the brand.

It is our hope that upon validation, our meaning resonance framework can provide not only improved understanding for brand equity theoreticians, but also enhanced utility

Table 3.1 Types of brand meaning resonance and the processes that give rise to these resonance forms

P1. Personal resonance:
The fit between a brand's claimed meaning portfolio and the person's broader life context

> **P1.1 Self-connection**: delivery against identity issues, themes, goals, and concerns
> **P1.2 Interdependence**: habits, rituals, and routines that entwine the brand's meanings seamlessly into the person's everyday life
> **P1.3 Intimacy**: awareness of intimate bits of knowledge not likely shared by brand 'outsiders'
> **P1.4 Personal co-creation**: consumer-generated elaborations on and changes to brand meanings; personal narratives about the brand
> **P1.5 Emotional vibrancy**: emotions, feelings, and hedonic experiences that become firmly attached to the brand

P2. Cultural resonance:
The degree to which a brand's claimed meanings reflect, echo, reinforce, and reshape the meaning fabrics of the broader socio-cultural world

> **P2.1 Cultural bedrock**: connection to durable, persistent, and reliable cultural categories and meaning-making foundations
> **P2.2 Currency value**: connection to fad, fashion, and trend meanings-of-the-moment that are 'hot' in the contemporary society
> **P2.3 Meaning opposition**: tensions and paradoxes surrounding the brand; potent juxtapositions against prevailing ideologies
> **P2.4 Role resonance**: emblematic linkages to acknowledged social roles and their cultural expressions
> **P2.5 Category resonance**: emblematic ties to quintessential and defining category-level meanings
> **P2.6 Cultural co-creation**: culturally-generated elaborations on and changes to brand meanings; culturally-authored narratives about the brand
> **P2.7 Multivocality**: broad and varied interpretations of the brand among different consumer segments
> **P2.8 Community**: in-group/out-group thinking and activities surrounding the brand

P3. Organizational resonance:
The degree to which the external expression of the brand aligns with the internal systems, structures, and behaviors of the firm

> **P3.1 Fit with the business model**: fit of the brand with the company's broader business model
> **P3.2 Intimacy and shared understanding**: accurate and consistent interpretation of brand meanings by employees
> **P3.3 Living the brand through employee co-creation**: execution of on-brand behaviors through daily performances and decisions
> **P3.4 Alignment of the internal-external promise**: fit between culturally-received and organizationally-delivered brand meanings

value to the managers who employ it. The framework can inform a range of management decisions across the brand life cycle, including the development of creative platforms, the refinement or definition of brand positioning strategies, the evaluation of alternative brand executions, and competitive tracking. The resonance framework can also be used to generate segments based on consumers' shared perceptions of the brand, offering a useful meaning-based tool for targeting decisions that may improve the utility of segmentation approaches overall (cf., Oakenfull et al., 2000; Wedel, 2001).

By articulating the meaning→strength and strength→value connections beyond the qualities of favorability, uniqueness, saliency and dominance, our proposed framework also offers brand stewards deeper insight into the factors influencing brand performance in the marketplace, and hence greater diagnostic value in the brand management task. Analysts can scrutinize facet profile scores to determine whether a given brand exhibits strength (dis)advantages because of contemporaneous links with culture, or through the habits and rituals that consumers have forged. Managers can determine where a brand's marketplace position is being compromised by internal misalignments. They can combine the different facets of resonance into a *cumulative resonance index* that will provide predictive capacity to inform marketing investment and strategy decisions.

DIRECTIONS FOR FUTURE RESEARCH

Going forward, the operationalization of core constructs in the model stands as an immediate and pressing goal. This is a challenging task, as the different facets present unique properties and measurement requirements. Measurement of the cultural bedrock facet, for example, requires the *a priori* determination of the emblematic character of particular socio-cultural meaning categories, such that consumers can rate a brand evoking those meanings according to the operative scheme. Co-creation as a property of the meaning web is a much more idiosyncratic quality that requires a different type of background research: namely, research specific to each brand's historical marketing programs that allows us to gauge consumer and cultural sources of meaning overall.

The brand's performance on other resonance facets can be determined using coders and judges who scrutinize the brand's elicited meaning portfolio for the presence of select resonance properties identified in the propositions above. Does the meaning web include paradoxical meanings, for example; are emotions manifest in the meaning web? Performance on yet other resonance facets can be derived directly from an analysis of the brand's claimed meaning web. Researchers might calculate the number and range of elicited meanings within and across subjects to represent multivocality, or to estimate the variance in the number of meanings elicited by consumers for each brand. Other facets could be rated by consumers directly. For example, scales for the assessment of self-connection could gauge the fit of the generated meaning web with operative identity projects for the consumer; the frequency, strength and quality of interactions between consumer and brand could reflect interdependency levels associated with the brand.

Importantly, assessments of resonance for a particular brand will also require determination of the nature and structure of the resonance model overall. Appropriate mathematical tools can specify whether the model adheres to the multi-faceted, tripartite structure proposed here. Is the model hierarchical in form with personal, cultural and organizational dimensions? Are these facets summative or proportionate in their contributions to the whole?

Research will also be needed to refine a system for brand meaning elicitation such that the resonant qualities of claimed meanings can be gauged. Measurement approaches that leverage online technologies and the visual communications channel (cf., Englis and Solomon, 2000; Grunert-Beckmann and Askegaard, 1997) are likely to possess great potential in expressing the meaning categories we propose and hence may prove most useful in eliciting gestalt brand meaning portfolios. These challenges are clearly time intensive, and will require significant experimentation toward systems development goals.

Through a structured research program that fixes conceptualization of the different meaning categories, a reliable method for meaning elicitation and coding, and valid metrics to quantify the different resonance facets for a brand, we hope to move the field beyond a functional description of what brands mean to a deeper and more managerially useful understanding of how they come to matter – for both consumers and the corporations that steward brands over time.

REFERENCES

Aaker, David A. (1991), *Managing Brand Equity: Capitalizing on the Value of a Brand Name*, New York: The Free Press.

Aaker, David A. (1995), 'Resisting temptations to change a brand position/execution: the power of consistency over time', *Journal of Brand Management*, **3**(4), 251–8.

Aaker, David A. (1996), *Building Strong Brands*, New York: The Free Press.

Aaker, David A. and Robert Jacobson (1994), 'The financial information content of perceived quality', *Journal of Market Research*, **31**(spring), 191–201.

Aaker, David A. and Erich Joachimsthaler (2000), *Brand Leadership*, New York: The Free Press.

Agres, Stuart J. and Tony M. Dubitsky (1996), 'Changing needs for brands', *Journal of Advertising Research*, **36**(1), 21–30.

Algesheimer, Rene, Utpal M. Dholakia and Andreas Herrmann (2005), 'The social influence of brand community: evidence from European car clubs', *Journal of Marketing*, **69**(July), 19–34.

Allen, Chris, Susan Fournier and Felicia Miller (2008), 'Brands and their meaning makers', in Curtis Haugtvedt, Paul Herr and Frank Kardes (eds), *Handbook of Consumer Psychology*, Mahwah, NJ: Lawrence Erlbaum Associates, pp. 781–822.

Altman, Irwin and Dalmas A. Taylor (1973), *Social Penetration: The Development of Interpersonal Relationships*, New York: Holt, Rinehart and Winston.

Arnould, Eric and Craig Thompson (2005), 'Consumer Culture Theory (CCT): twenty years of research', *Journal of Consumer Research*, **31**(March), 868–82.

Arvidsson, Adam (2005), 'Brands: a critical perspective', *Journal of Consumer Culture*, **5**(2), 235–58.

Aurand, Timothy, Linda Gorchels and Terence Bishop (2005), 'Human resource management's role in internal branding: an opportunity for cross-functional brand message synergy', *The Journal of Product and Brand Management*, **14**(May), 163–9.

Avery, Jill (2006), 'Saving face: consumers' collective negotiation of brand meaning change', doctoral thesis proposal at Harvard Business School.

Bedbury, Scott and Stephen Fenichell (2002), *A New Brand World: Eight Principles for Achieving Brand Leadership in the Twenty-first Century*, New York: Penguin Books.

Boyd, G. and M. Sutherland (2006), 'Obtaining employee commitment to living the brand of the organisation', *South African Journal of Business Management*, **37**(1), 9–20.

Business Week (2005), 'Keep up with the Jones, dude!', www.businessweek.com/innovate/content/oct2005/id20051026_869180.htm.

Carpenter, Gregory and Kent Nakamoto (1989), 'Consumer preference formation and pioneering advantage', *Journal of Marketing Research*, **26**(August), 285–98.

Chang Coupland, Jennifer (2005), 'Invisible brands: an ethnography of households and the brands in their kitchen pantries', *Journal of Consumer Research*, **32**(June), 106–18.

Christensen, Glenn and Jerry Olson (2002), 'Mapping consumers' mental models with ZMET', *Psychology & Marketing*, **19**(June), 477–501.

Court, David C., Anthony Freeling, Mark G. Leiter and Andrew J. Parsons (1997), 'If Nike can "Just Do It", why can't we?', *The McKinsey Quarterly*, **3**, 24–34.

Davis, Scott M. and Michael Dunn (2002), *Building the Brand-Driven Business*, San Francisco, CA: Jossey-Bass.

Deighton, John (2002), 'How Snapple got its juice back', *Harvard Business Review*, January, **80**(1), 47–53.

Doyle, Peter (2000), 'Value-based marketing', *Journal of Strategic Marketing*, **8**(4), 299–311.

Elliott, Richard (1994), 'Exploring the symbolic meaning of brands', *British Journal of Management*, **5**(2), 13–19.

Elliott, Richard and Kritsadarat Wattanasuwan (1998), 'Brands as symbolic resources for the construction of consumer identity', *International Journal of Advertising*, **17**(2), 131–44.

Elliott, Stuart (2006), 'Chevy tries a write-your-own-ad approach, and the potshots fly', *The New York Times Online*, 4 April.

Englis, Basil G. and Michael R. Solomon (1996), 'Consumption constellations: implications for advertising strategies', *Journal of Business Research*, **37**(3), November, 183–92.

Englis, Basil B. and Michael R. Solomon (2000), '*Life/Style OnLine*: a web-based methodology for visually-oriented consumer research', *Journal of Interactive Marketing*, **14**(February), 2–14.

Escalas, Jennifer and James Bettman (2000), 'Using narratives to discern self-identity related consumer goals and motivations', in S. Ratneshwar, David Mick and Cynthia Huffman (eds), *The Why of Consumption: Contemporary Perspectives on Consumer Motives, Goals, and Desires*, New York: Routledge, pp. 237–58.

Farquhar, Peter H. (2005), 'Editorial: "brand alignment across organisational boundaries"', *Brand Management*, **13**(2), 96–100.

Farquhar, Peter H., Julia Y. Han, Paul M. Herr and Yuji Ijiri (1992), 'Strategies for leveraging master brands', *Marketing Research*, **4**(3), 32–43.

Feldwick, Paul (2002), *What is Brand Equity Anyway?*, Oxfordshire: World Advertising Research Center.

Fournier, Susan (1998), 'Consumers and their brands: Developing relationship theory in consumer research', *Journal of Consumer Research*, **24**(March), 343–73.

Fournier, Susan (2001), 'Introducing New Coke', Harvard Business School Case 9-500-067, Boston, MA: Harvard Business School Publishing.

Fournier, Susan (2006), 'Starbucks: leveraging the brand for growth', Boston University Case Study.

Fournier, Susan and Kerry Herman (2006), 'Taking stock in Martha Stewart', Boston University School of Management Working Paper, No. 2006-10.

Fournier, Susan, Sylvia Sensiper, James McAlexander and John Schouten (2001a), 'Building Brand Community on the Harley-Davidson Posse Ride', Harvard Business School Case 9-501-009, Boston, MA: Harvard Business School Publishing.

Fournier, Susan, Laura Winig, Kerry Herman and Andrea Wojnicki (2001b), 'Martha Stewart Living Omnimedia (A)', Harvard Business School Case 9-501-080, Boston, MA: Harvard Business School Publishing.

Gladwell, Malcolm (1997), 'The coolhunt', *The New Yorker*, 17 March, pp. 78–88.

Goffman, Erving (1959), *The Presentation of Self in Everyday Life*, New York: Doubleday Anchor.

Grunert-Beckmann, Suzanne C. and Søren Askegaard (1997), 'Seeing with the mind's eye: an exploratory study of the use of pictorial stimuli in value research', in Lynn E. Kahle and Larry Chiagouris (eds), *Values, Lifestyles and Psychographics*, Hillsdale, NJ: Lawrence Erlbaum Associates, pp. 161–82.

Harris, Fiona and Leslie deChernatony (2001), 'Corporate branding and corporate brand performance', *European Journal of Marketing*, **35**(April), 441–56.

Hinde, Robert A. (1979), *Towards Understanding Relationships*, London: Academic Press.

Hirschman, Elizabeth C. and Morris B. Holbrook (1982), 'Hedonic consumption: emerging concepts, methods and propositions', *Journal of Marketing*, **46**(July), 92–101.

Hoch, Stephen J. (1988), 'Who do we know: predicting the interests and opinions of the American consumer', *Journal of Consumer Research*, **15**(December), 315–24.

Holt, Douglas B. (2002), 'Why do brands cause trouble? A dialectical theory of consumer culture and branding', *Journal of Consumer Research*, **29**(June), 70–90.

Holt, Douglas B. (2003), 'What becomes an icon most?', *Harvard Business Review*, **81**(3), 43–9.

Holt, Douglas B. (2004), *How Brands Become Icons: The Principles of Cultural Branding*, Boston, MA: Harvard Business School Press.

Holt, Douglas B. (2005), 'How societies desire brands', in David Glen Mick and S. Ratneshwar (eds), *Inside Consumption: Perspectives on Consumer Motives, Goals, and Desires*, London: Routledge, pp. 273–91.

Holt, Douglas B. and Craig Thompson (2004), 'Man-of-action heroes: the pursuit of heroic masculinity in everyday consumption', *Journal of Consumer Research*, **31**(September), 425–40.

Jung, Carl G. (1959/1980), *Archetypes and the Collective Unconscious*, Princeton, NJ: Princeton University Press.

Keller, Kevin (1993), 'Conceptualizing, measuring, and managing customer-based brand equity', *Journal of Marketing*, **57**(January), 1–22.

Keller, Kevin (2001), 'Building customer-based brand equity: a blueprint for creating strong brands', *Marketing Management*, **10**(2), 14–19.

Keller, Kevin (2003), 'Brand synthesis: The multidimensionality of brand knowledge', *Journal of Consumer Research*, **29**(March), 595–600.

Keller, Kevin, Brian Sternthal and Alice Tybout (2002), 'Three questions you need to ask about your brand', *Harvard Business Review*, **80**(9), 80–85.

Kozinets, Robert V. (2001), 'Utopian enterprise: articulating the meanings of Star Trek's culture of consumption', *Journal of Consumer Research*, **28**(June), 67–88.

Kumar, Nirmalya and Brian Rogers (2000), 'Easy everything: the Internet shop', Case Study GM 874 at International Institute for Management Development, Lausanne, Switzerland.

Larsen, Steen and Janos Laszlo (1990), 'Cultural knowledge and personal experience in the appreciation of literature', *European Journal of Social Psychology*, **20**(5), 425–40.

Lowry, Tina M., Basil G. Englis, Sharon Shavitt and Michael R. Solomon (2001), 'Response latency verification of consumption constellations: implications for advertising strategy', *Journal of Advertising*, **30**(1), 29–39.

Madden, Thomas, Frank Fehle and Susan Fournier (2006), 'Brands matter: an empirical demonstration of the creation of shareholder value through branding', *Journal of the Academy of Marketing Science*, **34**(2), 224–35.

Marketing Science Institute (2002), *2002–2004: A Guide to MSI Research Programs and Procedures*, Cambridge, MA: MSI.

McAlexander, James, John Schouten and Hal Koenig (2002), 'Building brand community', *Journal of Marketing*, **66**(January), 38–54.

McClelland, Steve (2006), 'No longer up for debate: engagement means money', *Adweek*, 8 May, p. 12.

McClelland, Steve and John Consoli (2006), 'At 4A's, harsh words and uncertain futures', *Adweek*, 6 May, pp. 6–7.

McCracken, Grant (1986), 'Culture and consumption: a theoretical account of the structure and movement of the cultural meaning of consumer goods', *Journal of Consumer Research*, **13**(June), 71–84.

McCracken, Grant (1989), 'Who is the celebrity endorser? Cultural foundations of the endorsement process', *Journal of Consumer Research*, **16**(December), 310–21.

McCracken, Grant (1997), *Plenitude, Volume 1: Culture by Commotion*, Toronto: Periph Fluide.

McCracken, Grant (2002), *Transformation, Volume 2: Culture by Commotion*, Toronto: Periph Fluide.

McCracken, Grant (2005), *Culture and Consumption II: Markets, Meaning, and Brand Management*, Bloomington, IN: Indiana University Press.

McCracken, Grant (2006), 'Chevy cocreation', blog entry dated 25 April, at www.cultureby.com/trilogy/2006/04/chevy_cocreatio.html.

McQuarrie, Edward and David Mick (1992), 'On resonance: a critical pluralistic inquiry into advertising rhetoric', *Journal of Consumer Research*, **19**(September), 180–97.

McQuarrie, Edward and David Mick (1999), 'Visual rhetoric in advertising: text-interpretive, experimental, and reader response analyses', *Journal of Consumer Research*, **26**(June), 37–54.

Michel, Stefan (2005), 'McDonald's adventure in the hotel industry', Case Study A02-05-0017 at Thunderbird School of International Management.

Mick, David and Claus Buhl (1992), 'A meaning-based model of advertising experiences', *Journal of Consumer Research*, **19**(December), 317–38.

Mick, David and Susan Fournier (1998), 'Paradoxes of technology: consumer cognizance, emotions, and coping strategies', *Journal of Consumer Research*, **25**(September), 123–43.

Mitchell, Colin (2002), 'Selling the brand inside', *Harvard Business Review*, **80**(1), 99–105.

Muniz, Albert M. and Thomas C. O'Guinn (2001), 'Brand community', *Journal of Consumer Research*, **27**(March), 412–32.

Muniz, Albert M. and Thomas C. O'Guinn (2005), 'Marketing communications in a world of consumption and brand communities', in Allan J. Kimmel (ed.), *Market Communication: New Approaches, Technologies and Styles*, London: Oxford University Press.

Muniz, Albert M. and Hope Schau (2005), 'Religiosity in the abandoned Apple Newton brand community', *Journal of Consumer Research*, **31**(March), 737–47.

Oakenfull, Gillian, Edward Blair, Betsy D. Gelb and Peter Dacin (2000), 'Measuring brand meaning', *Journal of Advertising Research*, **40**(5), 43–53.

O'Guinn, Thomas C. and Albert M. Muñiz Jr (2005), 'Communal consumption and the brand', in David Glen Mick and S. Ratneshwar (eds), *Inside Consumption: Perspectives on Consumer Motives, Goals, and Desires*, New York: Routledge, pp. 252–72.

Pinkett, Randal D. (2002), 'Toward social and cultural resonance with technology: case studies from the creating community connections project', *Proceedings of the International Symposium on Technology and Society (ISTAS): Social Implications of Information and Communication Technology*, Raleigh, NC: Institute for Electrical Engineers.

Ransdell, Eric (2000), 'The Nike story? Just tell it!', *Fast Company*, **31**, 44–52.

Reeves, Rosser (1961), *Reality in Advertising*, New York: Alfred A. Knopf.

Reisman, David (1969), *The Lonely Crowd: A Study of the Changing American Character*, New Haven: Yale University Press; originally published 1950.

Richardson, Melissa (2000), 'Letting the brand guide the people', *Journal of Brand Management*, **7**(4), 275–80.

Richins, Marsha L. (1994), 'Valuing things: the public and private meanings of possessions', *Journal of Consumer Research*, **21**(December), 504–21.

Ries, Al and Jack Trout (2001), *Positioning: The Battle for Your Mind*, New York: McGraw-Hill.

Ritson, Mark (2003), 'Brand bricolage', working paper, London Business School.

Schmitt, Bernd and Alex Simonson (1997), *Marketing Aesthetics: The Strategic Management of Brands, Identity, and Image*, New York: The Free Press.

Schouten, John W. and James McAlexander (1994), 'Subcultures of consumption: an ethnography of new bikers', *Journal of Consumer Research*, **22**(June), 43–61.

Sherry, John (2005), 'Brand Meaning', in Alice Tybout and Tim Calkins (eds), *Kellogg on Branding*, Hoboken, NJ: John Wiley & Sons, pp. 40–69.

Solomon, Michael R. (1989), 'Building up and breaking down: the impact of cultural sorting on symbolic consumption', in J. Sheth and E.C. Hirschman (eds), *Research in Consumer Behavior*, Greenwich, CT: JAI Press: pp. 325–51.

Solomon, Michael R. (2002), *Consumer Behavior: Buying, Having, and Being*, 5th edn, Upper Saddle River, NJ: Prentice Hall.

Solomon, Michael R. (2003), *Conquering Consumerspace: Marketing Strategies for a Branded World*, New York: AMACOM.

Solomon, Michael R. (2007), *Consumer Behavior: Buying, Having, and Being*, 7th edn, Upper Saddle River, NJ: Prentice Hall.

Solomon, Michael R. and Henry Assael (1987), 'The forest or the trees? A gestalt approach to symbolic consumption', in Jean Umiker Sebeok (ed.), *Marketing and Semiotics: New Directions in the Study of Signs for Sale*, Berlin: Mouton de Gruyter, pp. 189–218.

St. Clair, Robert (1998), 'Cultural wisdom, communication theory, and the metaphor of resonance', *Intercultural Communication Studies*, VIII-1, p. 9.

Studeman, Dave, Hayes Roth, Susan Nelson and Allen Adamson (2000), 'Landor ImagePower survey of top 250 technology brands determines market winners and losers', Landor Associates report, downloaded from www.landor.com.

Thompson, Craig J. and Diana L. Haytko (1997), 'Speaking of fashion: consumers' uses of fashion discourses and the appropriation of countervailing cultural meanings', *Journal of Consumer Research*, **24**(June), 15–42.

Thompson, Craig J., Aric Rindflesich and Zeynep Arsel (2006), 'Emotional branding and the strategic value of the doppelgänger brand image', *Journal of Marketing*, **70**(January), 50–64.

Turner, Victor (1969), *The Ritual Process: Structure and Anti-Structure*, Chicago, IL: Aldine.

Van Auken, Brad (2000), 'Developing the brand building organization', *The Journal of Brand Management*, **7**(4), 281–90.

Van Auken, Brad (2004), *The Brand Management Checklist*, London: Kogan Page.

Wasserman, Todd (2006), 'Intelligence gathering', *Brandweek*, 19 June, S9–S18.

Wedel, Michel (2001), 'Is segmentation history?', *Marketing Research*, **13**(4), 26–9.

Zaltman, Gerald (2003), *How Customers Think: Essential Insights into the Mind of the Market*, Boston, MA: Harvard Business School Press.

4. Brand identity: the guiding star for successful brands

Franz-Rudolf Esch

DO MANAGERS LIVE THEIR BRAND?

Managers are aware of the power of strong brands and they emphasize the importance of brands. Nowadays nearly every company pretends to be brand driven. But do managers really live their brand on a daily basis (Esch et al., 2006b)?

When discussing brand-related topics with managers it often becomes evident that they are sometimes under the impression that the brand simply stands for the logo and the nice pictures in their mass communication, and for nothing else. Accordingly, in large companies, marketing and the corporate communication departments are predominately responsible for product and/or corporate brands. Since their options are regularly limited, they concentrate mainly on mass communication and public relations.

Important consumer touchpoints with the brand, as well as those of other stakeholders, are often neglected (Davis and Dunn, 2002). This is the case in many insurance companies; salesmen are regularly unaware of the company's brand identity and thus do not act as brand ambassadors. In international corporations, the employees responsible for operations in different countries or those in different business units are not sensitive to the brand and definitely do not contribute to implementing the brand inside the company; this is supposed to be the task of the company's brand experts only.

Automotive manufacturers often develop and market cars without regard to the brand's identity. From their point of view, all that matters is selling as many cars as possible and securing jobs. This approach might work with strong car brands because they can buffer negative brand associations and prevent the brand from eroding for a period of time. However, weak brands are not able to buffer negative brand associations because they lack brand equity. On the other hand, best practices of other brands such as Procter & Gamble, BMW Group, Apple and Starbucks emphasize the worth of company-wide brand-driven decisions (Esch, 2007). For this reason brand identity must be the manager's point of reference for all their actions and decisions.

Brand identity is a concept that serves as the basis of brand strategy and corporate strategy. Whether brand strategy should drive corporate strategy or vice versa varies from company to company. Two pathways can be differentiated

Pathway 1: Aaker and Joachimsthaler (2000) state that 'brand strategy is the face of business strategy'. Although this statement might at first seem convincing, it must be looked at critically, as it implies that with every shift in business strategy, a company would have to adapt its brand strategy. Deutsche Bank has changed its slogan several times within the last ten years. Such actions typically result in confused stakeholders. Therefore from a marketing point of view, brand strategy should always be taken into account and serve to a greater or lesser extent as a guardrail for business strategy. This applies to all companies and can frequently be observed within the B2B market as well as in the industrial commodity sector. The recently developed brand identity and positioning of BASF states that BASF is a leading chemical corporation which contributes to the success of its business partners. The brand BASF serves as a guardrail for its business strategy. Business units that originally do not possess the chemical competence of BASF are not branded as BASF units (Esch, 2007).

Pathway 2: In this case the brand, and therefore brand identity, plays a pivotal role. Accordingly, the maxim is: 'brand strategy drives business strategy' (Esch, 2007). Brand identity serves as the basis of strategic guidelines. The BMW Group, as a strong corporate brand, could never sell cheap and powerless cars that do not take into account its brand promise: 'Sheer Driving Pleasure'. The BMW Group's brand strategy thus drives their business strategy. Beiersdorf, with brands like Nivea, adjusts its strategies for growth precisely on its brand identity. This company capitalizes its brand strengths by identity-driven brand extensions. Such a procedure should be employed in the case of consumer goods as well as by companies providing services (Esch, 2007).

BRAND IDENTITY PROVIDES THE BASIS FOR BRAND MANAGEMENT

Today's understanding of brand identity stems from the research into human identity. Domizlaff (1939) emphasized the connection between the identity of people and brands in the 1930s. Like every person, every brand has a unique face with characteristic features that make the brand recognizable at any time.

For centuries, there has been a serious discussion among philosophers about a person's identity and the crucial question of who we are (Weigert, 1986; van Rekom, 1998). The contemporary understanding of identity is significantly influenced by the work of John Locke (van Rekom, 1998; Noonan, 1989). Locke stresses the importance of human consciousness in the definition of a person's identity (Locke, 1991). By regularly thinking through his or her past and current actions, a person creates his or her own identity. In this process, basic questions like 'where am I coming from?' and 'where am I going?' are raised. Therefore, identity is rather introversive, as it focuses on a person's self-perception.

In addition to this subjective identity, Weigert (1986) defines two further facets of identity: the 'objective identity', which includes characteristic and identity-reflecting attributes of a person, and the 'intersubjective identity', which contains identity-reflecting criteria that are shared by a group of people.

Three fundamental criteria of brand identity can be derived from identity research:

1. Self-image, which refers to the subjective perception of brand identity. This self-image refers to managers' and employees' perception of the brand.
2. Identity-reflecting attributes, which comprise continuous and visible artifacts through which brand identity becomes perceivable for others. The target group comes into contact with the identity-reflecting attributes of the brand through personal as well as mass communication. For instance, brand identity can be expressed through

corporate design, company buildings, showrooms, packaging, advertisement, employee behavior, and so on.
3. Brand image describes the picture that is perceived by target groups and that has been formed through various contacts with a brand. The external image arises from the learning processes that are initiated by all brand experiences.

Analogous to a person's identity, brand identity expresses what a specific brand stands for or what it is supposed to stand for (Aaker and Joachimsthaler, 2000; Esch, 2007). It comprises the essential, characteristic and continuous attributes of a brand. Therefore, brand identity can be qualified as the roots of a brand, as it is the origin of all brand activities. Brand identity reflects a company's strategic thinking about the general direction of the brand (Kapferer, 2004).

Nokia connects people and enriches their life with inspiring state-of-the-art technology. The brand offers user-friendly and stylish mobile phones that are easy to deal with. Mercedes-Benz, on the other hand, is a traditional German automotive manufacturer of exclusive, prestigious, and safe cars (Esch, 2007).

FROM BRAND IDENTITY TO BRAND POSITIONING AND BRAND IMAGE IN STAKEHOLDERS' MINDS

Brand identity, brand positioning and brand image are closely related (see Figure 4.1). Brand identity is the cornerstone of brand strategy and is vital to brand management (Kapferer, 2004). It also serves as the basis for brand positioning. Positioning a brand involves emphasizing the distinctive characteristics of brand identity that differentiate it from other brands and make it attractive to stakeholders. Thus, brand positioning is the gist of brand identity (Esch, 2007).

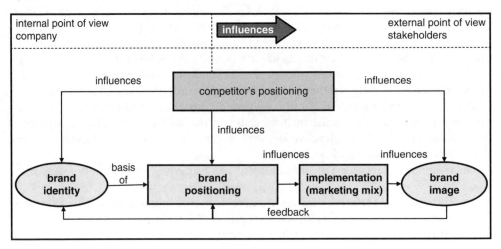

Source: Esch et al. (2005).

Figure 4.1   Relationship between brand identity, brand positioning and brand image

In order to position a brand properly, it is necessary to focus brand identity on relatively few points of difference due to today's predominant market and communication conditions, so that a communicative transformation of brand identity can actually take place. Those brand associations which mark a point of difference should be strong, unique, and favorable in order to create a competitive advantage. On the other hand, points of parity are those brand associations that are not exclusive to the brand (Keller, 2003). The BMW Group's points of difference are performance and sportiness in comparison to luxury cars like Mercedes-Benz, whereas safety or quality are points of parity with those cars. Rolls Royce and Bentley both offer exclusive cars; nevertheless they want to project different images by their brand positioning. While Rolls Royce is an icon of luxury and a car that people are typically chauffeured in, Bentley is the hand-built gentleman's sporting tourer and is an exhilarating car that is built to be driven by the owner.

Finally, brand image is the point of reference for the more or less successful transfer of brand positioning through marketing-mix activities. It provides information about the achievement of congruence between the brand identity and the brand image (Esch et al., 2005).

In other words, brand identity reflects the sender's side and presents the self-image of a brand that is actively created by a company. Whereas brand image, on the other hand, reflects the receiver's side and refers to the way in which stakeholders decode brand signals emanating from marketing-mix activities such as communication, services and products (Esch, 2007; Kapferer, 2004; Upshaw, 1995). Hence brand identity and positioning represent the company's action-level, whereas brand image stands for the impact level on the side of a company's stakeholders.

REQUIREMENTS FOR ESTABLISHING A BRAND IDENTITY

Brand identity is the starting point for creating clear brand images in people's minds. Mental images in consumers' minds are multilayered and refer to different kinds of knowledge. Brand knowledge structures are manifested in both hemispheres of the brain; therefore, approaches intending to establish a brand identity successfully need to consider insights from cognitive psychology. In terms of cognitive psychology, brand images are stored as schema (Esch, 2007). A schema is a mental framework for organizing knowledge which can be defined as a complex knowledge structure that represents categorical knowledge (Anderson, 2004; Rumelhart, 1980). Schemas encompass the typical attributes of objects, persons, relationships or events in the form of standardized beliefs (Alba and Hasher, 1983; Rumelhart, 1980; Rumelhart and Ortony, 1977). They contain different knowledge contents, facts and feelings as well as verbal and non-verbal elements attributed to a brand (Fiske, 1982; Marcus and Zajonc, 1985). Like any kind of knowledge, schemas can be visualized through semantic networks (Fiske/Pavelchak, 1986; Minsky, 1975) (see Figure 4.2).

Brand identity has to be described by considering hard and soft facts (feelings and emotions) as well as verbal and non-verbal elements. When conceptualizing brand identity, the following aspects have to be taken into account (Esch, 2007):

1. Brand identity is more than a mere addition of separate criteria; in the case of a brand identity 'the sum of the parts does not equal the whole'. Consequently, brand identity

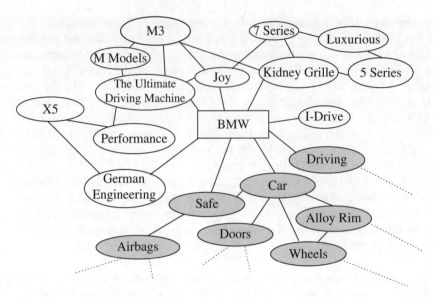

Figure 4.2 Semantic network of BMW

must reflect the 'big picture' of a brand instead of many details. Therefore, a central requirement for approaches intending to capture brand identity is that they should focus not only on single attributes but rather consider the brand identity holistically with correlations between single attributes. Brands evoke rational and emotional, as well as verbal and non-verbal associations. For this reason, it has to be guaranteed that brand identity attributes are situated in both hemispheres of the brain and evoke brand associations of different modalities. This is a necessary condition independent from the chosen brand identity approach. So, brand identity elements may not be unrelated. Rather, their integration should be considered because target groups regard brands holistically. The Mini claims to be the most exciting small car. All brand attributes such as the powerful engine, the suspension, as well as the size of the car contribute to the kart-like driving experience. Its brand personality of being a young, extroverted and funny car corresponds to those brand attributes. Furthermore, the advertising style, as well as the exterior and interior design elements, contribute to convey the brand identity consistently (see Figure 4.3).

2. For the development of strong brand associations, emotions and modality-specific impressions play a pivotal role. Strong brands evoke intense emotions, images and keen sensory experiences (Esch et al., 2006a). Hence, when developing a strong brand it is important to consider such soft facts because objective-rational brand features are usually not sufficient to differentiate a brand. Emotions and modality-specific impressions are typical of strong brands and become more important for their development.

3. Collect brand identity attributes completely and precisely; the collection approaches have to ensure that all continuous and important attributes of the brand have been considered. If an approach ignores the central roots of the brand, brand management runs the risk of dissociating from the actual brand identity, and

Source: www.mini.de, reproduced with kind permission from BMW Group.

Figure 4.3   Mini conveys its brand identity holistically

thereby losing relevance for purchase. The procedures used to gather brand identity features should intersect minimally. Otherwise, redundancies could emerge between different facets of a brand identity, which would restrict the practicability of the approaches. To take further steps effectively, brand identity must be concise and practicable, as difficulties could arise if a brand identity cannot be easily and correctly understood.

4. Use a practical brand identity approach; brand identity should guide all brand-related actions as well as every brand management process in the company. This implies that brand identity tools should reflect brand identity in such a manner that its content is easily applicable. To manage numerous interfaces effectively between all people involved in brand management (for example, brand managers, advertising agencies, and so on), simplicity and comprehensibility of brand identity is essential. The brand can only become alive inside the company if all employees and managers comprehend communicate, and 'live' the brand in a similar manner every day.

5. Consider the product spectrum; the product range of a brand influences the development of brand identity. This process is more challenging for a company that offers heterogeneous products (for example Siemens) than for a company that offers homogeneous products (for example the BMW Group). The more heterogeneous a product portfolio is, the less characterized the future brand identity is by specific brand benefits. In this case, it is necessary to find a common denominator for all offers, which encompasses as many features of the company as possible.

6. Analyze the relationship between brand identity and brand strategy; in the same way as the brand strategy has to fit the company's strategy, brand identity has to be embedded in the brand strategy. It makes a difference whether the company employs a 'house of brand' or a 'branded house' strategy (Aaker and Joachimsthaler, 2000). In the case of a house of brand strategy, it is important to differ selectively between separate brand identities so that an overlap between these different identities can be avoided.

DERIVING A BRAND IDENTITY BY USING THE BRAND STEERING WHEEL

The essential challenge is how to actually derive brand identity and use it for navigating the brand. In the 1990s, researchers dedicated themselves to developing theoretical brand identity approaches. Among these approaches, the better known include the approaches of Aaker (1996) and Kapferer (2004). At about the same time, the brand steering wheel was developed in Germany as an identity tool, and is nowadays successfully applied in a vast number of German and international companies.

The brand steering wheel was developed by Icon Brand Navigation and inspired by imagery and hemispheric research insights (Andresen and Nickel, 2005; Esch et al., 2005). Cerebral lateralization has often been characterized in terms of dichotomies such as 'logical versus intuitive', 'verbal versus visuospatial', and 'analytic versus holistic' (Gazzaniga et al., 2002). The left hemisphere is said to be predominantly responsible for linguistic-rational processes such as speech production and verbal processing, and involves linear, logical as well as analytic-sequential reasoning (Bryden, 1982; Hellige, 1990). The right hemisphere, on the other hand, is said to be predominantly responsible for visuospatial and non-verbal functions, the production and perception of emotions, as well as a holistic and intuitive processing style (Bryden, 1982; Hellige, 1990). Both hemispheres are linked to the corpus callosum and other smaller parts of the brain to coordinate localized functions (Liederman, 1998).

In spite of recent research insights which imply that the hemispherical specialization is rather heuristic than clear-cut, the brand steering wheel, with its reference to the hemisphere specialization, is still useful to structure a brand identity heuristically. From a managerial point of view, Esch's identity approach is well suited for deriving a brand identity. The brand steering wheel sensitizes managers to the fact that brand associations are more than objective, rational brand features and include emotions and feelings as well as non-verbal and modality-specific impressions. Furthermore, the approach helps managers apply and comprehend their brand easily. In addition the brand steering wheel is an appropriate tool for enabling and sustaining the process of implementing the brand inside the company as well as in the marketing mix.

The left-hand side of the brand steering wheel, referred to as the rational, logical side, consists of core brand attributes (what are the core brand attributes?) and the brand benefits (what does it offer?). The distinction between benefits and attributes plays an important role regarding the rational influence of the consumers, because they do not buy attributes but product benefits.

On the other hand, the right-hand side predominantly contains the soft facts, namely emotions, feelings and non-verbal impressions, that are connected to a brand. The brand

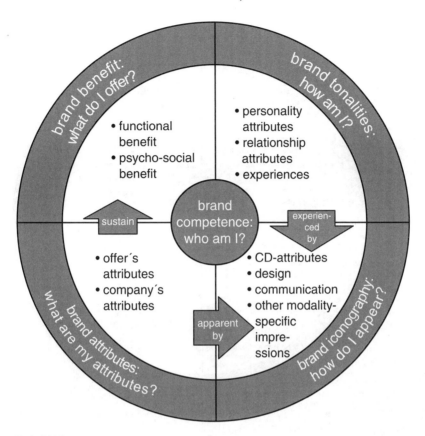

Source: Esch (2007).

Figure 4.4 The brand steering wheel

tonalities (how am I?) and the brand iconography (how do I appear?) constitute the right-hand side of the brand steering wheel (Esch, 2007; see Figure 4.4).

These four quadrants are strongly interrelated. Brand attributes support functional and psycho-social brand benefits. Like brand tonalities, they become apparent in the brand's iconography. The brand's iconography, in turn, is useful in controlling brand identity and its brand consistency.

Brand competence as an essence of brand identity is depicted at the center of the brand steering wheel. Competence answers the question: 'Who am I?' and gets at the root of the brand. Brand competence contains emotional as well as objective, rational aspects and is therefore located in the middle.

The BASF brand's steering wheel is a good example showing all four quadrants stringently intertwined (see Figure 4.5).

Brand Competence (Who am I?)

Brand competence captures central brand characteristics referring to:

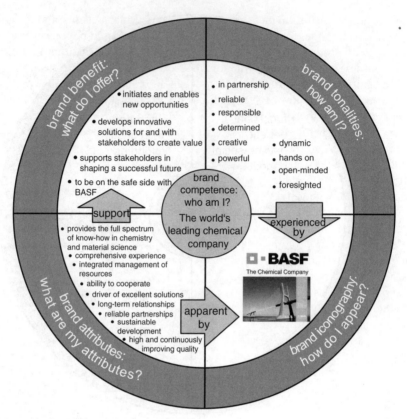

Source: Schubert, et al. (2006, p. 313).

Figure 4.5   Abstract of BASF's brand identity

1. A brand's history and the time the brand has enjoyed in the market: a company like
    Coca-Cola that has more than 100 years of experience in the market for beverages,
    doubtlessly possesses an adequate brand competence that may have a positive impact
    on the other quadrants of the brand steering wheel.
2. Origins of the brand: the country of origin is by no means unimportant for brands.
    Porsche is associated with positive values such as German engineering, performance
    and outstanding quality.
3. Role of the brand in the market: the market leader is often associated with reliability,
    whereas younger challengers are often linked with attributes like flexibility or moder-
    nity, which could be reflected in other quadrants of the brand steering wheel.
4. The brand's central assets: for example special methods of production, engineering,
    know-how from research and development.

Brand Benefits (What do I Offer?) and Brand Attributes (What are my Attributes?)

Regarding brand benefits and attributes, it is necessary to differentiate between attributes
and (relevant) benefits for the different target groups.

Brand benefits can be divided into objective-functional benefits and psychological-social benefits. Examples for objective-functional benefits could be convenient access to a broad variety of products on eBay, the especially good price–performance ratio of Dell, the rapid order processing of McDonald's, or the outstanding cleaning power of Mr Clean. Furthermore, situations of use can be considered as objective-functional benefits, Pringles Chips are perfectly suited for take-away consumption. Psycho-social benefits are reflected by softer facts such as feeling in good hands at the car insurance company, Geico, or being well taken care of as a customer of Body Shop or Bath & Body Works. It is easy to comprehend that psycho-social benefits are commonly more relevant for customers than the objective-functional benefits. However these psycho-social benefits are often hardly ascertainable by the customer.

Benefits can only be generated when there are qualities behind it – deriving from the company, its people, or the attributes of the product. Toyota offers reliable cars due to their outstanding quality and service. Mercedes-Benz is considered to be a safe car because it has, among other aspects, many airbags, good brake deceleration, and a solid passenger compartment. On the other hand Febreze is a reliable air freshener because of its odor-eliminating technology.

It is essential to visualize the relationship between benefits and attributes to gain an understanding of how one single benefit is substantiated and what could happen if the attribute is changed abruptly. A reduction of quality could therefore impact the durability and lifespan of a product as well as its reliability.

In this context, it is useful to establish – in terms of laddering analyses – means–end relations between attributes and benefits. The aim of laddering analysis is to ask questions that firstly evoke attributes, then benefits, and finally values (Gutman, 1984). This proceeds by repeatedly asking 'Why. . .?'; for example, 'Why do you buy a special product?' If the interviewee names an attribute, the interviewer continues with questions such as 'Why is this attribute of importance to you?' (Reynolds and Gutman, 1988). Using this procedure it is possible to identify relationships between attributes, benefits and values (see Table 4.1).

Another possibility is to use the T-schema. With the help of such a T-shaped schema, relationships between brand benefits and attributes can be illustrated. In this context benefits are presented on the left-hand side of the T-schema while the attributes that cause the benefits are on the right-hand side (Esch, 2007).

Brand Tonalities (How am I?)

Tonalities capture the emotions and feelings associated with a brand, which can be discovered by three central approaches:

1. Determining the brand personality.
2. Specifying brand relationships.
3. Determining relevant experiences.

These three approaches intersect, but also endorse each other and analyze the brand from different points of view.

Brands can possess personality traits like humans. Brand personality characterizes the sum of human attributes associated with a brand (Aaker, 1997). Due to experiences with

Table 4.1   Means–end relationships

Means–end model	Example of a luxury convertible car
Terminal value	Self-respect
Instrumental value	Experience exclusiveness
Psycho-social benefit	Relaxation
Functional benefit	Comfort
Abstract attribute	Modern technology
Concrete attribute	Retractable aluminum hardtop

Sources: Herrmann (2002) and Esch (2007).

a brand and the learning processes initiated by communication, consumers are able to describe brands with personality traits. These include demographic characteristics like sex, age or social class, and classic personality traits like intelligence and truthfulness (Aaker, 1997). Consistent and effective brand management anchors those attributes constantly and distinctively in the consumers' minds.

For consumers, brand personality is of importance in two respects:

1.   It reflects their identity and causes a positive attitude towards the brand.
2.   It comprises consumers' aspirations of an 'ideal' personality.

Singapore Airlines is perceived as a pleasant, caring and modern company, Apple as young and modern, whereas Harley-Davidson can be described as adventurous and all-American. Mini on the other hand is perceived as a young, extroverted and funny brand (see Figure 4.6). In order to figure out such personality traits, it helps to describe the brand as a person with distinct characteristics. Besides associating personality traits with a brand, consumers build relationships with them and vice versa (Fournier, 1998).

Principally relationships give people's lives a meaning by enriching and structuring them (Fournier, 1998). For a lot of consumers, brands can come alive and thereby be an active partner. In this context Biel (2001) points out that it is necessary – when talking about relationships between brands and consumers – to answer two questions:

1.   How do consumers perceive a brand?
2.   How does the brand perceive the consumer?

For example, Apple users describe their brand relationship as amicable. They often perceive Apple as a friend or partner.

Finally, consumers associate experiences with certain brands which become manifested through communication or personal experiences. Experiences become increasingly important in today's affluent society. While brands' objective and functional benefits are replaceable, emotions and feelings associated with brands gain in importance (Schmitt, 1999). Consumers are searching for new stimulations and experiences (Kroeber-Riel and Esch, 2004). Accordingly the exact formulation of a brand's experience is important. Singapore Airlines has thought through all of its customer touchpoints in terms of the

Figure 4.6   Mini's advertising projects its brand personality

brand experience (Schmitt, 2003). Consequently the brand is associated with an exotic and outstanding service experience. At Barnes & Noble consumers feel at home when reading a book in a relaxed atmosphere drinking a Starbucks coffee. At Häagen-Dazs Cafes customers enjoy the sensual pleasures of their world-famous ice cream (Schmitt, 1999). At the Hard Rock Cafe consumers experience an entertaining dinner accompanied by rock 'n' roll music.

Brand Iconography (How do I Appear?)

A brand's iconography is affected by many impressions, which have an impact on brand awareness (brand recognition, memory of the brand) or brand image. Such impressions are ascribable to personal and mass communication. Therefore it is possible to make visual brand impressions on salespeople, users and fans of the brand by designing buildings, sales rooms, packaging and products, sales information or brochures, websites, and all kinds of mass communication.

When designing the brand iconography, different sensory experiences have to be considered. These impressions are more than visual impressions and include sound, touch, smell as well as taste (Lindstrom, 2005). In the case of Marlboro, consumers typically associate the cowboy with the brand. Consumers will always remember the rich and intense taste of Tabasco's pepper sauce or the smell of the world-famous perfume Chanel No. 5. Likewise consumers associate the Intel brand when hearing the 'drumbone' tone. Furthermore consumers will always remember the shape of the original Coca-Cola bottle or that of an Absolut Vodka bottle (see Table 4.2).

Table 4.2   Sensory experiences of brands

Sensory experiences	Examples of everyday life	Examples of brands
Sight	Empire State Building	Ford Shelby
		Pillsbury Doughboy
	Chrysler Building	Marlboro Country
Sound	Sound of a phone	Intel's 'drumbone' tone
Smell	Smell of leather	Chanel No. 5
	Smell of a barbecue	Hawaiian Tropic
Touch	Sponge	Coca-Cola bottle
	Nylons	Absolut Vodka bottle
Taste	Taste of whisky	Tabasco
	Taste of lobster	Big Mac

Source: Andresen (1991).

SHORTCOMINGS IN DEVELOPING AND IMPLEMENTING BRAND IDENTITY

In order to develop and implement brand identity successfully, the following key lessons need to be considered (Esch, 2006; 2007).

Senior management buy-in: in order to implement brand identity successfully senior management commitment is of paramount importance. Thus senior managers need to support the ideas as well as the process of developing brand identity.

Do not underestimate the process of developing and implementing brand identity: the period specified for developing brand identity is usually too short. A lack of time for the process implies that necessary feedback loops to revise brand identity are neglected. In order to develop and implement brand identity successfully, the project team should also reflect all relevant areas of the company adequately, and start with an internal instead of an external analysis of the brand. The results of the internal analysis, which reflects the status quo of the brand identity, serve as the basis for interviewing external stakeholders. When consolidating the internal and external perspective in order to establish the brand's future identity, one needs to consider the brand's history as well as the company's future strategy.

Separate the wheat from the chaff: characteristic brand criteria must be differentiated from non-characteristic ones. This often causes problems, as central brand assets are often underestimated by managers due to the fact that they are often not aware of them. One hundred and forty years of experience within and for the chemical market are very important to BASF as these attributes support and convey the expertise of BASF as a leading chemical company in the world. Likewise these attributes reflect that BASF is a reliable and powerful partner that is 'here today' and will still be 'here tomorrow' to help shape the future of its business partners successfully.

Develop the brand's big picture instead of patchworking: brand identity includes the essential and characteristic traits of a brand. These traits reflect rational as well as emotional, verbal and non-verbal impressions. The brand steering wheel considers those facets necessary for developing the brand's big picture. The left-hand side of the brand steering wheel reflects the ratio and hard facts, whereas the right-hand side reflects the feelings and non-verbal brand impressions (Esch, 2007).

Raise awareness about the interrelations between the facets of the brand steering wheel: in order to develop a coherent brand identity, it is of paramount importance to make sure that the facets of the steering wheel are interrelated. Brand benefits must be reflected in brand tonalities as well as in the brand iconography which should convey the brand coherently and vice versa. In order to capture brand identity in such a holistic way, it is helpful to map the connections between the facets within a semantic network.

The grass is always greener on the other side of the fence: when developing a new brand identity, managers often want to possess the characteristics of strong competitor brands, although they actually do not match their own brand.

Fantasy world: since managers are often very positive about their companies, they argue that their brand possesses certain characteristics that are neither typical nor provable of that brand. Therefore brand characteristics need to be seriously questioned. Furthermore, it needs to be proven how those brand characteristics affect how employees think, feel and act.

Politics and trends: politics and trends play an important role when crafting brand identity. Nowadays every company wants to be sustainable, although sustainability is not often typical of a brand.

Implement brand identity inside the company: many companies are misled by the impression that brand management is primarily externally focused and that a nice advertising campaign is all that is needed in order to build strong brands. A brand can only unleash its potential when the employees live the brand inside as well as outside the company. The process of successfully implementing a brand depends on the employees' commitment of living the brand throughout their daily routine.

Overcome barriers: the implementation of a brand identity can be considered as a change-management process. Within this process, several barriers need to be overcome. Such barriers are rooted either within employees or in the situation itself. These barriers must be identified in order to solve them with appropriate measures.

Get organized for internal brand building: in order to implement brand identity effectively, it is extremely important to coordinate that process through a project team, which acts as a feedback and control authority and guides the process. Crucial questions that need to be considered when setting up a project group centre around their composition and persuasive power.

REFERENCES

Aaker, David, A. (1996), *Building Strong Brands*, New York: The Free Press.
Aaker, David, A. and Erich Joachimsthaler (2000), *Brand Leadership*, New York: The Free Press.
Aaker, Jennifer L. (1997), 'Dimensions of brand personality', *Journal of Marketing Research*, **24**, 347–56.
Alba, Joseph W. and Lynn Hasher (1983), 'Is memory schematic?', *Psychological Bulletin*, **93**(2), 203–31.
Anderson, John R. (2004), *Cognitive Psychology and its Implications*, 6th edn, New York: Worth Publishers.

Andresen, Thomas (1991), 'Innere markenbilder: MAX, wie er wurde, was er ist', *Planung and Analyse*, **18**(1), 28–34.

Andresen, Thomas and Oliver Nickel (2005), 'Führung von Dachmarken', in Franz-Rudolf Esch (ed.), *Moderne Markenführung, Grundlagen – Innovative Ansätze – Praktische Umsetzungen*, 4th edn, Wiesbaden: Gabler, pp. 765–96.

Biel, Alexander L. (2001), 'Grundlagen zum Markenwertaufbau', in Franz-Rudolf Esch (ed.), *Moderne Markenführung*, 3rd edn, Wiesbaden: Gabler, pp. 61–90.

Bryden, M. Philip (1982), *Laterality, Functional Asymmetry in the Intact Brain*, New York: Academic Press.

Davis, Scott M. and Michael Dunn (2002), *Building the Brand-Driven Business*, San Francisco, CA: Jossey-Bass.

Domizlaff, Hans (1939), *Die Gewinnung des öffentlichen Vertrauens: Ein Lehrbuch der Markentechnik*, Hamburg: Hanseatische Verlagsanstalt.

Esch, Franz-Rudolf (2006), 'Wachstum mit Marken: Marken dehnen und Allianzen bilden', *Thexis*, **3**, 11–15.

Esch, Franz-Rudolf (2007), *Strategie und Technik der Markenführung*, 4th edn, Munich: Vahlen.

Esch, Franz-Rudolf, Tobias Langner and Jan-Eric Rempel (2005), 'Ansätze zur Erfassung und Entwicklung der Markenidentität', in Franz-Rudolf Esch (ed.), *Moderne Markenführung, Grundlagen – Innovative Ansätze – Praktische Umsetzungen*, 4th edn, Wiesbaden: Gabler, pp. 103–29.

Esch, Franz-Rudolf, Tobias Langner, Bernd H. Schmitt and Patrick Geus (2006a), 'Are brands forever? How brand-knowledge and relationships affect current and future purchases', *Journal of Product & Brand Management*, **15**(2), 98–105.

Esch, Franz-Rudolf, Kristina Strödter and Alexander Fischer (2006b), 'Behavioral Branding – Wege der Marke zu Managern und Mitarbeitern', in Andreas Strebinger, Wolfgang Mayerhofer and Helmut Kurz (eds), *Werbe- und Markenforschung, Meilensteine – State of the Art – Perspektiven*, Wiesbaden: Gabler, pp. 403–33.

Fiske, Susan T. (1982), 'Schema-triggered affect: Applications to social perception', in Margaret S. Clark and Susan T. Fiske (eds), *Affect and Cognition*, Hillsdale, NJ: Erlbaum, pp. 55–78.

Fiske, Susan T. and Mark A. Pavelchak (1986), 'Category-based versus piecemeal-based affective responses. Developments in schema-triggered affect', in Richard M. Sorrentino and E. Tory Higgins (eds), *Handbook of Motivation and Cognition: Foundations of Social Behavior*, New York: Guilford Press, pp. 167–203.

Fournier, S. (1998), 'Consumers and their brands', *Journal of Consumer Research*, **24**(4), 343–73.

Gazzaniga, Michael, S., Richard B. Ivry and George R. Mangun (2002), *Cognitive Neuroscience: The Biology of the Mind*, 2nd edn, New York: W.W. Norton & Company.

Gutman, Jonathan (1984), 'Analyzing consumer orientation toward beverages through means-end chain analysis', *Psychology and Marketing*, **1**(3/4), 23–43.

Hellige, Joseph B. (1990), 'Hemispheric asymmetry', *Annual Review of Psychology*, **41**, 55–80.

Herrmann, A. (2002), 'Anwendurg smöglichkeit des MECCAS-modells am beispiel des SL-klasse?', unveröffentlicher Forschungsbericht.

Kapferer, Jean-Noel (2004), *The New Strategic Brand Management, Creating and Sustaining Brand Equity Long Term*, 3rd edn, London: Kogan Page.

Keller, Kevin L. (2003), *Strategic Brand Management: Building, Measuring, and Managing Brand Equity*, 2nd edn, Upper Saddle River, NJ: Prentice Hall.

Kroeber-Riel, Werner and Franz-Rudolf Esch (2004), *Strategie und Technik der Werbung*, 6th edn, Stuttgart: Kohlhammer.

Liederman, Jacqueline (1998), 'The dynamics of interhemispheric collaboration and hemispheric control', *Brain and Cognition*, **36**, 193–208.

Lindstrom, Martin (2005), *Brand Sense: Build Powerful Brands Through Touch, Taste, Smell, Sight, and Sound*, New York: The Free Press.

Locke, John (1991), *An Essay Concerning Human Understanding*, London: John W. Yolton.

Marcus, Hazel and Robert B. Zajonc (1985), 'The cognitive perspective in social psychology', in Gardner Lindzey and Elliot Aronson (eds), *The Handbook of Social Psychology: Theory and Method*, New York: McGraw-Hill, pp. 137–230.

Minsky, Marvin (1975), 'A framework for representing knowledge', in Patrick H. Winston (ed.), *The Psychology of Computer Vision*, New York: McGraw-Hill, pp. 211–80.

Noonan, Harold W. (1989), *Personal Identity*, London and New York: Routledge.

Reynolds, Thomas J. and Jonathan Gutman (1988), 'Laddering theory, methods, analysis and interpretation', *Journal of Advertising Research*, **28**(1), 11–31.

Rumelhart, David E. (1980), 'Schemata: the building blocks of cognition', in Rand J. Spiro, Bertram C. Bruce and William F. Brewer (eds), *Issues in Reading Comprehension*, Hillsdale, NJ: Erlbaum, pp. 33–58.

Rumelhart, David E. and Andrew Ortony (1977), 'The representation of knowledge in memory', in Richard C. Anderson, Rand J. Spiro and William E. Montague (eds), *Schooling and the Acquisition of Knowledge*, Hillsdale, NJ: Lawrence Erlbaum, pp. 99–135.

Schmitt, Bernd H. (1999), *Experiential Marketing: How to Get Customers to Sense, Feel, Think, ACT, Relate*, New York: The Free Press.

Schmitt, Bernd H. (2003), *Customer Experience Management: A Revolutionary Approach to Connecting with Your Customers*, New Jersey: John Wiley & Sons.

Schubert, Christian, Hans Kiefer, Franz-Rudolf Esch and Simone Roth (2006), 'Corporate brand identity', in Thomas Heilmann (ed.), *Manual of International Marketing*, Wiesbaden: Gabler Verlag, pp. 311–24.

Upshaw, Lynn B. (1995), *Building Brand Identity: A Strategy for Success in a Hostile Marketplace*, New York: John Wiley & Sons.

van Rekom, Johan (1998), *Corporate Identity: Development of the Concept and a Measurement Instrument*, Rotterdam: Erasmus University.

Weigert, Andrew J. (1986), 'The social production of identity: metatheoretical foundations', *The Sociological Quarterly*, **27**(2), 165–83.

PART II

Managerial concepts

In this part, the authors examine key managerial concepts from current practice in brand management. In linking theory to practice, the authors seek to address important issues in managerial practice, and assess impact of these concepts on the performance of companies and their brands.

Sexton addresses the importance of understanding the link between brand investment and shareholder value, the danger of investing insufficiently in branding when this link is not understood, and approaches to measuring the impact of branding on perceived value and demand curves.

Chang examines the importance of brand convergence and its challenges in an environment of media convergence between digital networks, technologies, services and devices; his 'dual convergence matrix' provides a tool for managing convergence within a brand portfolio.

Montaña, Guzmán and Moll identify how design can enrich the brand-building process, with design providing a source of differentiation, both in product and service development and in consistently managing all branding elements for clear communication to consumers.

Meyer, Brudler and Blümelhuber analyze the variety of target groups that a brand may have – both functional (the range of different stakeholders besides customers) and attitudinal (the range of biases besides a devoted brand follower) – and assess their impact on the establishment of brand relationships with consumers.

5. Brand investment and shareholder value

Donald Sexton

An organization's brands are likely to be their most valuable single asset – and their branding activities may be one of their most important investments.

Many studies have established that brands represent substantial monetary value. For example, CoreBrand tracks the brands of more than a thousand companies. For those companies, Jim Gregory, CoreBrand's founder and CEO, estimated that in 2006, on average, corporate brands accounted for 16.1 per cent of the market capitalization for companies producing home appliances, 14.1 per cent for motor vehicles, 11.6 per cent for aerospace, 8.3 per cent for computers and peripherals, 10.3 per cent for foods, 8.0 per cent for brokerage services, 7.0 per cent for telecommunications equipment, 5.8 per cent for pharmaceutical products, and 5.4 per cent for industrial equipment. CoreBrand corporate brand equity estimates for individual companies included \$69.0 billion for General Electric, \$62.9 billion for Exxon Mobil, \$53.3 billion for Microsoft, and \$42.1 billion for Toyota Motor.

The conclusions of other studies are similar: An organization's brands represent a significant portion of their market capitalization. This conclusion holds true for products and services and for business-to-consumer and business-to-business companies. Brand value as a percentage of market capitalization does vary by industry category and company, but it always represents a substantial amount of money.

That an organization's brands constitute a hugely valuable asset is completely consistent with standard financial concepts. Branding affects perceived value, which in turn affects overall demand. Demand affects price and sales and therefore contribution. Finally, contribution affects cash flow, which is the basis of shareholder value (see Figure 5.1).

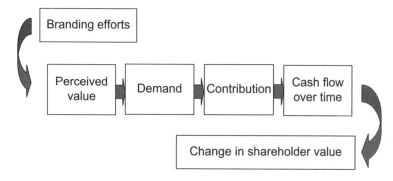

Source: Sexton (2007). Used with permission.

Figure 5.1   How branding affects shareholder value

Unfortunately, how branding efforts affect shareholder value is not always understood because the relationship rests on ideas from several disciplines – marketing, economics, statistics, accounting and finance. If managers do not understand the linkage between branding and shareholder value, they may not invest sufficiently in branding activities to the detriment of the shareholders.

BRANDING AND PERCEIVED VALUE

Perceived value is a key construct in understanding the impact of branding.

Perceived value is the maximum the customer will spend for a particular product or service (author's definition). It is *not* price – it is the *ceiling* on price. Perceived value is due both to the attributes of the product or service and to the attributes associated with the brand (see Figure 5.2).

Perceived value can be estimated in monetary terms by using statistical techniques known as *constrained choice models*. These methods have been used by companies such as DuPont, Gillette and Marriott to inform their design and pricing decisions.

To employ these techniques, data are gathered from customers regarding their preferences for comparable products or services with different attributes, including different brands and different prices. Not only can a customer's overall perceived value for a specific product or service be estimated in monetary terms, it is also possible to estimate the proportion each component – such as the brand – represents in the overall perceived value.

The brand proportion of perceived value does vary by product category. For example, Interbrand has estimated that brands represent about 98 per cent of the perceived value for fragrances and 90 per cent for cookies, while only 5 per cent for semiconductors. These category differences are part of the explanation as to why brand equity as a percentage of market capitalization varies by industry.

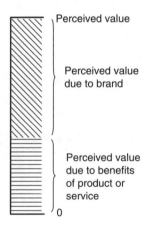

Source: Sexton (2007). Used with permission.

Figure 5.2   Components of perceived value

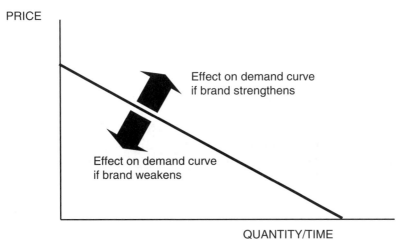

PRICE

Effect on demand curve
if brand strengthens

Effect on demand curve
if brand weakens

QUANTITY/TIME

Source: Sexton (2007). Used with permission.

Figure 5.3   Demand curve

PERCEIVED VALUE AND FINANCIAL RETURNS

In microeconomics, a demand curve displays the quantity in units of a product or service that will be purchased at different price points (see Figure 5.3). In other words, a demand curve depicts the distribution of all the perceived values associated with all the customers in the market. Some customers might evaluate the product or service as having high perceived value, others as having low perceived value. As price falls below the perceived value of each customer, in turn each buys the product or service and that leads to the downward slope of the demand curve.

Branding affects the demand curve by shifting it. If a brand strengthens, then the demand curve shifts to the right. If a brand weakens, the demand curve shifts to the left.

High perceived value means that a company can charge a higher price *or* sell more units *or* both. Strong brands do provide a price premium (some people define brand strength solely as price premium) but brands can and often do also provide a unit sales premium. The net effect is that a strong brand leads to higher revenue, which in turn typically leads to higher contribution, the difference of revenue and costs.

Cash flow is defined as cash in less cash out. Contribution is a significant component of cash flow, so strong brands are associated with higher cash flows. Finally, shareholder value depends on the anticipated cash flows from a company. A company that can be expected to manage its brands well should have higher shareholder value expressed as its market capitalization.

ISSUES IN EVALUATING BRAND INVESTMENTS

While conceptually straightforward, the process of estimating the impact of the brand on shareholder value is not necessarily easy in practice. Issues include:

1. Difficulties in estimating current cash flow due to brand. To make this estimate requires first an understanding of the impact of the brand on perceived value. Then it is necessary to develop the relationship of perceived value to the demand curve for the product or service during a given time period. Finally, changes in the demand curve need to be related to changes in contribution and cash flow. Each of these steps poses a statistical problem. There are feasible solutions for each step but they do require experience with multivariate statistics.
2. Difficulties in estimating future cash flow due to brand. Whenever one is forecasting, uncertainty is involved. In this case, a key estimate is how perceived value will change in the future. That depends not only on what the organization does, but also on what its competitors will do.
3. Need to analyze each market segment separately. The value of a brand should be estimated separately for each market segment (one definition of a segment is a group of customers who share a similar perceived value for a product or service). Focusing on specific segments leads to more precise brand value estimates.
4. Need to estimate costs and any changes in costs. While the estimates of perceived value are related to estimates of 'cash in', one must also estimate 'cash out'. Cash out includes all costs but especially the costs of building and maintaining a strong brand.
5. Evaluation of brand extensions. One reason one organization may pay more for a brand than another organization is that it sees more possibilities for brand extensions. The cash flows associated with those growth paths need to be incorporated into any valuation of a brand.
6. Accounting for effects on cash flow other than those due to demand. A strong brand not only affects demand, it may affect the organization in other ways. For example, strong brands can have a large positive effect on recruiting and retaining employees. In turn, those human resource effects may affect the cash flow of an organization and ideally should be considered when evaluating the investments in a brand.

Despite these possible difficulties in evaluating brand investments, it is possible to utilize the model described in Figure 5.1. Nonetheless, according to studies a few years ago by the Conference Board and by the American Productivity and Quality Center, many companies do not perform such research. Often what is not measured is not managed. The lack of measurement concerning brand investments can lead to inattention to brands or underinvestment in brands.

UNDERINVESTING IN BRANDS

Successful brands require both effective innovation and effective communications. Innovation concerns ongoing efforts to ensure that the design of the product or service matches the needs and expectations of the customer. Communications consists of making sure that the customers know the positive experience they will receive if they purchase or use the product or service.

Insufficient investment in product improvements can lead to the *hollowing out* of a brand. Often such a scenario occurs when a senior manager attempts to improve short-term financial performance by cutting back on investments in a product or service associated with a strong brand.

A hollowing-out strategy can work for a while – at least in the sense that financial results such as profit are increased in the short term. The danger of hollowing-out strategies is that they may damage the brand in the long term. Hollowing-out strategies can work in the short term because customers are likely to display loyalty to a strong brand. However, eventually those customers will realize that their brands have changed for the worse and stop purchasing – possibly not to purchase again. Hollowed-out brands often die.

Insufficient investment in branding may also mean insufficient communication to the customers regarding the benefits provided by the brand. One of the clear implications of research conducted by Young and Rubicam is that branding is not simply about building name awareness – it is about communicating what the brand stands for. A brand may have high awareness but the customer may be really saying, 'I know you and I don't like you'. Brand communications must make clear the positive aspects of the brand and continually reinforce them. Cutting brand communications to improve short-term financial results can have a negative effect similar to cutting product improvements – the loss of long-term customers and their revenue, profit and cash flow.

CONCLUSIONS

Strong brands represent an enormously valuable asset to organizations. As any asset, they need to be managed and maintained. The relationship between branding efforts and shareholder value is clear, and data and analytical tools are available to evaluate the impact of branding efforts. Investments in brands can and should be evaluated with the same financial thinking that is applied to other investments. Investment in branding is one of the most important investments an organization makes.

REFERENCE

Sexton, Donald E. (2007), 'How corporate and product brands affect shareholder value', presentation at the 2007 Corporate Image Conference, New York, 26 January.

6. Brand convergence

Dae Ryun Chang

In the increasingly connected and wireless world of the new millennium, marketing management has ventured beyond its traditional offline boundaries in order to take advantage of new technologies and media. This has resulted in a significant demand for a vast range and high quantity of content that in turn is putting pressure on brand management. Through the 'digital convergence' of networks, technologies, contents, services and devices that has occurred over the last decade, the delivery of brand information is now more diverse than ever before. What is often overlooked in digital convergence, however, is the need for 'brand convergence'. Even though a great deal of effort is made to integrate hardware, software and service features to enable digital convergence, fewer steps have been taken to guarantee a smooth integration of brand-related concerns. Brand convergence therefore is the strategic integration of brand associations that are created in the minds of consumers through the various media.

Brand convergence may be more difficult to achieve than digital convergence because consumer perceptions are driven less by technological or product integration than by the clarity and consistency of the brand. Brands are often defined as 'a network of associations'; and as the 'touchpoints' between a brand and consumers become more varied because of digital convergence, so does the difficulty of their integration.

Let us take for example the union between Sony and Ericsson. This partnership was designed to seamlessly combine the electronics expertise and reputation of the former with the experience and name of the latter as a wireless network and device vendor. Moreover, Sony's vast access to its ownership of contents in games, music and pictures added to the luster of the Sony-Ericsson co-branding strategy. From a consumer's perspective, however, 'Sony-Ericsson' as a brand represents a potential challenge. This is because Sony and Ericsson are two well-known brands that each have both positive and negative associations in their respective networks.

The issue of integrating brands is not a new problem. Even in the offline domain, similar questions arise when companies are merged or acquired.

THE DUAL CONVERGENCE MATRIX

Based on the notion that digital convergence is not the total solution to all the problems that a company faces, the following framework conceptualizes digital convergence and brand convergence as being two managerial tasks that interact to produce a variety of effects.

We see from Figure 6.1 that digital and brand convergence can be independently high or low. The two dimensions and their respective conditions result in four categories. The

Brand convergence

		Low	High
Digital convergence	High	Ubiquitous brand anarchy	Ubiquitous brand integration
	Low	Localized brand anarchy	Localized brand integration

Figure 6.1   The dual convergence matrix

first category is what can be called 'localized brand anarchy'. This is where both digital and brand convergence are low. In this state, the lack of brand integration leads to brand-related disorganization. However, due to the lack of digital convergence, the extent of this brand confusion is limited by its present technological boundary. For example, a company that provides a wide variety of offline games with many different brands can be said to be of this type. This situation may result from a company's haphazard strategy of developing its own games that is combined with using licenses from other popular gaming content providers. In other words, when sales maximization becomes the fore-most imperative, then inevitably brand building becomes very difficult. The second category is what can be called 'ubiquitous brand anarchy'. This is the situation where brand convergence is low but digital convergence is high. The key difference between this and the first category is the farther-reaching extent of the brand disorganization. Sticking with the gaming example, that same company could entertain thoughts of joining hands with a well-established Internet portal to offer their content online. The end result is that what was previously a contained problem may now be significantly more widespread. The Internet portal may be using any number of sub-brands for its various search engines, directories, community sites and other services. The gaming company must now deal not only with their own branding problems but also with problems related to the larger context of the Internet portal. The third category is what can be called 'localized brand integration'. This is where digital convergence is low but brand convergence is high. Even in situations where digital convergence has not yet been achieved, the need for brand convergence remains. The last category is what can be called 'ubiquitous brand integration'. This is where both digital and brand convergence is high. Although it was argued that digital convergence makes brand convergence difficult, this last category is realized when companies make a concerted effort to achieve not only a technological interface between the various digital media, but also a seamless integration of its branding interfaces.

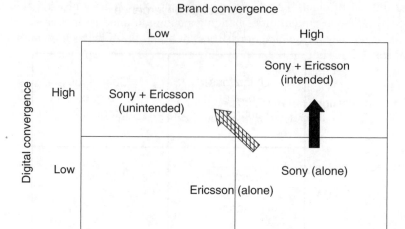

Figure 6.2   Sony-Ericsson migration patterns

BRAND CONVERGENCE AND BRAND MIGRATION

The dual convergence matrix explained above is a useful framework to understand the various dynamics that occur when digital and brand convergence interact. Moreover, we can use it to chart the migration of markets from one situation to another. Migration refers to the movement of consumers from one market to another. We commonly talk of migration only from a digital convergence standpoint but make the mistake of overlooking migration tasks for the brand. The Sony-Ericsson example discussed previously is shown in Figure 6.2. The idea for the union is to carry the customers successfully from both these networks.

The solid arrow indicates the intended migration path whereas the checkered arrow indicates the unintended migration of Sony and Ericsson users. One could posit that Sony-Ericsson's earlier trouble may have stemmed from the inability of these brands to carry their existing users over to the joint branding endeavor. Consumers are influenced not only by their perception of these two brands, but also by their preferences for competing brands in the targeted industries.

More recently, the Sony-Ericsson joint venture is showing very positive signs of life, especially in terms of sales. Using the dual convergence schema, their current success can be attributed to a combination of improved digital convergence and brand convergence. Sony-Ericsson has finally come out with timely integrated devices such as their popular T610 camera phone and also a bona fide 3G handset, the Z1010, which has received good reviews. Despite its original desire to converge its GSM and CDMA networks, Ericsson has 'bitten the bullet' by consolidating its effort on GSM and Japanese standards (Edström, 2004). For its part, Sony is consolidating its digital convergence efforts as well as its complete withdrawal of all its Clié and PDA category development efforts in the North American and European markets. In terms of brand convergence, the consolidation for both brands' technological efforts facilitates a tighter brand association network. In addition to that, Sony-Ericsson is making a conscious effort to present a unified 'face' to its portfolio of products. For example, its current Asian marketing campaign strongly reflects Sony-Ericsson's intention of building a common underlying user association for the brand. The newly formulated Sony-Ericsson brand promise has less emphasis on its technical capabilities but more on 'providing customers a new language of wireless, fun and ready to run' (Hamdi, 2004).

Brand migration is a useful tool for companies that are contemplating digital convergence. The primary implication is that the roadmap to successful digital convergence may be aided by brand convergence. Brands bridge different markets.

BRAND CONVERGENCE AND BRAND COMMUNICATION

An important function of a brand is that it is a very important medium for marketing communication. Brand communication can impact the branding strategy of digital convergence moves. One example is a study that the author conducted to look at how consumers reacted to the effect of branding on publicity related to digital convergence. Respondents in one situation were given ambiguous information about future convergence of mobile phones with other digital products. In another situation, different consumers were given explicitly clear information about how the digital convergence between products was better than their existing mobile phones as reported by some reputable news magazine. As Figures 6.3 and 6.4 establish, regardless of the ambiguity of the integrated

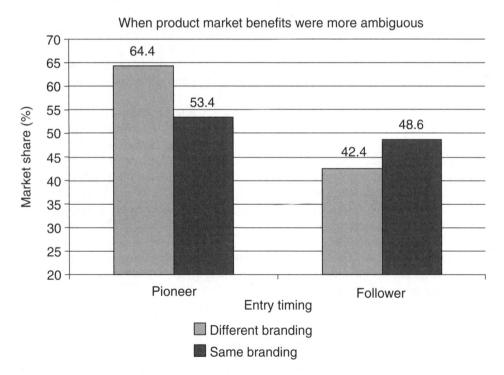

Figure 6.3   Brand effect when digital convergence benefits are unclear

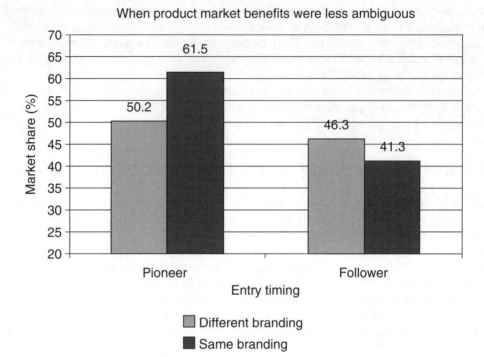

Figure 6.4   Brand effect when digital convergence benefits are clear

technology, it pays to be the first company to market the converged product. With respect to branding strategy, we can see that where there is ambiguity, there is an added bonus to using a different brand for the converged technology/service.

In the first case, we can infer that confusion about the technological superiority of the integrated solution is exacerbated when the same brand is used. In other words, the attribution by many consumers could be: 'I think the new product is better than the old one, but then again I am not so sure if the brands are the same'. The use of a different brand puts the consumer in a positive frame of mind that somehow the products must be different. In the latter situation we can speculate that the publicity surrounding the superiority of the integrated solution enables consumers to add other positive aspects, such as a well-known brand name that leads them to think such thoughts as 'that is what I expected from a leading brand'.

Companies that pursue digital convergence must be very proactive in integrating their brands and must utilize many more communication tools such as advertising and publicity in a clear and consistent manner.

CONCLUSION

As we have seen in the many examples cited above, many companies pursuing digital convergence must juggle many brands. The dual convergence matrix assists in pruning the brand portfolio. This process should be undertaken on a regular basis so that the brand architecture is aligned with consumer perception as well as with the company's other marketing communication components. Digital convergence, when achieved seamlessly and when consistent with consumer needs, may allow companies to radically reduce their number of brands.

BIBLIOGRAPHY

Bluetooth Homepage, www.bluetooth.org/bluetooth/landing/auto.php.
Cristol, S.M. and P. Sealey (2000), *Simplicity Marketing*, New York: The Free Press.
DeStefano, J. (2001), 'Telematics slowed by standards snarl', *EE Times*, 6 March.
Edström, A. (2004), 'Signs of life at Sony-Ericsson', *Fortune* (Europe), 23 February, **149**(3), p. 14.
Hamdi, R. (2004), 'New creative direction to put Sony-Ericsson on track', *Media Asia*, 27 February, p. 5.
Schmitt, B. (1998), *Experiential Marketing*, New York: The Free Press.

7. Branding and design management

Jordi Montaña, Francisco Guzmán and Isa Moll

Design as a source of differentiation has become a key element for brand building. Good design is important for branding not only because aesthetically pleasing products and services compete better for consumers' short attention span (Berkowitz, 1987; Page and Herr, 2002), but also because it may serve as the cohesive factor for all elements that configure a brand experience. Through design, the consistency of all brand elements can be achieved, allowing customers to understand better what a particular brand does for them and what it stands for.

Design is important to a firm and should be integrated with other business functions, even though its integration may be difficult, 'given the tension between the values of designers and the output and performance-focused business disciplines' (Beverland, 2005, p. 196). For this reason, design must be guided by the brand and a closer integration should exist between design and brand management (Beverland, 2005; Borja de Mozota, 2003; Kreuzbauer and Malter, 2005; Schmitt, 1999; Stompff, 2003; Svengren-Holm and Johansson, 2005). In recent years, brand building and design have become strategic for companies: while brands have become important organizational assets, design, by enhancing product aesthetics, produces positive effects on consumer preference and organizational performance. However, little attention has been placed on how design can enrich the brand building process.

This chapter examines issues in branding and design management. We analyze the importance of design for brand building, and the importance that strategic design management can have for brand management. Design not only enriches products themselves, but also enriches the process by which products are made. We consider design management to be a holistic process of creation and decision-making that enhances both managerial and strategic decisions (Borja de Mozota, 2003), and whose effectiveness depends especially on how it is coordinated with other managerial functions (Vazquez and Bruce, 2002). The discussion in this chapter will present some academic progress in this area, as well as some real examples.

The chapter is organized as follows. First, we discuss how and why brands have evolved to the point they are at today. Second, we analyze some basic design management concepts and talk about their importance for branding and new product development (NPD). Third, we introduce a design management model. We then present a case study. Finally, we present the managerial implications of integrating branding and design management.

HOW BRANDING HAS EVOLVED

In the last decade, brand building has experienced a dramatic shift. The original conception that a brand's primary function is to identify a product has evolved. Brands today are conceived as much more than mere identifiers that allow products to distinguish themselves from the competition; brands even stand above the products or services they help identify. Brands have evolved from being a tactical element of a product to a strategic asset for many organizations, and therefore the focus of brand management has shifted from increasing sales to developing brand equity or value (Aaker and Joachimsthaler, 2000). In summary, brands have become firms' 'strategic platforms for interacting with their customers' (Urde, 1999).

By analyzing several definitions of a brand, it is possible to understand how the conception of a brand has evolved. The American Marketing Association (AMA) defines a brand as 'a name, term, sign, symbol, or design, or a combination of them, intended to identify the goods or services of one seller or group of sellers and to differentiate them from those of competitors'. The AMA's definition distinguishes brands' main function as identifiers; however, a brand is much more than this, as it serves utilitarian and symbolic needs. Keller (2003) argues that a brand adds dimensions that differentiate products or services designed to satisfy the same needs, while Kotler (2000) states that a brand is a product offer from a known source. Taking into consideration these two perspectives, it is possible to see that brands not only serve as identifiers, but provide additional information about where they come from, what and who is behind their production, and help distinguish between two apparently equal solutions for a certain need. As Kapferer (1997) suggests, brands become a source of value for customers given that they reduce the perceived risk of consumption, and serve a variety of both utilitarian and symbolic functions. Brands, therefore, are a set of promises, an intangible but critical component for defining what a firm means (Davis, 2002). Or as Bedbury (2002) would argue, a brand is the result of a synaptic process in consumers' brains because they are sponges for content, images, feelings, sensations and experiences.

From analyzing the previous definitions we can see how brands have evolved from being conceived as mere identifiers of products and services to psychological concepts that reduce perceived risk, offer value, and embody a whole experience. Since brands reside in consumers' minds, achieving a consistent brand image or brand positioning is a very complicated task for brand managers, as each individual can potentially perceive things in a different manner. Therefore, it is critical for a brand to identify and understand its target customers clearly in order to become and remain appealing to them. Furthermore, since customers are heterogeneous, a brand must have a clear and functional segmentation of its target public in order to be capable of managing the perceptions of each of its different customer segments, as each segment might expect different things from the same brand. In other words, a brand needs to capture the expectations of, and represent the set of promises for, each of its target segments (Guzmán et al., 2006). A brand can, therefore, be defined as a portfolio of meanings, and design can play an important role in creating coherence within this portfolio.

THE MELDING OF BRANDING AND DESIGN

As discussed, brands live in the consumer's mind and therefore a strong brand is one that is able to gain an important and consolidated space in it. However, building a strong brand alone is not enough to establish a strong position in consumers' minds. In the end, the product (quality, functionality and design) has to offer added value to the customer in order to differentiate the whole brand experience from the competition. Nowadays, transcending the product-only relationship and connecting the brand to powerful emotions makes it distinct, but meaningful product innovation can never be replaced (Bedbury, 2002). A product that generates a positive interaction with a customer by delivering the promised value reinforces the brand experience like nothing else can (Oppenheimer, 2005). Design is vital for enhancing this interaction, and, consequently, consumer-centered product design is emerging as a best practice in many industries (Lojacono and Zaccai, 2004; Siedel and Pinto, 2005; Veryzer and Borja de Mozota, 2005). Market research techniques that help designers and brand managers understand consumer lifestyles and translate data into sensory dimensions, such as ethnography, anthropometrics and other observational techniques, are playing an ever more important role in the new product development process (Cooper and Evans, 2006).

The heart of branding lies in a key idea around which the brand-building strategy can be developed. This idea should be inspired by the consumer's sweet spot – 'the part of his or her life that represents significant involvement and commitment and/or expresses who they are' (Aaker and Joachimsthaler, 2000, p. 264). Design for the product, its production process, and for the brand-building program itself, plays a crucial role in reaching the customer's sweet spot, as it is able to bring to light the emotional meaning of products and services (Lojacono and Zaccai, 2004). Creusen and Schoormans (2005) distinguish six roles that design and product aesthetics have for consumers, and show that these roles are relevant for them in a consumption decision: design and aesthetics draw the consumer's attention; allow consumers to categorize and differentiate products; serve as a cue for features, functionality and technical quality; show the consumer–product interaction; relate the product's fit with other products owned; and serve as a basis for symbolic product association by communicating brand image.

Design has evolved from a two-dimensional graphical approach for creating identities to a tool for creating three-dimensional, intense, holistic brand experiences (Kent, 2003). Since visual symbols have acquired greater potential than words in the marketplace (Borja de Mozota, 2003), brands have become symbolic signs on an expressive level that, instead of focusing so much on storytelling as before, focus on the production of impressions and experiences that rely more on images and visual signs (Salzer-Mörling and Strannegard, 2004). Within this aesthetic and holistic context, design management acquires utmost importance in the brand-building process. Additionally, since brands have become important signs that help customers express who they are, the values brands convey have increased in importance. Corporate social responsibility (CSR), for example, has become an important source of brand differentiation and another factor that helps create a holistic brand experience. Strategic CSR can, therefore, enhance the brand-building process as long as there is a strategic fit between the values of the brand and the values of the CSR initiative it is associated with (Guzmán and Montaña, 2006). In other words, CSR can be an effective element of the brand-building process as long as it is used as more than a communication tactic. In this process, a CSR branding strategy can rely on design in order to bring social responsibility to life (Cooper, 2005). Responsible design, therefore, is part of responsible business (Sethia, 2005), and it can help enhance the brand-building process and enrich the brand experience as it makes a positive contribution to society, to lifestyles, and to the environment in general (Cooper, 2005).

Likewise, the aesthetic aspects of design can be important in determining the consumer's selection of products (Veryzer, 2000). These aspects, which create satisfiers in the consumers' experiential worlds, are able to create loyalty, foster a sense of exclusiveness or distinction, and help a brand avoid competitive attacks. Aesthetically appealing product designs lead to positive brand evaluations, facilitate product and brand categorization, and facilitate consumer interaction (Kreuzbauer and Malter, 2005). Aesthetics, through product design, communications research design and spatial design, offers added value for the customer (Schmitt and Simonson, 1997) and produces positive effects on organizational performance (Berkowitz, 1987; Kreuzbauer and Malter, 2005). In other words, design enhances not only the aesthetics of a product but, as we have already mentioned, the whole customer experience. Even though little work has been done in this field (Berkowitz, 1987; Beverland, 2005; Bloch, 1995; Jevnaker, 2000; Vazquez et al., 2003, Veryzer and Borja de Mozota, 2005), product design and aesthetics have been acknowledged as strategic tools for firms seeking a competitive advantage (Borja de Mozota, 2002; Creusen and Schoormans, 2005; Kotler and Rath, 1984; Hertenstein et al., 2005; Page and Herr, 2002; Peters, 1989; Vazquez and Bruce, 2002). Despite few studies about how design influences the brand-building process, it seems to be an ever more crucial element in the quest to build a differentiated brand.

The brand-building process can be greatly enriched by combining marketers' more quantitative and objective approaches with designers' more intuitive and subjective methods. Design should be integrated with other organizational functions (Beverland, 2005). Some suggest integration at the product design and innovation level (Bedbury, 2002; Bloch, 1995; Godin, 2003; Jones, 2001; Leonhardt and Faust, 2001; Ries and Ries, 2002; Stompff, 2003), including the novel process of reverse product design when a customer designs his/her own products (Kotler et al., 2002); others have focused on integration of design in communications strategy (Bedbury, 2002; Jones, 2001; Leonhardt and Faust, 2001; Ries and Ries, 2002); and still others focus on the integration of design at the brand level (Aaker and Joachimsthaler, 2000; Kapferer, 1997; Keeley, 2001; Schmitt and Simonson, 1997; Stompff, 2003).

A brand will not capture a distinctive position in a consumer's mind if it does not create a sensory experience (Schmitt and Simonson, 1997). Aesthetics and design have become a crucial part of any marketing and brand-building activity. Brand design does not limit itself to the product but to the experience created, given that product form and aesthetics affect the quality of life of customers by improving the product or service (Svengren-Holm and Johansson, 2005), by providing sensory pleasure and stimulation (Bloch, 1995), and creating additional perceived value for customers (Brown et al., 2002).

THE BRAND DESIGN MANAGEMENT MODEL

By viewing design as a part of a firm's business strategy, we support a holistic approach to integrating design with the marketing and branding processes, an approach that incorporates design from the first steps of the new product development process and consequently reflects the orientation and philosophy of the organization. Since design can be considered a form of innovation, this design management model is based on Tidd et al.'s (1997) innovation management model.

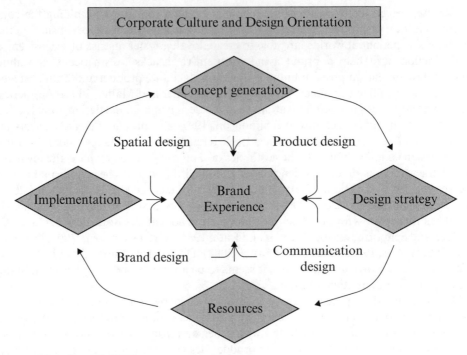

Source: Montaña, et al. (2007).

Figure 7.1   Design management model

Design is a sub-process, or a set of processes, within the innovation process of a firm. As a consequence, design intervenes, in a lesser or greater degree, in all the basic activities that configure the innovation process: new product development, development of new concepts, redefinition of production processes, redefinition of commercialization processes, and knowledge and technology management. Design is also linked to the firm's innovation strategy, which can be divided into four activities: *concept generation*, which consists of the collection of internal and external information and stimuli in order to develop a potential offering; *design strategy*, which includes defining the activities necessary for perfecting the potential offering; *resource procurement*, during which the team tries to assemble all of the external and internal resources necessary for realizing the design process; and *implementation* of the strategy. All of these activities are framed by the design culture or orientation of the firm. The design management model (Montaña and Moll, 2003) is illustrated in Figure 7.1.

1. *Corporate culture and design orientation*: It is crucial for the firm's management and ownership to be involved in design management, as it is critical to managing the design process in an efficient manner. Hence, it makes no sense to consider design a sporadic action with little relationship to the corporate strategy. A design-oriented company, for example, understands the potential for enhancing the NPD process and improving financial performance by appropriately managing the design function.

2. *New concept generation*: The beginning of the design process consists of analyzing the ways that design can be involved in generating new ideas, defining new product concepts, managing the marketing process, and leveraging other organizational functions and departments to take advantage of internal strengths. New ideas must be converted into concepts, and a minimum of 60 initial ideas have been calculated to be necessary before a product – once it has gone through the whole development process – finally gains acceptance in the market (Montaña, 1990). Designers play a crucial role in defining these concepts, making them perfectly understandable, and helping them to be shared by the whole organization in order to make the NPD process as efficient as possible.
3. *Design strategy*: This consists of analyzing design's role within the business, new product development, and branding strategies of the firm. Design strategy can have three levels of involvement within the business strategy. It can play a minor role in the NPD process by acting as a separate function subordinate to the marketing department; under this first scenario, design is limited to typical design activities such as developing the visual, aesthetic and technical aspects of the offering. Design can be part of a multifunctional team and assume a more central role in the innovation process; under this second scenario design is involved through the whole NPD process and designers play a key role as they help establish relationships with other actors involved in the process. Finally, design can be the leader of the whole NPD process; under this third scenario, typical of design-oriented firms, design is seen as the principal driver of innovation, and designers guide the whole development process of the offering.
4. *Resource procurement*: This refers to defining how design resources are managed, how internal and external design teams are used, how existing needs are managed within the firm in order to develop human resources, and how knowledge is created, used and protected. For example, a design-oriented firm's top management generally supervises the whole NPD process, considers the creative potential of its employees, and invests in training and developing designers' specific capabilities.
5. *Implementation*: Implementation refers to the execution and culmination of the design process. It allows for measuring the degree of novelty and innovation that design has within the firm, understanding how different design processes are coordinated, and evaluating design and its results for the firm. Since costly and time-consuming unexpected technical and market difficulties may occur during this activity, it is crucial that design be properly involved within the NPD process in order to reduce the impact of these circumstances. The success of this activity depends primarily on the integration of all organizational functions.

This model was originally developed considering design management as part of the new product development process (Montaña and Moll, 2003). Later on, it was adapted in order to make it a design management model for the whole company, considering not only product design, but also space, communications and brand design. During the summer of 2005 we developed a research project, funded by the Spanish Federation of Promotion Design Agencies[1] (FEEPD), with the objective of analyzing how Spanish companies that were considered excellent in design and performance managed the design process. Thirty-one companies, proposed by the FEEPD, from the furniture, electronics and tourism industries served to verify our design management model. The research methodology consisted of in-depth interviews with the owners and/or top management as well as nonintrusive observational techniques. Every interview had a duration of between two and four hours and was followed by a tour of the company's facilities. Each interview was transcribed and thoroughly analyzed; the process was repeated until the saturation criteria were achieved. The study served to verify our design management model, offered a view of the design strategy used by the analyzed firms, and identified the characteristics of the optimal design strategies within these sectors. Within this process, it was possible to study the relationship between brand building and design management.

The design management model was applied to 31 companies: nine from the furniture industry, nine from the electronics industry, and 13 from the tourism industry. The model was verified despite the size, specialization and strategic orientation differences between each of the analyzed firms. Each industry has its own specific design characteristics. For example, in the furniture industry, design is a traditional activity for most companies. We can even affirm that modern design in Spain began with furniture, illumination and home accessories. Some of the studied companies, however, still use their design resources inefficiently, and, despite being selected because of the quality of their design, they admitted to having years of work ahead in order to optimize their whole design management process. In the electronics industry there is a decisive focus towards research and development (R&D), which means that more attention and resources are channeled to technological research and development than to design, which is perceived as a differentiating tool. In the hotel and restaurant sector, the largest sector within the tourism industry, the intangible elements of offerings are more important than the tangible ones despite the fact that the latter facilitate service. The companies we analyzed were of all types and had different levels of design orientation. They represented firms producing industrial products and services within both consumer and business-to-business markets. Given these characteristics, it was initially assumed that the industries' differences would lead to different models; however, the fieldwork led to a consistent design management model.

CASE STUDY: INTEGRATING DESIGN STRATEGY AND BRAND BUILDING

This study analyzes the influence of design on brand building. In it, we discuss the example of Axel Hotel, which has a strategy in which the value of its brand transcends its products and services. The hotel is conscious of the value of a brand, and, as a consequence, all of its brand-building instruments are completely coordinated. Brand strategy and design decisions are always made by top management, allowing for an integrated strategy.

Axel Hotel: The 'Heterofriendly' Hotel

Axel Hotel is a three-star, gay-focused hotel in Barcelona. In the spring of 2005 it had 66 rooms and 40 more were under construction. The hotel is a success, with an average occupancy rate of 80 per cent (100 per cent during the weekends) and plans to open a second hotel in Buenos Aires, Argentina in September 2006, and five other hotels around the world over the next five years. Axel Hotel is unique in its positioning, given that other existing hotels targeted to the gay community are mainly holiday resorts. Axel Hotel's rooms offer a high-speed Internet connection that can be accessed from a plasma TV, a special area named Axel Business with computers and color printers free of charge, and a convention room.

The company started in 2003, when its founder and owner, Juan Juliá, after years of experience as a marketing executive in several multinational companies, decided to enter the hotel business. As he expresses on the hotel's web page: 'everything began as a dream . . . opening a hotel targeted to the gay world, my world.'

Design played an important part in this hotel's development. Accordingly the hotel's building has the typical façade of the buildings in the Eixample district, perfectly restored exterior stained-glass windows, and modern rooms equipped with modern bathrooms, large beds and many amenities. The building's restoration was done in order to maintain the original façade and the harmony between the hotel and the neighboring buildings. The hotel's interior design was Mr Juliá's responsibility, and he described (in a verbal communication) what he wanted to the interior designers as follows:

Imagine that I had to live in the hotel for six months of every year. Create a hotel in which I would be comfortable . . . do not put any carpet, I hate it, nor day bed covers. I want risky proposals, no whites, blacks, or gray . . . I want color. The gay public will accept it, they will not accept a boring place; they will accept a risky proposal with different colors and different materials.

The hotel targets the gay community that visits Barcelona either for business or leisure and is looking for an adequate environment. According to Mr Juliá,

A gay hotel is like any other hotel that tries to adapt to the specific needs of its clients. In a golf hotel they will indicate to clients where the best golf courses are, and which are easier or more difficult. A gay hotel gives information, for example, about where to party and where to meet people. It should offer an atmosphere where gay people feel comfortable . . . like being at home.

Axel Hotel not only appears to be 'gay-friendly', but also, as it explicitly defines in its graphic material, to be 'heterofriendly'. In other words, it does not impede the entrance of heterosexual guests, though its objective is to make gay guests perfectly comfortable in the hotel's environment.

The hotel's webpage is very well related to Axel's visual and graphic identity: graphic descriptions, little text, and elegant visual images. The webpage contains letters and testimonials from clients. Axel Hotel's logo, corporate identity symbols, and graphic material mirror the multicolor mosaic that decorates the hotel's floor and is a modern version of a typical hydraulic modernist[2] mosaic. The design of the hotel's interior and all its objects and accessories is directly related to the corporate strategy. For example, the rooms have substituted typical wooden wardrobes with doors with open metallic structures where clothes can be hung, in keeping with the philosophy that clothing should be visible. The sound insulation installed between each room, following Mr Juliá's orders, is twice as thick as what is considered to be standard and acceptable. As Mr Juliá says, 'if you sleep well and the room is nice, you will be fascinated. Therefore, we should not lose the basic business objective: offering a good night's sleep.'

Being at Axel Hotel is an experience. 'The environment, the atmosphere created by the interior design, the surrounding accessories, and the hotel's staff, create the basic conditions for the creation of experiences: theme, impressions, and effects', explains Mr Juliá.

> The hotel's theme is unique: a cool environment for the gay community. The impressions are based on a warm and exclusive atmosphere created by the architectural, interior, and accessory design, together with all of the visual identity signs. The total affects every sense and every strategic experiential module: sensations, feelings, thoughts, behaviors, and relations.

The coordination of every single design element the restaurant has allowed Mr Juliá to create a unique brand experience: the Axel brand experience.

MANAGERIAL IMPLICATIONS

Design is part of corporate management, and, more concretely, it forms part of the culture of the business owner. Successful companies recognize that creativity and innovation are a common denominator in the constant search for new concepts. Integrated design strategies allow for building brands and brand experiences. The successful implementation of design strategy is carefully supervised by management in order to guarantee consistency and coherence in every detail. These companies also focus on social responsibility and the environment in the development of their design strategies. In short, their design strategies are focused on the creation of an experience, and their brands are shaped by the experiences offered.

Several managerial implications can be extracted from this analysis. All of the brand elements (for example, the name, the symbol, the product or service, the packaging or facility, the communication, the pricing, the distribution) must be designed so as to strengthen the brand's positioning. Each of these elements must be designed by different professionals: industrial designers, interior designers, graphic designers, architects, engineers, and so on. Some of them might work internally and others as freelancers, but what is key is that all of them work together. As design decisions for different brand elements are usually taken on by different managers at different hierarchical levels, the design process becomes even more complex. A coordinated design management strategy becomes a must. To build a strong, well known, and well regarded brand it is necessary to coordinate every single brand message in order to have a consistent portfolio of meanings. Design plays a pivotal role in this task. Design can function as a manager of consistency and coherence, but in order to do so it must be understood by the whole company.

In summary, design management can positively enhance the brand-building process by:

- Increasing brand equity.
- Improving a company's performance.
- Influencing strategic positioning and the creation of competitive advantages.
- Making a company's strategy visible.
- Influencing corporate culture and promoting innovation.
- Augmenting internal efficiencies by improving management through the coordination of the marketing, R&D, production and process transformation functions.

NOTES

1. The FEEPD groups all the organizations that operate within all of Spain's Autonomous Communities. Its purpose is to introduce design in small and medium firms in order to increase their competitiveness. This research was funded by the FEEPD with regional and European funds.
2. Modernism in Catalonia was an architectural and decorative movement, between the end of the nineteenth and beginning of the twentieth centuries, characterized by the predominance of curves, dynamic and asymmetrical forms, and exuberant decoration, which were usually inspired by nature.

REFERENCES

Aaker, D.A. and E. Joachimsthaler (2000), *Brand Leadership*, London: Free Press.

Bedbury, S. with S. Fenichell (2002), *A New Brand World: Eight Principles for Achieving Brand Leadership in the 21st Century*, New York: Viking.

Berkowitz, M. (1987), 'Product shape as a design innovation strategy', *Journal of Product Innovation Management*, **4**, 274–83.

Beverland, M.B. (2005), 'Managing the design innovation–brand marketing interface: resolving the tension between artistic creation and commercial imperatives', *Journal of Product Innovation Management*, **22**, 193–207.

Bloch, P.H. (1995), 'Seeking the ideal form: product design and consumer response', *Journal of Marketing*, **59** (July), 16–29.

Borja de Mozota, B. (2002), 'Design and competitive edge: a model for design management excellence in European SMEs', *Design Management Journal Academic Review*, **2**(1), 88–103.

Borja de Mozota, B. (2003), *Design Management: Using Design to Build Brand Value and Corporate Innovation*, New York: Allworth Press.

Brown, K., H. Schmied and J. Tarondeau (2002), 'Success factors in R&D: a meta-analysis of the empirical literature and derived implications for design management', *Design Management Journal Academic Review*, **2**(1), 72–87.

Cooper, R. (2005), 'Ethics and altruism: what constitutes socially responsible design?', *Design Management Review*, **16**(3), 10–18.

Cooper, R. and M. Evans (2006), 'Breaking from tradition: market research, consumer needs, and design futures', *Design Management Review*, **17**(1), 68–74.

Creusen, M.E.H. and J.P.L. Schoormans (2005), 'The different roles of product appearance in consumer choice', *Journal of Product Innovation Management*, **22**, 63–81.

Davis, S.M. (2002), *Brand Asset Management: Driving Profitable Growth through your Brands*, San Francisco, CA: Jossey Bass.

Godin, S. (2003), *Purple Cow: Transform your Business by being Remarkable*, New York: Portfolio.

Guzmán, F. and J. Montaña (2006), 'Construir marcas mediante la asociación a servicios públicos', *Harvard Business Review (América Latina)*, **84**(4), 46–51.

Guzmán, F., J. Montaña and V. Sierra (2006), 'Brand building by associating to public services: a reference group influence model', *Journal of Brand Management*, **13**(4/5), 352–62.

Hertenstein, J.H., M.B. Platt and R.W. Veryzer (2005), 'The impact of industrial design effectiveness on corporate financial performance', *Journal of Product Innovation Management*, **22**, 3–21.

Jevnaker, B.H. (2000), 'Championing design: perspective on design capabilities', *Design Management Journal Academic Review*, **1**(1), 25–39.

Jones, R.H. (2001), 'The big idea', *Design Management Journal*, **12**(1), 29–33.

Kapferer, J. (1997), *Strategic Brand Management*, London: Kogan Page.

Keeley, L. (2001), 'New! Improved! (Uh huh, yeah sure, whatever . . .) A look at the modern dynamics of brands', *Design Management Journal*, **12**(1), 14–18.

Keller, K.L. (2003), *Strategic Brand Management: Building, Measuring, and Managing Brand Equity*, Upper Saddle River, NJ: Prentice Hall.

Kent, T. (2003), '2D23D: management and design perspectives on retail branding', *International Journal of Retail & Distribution Management*, **31**(3), 131–42.

Kotler, P. (2000), *Marketing Management. The Millennium Edition*, Upper Saddle River, NJ: Prentice Hall.

Kotler, P., D.C. Jain and S. Maesincee (2002), *Marketing Moves. A New Approach to Profits, Growth, and Renewal*, Boston, MA: Harvard Business School Press.

Kotler, P. and G.A. Rath (1984), 'Design: a powerful but neglected strategic tool', *The Journal of Business Strategy*, **5**(2), 16–21.

Kreuzbauer, R. and A.J. Malter (2005), 'Embodied cognition and new product design: changing product form to influence brand categorization', *Journal of Product Innovation Management*, **22**, 165–76.

Leonhardt, T. and B. Faust (2001), 'Brand power: using design and strategy to create the future', *Design Management Journal*, **12**(1), 10–13.

Lojacono, G. and G. Zaccai (2004), 'The evolution of the design-inspired enterprise', *MIT Sloan Management Review*, **45**(3), 75–9.

Montaña, J. (1990), *Marketing de Nuevos Productos. Diseño, Desarrollo y Lanzamiento*', Barcelona: Editorial Hispano Europea, pp. 103–5.

Montaña, J. and I. Moll (2003), *Guia per Gestionar la Innovació. Desenvolupament de Producte: La Gestió del Disseny*, Barcelona: CIDEM, Generalitat de Catalunya.

Montaña, J., F. Guzmán and I. Moll (2007), 'Branding and design management: a brand design management model', *Journal of Marketing Management*, **23**(9–10), 829–40.

Oppenheimer, A. (2005), 'From experience: products talking to people – conversation closes the gap between products and consumers', *Journal of Product Innovation Management*, **22**, 82–91.

Page, C. and P.M. Herr (2002), 'An investigation of the processes by which product design and brand strength interact to determine initial affect and quality judgments', *Journal of Consumer Psychology*, **12**(2), 133–47.

Peters, T. (1989), 'The design challenge', *Design Management Journal*, **1**(1), 3–7.

Ries, A. and L. Ries (2002), *The Fall of Advertising and the Rise of PR*, New York: Harper Business.

Salzer-Mörling, M. and L. Strannegard (2004), 'Silence of the brands', *European Journal of Marketing*, **38**(1/2), 224–38.

Schmitt, B.H. (1999), *Experiential Marketing: How to get Customers to Sense, Feel, Act and Relate to your Company and Brands*, New York: Free Press.

Schmitt, B.H. and A. Simonson (1997), *Marketing Aesthetics: The Strategic Management of Brands, Identity and Image*, New York: Free Press.

Sethia, N. (2005), 'At the bottom of the pyramid: responsible design for responsible businesses', *Design Management Review*, **16**(3), 42–9.

Siedel, V. and J.P. Pinto (2005), 'Social science strategies for user-focused innovation and design management', *Design Management Review*, **16**(4), 73–9.

Steinbock, D. (2005), 'Design and mobile innovation', *Design Management Review*, **16**(4), 55–62.

Stompff, G. (2003), 'The forgotten bond: brand identity and product design', *Design Management Journal*, **14**(1), 26–32.

Svengren-Holm, L. and U. Johansson (2005), 'Marketing and design: rivals or partners?', *Design Management Review*, **16**(2), 36–41.

Tidd, J., J. Bessant and K. Pavitt (1997), *Managing Innovation. Integrating Technological, Market and Organizational Change*, Chichester, UK: Wiley and Sons.

Urde, M. (1999), 'Brand orientation: a mindset for building brands into strategic resources', *Journal of Marketing Management*, **15**, 117–33.

Vazquez, D. and M. Bruce (2002), 'Exploring the retail design process within a UK food retailer', *International Review of Retail, Distribution and Consumer Research*, **12**(4), 437–48.

Vazquez, D., M. Bruce and R. Studd (2003), 'A case study exploring packaging design management process within a UK food retailer', *British Food Journal*, **105**(9), 602–17.

Veryzer, R.W. (2000), 'Design and consumer research', *Design Management Journal*, **1**, 64–73.

Veryzer, R.W. and B. Borja de Mozota (2005), 'The impact of user-oriented design on new product development: an examination of fundamental relationships', *Journal of Product Innovation Management*, **22**, 128–43.

8. Everybody's darling? The target groups of a brand

Anton Meyer, Benjamin Brudler and Christian Blümelhuber

INTRODUCTION

Almost any industry is faced with the threat of commoditization. The threat of new market entrants who may provide almost identical products and services cheaper, faster, or more simply (that is, 'no frills' concepts) is omnipresent. How can marketers preserve and expand their current customer base in this turbulent environment?

One possible answer is the development of brands. Brands fulfill various tasks for consumers. They add emotional values to functional products, serve as a signal of quality, and reduce the buyer's (perceived) risk. Therefore, they help to shape consumers' preferences and buying behavior. Against this background, brands are much more than just another marketing instrument or a single field of action in a firm's market communication or product policy. They are central resources and assets (Hall, 1992), organizational coordination units, drivers of customer equity, and therefore drivers of firm value (Rust et al., 2000).

Taking this into account, the current popularity of the concept of brands is not surprising. A concept that emerged from the consumer goods sector is now common practice in almost all organizations and institutions. Corporations, but also political parties, NGOs, even countries, regions or celebrities like to view themselves as brands and make efforts to tap the full potential of their brands. Creating, maintaining and enhancing the strength of brands has become a growing management imperative in all sectors. Consequently, a legion of researchers, consultants and management gurus attends to this topic. Concepts of the last few years include emotional branding (Travis, 2000), cult branding (Atkin, 2004), fusion branding (Wreden, 2002), even passion brands (Edwards and Day, 2005) and fire brands (Millison and Moon, 2000), and are marketed as brands themselves. Although it cannot be denied that all these works contributed to an adequate consideration of brands among marketing practitioners, it is questionable whether this glut of ideas did not also cause confusion (Schultz and Schultz, 2004).

Therefore, it is not our intention to add yet another magic formula for overwhelming brand success to the available stock. In contrast, we present an integrated view on brand management combining three important approaches from a managerial perspective. This conception serves as a basis to draw attention to a topic in brand management that seems to be underrepresented in current research, that is, the variety of target groups of a brand. The majority of prior research places emphasis on customers but disregards other stakeholders. Also, there is an unreasonable simplification in brand research based upon the presumption that consumers are positively biased towards brands: 'Academic marketing theorizes away conflicts between marketing and consumers. Such conflicts result only when firms attend to their internal interests rather than seek to meet consumer wants and needs' (Holt, 2002, p. 70). As we will show, the simple algorithm '*If* the brand management is professional . . . *then* the consumer is happy' does not hold any more. Consumers have become branding experts in recent decades and thus show different, 'unconventional' ways of perceiving brands, some being very critical towards them.

The purpose of this chapter is to discuss the complex nature of the relationship between companies, people and brands. A framework of the various stakeholders and target groups of a brand is developed, both from a functional (for example journalists, suppliers, staff) and from an attitude-based (for example 'devotees', 'saboteurs') point of view. We identify four types of attitudes towards brands and present their role in brand management. The consequences of the framework for brand management are discussed. The chapter is conceptual in its approach and is intended to draw attention to a relevant topic in brand management and research.

AN INTEGRATED VIEW ON BRANDS

As mentioned above, brand research has produced a vast number of definitions and concepts. Besides the popular writings by marketing practitioners, there are numerous academic propositions (see de Chernatony and Dall'Olmo Riley, 1998 for an overview). Unfortunately, many of the existing definitions and models just focus on one aspect of the brand phenomenon.

The first concept can simply be called 'branding'. This term represents the traditional view on brands still reflected in the AMA (American Marketing Association) definition of a brand: 'A name, term, design, symbol, or any other feature that identifies one seller's good or service as distinct from those of other sellers. The legal term for brand is trademark' (American Marketing Association, 2007). This definition focuses on the differentiability of products achieved through branding. Furthermore, it underlines its legal importance. In any case, it is based on the underlying presumption that a firm has, or at least should have, almost perfect control over its brands. It is significant that customers and their perceptions are not mentioned in this definition. The definition is quite one-sided, since brand equity can only arise from consumers' preferences and buying decisions (Hallberg, 1995). Anyway, it indicates two important characteristics of brands, namely their ability to build a real competitive advantage (that is valuable, rare, imperfectly imitable and sustainable; Barney, 1991) by 'being different', and the right to defend this advantage by legal means.

The second concept is called 'knowledge' and provides a reverse way of looking at brands. Instead of viewing brands as controllable assets, this school focuses more on the consumer's side and defines brands as 'simply a collection of perceptions held in the mind of the customer' (Fournier, 1998, p. 345). It is widely accepted that customer-based brand equity only 'occurs when the consumer has a high level of awareness and familiarity with the brand and holds some strong, favorable, and unique brand associations in memory' (Keller, 1998, p. 50). Various factors contribute to consumer brand knowledge; Keller

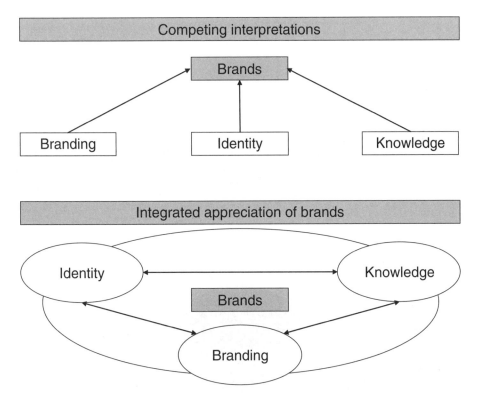

Figure 8.1   An integrated view on brands

identifies eight key dimensions: awareness, attributes, benefits, images, thoughts, feelings, attitudes and experiences (Keller, 2003). The 'brand knowledge' approach is dominant in current research and of special importance for established brands. While new brands arise from deliberately planned, executed and controlled marketing measures such as market communications, control gets lost after a while because more information is attached to the brand: 'Over time, however, the consumer becomes more involved in this process [of branding], and this presents a challenge to firms as they must learn how to work with consumers' (McEnally and de Chernatony, 1999). What we take from this approach is the key learning that brands are not perfectly controllable, have no objective reality, and can only be managed effectively by seeing them through the eyes of the customer (Lederer and Hill, 2001).

The third concept comes from the 'identity' school, which mainly emerged in Europe (Kapferer, 1986; Meffert and Burmann 1996). This is in keeping with the notion that identity precedes image (Kapferer, 2004, p. 99). In this process, there are several uncontrollable and disturbing factors (for example competitors' actions, norms, trends, and so on). Discrepancies between intended and real images are exposed through market research. Finally, necessary adaptations are made to the brand identity and/or the positioning.

A combination of the identity, branding and knowledge concepts results in an integrated approach to brands (see Figure 8.1) as mirrored in our definition: 'A brand is . . .

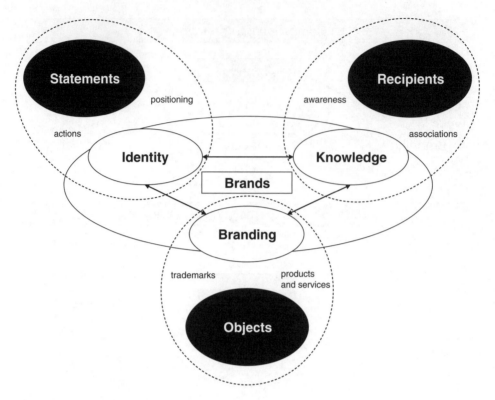

Source: Blümelhuber et al. (2004).

Figure 8.2   Aspects of integration

- a holistically planned and managed (identity approach),
- through specific signs recallable (branding approach)
- schema (knowledge approach).'

Schemas are cognitive structures, on the one hand representing the expectations one has about an object, and on the other hand moderating the processing of new information related to the object (Bettman, 1979).

This definition of brands gives an answer to the 'meaningless discussion' (Schultz and Schultz, 2004, p. 20) as to whether the brand belongs to the firm or the customer.

Of course, to tap the full potential of this approach, marketing practitioners do not only need an integrated understanding of brands, but also an integrated management of brands.

Figure 8.2 shows some aspects of integrated brand management (Blümelhuber et al., 2004). Since we cannot discuss all aspects of integration in this chapter, we focus on one point that is both crucial for success and often disregarded in contemporary research: an understanding of the various target groups, or 'recipients', of a brand. This aspect is located primarily in the corner represented by 'knowledge'. Therefore, let us examine the development of brand knowledge in further detail.

BRAND 'BRICOLEURS'

As we have already mentioned, brands neither have a material existence nor an objective reality. According to interpretive approaches to reality (Burrell and Morgan, 1979, pp. 227–78 for an overview), each individual constructs his or her own effigy of reality. This image does not mirror sensual perceptions only, but is influenced by personal acts of selection, classification and estimation. This process is typically unsystematic. In Lévi-Strauss's analysis of the 'bricoleur' (Lévi-Strauss, 1966) we see an analogy to the creative process of tinkering. Instead of the systematic approach of a DIY-worker, the bricoleur does not have a clear goal for his/her work but takes material which is incidentally available. Similarly, individuals assemble their attitude towards a brand from various contact points with the brand, whether they are marketing driven or not.

This constructed brand image is temporary in nature. Cognitive structures are constantly modified and adopted to personal experiences. As long as the new information is congruent with the existing schema of the brand, these changes are only slight and the knowledge base is strengthened (Fiske and Taylor, 1984). But if the new information is not congruent either with the product category or the former image, the brand knowledge will alter significantly (Meyers-Levy and Tybout, 1989; Lee, 1995). Almost any information that is linked to the brand can trigger this process (Hoch and Deighton, 1989; O'Shaughnessy and O'Shaughnessy, 2003). Also, this process can be negative (for example, a bad service experience spreading through the blogosphere) or positive (for example, a successful relaunch).

This process gave birth to a concept of brand management that manages all contact points so that a consistent brand image develops (Chattopadhyay and Laborie, 2005). Another popular concept is the idea of integrated marketing communications (Schultz et al., 1993). These concepts, however, neglect the fact that many contact points are not directly controllable (see Figure 8.3).

A FRAMEWORK OF BRAND STAKEHOLDERS AND TARGET GROUPS

We develop a framework which gives marketing practitioners an understanding of a brand's stakeholders and target groups.

Stakeholder theory tells us that a firm relies on a network of relations among various groups in its environment. Therefore the goal of strategic management is to exert influence on these relations so that they help the firm achieve its goals (Freeman, 1984).

Brand managers should broaden their view and understand the role all stakeholders play in the creation of brand equity. Figure 8.4 shows a typology of brand stakeholders according to Jones (2005).

The stakeholder approach is a very broad one and integrates other concepts such as internal branding, supplier branding and so on. It can be a very useful tool for managers since brand equity may in some cases depend heavily on groups other than the customer. For example, consider a typical low-involvement consumer good such as flour. For the producer, it is probably more relevant to gain access to important sales channels such as retailers than to develop a unique brand image among potential customers.

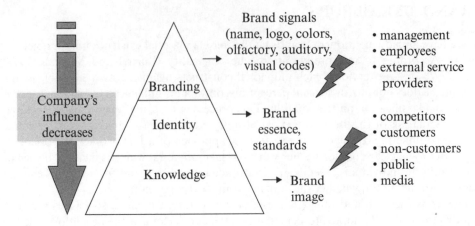

Figure 8.3   Company's control over different brand levels

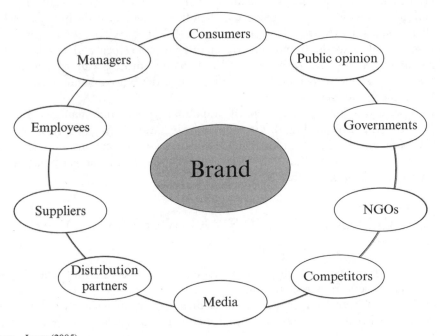

Source: Jones (2005).

Figure 8.4   Stakeholders of a brand

In fact, it is better for brand managers to identify their stakeholders and rank them on dependency, strategic significance, actuality and attractiveness (Jones, 2005). On this basis, the effectiveness and efficiency of brand management might be improved. Of course, this is quite a bold venture since the various stakeholders expect and perceive different kinds of benefits, experience different aspects of a brand, and evaluate contact points in a different way. Furthermore, the stakeholder approach is quite hard to measure.

Research on reputation management shows interesting new ways to quantify these effects (Eberl and Schwaiger, 2005).

The stakeholder approach is an important step towards a holistic understanding of brands. However, it leaves some important questions open. Why do people react so differently towards brands? While some consumers seem to be obsessed with brands, others feel oppressed by them or seem to ignore them completely. A clear pattern is not visible. The next section explores consumer attitudes and derives implications for branding.

THE ATTITUDE-BASED VIEW: BRAND TARGET GROUPS

We use the term 'target group' in a somewhat unusual way. While it normally describes well-defined consumer segments, we deliberately include non-consumers in our framework. Additionally, we suggest a concept of brand target groups based on attitudes towards the brand.

As we have already mentioned, the traditional idea of 'brand-friendly' consumers is a bit outdated. Consumers do not always have a positive bias towards brands. They use them in ways not intended by brand managers, show active resistance, or even boycott brands (Holt, 2002).

A starting point for our framework can be found in the literature on 'brand relationships'. In an interesting analogy to human relationships, the different types of relationships range from 'arranged marriages' to 'secret affairs' and 'best friendships' (Fournier, 1998). Further, we also draw upon Hirschman's theory of 'exit, voice and loyalty' (Hirschman, 1970). Accordingly, we distinguish between three basic feedback mechanisms (related target groups in parentheses):

- Exit: describes a consumer who shows little interest in the brand's activities, hardly trusts the brand, and therefore frequently switches brands (Unconcerned)
- Voice: describes an 'angry' consumer, either critical towards the brand or disappointed (Saboteur)
- Loyalty: describes a consumer who is very interested in the brand, and shows a lot of commitment: the brand is an important part of his self-concept (Devotee)

Furthermore, we add to Hirschman's framework with the idea of 'twisting' (Cova and Cova, 2001) in describing the following feedback mechanism:

- Twist: a self-conscious consumer who relates to the brand in a manner different from the brand's established image (Twisters)

Further, we allow for the fact that an individual can take up different roles when confronted with different brands. Figure 8.5 shows the different target groups.

Unconcerneds: Logo. So?

Apart from a lack of motivation towards understanding the brand, price sensitivity can also explain this target group.

Figure 8.5　Brand target groups and stakeholders

Saboteurs: No Logo!

Some consumers express distrust and active resistance against brands. Prominent examples include Naomi Klein's widely discussed book *No Logo!*, the Canadian magazine *Adbusters*, and the 'Attac' movement. Paradoxically, this segment has been converted into a target group for specific 'anti-establishment' brands such as 'No Sweat™' apparel.

Research has identified various sources of distrust towards branding (Ozanne and Murray, 1995; Holt, 2002). Recent findings suggest that 'emotional' brands that lack authenticity in the consumer's eye are susceptible to these reactions (Thompson et al., 2006). Managers should be especially careful in addressing the distrust of this target group.

Devotees: Pro Logo!

This target group consists of passionate, loyal customers for whom the brand is an integral part of life and who engage in active word-of-mouth about the brand. Consumers choose brands that enhance their self-concept and give them the potential to communicate to others (Elliott and Wattanasuwan, 1998; Belk, 1988). Luxury goods benefit from this motive (Bearden and Etzel, 1982).

Twisters: ' My' Logo!

The concept of twisting – as a creative process – becomes particularly explicit in art. From Andy Warhol's 'Campbell's Soup' to Wang Guangyi's 'Great Criticism', visual artists have used brands as a modern cultural resource. Other examples include the brand obsession of many Hip-Hop artists.

One famous precursor of the twisting phenomenon is the French designer Ora-ïto who produced several designs for luxury brands, such as the 'Back Up Vuitton' backpack for Louis Vuitton and the camouflage printed 'Hack Mac' laptop for Apple.

While some 'brand twisters' can be understood as the creative type of 'saboteurs', others are in fact real fans of the brand. These consumers prefer to redefine the brand's meaning. The firm can, and in many cases does, encourage this behavior (including several firms that indulge in 'send us your own slogan for the brand' type campaigns).

Marketing should be concerned with the co-creation of value and the establishment of relationships (Vargo and Lusch, 2004; Lusch et al., 2006). 'Co-creating' can only be successful if both partners are considered equal. In the age of 'bricolage', it is the consumers who attach meaning to brands. On the other hand, the firm should still try to create some 'concurrent areas' to manage the core elements of its brand consistently.

REFERENCES

Algesheimer, René, Utpal M. Dholakia and Andreas Hermann (2005), 'The social influence of brand community: evidence from European car clubs', *Journal of Marketing*, **69**, 19–34.

Ambler, Tim, Chitrabhan B. Bhattacharya, Julie Edell, Kevin L. Keller, Katherine N. Lemon and Vikas Mittal (2002), 'Relating brand and customer perspectives on marketing management', *Journal of Service Research*, **5**, 13–25.

American Marketing Association (2007), 'Marketing Terms Dictionary: definition of "brand", www.marketingpower.com/mg-dictionary-view329.php.

Atkin, Douglas (2004), *The Culting of Brands: When Customers Become True Believers*, New York, US and London, UK: Penguin.

Barney, Jay (1991), 'Firm resources and sustained competitive advantage', *Journal of Management*, **17**, 99–120.

Bearden, William O. and Michael J. Etzel (1982), 'Reference group influence on product and brand purchase decisions', *Journal of Consumer Research*, **9**, 183–94.

Belk, Russell W. (1988), 'Possessions and the extended self', *Journal of Consumer Research*, **15**, 139–68.

Bettman, James R. (1979), *An Information Processing Theory of Consumer Choice*, Reading, MA: Addison-Wesley Publishing Company.

Block, Ryan (2007), 'Live from Macworld 2007: Steve Jobs keynote', www.engadget.com/2007/01/09/live-from-macworld-2007-steve-jobs-keynote/.

Blümelhuber, Christian, Michael Maier and Anton Meyer (2004), 'Integriertes Markenverständnis und-management', in Manfred Bruhn (ed.), *Handbuch Markenführung*, vol. 2, 2nd edn, Wiesbaden, Germany: Gabler, pp. 1365–84.

Burrell, Gibson and Gareth Morgan (1979), *Sociological Paradigms and Organisational Analysis*, London, UK: Heinemann.

Chattopadhyay, Amitava and Jean-Louis Laborie (2005), 'Managing brand experience: the market contact audit™', *Journal of Advertising Research*, **45**, 9–16.

Coulter, Robin H. and Gerald Zaltman (1994), 'Using the Zaltman metaphor elicitation technique to understand brand images', *Advances in Consumer Research*, **21**, 501–7.

Cova, Bernard (1997), 'Community and consumption: towards a definition of the "linking value" of product or services', *European Journal of Marketing*, **31**, 297–316.

Cova, Bernard and Stefano Pace (2006), 'Brand community of convenience products: new forms of customer empowerment – the case of "my Nutella The Community"', *European Journal of Marketing*, **40**, 1087–105.

Cova, Veronique and Bernard Cova (2001), ' "Exit, voice, loyalty and . . . twist": consumer research in search of the subject', in Suzanne C. Beckmann and Richard H. Elliott (eds), *Interpretive Consumer Research*, vol. 2, Copenhagen: Copenhagen Business School Press, pp. 25–45.

de Chernatony, Leslie and Francesca Dall'Olmo Riley (1998), 'Defining a "brand": beyond the literature with experts' interpretations', *Journal of Marketing Management*, **14**, 417–43.

Eberl, Markus and Manfred Schwaiger (2005), 'Corporate reputation: disentangling the effects on financial performance', *European Journal of Marketing*, **39**, 838–54.

Edwards, Helen and Derek Day (2005), *Creating Passion Brands: Getting to the Heart of Branding*, Sterling, VA, US and London, UK: Kogan Page.

Elliott, Richard and Kritsadarat Wattanasuwan (1998), 'Brands as symbolic resources for the construction of identity', *International Journal of Advertising*, **17**, 131–44.

Firat, A. Fuat and Alladi Venkatesh (1995), 'Liberatory postmodernism and the reenchantment of consumption', *Journal of Consumer Research*, **22**, 239–67.

Fiske, Susan T. and Shelley E. Taylor (1984), *Social Cognition*, Reading, MA, US: Addison-Wesley.

Fournier, Susan (1998), 'Consumers and their brands: Developing relationship theory in consumer research', *Journal of Consumer Research*, **24**, 343–73.

Freeman, R. Edward (1984), *Strategic Management: A Stakeholder Approach*, Boston, MA, US: Pitman.

Hall, Richard (1992), 'The strategic analysis of intangible resources', *Strategic Management Journal*, **13**(2), 135–44.

Hallberg, G. (1995), *All Consumers are not Created Equal: The Differential Marketing Strategy for Brand Loyalty and Profits*, New York, US: John Wiley & Sons.

Hirschman, Albert O. (1970), *Exit, Voice, and Loyalty: Responses to Decline in Firms, Organizations and States*, Cambridge, MA, US: Harvard University Press.

Hoch, Stephen J. and John Deighton (1989), 'Managing what consumers learn from experience', *Journal of Marketing*, **53**, 1–20.

Holt, Douglas B. (2002), 'Why do brands cause trouble? A dialectical theory of consumer culture and branding', *Journal of Consumer Research*, **29**, 70–90.

Jones, Richard (2005), 'Finding sources of brand value: developing a stakeholder model of brand equity', *Journal of Brand Management*, **13**, 10–32.

Kapferer, Jean-Noël (1986), 'Beyond positioning, retailer's identity', *Esomar Seminar Proceedings*, Brussels, 4–6 June, pp. 167–76.

Kapferer, Jean-Noël (2004), *The New Strategic Brand Management: Creating and Sustaining Brand Equity Long Term*, Sterling, VA, US and London, UK: Kogan Page.

Keller, Kevin L. (1998), *Strategic Brand Management: Building, Measuring and Managing Brand Equity*, Upper Saddle River, NJ, US and London, UK: Prentice Hall.

Keller, Kevin L. (2003), 'Brand synthesis: the multidimensionality of brand knowledge', *Journal of Consumer Research*, **29**, 595–600.

Lederer, Chris and Sam Hill (2001), 'See your brand through your customers' eyes', *Harvard Business Review*, June, pp. 125–33.

Lee, Moonkyu (1995), 'Effects of schema congruity and involvement on product evaluations', *Advances in Consumer Research*, **22**, 210–16.

Lévi-Strauss, Claude (1966), *The Savage Mind*, London, UK: Weidenfeld & Nicolson.

Lusch, Robert F., Stephen L. Vargo and Alan J. Malter (2006), 'Marketing as service-exchange: taking a leadership role in global marketing management', *Organizational Dynamics*, **35**, 264–78.

McAlexander, James H., John W. Schouten and Harold F. Koenig (2002), 'Building brand community', *Journal of Marketing*, **66**, 38–54.

McEnally, Martha and Leslie de Chernatony (1999), 'The evolving nature of branding: consumer and managerial considerations', *Academy of Marketing Science Review*, **99**(2), www.amsreview.org/articles/mcenally02-1999.pdf.

Meffert, Heribert and Christoph Burmann (1996), 'Towards an identity-orientated approach of branding', Working Paper No. 18, Judge Institute of Management Studies, University of Cambridge, UK.

Meyers-Levy, Joan and Alice M. Tybout (1989), 'Schema congruity as a basis for product evaluation', *Journal of Consumer Research*, **16**, 39–54.

Mikunda, Christian (2004), *Brand Lands, Hot Spots and Cool Places: Welcome to the Third Place and the Total Marketing Experience*, Sterling, VA, US and London, UK: Kogan Page.

Millison, Doug and Michael Moon (2000), *Firebrands: Building Brand Loyalty in the Internet Age*, Berkeley, CA, US: Osborne/McGraw-Hill.

Muniz Jr., Albert M. and Thomas O'Guinn (2001), 'Brand community', *Journal of Consumer Research*, **27**, 412–32.

O'Shaughnessy, John and Nicholas J. O'Shaughnessy (2003), *The Marketing Power of Emotions*, Oxford, UK: Oxford University Press.

Ozanne, Julie L. and Jeff B. Murray (1995), 'Uniting critical theory and public policy to create the reflexively defiant consumer', *American Behavioral Scientist*, **38**, 516–25.

Rust, Roland T., Valarie A. Zeithaml and Katherine N. Lemon (2000), *Driving Customer Equity: How Customer Lifetime Value is Reshaping Corporate Strategy*, New York, US and London, UK: The Free Press.

Schindler, Robert M. (1992), 'The real lesson of New Coke: the value of focus groups for predicting the effects of social influence', *Marketing Research*, **4**(4), 22–7.

Schultz, Don E. and Heidi F. Schultz (2004), *Brand Babble: Sense and Nonsense about Branding*, Mason, OH, US and London, UK: Thomson Learning.

Schultz, Don E., Stanley I. Tannenbaum and Robert F. Lauterborn (1993), *Integrated Marketing Communications: Putting it Together & Making it Work*, Lincolnwood, IL, US: NTC Business Books.

Specht, Nina, Sina Fichtel and Anton Meyer (2007), 'How the service provider's effort and abilities affect customer satisfaction within the service encounter', *International Journal of Service Industry Management* (forthcoming).

Thompson, Craig J., Aric Rindfleisch and Zeynep Arsel (2006), 'Emotional branding and the strategic value of the Doppelgänger brand image', *Journal of Marketing*, **70**, 50–64.

Travis, Daryl (2000), *Emotional Branding: How Successful Brands gain the Irrational Edge*, Roseville, CA, US: Prima.

Vargo, Stephen L. and Robert F. Lusch (2004), 'Evolving to a new dominant logic for marketing', *Journal of Marketing*, **68**, 1–17.

Wreden, Nick (2002), *FusionBranding: How to Forge your Brand for the Future*, Atlanta, US: Accountability Press.

PART III

Concepts and frameworks of experience management

In this part, the authors present concepts and frameworks for customer experiences, experiential marketing and experience economies, examining each and describing areas for continued research to further our understanding of experience management.

Schmitt examines the concept of experience and its relevance to marketing and branding, and presents a framework for managing customer experiences based on a set of five 'experiential modules' and on the use of various 'experience providers' to activate these experiences.

Raghunathan examines the emergence of economies focused on selling experiences and analyzes the reasons underlying this shift, whether there is a qualitative difference between traditional and experiential goods and services, and the future of what has been called the 'experience economy'.

Brakus presents an empirically testable theory of consumer experiences based on a cognitive science framework that serves as an alternative to the mainstream marketing paradigm of information processing and choice, and shows how it can be used to address strategic marketing issues.

9. A framework for managing customer experiences

Bernd H. Schmitt

Managers have applied the practice of experiential marketing to great success in a wide variety of industries. New trends in media, technology and society seem to be driving a move towards marketing experiences and not just the functional aspects of their products and services. There is, however, a more fundamental reason why any marketer should consider experiences and not only functional features and benefits.

For centuries, philosophers from Aristotle to Kant, psychologists from William James to Carl Rogers, and other popular thinkers from Steve Covey to Woody Allen, have repeatedly asked the questions: What motivates people? What makes life worth living? What is a good life?

And the (admittedly vague but important) consensus is: something beyond mere need satisfaction; something beyond the constraints of 'stimulus-response' reactions; something that somehow transcends our lives. Mihaly Csikszentmihalyi, a professor and former chairman of the Psychology Department at the University of Chicago, calls this something *Flow*. For Csikszentmihalyi, 'Flow' is about optimal experiences and enjoyment in life: 'flow through the senses', 'the flow of thought', 'the body in flow', 'other people as flow', and (yes!) 'enjoying work as flow'. Flow is in the mind, it is about 'the making of meaning'; the ultimate goal is 'turning all life into a unified flow experience' (Csikszentmihalyi, 1991). Interestingly enough, the German word for experience, *Erlebnis*, is etymologically related to the verb 'to live' (*leben*).

Don't let the 'new age' terminology disturb you. You can change the terms. The bottom line for managers remains: you have to somehow enrich people's lives and provide enjoyment for your customers. To define the purpose of marketing in terms of need satisfaction, problem solution, or benefit delivery is too narrow. The ultimate – if you will, humanistic – goal of marketing is providing customers with valuable (that is, optimal) experiences.

Peter Drucker wrote: 'There is only one valid definition of business purpose: to create a customer' (Drucker, 1954: 37). Similarly, there is only one valid definition of the purpose of marketing: to create a valuable customer experience. And it is good business: your customers will thank you for it, stay loyal to your business, and pay a premium for it.

In this chapter, I provide a conceptual framework for managing customer experiences. The framework focuses on two key concepts: strategic experiential modules (SEMs) which constitute different types of experiences with their own distinct structure and principles, and experience providers (ExPros) through which the SEMS are created. However, before I discuss the framework, let us first focus on more philosophical and definitional issues.

WHAT EXACTLY IS AN EXPERIENCE?

Experiences are private events that occur in response to some stimulation (for example, as provided by marketing efforts before and after purchase). Experiences involve the entire living being. They often result from direct observation and/or participation in events – whether they are real, dream-like or virtual. As philosopher Merleau-Ponty put it in his well-known book *Phenomenology of Perception*, 'The world is not an object such that I have in my possession the law of its making; it is the natural setting of, and field for, all my thoughts and all my explicit perceptions' (Merleau-Ponty, 2002). In other words, as a marketer you need to provide the right environment and setting for the desired customer experiences to emerge.

Experiences are usually not self-generated but induced. Or, as philosophers and psychologists in the phenomenological tradition have called it, experiences are 'of' or 'about' something; they have reference and intentionality (Husserl, 1931; Brentano, 1973). This basic fact of experiences is clearly reflected in language. As psycholinguists Roger Brown and Deborah Fish have demonstrated, verbs that describe experiences (such as 'like', 'admire', 'hate', 'attract') typically describe the stimulus that produces the experience as opposed to the person who has the experience (Brown and Fish, 1983). To demonstrate this, they showed people simple sentences of the type 'X likes Y' and asked: 'Is this because X is the kind of person who generally likes other people, or is this because Y is the type of person who other people typically like?' Brown and Fish found that people tend to assume the latter, and not only for 'like' but for most other experience verbs (such as admire, hate, attract). Indeed, language reflects this assumption: derivatives of these experience words such as 'likeable', 'admirable', 'hateful', and 'attractive' all refer to the stimulus – not to the person who has the experience. This is true not only for English, but also many other languages psycholinguists have researched.

As a marketer, you provide stimuli that result in customer experiences: you are an experience provider. You are in charge. You provide the experience, and, as a result, your company and brand are seen as more or less likeable, admirable or attractive. This does not mean that the consumer is passive. It means that you have to take the first action. This is how the world works, and it has been incorporated as general action and experience schemata into our languages.

One last point about experiences. Experiences may be viewed as complex, emerging structures (Holland, 1998). Emerging structures in the physical world typically display what is called 'perpetual novelty'. That is, no two experiences are exactly alike. But, as we will see, they may nonetheless be categorized in terms of their generic emerging properties into different types of experiences. Therefore, as a manager, rather than being concerned with any particular individual experience, you need to ask yourself the more important strategic question of what types of experiences you want to provide, and provide them with perpetually fresh appeal.

EXPERIENCES AS TYPOLOGIES OF THE MIND

To use experiences as part of marketing strategy and practice, it is essential to discuss some key neurobiological and psychological facts regarding experiences. The idea that there are distinct functional areas in the brain that correspond with distinct experiences has been called the 'modular view of the mind'.

> The word 'module' brings to mind detachable, snap-in components, and that is misleading. Mental modules are not likely to be visible to the naked eye as circumscribed territories on the surface of the brain, like the flank steak and the rump roast on the supermarket cow display. [. . .] Modules are defined by the special things they do with information available to them, not necessarily by the kinds of information they have available (Pinker, 1997).

In other words, the physical substrate is always identical, no matter what and how you experience it: it is always a matter of nerve cells forming connections among information by relaying chemical and electric impulses. However, in terms of the phenomenology of experience, there are several distinct functional areas.[1]

First, there is a perceptual or sensory system located in the thalamus. This system processes the sensory input in the form of lightwaves, soundwaves, haptic and textile information that reach the retina, the ear, and other sensors. Then there is an affective system, which is housed in two separate locations: first, in the limbic system and a nearby region called the amygdala, as well as in the neocortex. The 'lower systems' of the limbic system and the amygdala produce a fast 'gut' affective response without much thought and analysis, whereas the neocortex can produce more complex emotions. Finally, there are other parts of the neocortex which are the seats of elaborate cognition, thinking and creativity (Goleman, 1995; LeDoux, 1994; Damasio, 1994).

Think of it this way. Pick up a knife, and have a look at it. It is impossible for you to look at the knife and see it suddenly bending or turning blue or red (even if you are color-blind). You can try as hard as you like; it won't work. So your perception is constrained by your perceptual system – it is not really under your voluntary control. Light waves hit your retina and produce a certain impression that you cannot control. But of course you can imagine the knife flying up and out of the window and describe to others how it may land on people who walk by. But that is cognition, that is, a thought process of your creative imagination. It is not sensory perception. And, if a mugger ever broke into your house and tried to stab you with this knife, you may still have a weird response in your stomach each time you see it – you can't help it. That is affect, and you can see that affect, like sensation, is partly independent from cognition. In other words, these three systems – sensation, cognition and affect – have their own structures and principles although they interact to produce one coherent sensory perception, feeling and thought. Consequently, as we will see later, if our goal as marketers is to appeal to the senses, we need to employ different strategies than if we target the senses, feelings or creative thinking.

In addition to these internal processes, social psychologists and sociologists often add two more experiential components: first, the individual's actions extended over time (ranging from physical experiences to broader patterns of behavior and lifestyles), and, second, a relational experience, that is, the individual's experience of belonging to a group, society or culture.

THE EXPERIENTIAL MARKETING FRAMEWORK

These philosophical insights as well as neurobiological, psychological and sociological models provide a solid foundation for developing a conceptual framework for managing customer experiences. Unlike features and benefits marketing, which lacks a fundamental basis and insightful understanding of customers, experiential marketing is grounded on psychological, yet practical, theory of the individual customer and his/her social behavior. The framework has two aspects: strategic experiential models (SEMs), which form the strategic underpinning of experiential marketing, and experience providers (ExPros) which are the tactical tools of experiential marketing.

THE STRATEGIC UNDERPINNINGS OF EXPERIENTIAL MARKETING: SEMS

Modularity of the mind, that is, the view that the mind is composed of specialized functional parts, provides a wonderful metaphor and practical lesson for experiential marketing: experiences may be dissected into different types, each with their own inherent structures and processes. As a manager you may view these different types of experiences as strategic experiential modules (SEMs) that constitute the objectives of your marketing efforts.

Let me provide a brief description of the five types of customer experiences that form the basis of the Experiential Marketing Framework:

SENSE

SENSE marketing appeals to the senses with the objective of creating sensory experiences through sight, sound, touch, taste and smell. SENSE marketing may be used to differentiate companies and products, to motivate customers and to add value to products. As we will see, one of the key principles of SENSE is 'cognitive consistency/sensory variety', that is, the ideal SENSE approach provides an underlying concept that is clearly detectable but appears always fresh and new. Moreover, a successful SENSE campaign requires an understanding of what stimuli are most appropriate for sensory impact.

RICHART, a maker of luxury chocolates, employs an integrated SENSE marketing approach that fully exploits the experiential nature of chocolate purchase and consumption ('Counter culture', 1997; Fabricant, 1997). This approach starts with the name of the company itself: RICHART Design et Chocolat – RICHART bills itself as a design company first, a chocolate company second. Attention to design is carried through all the marketing and packaging materials and into the products themselves. The RICHART logo is done in an art-deco typeface with a distinctive leaning 'A' that graphically demarcates the words 'rich' and 'art'. RICHART chocolates are sold in a showroom that resembles that of a fine jeweler, with items displayed in glass cases on a spacious, brightly lit salesfloor. They are also available through a catalogue reminiscent of an up-market clothing or jewelry designer, labeled 'Collection 97/98'. Products are lit and photographed in the catalogue as if they were fine pieces of art or jewelry. Headlines in the catalogue are in French and English. Promotional materials are printed on smooth, heavy papers.

The packaging is no less elegant. Chocolate boxes are pure glossy white, with gold or silver embossed lettering. Red cloth ribbons seal the packages. Box liners are segmented so that each work of chocolate art is displayed in its own compartment.

The chocolates themselves are a feast for the visual sense. Beautifully shaped and decorated with different patterns and colors of ornamentations (a special line displays a charming set of children's drawings), they look too beautiful to eat. Special chocolate plaques can be made to customers' specifications. So precious are these chocolates that RICHART even sells a burlwood chocolate vault with temperature and humidity gauges, for $650. And British *Vogue* magazine called RICHART Chocolates 'the most beautiful chocolates in the world'.

Many more examples of SENSE marketing can be found, including Gucci, Nokia, Tiffany and British Airways.

FEEL

FEEL marketing appeals to customers' inner feelings and emotions, with the objective of creating affective experiences that range from mildly positive moods linked to a brand (for example, for a non-involving, non-durable grocery brand or service or industrial product) to strong emotions of joy and pride (for example, for a consumer durable, technology, or social marketing campaign). As we will see, most affect occurs during consumption. Therefore standard emotional advertising is often inappropriate because it does not target feelings during consumption. What is needed for FEEL marketing to work is a close understanding of what stimuli can trigger certain emotions as well as the willingness of the consumer to engage in perspective-taking and empathy.

An example of FEEL marketing is Clinique's fragrance 'Happy'. Videos at the point of purchase reinforce the name's message, reflecting the product's sunny orange packaging, showing the jumping, joyfully smiling figure of model Kylie Bax. Television ads incorporate movement and music with lively camera work. In mounting the first 'Happy' campaign, Clinique rode a growing anti-grunge wave that was sparking a trend toward more cheerful fashions. As a tie-in, Clinique produced a limited-edition CD of 'happy' songs, including Judy Garland's 'Get Happy' and the Turtles' 'Happy Together' (Elliott, 1997).

More examples of FEEL marketing include Häagen-Dazs Cafes in Europe and Asia, Campbell's Soup, and the Colvert Group of Mutual Funds.

THINK

THINK marketing appeals to the intellect with the objective of creating cognitive, problem-solving experiences that engage customers creatively. THINK marketing appeals to target customers' convergent and divergent thinking through surprise, intrigue and provocation. THINK campaigns are common for new technology products. But THINK marketing is not restricted only to high-tech products. THINK marketing has also been used in product design, retailing and in communications in many other industries.

A good example is Microsoft's multi-million dollar 1996 campaign, 'Where Do You Want to Go Today?' created by Widen & Kennedy, the ad agency best known for its 'Just Do It' campaign for Nike. As a symbol for the campaign, the slogan did a brilliant job of encompassing all of Microsoft's many ventures and activities. Microsoft is closely associated in consumers' minds with the explosion in computers and the feeling that with technology anything is possible. With this slogan, Microsoft positions itself as the company responsible for these infinite possibilities – it's just a matter of naming your destination, and Microsoft will get you there. Indeed, the objective of the approach was 'to creatively understand what it means for people to use computers . . . in the 90s'. The spatial metaphor linked well with the geographical metaphors of the Internet – web pages are spoken of as 'sites' that can be 'visited' – and Microsoft's products for the net. The question 'where do you want to go today?' could be taken literally for Microsoft's Expedia, the travel services website, or its Sidewalk, the city site guide (Cox, 1998).

THINK marketing examples include Genesis Eldercare, Apple Computers, Siemens, RCN and Finlandia Vodka.

ACT

ACT marketing aims to affect behavior, lifestyles and interactions. ACT marketing enriches customers' lives by targeting their physical experiences, showing them alternative ways of doing things (for example, in business-to-business and industrial markets), alternative lifestyles, and interactions. As I will show, analytical, rational approaches to behavior change (that is, theories of reasoned actions) are only one of many behavioral change options. Changes in lifestyles and behaviors are often more motivational, inspirational and emotional in nature and brought about by role models (for example, movie stars or famous athletes).

Nike sells more than 160 million pairs of shoes a year – almost one of every two pairs sold in the US. One major part of the success of the company has been the brilliant 'Just do it' campaign. Frequently depicting famous athletes in action, it is a classic of ACT marketing. The ads transform the experience by appealing to the need to identify with celebrity role models, thus enticing the customer to action (Egan, 1998).

More ACT marketing examples include the Gillette Mach3, the Milk Moustache campaign, and Martha Stewart Living.

RELATE

RELATE marketing contains aspects of SENSE, FEEL and THINK marketing. However, RELATE marketing expands beyond the individual's personal, private feelings, thus relating the individual to something outside his/her present state.

RELATE campaigns appeal to the individual's desire for self-improvement (for example, a future 'ideal self' that he or she wants to relate to). They appeal to the need to be perceived positively by individual others (for example, one's peers, girlfriend, boyfriend, or spouse; family and colleagues). They relate the person to a broader social system (a subculture, a country, and so on), thus establishing strong brand relations and brand communities.

RELATE campaigns have been used in a variety of industries, ranging from cosmetics, personal care and lingerie (to create fantasies about the other sex), to national image improvement programs. The American motorcycle Harley-Davidson is a RELATE brand par excellence. From the physical experience of riding a Harley to the psychological devotion that the product commands, Harley transcends the consumption experience. Harley is a way of life. From the bikes themselves to Harley-related merchandise to Harley-Davidson tattoos on the bodies of enthusiasts (who cut across all social groups), consumers see Harley as a part of their identity. The Harley webpage gets to the heart of the matter:

> Suppose time takes a picture – one picture that represents your entire life here on Earth. You have to ask yourself how you'd rather be remembered. As a pasty, web-wired computer wiz, strapped to an office chair? Or as a leather-clad adventurer who lived life to the fullest astride a Harley-Davidson? You can decide which it is, but think quickly. Time is framing up that picture, and it's got a pretty itchy shutter finger.

More examples of RELATE marketing campaigns include Tommy Hilfiger, the Wonderbra, and Michael Jordan fragrance.

EXPERIENTIAL HYBRIDS AND HOLISTICALLY INTEGRATED EXPERIENCES

Experiential appeals rarely result in only one type of experience. Many successful corporations employ experiential hybrids that combine two or more SEMS in order to broaden the experiential appeal.

An automotive hybrid was the Volvo C70 coupé. Traditionally, Volvo cars have been built – and marketed – based on their solid reputation for safety. In 1997, when I spoke to a group of Volvo executives on their branding approach, they told me that safety alone was no longer enough: consumers rated key competitors' cars (Mercedes, BMW, Lexus) as just as safe. As a result, Volvo re-styled itself to incorporate a sexier, more sensual image, while not giving up its claim to be one of the safest cars on the planet. The C70 coupé showed off its sleek and beautiful lines on a series of outdoor installations, with the advertising neatly and wittily encompassing both THINK and SENSE appeals: 'For those who combine a passion for living, with a passion for living'; 'A surge of adrenaline, then a surge of peace-of-mind'; 'Ah, the sun, the moon, the side impact protection system . . . '; 'The new Volvo C70 convertible: Ingenious new hair dryer from Sweden'; 'Protect the body, ignite the soul'. The hybrid appeal was explicitly spelled out in corporate promotions: 'Call it a racecar for the rational. Or the blissful marriage of safety and sensually-sculpted beauty. Either way, the new Volvo C70 will move you in ways Volvo never has.'

Ideally, marketers should strive strategically for creating holistically integrated experiences that possess, at the same time, SENSE, FEEL, THINK, ACT and RELATE qualities. Think of Singapore Airlines. The goals of the company are entirely holistic: to be a fresh, new and elegant airline (SENSE), a kind and hospitable airline (FEEL), innovative and creative (THINK), service and action oriented (ACT), and international and Singaporean at the same time (RELATE).

Strategically, there are several questions regarding the creation of holistically integrated experiences. First, how can we enrich an existing type of experience? Second, how should we manage the transition from one type of experience to another? Third, how can we add new types of experiences to an existing experiential brand?

THE INTERNAL STRUCTURE OF SEMS

The five types of SEMs all have their own inherent structure and principles.

For example, a SENSE TV ad campaign typically dazzles viewers' senses with fast-paced, fast-cut images and music. It is dynamic and attention-getting and may leave a strong impression after just 15 seconds.

FEEL TV ads, in contrast, are often slice-of-life ads that take time to draw the viewer in, building emotion gradually. Successful Hallmark ads, the quintessential FEEL spots, all last for more than a minute.

THINK campaigns are often sedate. They begin with a voiceover, then move to text on the screen.

ACT campaigns show behavioral outcomes or lifestyles.

RELATE campaigns typically show the referent person or group that the customer is supposed to relate to.

In sum, like mental modules, each strategic marketing module has its own structure.

But how are the SEMs instantiated? Or conversely, what is the 'physical substrate' from which they arise? What's the equivalent in strategic marketing terms for the brain tissue or neurons that produce what we call 'the mind'?

THE INSTANTIATION TOOLS OF EXPERIENTIAL MARKETING: EXPROS

The instantiation of the strategic SENSE, FEEL, THINK, ACT and RELATE modules occurs by means of what I call 'experience providers' (or ExPros). ExPros are components that are at the disposal of the marketer for creating a SENSE, FEEL, THINK, ACT or RELATE campaign. They include communications, visual and verbal identity and signage, product presence, co-branding, spatial environments, electronic media, and people.

Communications

Communications ExPros include advertising, external and internal company communications (such as magalogs, internal and external brochures and newsletters, annual reports, and so on), as well as public relations and event planning. I will first discuss advertising – one of the most important communications ExPros for many companies – and then turn to two more unusual communication ExPros: magalogs and annual reports.

Advertising

Like other ExPros, advertising can create any of the five different strategic modules of SENSE, FEEL, THINK, ACT and RELATE. Communications can be used effectively to create all different types of experiential connections. Let us look at an example of an advertising campaign for each one of the SEMs.

SENSE   A powerful SENSE advertising campaign paved the way for the renaissance of a classic brand: Clairol Herbal Essences Shampoo (Brand Strategy, 1997). Clairol Herbal

Essences was the first natural botanical shampoo in the US market. After a strong showing in the 1970s, when it attained an 8 per cent market share, by 1994 it had slipped to about 2 per cent of the market. Surveys found, though, that 80 per cent of American women retained fond memories of the product, and Clairol decided to re-launch the line of naturally-based shampoos.

Wells Rich Greene BDDP launched a tremendously successful SENSE campaign for Herbal Essences. Rather than making the conventional claim that the product would promote beautiful shiny hair, they marketed the experience of using the product, with the tag line, 'A Totally Organic Experience'. The campaign featured a TV spot that imitated a scene from the film 'When Harry Met Sally' in which Meg Ryan dramatizes an orgasm. In the commercial, a woman steps into the shower and begins to shampoo her hair. The shampoo smells great, and she responds with gasps of enthusiastic pleasure. The ad then cuts to a bored couple watching this scene on television, and the wife comments, 'I wanna get the shampoo *she's* using.'

Print ads echoed the experiential message. Colorful layouts showed a bottle of Herbal Essences, with wildflowers and herbs bursting out of them, with the headline, 'When was the last time you had a totally organic experience?'

FEEL   A compelling print advertising example for a FEEL brand is the advertising for the luxury watchmaker Patek Philippe. Patek Philippe is one of the world's oldest and most expensive watches – a luxury and status brand known the world over, and a significant investment. In ads created by London ad agency Leagas Delaney, an attractive and well-groomed young woman, dressed in a casual leather jacket, is sitting on a bench. Climbing up behind her is a little girl, perhaps five years old, dressed in a plaid jumper, covering the woman's eyes in a happy game of 'guess who?' Mother and daughter are both smiling and laughing. The picture is one of relaxed affluence. The young mother is wearing a simple gold wedding band – and no visible watch. The ad headline reads, 'You never actually own a Patek Philippe. You merely look after it for the next generation. Begin your own tradition.' The message is two-fold: a sense of present happiness combined with the notion that a Patek Philippe is an heirloom to be passed from mother to daughter, an enduring emblem of family happiness and security. The ad combines a strong traditional feeling with a contemporary one, ringing changes on the notion that fine watches are passed down from father to son (Canedy, 1998).

THINK   A three-year THINK advertising campaign was launched by the Newspaper Association of America, with the help of Jerry Della Femina and his team at Jerry & Ketchum (NAA.org, 2007).

The purpose of the campaign was to promote literacy and encourage readership by showcasing newspapers as a vibrant and relevant medium. The campaign's main theme was the important role that newspapers can play in learning by young people. The ads showed celebrities reading a newspaper with the lines 'Encourage your children to read every day', and 'It all starts with newspapers'.

The campaign had broad appeal through its use of a wide variety of spokespersons, who encouraged us to think of newspapers and daily reading as an integral part of life. These included former presidents George H.W. Bush and Jimmy Carter, retired general Norman Schwarzkopf, MTV journalist Tabitha Soren, Super Bowl quarterback John

Elway, and rapper LL Cool J. Newspapers were also encouraged to give the campaign local flavor through use of local celebrities.

RELATE   Rather than arguing for the health benefits of orange juice, Tropicana Pure Premium Orange Juice ran a series of RELATE print ads customized for various magazine audiences. One ad that appeared in *Golf Digest* magazine shows an athletic-looking man in workout clothes, sitting on an apartment terrace with a city skyline in the background. He is surrounded by exercise equipment, taking a break from his morning workout to have some OJ. The photo is in black and white, except for the bright orange juice. Superimposed over this shot are floating slices of juicy orange, and across the bottom of the spread a rich ocean of orange juice. The tagline reads, 'Morning without Tropicana Pure Premium? Not an option.'

ACT   'Gentlemen, Start Your Follicles'. This one-line tag appeared in a print advertisement for Rogaine, the medication designed to stimulate the growth of thinning hair. The key word in this ACT marketing campaign is 'Start'. Consumers get a 'starter kit', which includes a video called 'Getting Started'. The slogan is a powerful allusion to the masculine world of auto racing, and the thrilling words that traditionally begin the Indianapolis 500: 'Gentlemen, start your engines'. The campaign appeals to male consumers who may be feeling inadequate due to hair loss, and empowers them to ACT by evoking the manly sport of auto racing.

Magalogs
Another form of communications ExPro is the magalog. As its name suggests, the magalog is a cross between a magazine and a catalog. Magalogs typically offer a mix of features ranging from catalogue-like spreads of products and prices to evocative art photography to articles about lifestyle and image issues. The premier issue of Abercrombie & Fitch's magalog, *A&F Quarterly*, included features on choosing the right dog ('Must-Have Mongrels', which offered the advice 'Similar to the golden rules of human courtship, never pick a dog that's too desperate or too eager'), cool cars and trucks (including the new Beetle and Mercedes' new SUV), the coolest beers and wines, and a travel note called 'Sun, Surf, Sex, and Sydney'. In sum, the magalog was part of the company's lifestyle branding.

A distinctly different lifestyle is targeted by the Hermès magalog, *Le Monde D'Hermès*. The Spring-Summer 1998 issue honored trees, and the magalog is prefaced by an experiential message from Hermès president Jean Louis Dumas-Hermès:

> Where would we be without trees? Hermès is celebrating the tree all through 1998. This issue of *Le Monde D'Hermès* is dedicated to it. A haiku tells us to 'look at a tree and become that tree', so let us encourage our young shoots, draw up the sap from our living roots, raise our eyes toward the distant horizons that beckon from the high boughs. And may our actions bear rich fruit! Hermès: fine tree of rare yet simple descent seeks connoisseurs for fruitful and pleasant relationship.

The rest of the magalog does indeed resemble a magazine for the connoisseur, sort of an upscale *Smithsonian*. Printed on glossy stock with copious color photography, it includes features on bronze and pottery horses from the Han and Tang dynasties, mythologies of the tree, and the Gregoire Technical Training Center, where young people learn the art of saddlery and leatherworking. Hermès products are featured in lavish and beautiful fashion-photography spreads that carry through the 'tree' theme, and beautiful photos of ancient trees appear throughout the publication. Even the advertising from other retailers included in the magalog echoes the theme: an ad from the Discount Bank and Trust Company shows two little boys walking along a forest path; another, from Louis Roederer champagne, features decorative trees around a piazza at the Villa Medici in Rome.

Magalogs are an increasingly popular way for retailers to establish experiential connections between themselves and targeted consumers, and even traditional mail-order marketers like Williams Sonoma and Land's End incorporate more editorial materials – such as recipes and fiction – into their catalogs.

Annual reports

Even the stodgiest of corporate communications, the annual report, is becoming an experiential tool. Victor Rivera, creative director of Addison, highlighted a few of his favorites in the 1997 issue of *Addison Magazine*. In an early example, in 1984 H.J. Heinz Company marked 20 consecutive years of financial growth by issuing an annual report celebrating the tomato. The firm commissioned 11 famous artists, including Red Grooms, to contribute their own visions of the tomato. According to Rivera, the result is an annual report that is a work of art and a tribute to the mainstay of over 500 Heinz products. Another is Duracell's 1994 report that positions the firm as a true global player by styling the entire report as a passport, complete with stamps, pictures from different countries, and employee photos taken at picture booths around the world.

Identity and Signage

Like communications and other ExPros, verbal and visual identity and signage can be used to create SENSE, FEEL, THINK, ACT and RELATE brands. The set of visual-identity ExPros consists of names, logos and signage. Visual identity is the prime domain of so-called corporate identity consultants.

Brand names

Of course, there are numerous experiential brand names for products, such as Sunkist (citrus fruits), Skin-So-Soft (an Avon product), Silverstone (a Dupont non-stick cooking surface), Tide and Cheer (detergents), and Jolt (a high-caffeine cola). Experiential names are less common for companies, which often prefer the name of initial owners, acronyms or descriptive, functional names. However, there are some, especially in the high-tech industry: Amazon.com, Zipcar and YouTube, to name a few.

Logos

When it comes to logos, Ciba, a spinoff from the giant Ciba Geigy, took an experiential approach to its logo and visual identities from its inception. The logo was shaped like a butterfly, used as a symbol for Ciba's transformation and appropriate to represent the company's continued development into the future. The butterfly itself was made up of a collection of colored pixels of various sizes, each color representing a different division of Ciba's business: blue representing Additives, aqua representing Consumer Care

Chemicals, green representing Textile Dyes, and so on. The overall corporate color, violet, was chose to represent nobility and strength.

Another unusual and creative use of experiential logos and signage comes from Nickelodeon, the children's cable network. 'Nick' set a few guidelines for logo design: all logos are to be in Pantone 021 orange with white lettering, the font is always Balloon Bold in all caps, and the lettering of the word 'Nickelodeon' is always the same. Beyond that, designers have free rein to create different shapes and designs for the Nick logo, ranging from animal shapes to footprints to spaceships to exploding firecrackers and on and on. The creativity in the logo design policy mirrors the company's connection with kids and their imaginative energy – kids can even design their own Nick logos!

Product Presence

Like communications, logos, and other ExPros, product presence can also be used to instantiate an experience. Product presence ExPros include product design, packaging and product display, brand characters that are used as part of packaging, and point-of-sales materials.

Product design

An excellent example of experiential product design comes from a Philips product, the Satinelle epilator. Created for women, the product design conveys femininity on a number of levels: the overall shape is suggestive of female anatomy and the subtle shading of colors suggests the petals of a tulip. The feminine RELATE appeal is carried through in the product name, Satinelle, and the descriptor, 'sensitive', printed beneath the name.

Packaging

An obvious place to look for sensory messages is in packaging. Indeed, consumers have become increasingly attentive to packaging and have higher and higher expectations of it. According to Paul Lukas writing in *Fortune* magazine, 'On merchandise ranging from chocolate-covered raisins to toilet paper, more and more packages are now explicitly calling attention to themselves, as if to suggest that consumers are more interested in the packaging than in the product itself' (Lukas, 1998).

Consider packaging for beverages. The beverage formulation certainly matters, and beverage manufacturers are constantly inventing new formulas and trends (the 'fruit smoothie' rage being one of the latest). But, asks Ken Miller, Vice President of IDI, a packaging innovation consultancy which designed the Whipper Snapple bottle, Snapple's entry into the smoothie category, 'What is it that makes these and the tried-and-true beverages really sing? Packaging . . . It [the packaging] has become worthy of serious investment because major players have found it pays off big' (Miller, 1988).

Wallace Church, a New York City based design consultancy and leader in experiential packaging, claims that 70 per cent of all grocery purchase decisions are made at the shelf. The company redesigned the product identity of Jack & Jill ice cream to evoke the 'ice cream man' that many of us remember from childhood. The new brand logo resembles an embroidered emblem that might have been on the ice cream man's uniform. The background illustration on the packaging depicts a nostalgic neighborhood scene of children eagerly waiting for a treat next to an old-fashioned ice cream truck. The shape of the packaging was also redesigned, creating a distinctive oval half-gallon that suggests a traditional hand-packed tub. In this integrated revamping of the brand, Wallace Church recaptured the emotion rooted in the brand's history, from an era when the product was originally sold by the ice cream man.

Brand characters

Wallace Church was also quick to see the FEEL value in the Pillsbury doughboy when they inherited this venerable spokescharacter. The doughboy was slimmed down and given a more dynamic expression; his engaging persona 'celebrates anew the essence of family fun that is central to the brand's congenial personality'.

Wallace Church has revamped several other old-fashioned brand characters with a new experiential feel. To celebrate Cracker Jack's 100th anniversary, for example, Sailor Jack was transformed from a sailor to a *little league* baseball player wearing a sailor hat – the redesign echoes the product's baseball connections and has a strong RELATE appeal for kids of all ages. Even the Kool-Aid pitcher-man has been streamlined and turned into an ACT marketing tool – he can now be seen playing tennis, spilling a bit of Kool-Aid as he returns a serve.

Point-of-sale product displays often tie into popular characters. For example, videos of the re-released Star Wars trilogy were displayed in a life-sized cardboard Darth Vader display. (So realistic was the display that the thrill of experiencing the Dark Lord up close was a bit too much for one small child, who was seen crying and hiding behind his mother in a video store!)

Co-Branding

Like other ExPros, co-branding can be used to develop any of the five strategic experiential modules. Co-branding ExPros include event marketing and sponsorship, alliances and partnerships, licensing, product placements in movies, co-op campaigns and other types of cooperative arrangements. Let me discuss two of the co-branding techniques in more detail: event marketing/sponsorship and product placements.

Event marketing/sponsorships

As Mava Heffler, Mastercard's senior vice president of global promotions and sponsorships put it, 'It is not enough for a brand to be seen or heard, it has to be experienced. Sponsorships are an important catalyst and component of that experiential marketing' (Coulton, 1997).

To celebrate its 125th anniversary in 1998, Zurich Insurance Company sponsored a series of events, including a fireworks display over Zurich's famous lake, a series of cultural workshops in conjunction with UNICEF, a series of internal events for employees and management, and the opening of new outdoor fitness trails sponsored by the company itself.

The purpose of event marketing, according to Mark Dowley, CEO of Momentum Experiential Marketing Group, is 'forging an emotional and memorable connection with consumers where they live, work, and play'.[2]

Event marketing requires a qualitative understanding of the appropriateness of a particular event as well as quantitative research to demonstrate its effectiveness in reach (for example, in terms of cost-per-thousand) and frequency. In general, special events tend to be more effective and less costly than media advertising. Media advertising is often characterized by huge clutter. Also, it may get awareness up – but rarely purchase intention or purchase. Therefore, to supplement media advertising, more and more marketers are turning to event marketing to create ACT. Guinness used the Guinness Fleadh (pronounced 'flah') events in New York, San Francisco and Chicago to create an 'Irish Village' theme with pre-event point-of-purchase efforts to retailers and promotions and lots of beer sampling during the events (Fitzgerald, 1998). BMW uses event marketing to get customers to buy their cars by traveling to cities with its Ultimate Driving Experience.

Or consider the Olympic Games, according to Mark Dowley 'the greatest marketing orgy of all times'. During the Atlanta Olympics about 3800 spots were shown by some of the best marketers in the world. Out of these 3800 spots, a major sponsor like GE may get 100–125 only for a hefty price tag of $20 million. Instead of media advertising, sponsoring the torch run may be more effective. During the Atlanta Olympics, Coca-Cola provided a strong FEEL appeal by sponsoring the Coca-Cola 1996 Olympic Torch Relay. The objective here was to 'share the Olympic Games with America', and the sponsorship included a 15 000-mile rolling street party along the path of the Olympic Torch runners. As a result, Coca-Cola experienced a 10 per cent sales gain; over 3 000 000 Cokes were sold along the Torch Relay, and an estimated 500 000 000 media impressions were made. It was the largest public relations event ever sponsored by Coca-Cola.

Product placement
Product placement in movies is becoming an increasingly rich source of co-branding. According to *The Hollywood Reporter*

> Even before paid advertising began appearing for the holiday release of 'Tomorrow Never Dies', the image of actor Pierce Brosnan as James Bond was being seen in commercials. There was 007 dashing around in his BMW, wearing his Omega watch, and using his Ericsson cell phone. The Bond movie was also featured in ads for Visa International, Smirnoff Vodka, and many others. Those commercials signaled a breakthrough – never before had a studio been so accommodating in sharing movie images and properties (Friedman, 1998).

Tie-ins have been a staple of studios like Disney and partners like McDonald's for many years. But the growth of 'event' movies has lured more and more new promotional partners to Hollywood, including Reebok, Sony, Casio and Shell. And promotional tie-ins are no longer limited to children's movies – new partnerships have included Tanqueray gin and 'Volcano', Holland America and 'Out to Sea', Gulden's mustard and 'Picture Perfect', and Apple and 'Mission Impossible'. Ray-Ban tripled sales of its Predator 2 line of dark glasses through its tie-in with 'Men in Black'. Even restricted viewing R-rated movies, traditionally harder to sell, are getting in on the act, although six airlines and Bekins Moving passed on the noir hit 'L.A. Confidential'. Microsoft, Packard-Bell and the Sci-Fi Network were apparently made of stronger stuff and forged partnerships with the dark and gory 'Starship Troopers'.

Spatial Environments

Spatial environments include buildings, offices and factory spaces; retail and public spaces; trade booths and corporate events.

Experiential environments are often the most comprehensive expression of what John Bowen, the chairman of Bowen Consulting, calls 'brand culture', the values and behaviors of the managers behind a brand (Bowen, 1998). IBM's corporate headquarters in Armonk, New York, expresses through architecture and landscaping the way the company perceives itself and the experience it wants to create for its customers and employees (*The Economist*, 1998). Situated on the site of its old, shoebox-like headquarters, the new building lies close to the ground, following the configurations of the landscape. An example of corporate downsizing, the building is 120 000 square feet smaller than the old headquarters, housing a third fewer employees. The new site represents spatially 1990s ideas about corporate hierarchy, with fewer office doors that close, and more cubicles with windows that overlook the surrounding woodlands. Among the cubicles are loose arrangements of chairs used for brainstorming. Car parks are hidden from view, and a jogging trail rings the grounds. Both exterior and interior convey IBM's vision of itself. The design, by the Manhattan firm of Kohn Pedersen Fox Associates PC, is close to the ground, close to nature, compatible with its natural surroundings; the interiors, by Swanke Hayden Connell Architects, are simple, adaptable, and unstructured.

Experiential marketing is also becoming common in retail spaces. Just think about Pottery Barn, Starbucks, Niketown, and theme stores and restaurants (such as Disney, Warner Brothers, Planet Hollywood, Harley Davidson Cafe), as well as numerous designer boutiques and department stores. The challenge for experiential marketers using retail branding is to make sure that each store follows the experiential marketing approach. This task can easily be overwhelming when you are dealing with several thousand store owners as part of a franchise system.

'Traditionally, retail management has said "Quality, Service, Style, Selection" – if we do those things right and get the pricing right, we will be fine', states Gerald Lewis, chairman of New York-based CDI Group Inc. 'But the customer says, "I want an experience"' (PR Newswire, 1997).

'In a store or restaurant, the customer's experience is vital: one bad encounter, and you've lost a customer for life', writes Howard Schultz, CEO of Starbucks Coffee (Schultz and Jones, 1997).

As retail spaces become more experiential, product displays become more important ExPros. Home furnishings stores like Pottery Barn have created comfortable, home-like atmospheres where products are displayed as they might appear in your home. More relaxed than traditional furniture showrooms, these sales spaces allow customers to plop down on sofas and take their time making decisions. Smaller products, such as clocks and glassware, are integrated into these environments, making the whole retail space a kind of mega-product display. And Pottery Barn's experiential space doubles as a Design Studio, where the look and products you like can be immediately tailored to your own home environment.

Trade booths at conventions and trade shows are also becoming increasingly experiential. Examples include trade designs that appeal to our senses and feelings, those that bombard us with 'Think' messages and slogans, and trade booths that invite us to experience the products in virtual reality settings.

Mass transportation vehicles from subway cars to airplanes are becoming vehicles for total immersion and experience creation. For example, in the mid-1990s, the advertising space in New York subway cars was allocated in a new way and priced higher. For most subway cars, advertisers were required to buy ad space for the entire car. This change in policy attracted national advertisers who were now able to install experiential spaces for their brands in a setting where it is easy to catch consumers' attention. The new policy increased revenues tremendously because these national advertisers are able to pay higher rates than the old subway advertisers – mainly small businesses advertising their mouse-trap and tattoo-removal services.

In the spring of 1998, on a flight from New York to Rome, I saw the same approach being used in a co-op promotion by Al'Italia and Baci Chocolates. The 'Baci dall'Italia' (With Baci to Italy) plane had been painted in the blue-and-white color scheme of Perugina's famous Baci chocolate wrappers. Baci chocolates were handed out to passengers on board. And romantic, touchy-feely Baci slogans were posted in English and Italian all over the interior of the plane.

Websites and Electronic Media

The world wide web's interactive capabilities provide an ideal forum for many companies to create experiences for consumers. Unfortunately, many companies still use their website mainly as an information-posting device rather than an opportunity to entertain or otherwise relate to customers through experiential marketing.

In some industries, electronic media are in the process of replacing live experiences and creating new ones. The web has been used to engage in transactions without ever seeing or talking to real salespeople; the web has also been used for chat rooms instead of face-to-face or spoken phone conversations (Kaplan, 1998).

Club Med's early website, whose slogan was 'Do it your way', focused on providing a customized holistic experience for each person. Visitors to the website were asked to select the location they were interested in, and to click on jaunty cartoon figures indicating whether they planned to travel as a family, a single person, or a couple. The site took it from there. The page 'Village Vibes' linked to virtual villages that browsers could experience before they actually booked their vacations. 'Visions of a Club Med Vacation' led you on a guided fantasy about your ideal vacation:

> Close your eyes and picture your dream vacation! Where do you see yourself? On a sunny island in a clear blue tropical sea? Exploring pristine countryside, mountains, and valleys? Let's take a short trip together to some of our interactive villages. We've grouped them according to setting and climate. You'll have fun and you can get an idea of what a vacation at a real Club Med village is like!

Clicking on the Mediterranean Village led you to a screen where you could choose from tennis, snorkeling, boating, dancing, children's activities, fitness, horseback riding or waterskiing. Links took you to a map of the site or showed you schedules for daytime and night-time activities. Each page was lavishly illustrated by color photos and bright cartoons. The site offered a huge amount of information, easily accessible by village or by activity, including special packages and weather information, and visitors could make reservations and book flights online. Visiting the Club Med website was like a little vacation all its own, the essence of experiential marketing (Clubmed.com, 2007).

People

The final ExPro, people, can be a powerful provider of experience in all five experiential modules. People include salespeople, company representatives, service providers, customer service providers, and anybody else who can be associated with a company or a brand.

High-end designer boutiques understand the power of salespeople in creating consumer experiences. Not long ago, I had a first-hand taste of how a salesperson can turn a simple transaction into a holistically satisfying experience. During a recent trip to Los Angeles, I wandered into a chic Rodeo Drive boutique called Sulka. I was approached by a very friendly, well-dressed and attentive sales associate, Sheila. After greeting me, Sheila brought me a cup of delicious coffee, just the pick-up I needed after window shopping for a few hours. While enjoying the coffee, I mentioned I might be interested in a tie and a couple of shirts. Sheila lavished me with attention and took great care in helping me find the just the right things. She even got me to think a bit beyond my usual sense of style, showing me how a striped tie could be made to work with a striped shirt – a combination I had previously thought forbidden. Even this relatively modest contact with the world of designer boutiques made me feel like I was part of a different world. Suddenly I could relate to the crowd who haunts Rodeo Drive, Madison Avenue, Via Napoleona, Faubourg Saint-Honoré, Bond Street, Saville Row, Ometesando (Direction Ginza, NOT Meiji Shrine)!

Shortly after I returned to New York, this handwritten note, on Sulka letterhead, arrived in the mail:

Dear Mr Schmitt:

I hope this note finds you in the best of health and spirits. I would like to take this opportunity to thank you for your patronage at SULKA and also for giving me the privilege of being of service to you. I hope you are enjoying your new shirts and tie. It was a real pleasure to meet you, and please feel free to call if I can be of any assistance in the future.

I hope the star of happiness always shines upon your days.

Most sincerely,
Sheila

P.S. I found the tie that you saw in our catalogue; if you are interested, please call me and I will send it to you!

SUMMARY

In this chapter, I have presented a framework for managing experiences and for planning experiential campaigns. The framework centers around five types of strategic experiential modules (SEMs) of SENSE, FEEL, THINK, ACT and RELATE, and seven types of experience providers (ExPros). Each SEM has its own structures and principles that managers need to be familiar with to target these experiences and to create experiential hybrids and holistic experiences.

NOTES

1. One of the clearest expositions has been presented by Steve Pinker, a professor of psychology and director of the Center for Cognitive Neuroscience at MIT. In his book *How the Mind Works* (1997), Pinker dedicates one chapter each to the faculties of the mind: sensory perception ('The Mind's Eye'), feelings and emotions ('Hotheads'), creativity and reasoning ('Good Ideas'). Moreover, he adds social relations ('Family Values'). (Unlike other psychologists, Pinker leaves out a motivational or action component because he is interested primarily in mental computation rather than behavioral action.) Describing the specific structures of each module, Pinker subscribes to a computational theory of the mind, which is controversial. In contrast to Pinker's view, the alternative 'embodied cognition' view claims that the mind is a *perceptual* symbol system rather than a *computational* one (see Barsalou, 1999). However, this view does not necessarily call into question the notion that the mind is organized in a modular fashion. That is, the debate regarding computation vs. perceptual symbols is a psychology debate that is largely irrelevant to the objectives of this book.
2. I thank Mr Dowley who spoke in my Corporate Identity class at Columbia Business School in the spring of 1998 and provided useful materials on event marketing.

REFERENCES

Barsalou, L. (1999), 'Perceptual symbol systems', *The Behavioral and Brain Sciences*, **22**, 577–609.

Bowen, John (1998), 'Brand culture: going beyond brand positioning to enhance consumer loyalty and trust', speech at 'Branded Environments' Conference, The Strategic Research Institute, Orlando, Florida, 3–4 December.

Brand Strategy (1997), 'New brands/brand extensions', 23 May, 18–27.

Brentano, Franz (1973), *Psychology from an Empirical Standpoint*, London: Routledge and Kegan Paul.

Brown, Roger and Deborah Fish (1983), 'The psychological causality implicit in language', *Cognition*, **4**(3), 237–73.

Canedy, Dana (1998), 'The media business: Advertising', *New York Times*, 2 July, D6.

ClubMed.com (2007), Club Méditerranée Group, www.clubmed.com.

Coulton, Antionette (1997), 'With sports alliances, cards make big play for fans', *American Banker*, 2 October, p. 1.

Cox, Ana Marie (1998), 'Microsoft is trying to make you forget about its nerdy CEO through a multimillion-dollar sleight of hand', *Mother Jones*, **23**(1), p. 42.

Csikszentmihalyi, Mihaly (1991), *Flow*, New York: Harper Collins.

Damasio, Antonio (1994), *Descartes' Error: Emotion, Reason and the Human Brain*, New York: Grosset/Putnam.

Drucker, Peter (1954), *The Practice of Management*, New York: Harper and Row, Publishers Inc.

Economist, The (1998), 'Blue is the color', 6 June, p. 65.

Egan, Timothy (1998), 'The swoon of the swoosh', *The New York Times*, 13 September, p. 66.

Elliott, Stuart (1997), 'Clinique is introducing scent in bid for share of premium market', *The New York Times*, 30 September, D. 6.

Fabricant, Florence (1997), 'Food stuff', *The New York Times*, 15 October, F. 2.

Fitzgerald, Kate (1998), 'Sampling & singing', *Advertising Age*, 8 June, **69**, p. 32.

Friedman, Wayne (1998), 'Promo power fueling H'wood', *The Hollywood Reporter*, 19 January.

Gell-Mann, Murray (1994), *The Quark and the Jaguar: Adventures in the Simple and the Complex*, New York: Freeman.

Goleman, Daniel (1995), *Emotional Intelligence*, New York: Bantam.

Holland, John (1998), *Emergence: From Chaos to Order*, Reading, MA: Addison-Wesley.

Husserl, Edmund (1931), *Ideas: General Introduction to a Pure Phenomenology*, London: Allen and Unwin.

Kaplan, James (1998), 'Designer by design', *New York Magazine*, 20 July, pp. 34–40.

LeDoux, Joseph (1994), 'Emotional memory systems in the brain', *Behavioral Brain Research*, **58**, 20 December, 69–79.

Lukas, Paul (1998), 'New headline, same great column', *Fortune Magazine*, 16 February, 42.

Merleau-Ponty, Maurice (2002), *Phenomenology of Perception*, London: Routledge and Kegan Paul.

Miller, Ken (1988), 'What's next in beverage packaging?', *Brand Packaging*, October/November, 12–14.

NAA.org. (2007), Newspaper Association of America, www.naa.org.

Pinker, Steven (1997), *How the Mind Works*, New York: Norton.

PR Newswire (1997), 'Oil companies must look beyond own industry to stand in increasingly crowded C-Store field', 14 July, www.prnewswire.com/.

Schultz, Howard and Dori Jones Yang (1997), 'Reinventing the coffee experience', in H. Schultz and D. Jones Yang, *Pour Your Heart Into It: How Starbucks Built a Company One Cup at a Time*, New York: Hyperion.

South China Morning Post (1997), 'Counter culture', 16 November, p. 18.

10. Some issues concerning the concept of experiential marketing

Rajagopal Raghunathan

INTRODUCTION

The concept of experiential marketing, first introduced in the work of Pine and Gilmore on experience economy (1997)[1] and Schmitt on experiential marketing (1999), has gained significant traction, both among marketing academics and among practitioners (for example, Pine and Gilmore, 1999; Schmitt, 2003). Experiential marketing is said to occur 'when a company intentionally uses services as the stage and goods as props to engage individual customers in a way that creates a memorable event' (Pine and Gilmore, 1997, p. 98). One of the major benefits said to accrue from a well executed experiential marketing strategy is an increase in profit margins: companies that offer experiences – as opposed to mere products or services – the argument goes, are able to charge a higher premium for their offerings because customers are willing to pay the higher prices. The case of Starbucks (for example, Pine and Gilmore, 1999, p. 2; see Figure 10.1) and Volkswagen Beetle (for example, Schmitt, 1999, p. 214) are often touted as exemplifying how a well executed experiential marketing strategy can bear significant rewards.

Without questioning the potential usefulness of pursuing an experiential marketing strategy for improving firm profits (there is emerging empirical evidence for that; see Brakus et al., 2004), this chapter seeks to address three other, hitherto unanswered, conceptual issues concerning experiential marketing. The first issue concerns the reasons underlying the evolution of the economies: proponents of experiential marketing provide little rationale for *why* the economies have evolved over time – from commodities, to goods, to services, to experiences (cf. Pine and Gilmore, 1997). That is, while there is a general acceptance that businesses now operate in an experience economy, it is unclear what the underlying drivers are (or were) in the evolution of the economies. As we will see, addressing this issue enables us to derive intelligent predictions about where a particular economic system (for example, a third world country) stands on the continuum from the commodity to the experience economy.

Second, it is unclear whether there has been a truly *qualitative* change in the nature of offerings in this so-called 'experience economy'. A skeptic might argue, for instance, that the products or services that are thought of as experiential offerings (for example, Starbucks' coffee) are no more than 'very good' or even 'exceptional' products/services. That is, a case may be made that the present-day 'experiential' offerings are not that different from those that came before. As such, one may question the need for an elaborate framework of experiential marketing. As will become evident shortly,

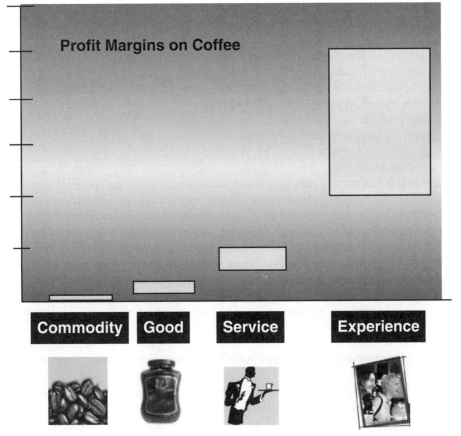

Profit Margins on Coffee

Commodity   Good   Service   Experience

Source: Adapted from Pine and Gilmore (1997).

Figure 10.1 Profit margins on coffee as a function of the nature of offering: the case of coffee

addressing this issue reveals a potentially novel and important rationale for why the concept of experiential marketing may yet prove useful to practitioners – even if there is no hard evidence that an experiential offering is significantly different from a service offering.

The third and final issue – one that is perhaps most important from a substantive viewpoint – concerns the future of experience economy: is it here to stay? Or is it just a passing fad? Understanding what lies ahead is important since the success of businesses depends critically on being able to accurately predict trends of the future.

The rest of this chapter is organized as follows. I start by providing a customer-centric explanation for the evolution of the economies. Then, I turn to the issue of whether the present-day experiential offerings can be thought to be qualitatively different from those that came before, and what implications this has for the concept of experiential marketing. Finally, I turn my attention to what we may expect in the future.

A CUSTOMER-CENTRIC PERSPECTIVE OF THE EVOLUTION OF THE ECONOMIES

So, why are we in an 'experience' economy? Why not in a 'super service' economy or, in a 'design' economy? In other words, what has led several thinkers to agree that the term 'experience' best reflects the current customer–firm interaction environment? Schmitt (1999) offers some compelling reasons for the choice of this term. He argues that, among others, two major trends have shaped the characteristics of present day customer–firm interactions: (1) omnipresence of information technology, and (2) ubiquity of integrated communications and entertainment. The first trend, in Schmitt's (1999) opinion, has facilitated information transfer from customers to companies, thereby making companies more capable of developing offerings closer to the consumers' ideal point. This trend, in conjunction with the second trend – the change in media towards entertaining rather than merely informing the customer (for example, consider the rising popularity of the Daily Show with Jon Stewart and the declining popularity of more traditional news programs) – has resulted in a new set of norms by which firms interact with customers. A core element of this norm is that firms seek to entertain customers in even the most functional domains of consumption, including laptops (for example, Apple), banks (for example, ING Bank), and retail stores (for example, Nike with Niketown); the term 'experience' thus appears well suited to capture the combination of emotional and functional benefits that the present day consumption offerings strive to provide.

A Customer-centric Perspective on the Experience Economy

Schmitt's (1999) perspective is arguably a *context*-centric view of why we are in an experience economy, since it builds on the idea that environment changes (technological advancements and changes in media) have resulted in the experience economy. There is yet another, more customer-centric, perspective that may be adopted to explain the same phenomenon. This view hinges on the following well accepted ideas in psychology: (1) the achievement of goals or needs[2] leads to the experience of emotional benefits (pleasure), and (2) goals are structured in a hierarchical fashion such that, once a lower order goal is met, emotional benefits can only be derived from the fulfillment of higher order goals. Maslow's (1962) needs hierarchy (depicted in Figure 10.2), provides perhaps the most commonly accepted view of how goals are typically structured. To elaborate, Maslow (1962) suggests that people (consumers) seek the fulfillment of physiological needs (such as those for food, water, clothing, and so on) first, and thereafter seek the fulfillment of security needs, and so on, until the only relevant goal that remains, when all else has been fulfilled, is the need for self-actualization.

Mapping from the Need Hierarchy to the Evolution of the Economies

Just as the status of an individual on the Maslow (1962) needs hierarchy provides a snapshot of this individual's primary concerns, the status of a society on the needs hierarchy may be thought to reflect this society's primary concerns.[3] For example, a society could be thought to belong to the physiological stage when most of its members seek the fulfillment of the basic needs of food, shelter and clothing; one could characterize certain

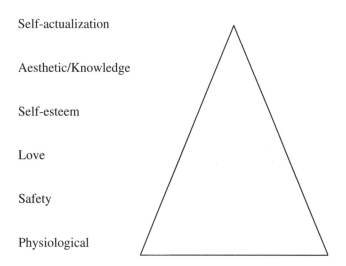

Self-actualization

Aesthetic/Knowledge

Self-esteem

Love

Safety

Physiological

Source: Maslow (1962).

Figure 10.2   Maslow's need hierarchy

economies (for example, third world countries) as being primarily concerned with the fulfillment of 'physiological' and 'security' needs. Likewise, one may characterize certain other economies (for example, Scandinavian countries) as being primarily concerned with the fulfillment of aesthetic or knowledge needs, and so on.

When most of the members in a society seek physiological needs, the offerings of that society will (naturally) consist largely of physical commodities such as food, building materials, clothing, and so forth. As such, the society can be conceptualized as belonging to a commodities economy. When a society's members seek assurance that the consumption offerings live up to a certain expected standard, the society may be thought to be concerned about seeking security (through reducing uncertainty about the quality of that society's consumption offerings). Because branding products/services is an important means of assuring quality, and because branding is thought to be an important element of a goods economy, a society that seeks security needs may be thought to belong to a goods economy. When a society has progressed beyond seeking security to seeking the fulfillment of the higher-order goals of love or self-esteem, the offerings in that society need to be of an intangible nature. Such a society may be thought to have progressed to a services economy. That is, one may draw a one-to-one mapping between the hierarchy of needs and the evolution of the economies from commodities to services, as depicted in Figure 10.3.

The question then is, which term best characterizes the needs of a society that has progressed beyond seeking self-esteem and love? According to Maslow (1962), such a society would be primarily concerned with the fulfillment of both knowledge and aesthetic needs. To the extent that knowledge and aesthetics are two separate categories of needs, it would appear that two separate terms are needed to characterize the concerns of such a society – unless one can think of an overarching term that captures the desire for both (knowledge and aesthetics).

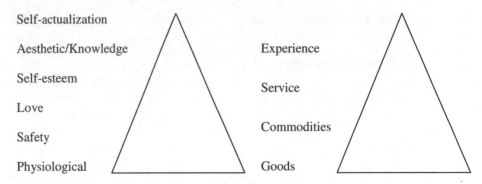

Self-actualization

Aesthetic/Knowledge   Experience

Self-esteem
                                                 Service
Love
                                                 Commodities
Safety
                                                 Goods
Physiological

Figure 10.3   Mapping of the hierarchy of needs to the evolution of the economies

Two terms readily lend themselves as appropriate for capturing knowledge needs: 'knowledge economy', and 'information economy'. These terms have a tradition of use in economics and business. According to proponents of the knowledge economy (for example, Romer, 1990), economic systems that align their incentives towards rewarding producers of knowledge will stand to gain in the future. Likewise, according to proponents of the information economy (for example, Toffler, 1970), technological advancements shorten the time taken for information exchange (between organizations), facilitating faster turnover of money and ultimately resulting in more rapid economic growth; thus, firms that invest in the acquisition of systems that facilitate efficient information transfer would stand to gain most. Note that both conceptualizations offer a firm-centric, rather than a customer-centric, view of economic trends. That is, both perspectives theorize about what firms (rather than customers) value.[4,5] Maslow's (1962) hierarchy, in contrast, is better suited as depicting the structure of *customers'* needs. Thus, at least in its current from, neither the term knowledge economy nor the term information economy appear appropriate for capturing the needs of customers. Further, both terms suffer from the limitation of not capturing the aesthetic needs that customers in a society that has advanced beyond love and self-esteem would presumably seek.

The question is whether the term 'experience economy' is suitable, that is, whether it captures the idea that customers in a society that has advanced beyond love and self-esteem seek knowledge and aesthetics. The term, on first blush, appears better suited to capture the desire for aesthetics than that for knowledge. In both the Pine and Gilmore (1997) and the Schmitt (1999, 2003) conceptualizations, the aesthetic elements are thought to be crucial to the execution of a memorable experience. In Schmitt's (1999) conceptualization, for example, the SENSE elements (sight, sound, taste, touch and smell) are considered the bedrock upon which experiential (emotional, cognitive, conative and relational) appeals rest.

A broader, more inclusive view of the term 'experiences', however, does allow for the inclusion of both knowledge and aesthetic needs. Experiences are not always just emotional in nature, but can also be of a thought-provoking nature. (For example, we may have a great experience attending a stimulating lecture on astrophysics.) Thus, to the extent that an experiential framework allows for the inclusion of knowledge, or thought-oriented, needs, the term 'experience' may be considered well suited to capture the twin desires of knowledge and aesthetics that characterize consumers in societies that have advanced beyond love and self-esteem needs. Consistent with this view, in both the Pine and Gilmore (1997) and the Schmitt (1999) frameworks, experiences are conceptualized as appealing not just to the senses and to feelings, but also to cognitions.

Nevertheless, to the extent that the term 'experience' connotes an affective (rather than a cognitive) appeal, the term may not be a perfect representative for capturing the primary consumption desires of societies that have advanced beyond love and self-esteem. Put differently, marketers who wish to pursue an experiential strategy need to explicitly recognize that customers in an experience economy not only seek aesthetic needs, but also knowledge needs, and that creating thought-oriented appeals is a legitimate route to creating memorable experiences.

Summary and Implications

In sum, I have presented an alternative (customer-centric) view of the underlying reasons for the evolution of the economies – from commodities to goods to services to experiences. Building on Maslow's (1962) hierarchy, I have suggested that customers who have advanced beyond seeking love and self-esteem seek knowledge and aesthetic needs, and that the term 'experience' appears well suited to capture this evolution in customer needs. Because the term 'experiences' better captures the *aesthetic* concerns (and de-emphasizes the knowledge concerns), practitioners need to recognize that a broader conceptualization of the term 'experiences' – one that explicitly incorporates cognitive elements – may be in order.

Relating the evolution of the economies to Maslow's (1962) hierarchy permits marketers to assess whether a particular country or economic region is ready for the experience economy. Since it is necessary to have progressed beyond the fulfillment of love and safety to seek the experiential needs of knowledge and aesthetics, it is unlikely that the third world countries (such as India or Indonesia) or even the 'second world' ones (such as Brazil or Russia) are ready for the experience economy. Careful monitoring of the progress of these economies can, however, provide indications of when they will be ready, therefore allowing firms to prepare for this potentiality.

ARE THE PRESENT-DAY 'EXPERIENTIAL' OFFERINGS ANY DIFFERENT?

Although proponents of experiential marketing offer convincing illustrations of how many products and services have evolved over time – the birthday cake example from Pine and Gilmore (1997, p. 97; see Table 10.1) stands out as a particularly illuminating example – one may wonder whether there has truly been a *qualitative* change in the nature of offerings. Put differently, one may wonder whether what we now refer to as an experience is really only 'very good' (or even 'exceptional') service.

Consider, for instance, how Rainforest Café purportedly operationalizes its experiential strategy: by asking customers if they are prepared 'for their adventure to begin' and through channeling audio clips of animal sounds in strategically placed speakers. In what ways does Rainforest Café's execution differ from, say, McDonalds' (which creates an exciting environment for children to play in), or from what Williams Sonoma has been doing for years (creating an inviting environment through placing cinnamon buns near its

Table 10.1   Evolution of the birthday cake across the economies

Time Period	Source of Materials	Profit Margin
100+ years back	From scratch (eggs, flour, etc.)	A few dimes
75 years back	Pre-mixed ingredients (e.g., Betty Crocker mix)	$1–$2
50 years back	Bakery	$5–$10
Now	Event Management Team	$50+

Source: Adapted from Pine and Gilmore (1997).

entrance)? Is there anything qualitatively different about Rainforest Café's execution of its experiential strategy?

Pine and Gilmore (1997) argue that part of the difference between the offerings in a service vs. an experience economy is quantitative. For example, these authors suggest that, while the attribute in a service economy is 'customized', that in an experience economy is 'personalized' (Pine and Gilmore, 1997, Table 2). The idea of customer portfolio management, whereby customers get a level of service commensurate with their *individual* lifetime value, rather than the lifetime value of the segment that they belong to (for example, Zeithaml et al., 2001) is reflective of a trend towards personalization. Few would argue against the proposition that experiential offerings differ in a quantitative way from service offerings.

More debatable is the suggestion that experiential offerings are *qualitatively* different from those that came before them. Indeed, most differences between the experience and service economies appear qualitative, rather than quantitative (see Table 10.2). For example, Pine and Gilmore (1997) argue that whereas the offering in a service economy is 'intangible', that in an experience economy is 'memorable'; likewise, whereas the customer purportedly demands 'benefits' in a service economy, she or he demands 'sensations' in an experience economy.

The thesis that experiential offerings are qualitatively different from those that came before is, in my opinion, untenable. This is because there is no well-accepted set of (necessary and sufficient) conditions that can be applied to assess whether a consumption offering is an exceptional service or a great experience. Service providers should ultimately aim to deliver beyond customer expectations (Oliver, 1997), as must the stager of memorable experiences (Schmitt, 1999). The difference between experiences and services may, therefore, potentially be a matter of degree – staging a memorable experience may involve going the extra mile or being more creative than when delivering a great service – which points to a quantitative (rather than a qualitative) difference.

The Metaphorical Value of the Concept of Experiential Economy

In my view, the usefulness of the concept of experiential economy does not lie in being able to demonstrate that experiential offerings are indeed qualitatively different from service offerings. Rather, its usefulness lies in the set of *metaphors* that the term 'experience' evokes in the minds of the employees. Speaking of one's offering in terms of experience evokes a set of concepts and images that would not have been evoked if the same offering were conceptualized as a good or a service. For example, an employee of

Table 10.2 Differences across economies

	Commodities	Goods	Services	Experiences
Economy	Agrarian	Industrial	Service	Experience
Function	Extract	Make	Deliver	Stage
Offering	Fungible	Tangible	Intangible	Memorable
Attribute	Natural	Standardized	Customized	Personalized
Supply method	Stored in bulk	Inventoried	Delivered	Revealed
Seller	Trader	Manufacturer	Provider	Stager
Buyer	Market	User	Client	Guest
Demand	Characteristics	Features	Benefits	Sensations

Source: Pine and Gilmore (1997, p. 98).

Wendy's trained to treat their customer as a 'client' would interact differently with customers than one told to treat the customer as a 'guest'. In the former case, the customer is treated more formally, and held at arm's length, since the term 'client' conveys the connotation that the interaction should be primarily viewed as an economic transaction. In the latter case, the customer is invited to share one's personal space, and the interaction is viewed as an emotionally fulfilling one, since the interaction is viewed as a symbolic, rather than as an economic transaction (cf. Belk and Coon, 1993). Likewise, the concepts and ideas that are generated in the employee's mind when he/she seeks to *stage* an experience is different from that when he/she seeks merely to *deliver* it. When staging an experience, the image of being on a stage – in the limelight – is evoked; by contrast, delivering a service evokes the image of being on an equal footing with the customer. In the former, there is potentially greater self-consciousness, with more at stake, and there is an explicit focus on entertaining the 'audience' (customers). In the latter, there is an element of instrumentality to the interaction – again, the interaction has a flavor of being more instrumental than symbolic.

The set of metaphors associated with the concept of experiential marketing allows for what I term 'goal abstraction' to occur spontaneously. Goal abstraction occurs when goals that are higher up on the needs hierarchy (for example, Maslow's) are fulfilled. In a consumption context, this can result in greater customer satisfaction and, in turn, to greater profitability, as depicted in the context of coffee in Figure 10.4. This is because the amount of value delivered to the customer is greater when both lower- and higher-order goals are fulfilled than when only lower-order goals are fulfilled. For example, a grocery store that caters not just to experiential customers' convenience needs, but also to their need for knowledge (for example, learning about food products or about new recipes) will probably be more satisfied – even delighted – by visiting the store. This is potentially one reason why Central Market, a grocery store in Texas, which offers a unique customer retail experience in the grocery context is able to charge a significant premium for its produce over its competition.

I argue that goal abstraction occurs relatively spontaneously when the language associated with experiential marketing is used to convey, to the employees, the nature of customer interactions that the firm desires. Consider the above example of an employee of Wendy's who is instructed to treat customers as 'guests' as opposed to 'clients'. Such an employee would probably cater not just to the customer's hunger (which, to be sure, is

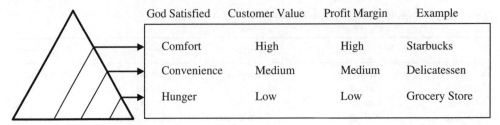

God Satisfied	Customer Value	Profit Margin	Example
Comfort	High	High	Starbucks
Convenience	Medium	Medium	Delicatessen
Hunger	Low	Low	Grocery Store

Figure 10.4   Enhancing experiences through goal abstraction: From customer value to firm value in the category of coffee

likely to be the customer's primary concern), but also to their other needs, such as that of being treated with genuine warmth and interest, or that for being in a clean, well-designed, aesthetically pleasing environment. By contrast, the employee would probably focus almost entirely on catering to the employee's hunger needs alone when asked to treat customers as 'clients'.

Summary and Implications

In summary, the argument that experiential offerings are *qualitatively* different from those in a service or a goods economy, a view implied in Pine and Gilmore's (1997, Table 2) framework, is, in my opinion, difficult to defend. Nevertheless, I believe that there is still value in using the experiential marketing framework. I argue that one of the main advantages of using the framework lies in the set of metaphors that the concepts associated with experiential marketing evoke. Just as a physical prototype can be useful in communicating to others (co-workers and customers) what the product is expected to do and how, and indispensable in the lead-up to the product development, the concept of experiential marketing is useful in communicating to others the vision of an experiential marketing strategy, and indispensable in honing employee–customer interactions in eliciting precisely the intended nature and intensity of customer reactions.

IS THE EXPERIENCE ECONOMY HERE TO STAY?

Let's now turn our attention to the final issue: is the experience economy here to stay or is it just a passing fad?

Critical to addressing this question is to address an even more fundamental one: can experiences become commoditized? Or can marketers constantly keep experiential campaigns fresh? The answer to this question lies in gaining an appreciation of two basic principles of human nature: 1. Adaptation-level principle, and 2. The more abstract (higher order) the goal, the greater the number of pathways to fulfilling it.

Principles of Human Nature and the Longevity of Economic Phases

The adaptation-level principle, first introduced by Helson (1947), refers to the idea that people adapt to a given level of stimulus, such that more of that stimulus is needed to maintain the same level of the experience. For example, the positive reaction that an employee experiences from an increase in wages will, over time, recede as the employee gets used to his/her new level of pay. Therefore, further increases in wages are needed to produce the same level of positive reaction that the employee felt from the first wage increase. The adaptation level principle has been replicated in a variety of domains, including that of money and physical ailments (Brickman et al., 1978) and, more relevant to the focus in this chapter, consumption experiences (for example, Raghunathan and Irwin, 2001). For example, Raghunathan and Irwin (2001) found that an average consumption stimulus was rated more poorly when it followed a set of superior experiences than when it followed a set of inferior experiences. Thus, a Toyota Camry was rated lower when raters were used to cars of the quality of Lexus and BMWs than when they were used to cars of the quality of Kia and Hyundai.

While seemingly an unfortunate aspect of human nature – the fact that we adapt to any level of stimulus suggests that no stimulus is capable of consistently providing a sustained level of happiness – the adaptation principle is useful in helping us get over negative events. It does suggest, however, that consumers are likely to adapt to experiential marketing campaigns, that the novelty of experiential campaigns is likely to wear off over time. As such, the adaptation level principle suggests that, as with the commodities, goods and service economies, the experience economy is merely a passing phase that will be replaced by some other type of economy in the future.

Does this mean that marketers would be better off focusing attention on what's coming next than on honing their experiential marketing techniques and skills? Not really, since although the experience economy is likely to be replaced by a new type of economy in the future, the experiential phase is likely to last quite a while. This is because of the second principle of human nature – the fact that there are a greater number of pathways to achieving higher-order (vs. lower-order) goals.

As mentioned earlier, as the economies evolve – say, from commodities to goods to services to experiences – customers' needs change towards seeking more abstract, higher-order goals. For example, whereas customers in a commodities economy seek the fulfillment of basic needs such as hunger and shelter, those in an experience economy seek the fulfillment of such higher-order needs as knowledge and aesthetics (see Figure 10.2). It follows, then, that the longevity of a particular type of economy – commodity, good, service or experience – will depend on the number of ways in which the primary set of needs associated with that economy can be fulfilled. As an example, the more ways in which consumers can seek the fulfillment of a particular need (say, hunger), the greater the number of options available to marketers for fulfilling that need, and hence, the higher the potential longevity of the type of economy in which that need is primary.

By this logic, the experience economy has the potential to last longer than the economies that came before. This is because the more abstract (higher order) the goal, the greater the number of pathways to fulfilling it. Because consumers in the experience economy are concerned with the fulfillment of very abstract (higher order) goals, such as that of knowledge and aesthetics, the greater the number of options available to marketers for fulfilling them. As an illustration of this point, consider a consumer who is primarily concerned with hunger and unconcerned about other higher-order needs, versus one who is relatively less concerned about hunger and more concerned about aesthetics. The number of ways by which a marketer can satisfy the former customer's need for hunger is limited by the number of food items (perhaps a few hundred types of dishes) viewed as acceptable in that society. In contrast, the marketer has the freedom to explore many more pathways to satisfying the latter customer's need of hunger *plus* the need for aesthetics. For example, whereas the former customer is unlikely to value the manner in which food is presented (a fish is a fish is a fish), the latter is likely to appreciate it. Likewise, where the former customer is unlikely to value ambience, the latter will, and so on.

The advantage of being able to choose among multiple pathways to fulfill higher-order needs, however, comes at the cost of having to learn about these pathways. A marketer who is only used to following a recipe and knows little about presentation of food, for example, is less likely to reap the benefits of being in an experience economy. Further, because higher-order goals are more difficult to define – aesthetics, for example, is often a matter of taste, whereas there is greater uniformity in how hunger is manifested – the marketer needs to be acutely aware of all the factors that impact the ways in which a higher-order goal can be fulfilled. For example, new trends in design (for example, which colors are 'in') can have a significant impact on how the marketer's offerings are perceived. A marketer in an experience economy is potentially more susceptible to the vagaries of the customer's perceptions than is one in a goods or a service economy.

Summary and Implications

To summarize, I believe that the experience economy is here to stay – at least for the foreseeable future. This also means, however, that it is important for marketers to become aware of the various ways in which customer's knowledge and aesthetic needs can be fulfilled. Further, marketers need also to become aware of how cultural and other (political) trends are likely to impact customers' definitions of knowledge and aesthetics and incorporate this into their experiential marketing strategies. This clearly calls for a rather exalted level of ability for the marketer hoping to succeed in the experience economy.

I conclude with a conjecture about what type of economy is likely to replace the experience economy. If Maslow's hierarchy is a veridical representation of consumers' needs, then it appears that the fulfillment of knowledge and aesthetic needs will be followed by the desire to seek self-actualization. As such, the experience economy is likely to be followed by an 'actualization' economy. It may thus be worthwhile for marketers to ascertain what 'actualization' means. As Rogers (1961) defines it, actualization means achieving one's true potential. This means that consumers are likely to pursue their 'true' interests without much regard for extrinsic rewards. Thus, consumers in the actualized economy are likely to make their hobbies their vocation, and are also likely to only 'work' on their hobbies to the extent that it interests them. Such consumers are unlikely to overwork themselves to the point of exhaustion for the sake of making more money, earning more fame or for the sake of increased power and control over others. Perhaps what is in store for us is the 'Utopian Economy'.

NOTES

1. Because the concept of the experience economy shares significant common ground with the concept of experiential marketing (first introduced by Schmitt, 1999), the term experiential marketing will be used to

refer to the set of marketing techniques that are expected to succeed in the context of the experience economy.

2. I use the terms 'goals' and 'needs' interchangeably.

3. Although Maslow's (1962) thesis was originally intended to depict the structure of goals at the individual level, one may extrapolate it to the societal level. Specifically, aggregating across each individual member's goal structure provides a good approximation to the goal structure of the society as a whole. Similar to this idea, one may arrive at the *status* of a society on the needs hierarchy by aggregating the status of each of its individual members.

4. Other terms, such as the 'Creative Economy' (for example, Coy, 2001), have also been used to refer to what firms seek in its employees, rather than what customers seek from first.

5. It is another matter whether the citizens of societies that have progressed beyond love and self-esteem desire knowledge. Is there evidence, for instance, that the citizens of developed countries (who are most likely to have advanced beyond the self-esteem and love needs) are more likely (than those in underdeveloped or developing countries) to seek knowledge? To the extent that conventional education represents knowledge, the rising demand for education in developed countries does appear to reflect a collective evolution towards seeking knowledge. Knowledge can, of course, be defined more broadly – to refer not just to the declarative kind (which is the type of knowledge that conventional education typically focuses on), but also procedural knowledge (the 'how to' of things). Hobbies as a whole also appear to have been growing in developed countries – another indication of the desire for knowledge. Although these mega trends offer preliminary evidence consistent with the view that we are presently in a (customer-centric) knowledge economy, more evidence is clearly needed to conclude that there is an emerging trend towards seeking knowledge.

REFERENCES

Belk, Russell W. and Gregory S. Coon (1993), 'Gift giving as agapic love: an alternative to the exchange paradigm based on dating experiences', *Journal of Consumer Research*, **20** (December), 393–417.

Brakus, Josko, Bernd Schmitt and Shi Zhang (2004), 'The role of experiential attributes in consumer judmgnet and choice', *working paper*, Columbia University.

Brickman, Philip, Dan Coates and Ronnie Janoff-Bulman (1978), 'Lottery winners and accident victims: is happiness relative', *Journal of Personality and Social Psychology*, **36** (August), 917–28.

Coy, Peter (2001), 'The creative economy', *Business Week*, 21 August.

Helson, Harry (1947), 'Adaptation-level as frame of reference for prediction of psychophysical data', *American Journal of Psychology*, **60** (Spring), 1–29.

Maslow, Abraham (1962), *Toward a Psychology of Being*, Oxford: Van Nostrand.

Oliver, Richard (1997), *Satisfaction: A Behavioral Perspective on the Consumer*, New York: McGraw-Hill.

Pine, Joseph B. and James H. Gilmore (1997), 'The experience economy', *Harvard Business Review*, January–February, pp. 91–101.

Pine, Joseph B. and James H. Gilmore (1999), *The Experience Economy*, Boston, MA: Harvard Business School Press.

Raghunathan, Rajagopal and Julie R. Irwin (2001), 'Walking the hedonic product treadmill: default contrast and mood-based assimilation effects in judgments of predicted happiness with target product', *Journal of Consumer Research*, **28**(3), 355–68.

Rogers, Carl R. (1961), *On Becoming a Person*, Boston, MA: Houghton Mifflin.

Romer, Paul (1990), 'Human capital and growth: theory and evidence', in A.H. Melzer (ed.), *Unit Roots, Investment Measures and Other Essays*, Carnegie Rochester Conference Series on Public Policy, **32**, Spring, 251–86.

Schmitt, Bernd H. (1999), *Experiential Marketing*, New York: Simon & Schuster, Free Press.

Schmitt, Bernd H. (2003), *Customer Experience Management*, Hoboken, NJ: Wiley and Sons.

Toffler, Alvin (1970), *Future Shock*, New York: Bantam.

Zeithaml, Valerie A., Roland T. Rust and Katharine N. Lemon (2001), 'The customer pyramid: creating and serving profitable customers', *California Management Review*, **43**(4), 118–42.

11. Embodied cognition, affordances and mind modularity: using cognitive science to present a theory of consumer experiences

J. Joško Brakus

Marketing theories typically explain product success by factors such as product differentiation based on functional features and benefits and a unique value proposition (Kotler, 1997; Porter, 1985). But what explains the dramatic success of such 'cool' new product concepts as the 'funky' Volkswagen Beetle, the colorful Nokia telephones or the Razor scooters? How do we explain the explosion of new product launches in product categories that are almost perfect commodities such as water or vodka?

Each of these new products arguably includes some sort of new product feature, a new functional benefit and perhaps a value proposition that is somewhat different from competitors'. However, if we look at the advertisements for these products, it seems that the main 'features' and 'benefits' of these products are 'superficial' characteristics such as colors and shapes. As a result, communications for these products do not follow the classic 'problem–solution' approach, but are full of peripheral components such as music, graphics and visual effects. Moreover, colors, shapes, visual effects and attractive music do not only appear in advertisements. Increasingly they are being used with great success to attract consumers' attention as part of a product design, packaging, website and retail space.

However, even though such elements have been used in marketing for a long time and can produce dramatic success, marketing theorists have had difficulties coming to grips with them. The prevailing view in marketing and strategy is that product success requires product differentiation on attributes that are meaningful, relevant and valuable (Kotler, 1997; Porter, 1985). Yet marketing researchers characterize attributes such as the color and shape of a computer or car, or 'flaked coffee crystals' in coffee, or the lighting of a store, or the graphic elements of a website as 'irrelevant', 'meaningless', or 'peripheral' (Carpenter et al., 1994) or, at best, as some unexplainable sort of 'puffery', 'image' or 'atmospheric' factors (Alba et al., 1992; Simonson and Nowlis, 2000). As a result, researchers seem to be surprised that marketing practitioners can create, as one award-winning article put it, 'meaningful brands from meaningless differentiation' (Carpenter et al., 1994). Indeed, the result that 'an irrelevant attribute is valued positively in a surprising number of cases' (Carpenter et al., 1994, p. 347) is considered to be 'somewhat disquieting for the model of rational choice' (p. 348). Thus, researchers need to evoke a complex inferential process to make sense of the results: 'We argue that adding an irrelevant attribute to one brand changes the structure of the decision consumers face, especially if the differentiating attribute is difficult to evaluate . . . As a result, consumers may infer the attribute's value and, in some cases, conclude that it is valuable.' (p. 339)

In this chapter, we argue that the attributes labeled as 'irrelevant', 'meaningless' or 'peripheral' deserve such labels only if viewed from the perspective of a particular paradigm – namely, the mainstream marketing paradigm of information processing and choice. However, attributes such as 'flaked coffee crystals', 'silk in the shampoo bottle', 'Milanese-style pasta', 'Alpine-class down-filled jackets' and 'studio-designed signal processing systems for compact disc players' – stimuli and examples used as 'irrelevant' and 'meaningless' attributes in the Carpenter et al. study – are very relevant and inherently meaningful if viewed from the alternative cognitive-science paradigm that we advocate in this chapter. Moreover, as we will show, the mechanism by which they create value for the individual is straightforward and does not require a complex inferential process.

More generally, we argue that the mainstream marketing paradigm of information processing and choice (for example, Bettman, 1979; Howard and Sheth, 1969) unnecessarily constrains domains of inquiry by imposing a frame of assumptions that may be inappropriate for the tasks at hand and increasingly fails to provide relevant explanations for some of the most important marketing campaigns today. The mainstream view may have provided research direction and focus in the past. However, now that the paradigm has entered the 'normal stage of science' (Kuhn, 1996), its assumptions have become restrictions that hinder further conceptual progress and practical applications, and it is time to explore alternatives.

In this chapter we present a framework that serves as an alternative to the mainstream marketing paradigm of information processing and choice. The framework is based on cognitive science, which in turn is based on evolutionary biology, and focuses on understanding consumer cognition and behavior. We also use the framework to present an empirically testable theory of consumer experiences. The theory describes and explains how consumers respond to a broad variety of experiential 'marketing stimuli' such as logos and signage, packaging, advertising and other communications, retail environments, and websites.

Specifically, cognitive science, derived from recent work in evolutionary biology, is guided by the notion that cognition is 'embodied', that is, that the mind evolved in the organism's natural environment and was shaped and conditioned by that environment (Clark, 1997; Harman, 1993; Varela et al., 1997). As a result, the mind responds to specific environmental cues, called 'affordances' (Gibson, 1966, 1979), that offer perceptual clues to the organism by virtue of the specific organism–environment interaction. Most importantly, the framework proposes that the mind is not a universal information-processing device but rather is specialized for certain environmental cues; that is, the mind is modular, and mental modules have their own structures and principles (Fodor, 1983; Pinker, 1997; Plotkin, 1998).

After presenting the framework, we propose an empirically testable theory of consumer experiences. The theory consists of five types of modular experiences (sensory, affective, intellectual, bodily and social). These experiences occur on two separate response levels – a primary level at which responses are fairly instinctual and automatic and a secondary level at which responses are learned and acquired. Toward the end of the chapter, we discuss methodological issues and show how the theory can be tested empirically. Finally, we discuss how to apply the theory to strategic management and public policy issues.

In the following section, we discuss the key assumptions of mainstream information processing and choice. We then discuss specific critiques of the information processing paradigm presented by a variety of research programs including behavioral decision theory, research on mood and affect, and interpretive approaches. Yet, as we will show, none of these research programs has presented a comprehensive alternative to the mainstream model of information processing and choice.

THE MAINSTREAM MARKETING PARADIGM AND ITS CRITICS

Core Assumptions

The mainstream marketing paradigm consists of several general models of consumer behavior and choice (Bettman, 1979; Engel et al., 1990; Howard and Sheth, 1969). These models are guided by certain core assumptions about consumers and how they process information and make a choice. In the context of managerial decision-making, these same assumptions have also been used to explain how experts, for example, executives or industrial buyers, process information and make choices and decisions. These assumptions are seldom presented explicitly, but they are implied in the 'habitus' (Bourdieu, 1990) of marketing researchers, that is, these assumptions affect how marketing issues are conceptualized and empirically investigated.

First, the information-processing paradigm views consumers as problem-oriented decision makers, and consumer cognition and behavior as a series of decision steps. These steps range from problem solving and information search to the formulation of consideration, choice sets, choice and, ultimately, behavior and usage. The number of processing steps, the degree of processing, and the degree of elaboration and inference differ slightly from model to model; moreover, they may depend on factors that are external to these decision steps such as degree of involvement or need for cognition (Howard, 1977). However, some sort of step-by-step processing always occurs.

Second, consumer information processing is viewed as goal-driven and task-oriented (Bettman et al., 1991; Newell and Simon, 1972). Examples of goals and tasks may include impression formation of a product (Fishbein and Ajzen, 1975), attitude formation about a brand (Johar et al., 1997), or assessing the degree of satisfaction with a product after purchase (Anderson and Sullivan, 1993; Oliver, 1980). Outcomes of the processes of impression and attitude formation and satisfaction are often conceptualized as a comparison between 'priors' (such as probabilities or expectations) and 'posteriors' (for example, perceived performance or experience).

Third, information processing is conceptualized as mental representations on which consumers perform a series of operations as part of a universal cognitive process (Mitchell, 1983). As such, the process is not stimulus-specific but rather propositional in nature. The type of 'input' is considered irrelevant to the subsequent processing: whether consumers are viewing a colorful logo, reading words on a website, or examining the packaging of products in a supermarket, the processing is the same. In each case, a universal mental processor similar to the processor inside a computer will process the information contained in the stimulus.

Fourth, information processing and choice theories take a disembodied view of the mind. That is, the information-processing paradigm assumes that categorization, concept formation and reasoning are separate from and independent of how we are evolved as an organism and what we do with our bodies in our physical environments (Clark, 1997; Lakoff and Johnson 1999; Varela et al., 1997). As a result, the cognitive processes by which mental categories are manipulated can be isolated and studied in a decontextualized manner.

Fifth, most models of information processing and choice are rational and functional in nature. Choice situations are conceptualized as mental matrices consisting of the functional features of various products (Bettman et al., 1991; Johnson and Payne, 1985; Svenson, 1979). In these matrices, consumers perform mental operations that focus on weighing and rating certain attributes, combining features, calculating utilities based on weights and ratings, assigning cut-off values and so on. These operations result in choice outcomes based on certain choice rules (based on the multi-attribute model, or conjunctive and disjunctive choice rules).

Critiques

A variety of research programs have offered critiques of the mainstream marketing paradigm. Behavioral decision theory (BDT) researchers have pointed out that most processing is much simpler due to cognitive limitations and trade-offs between effort and accuracy (Bettman et al., 1991; Einhorn, 1971; Johnson and Payne, 1985; Payne, 1976; Svenson, 1979). As a result, consumers often do not follow a rational, step-by-step decision model. Instead, they use heuristics and simple rules of thumb in decision-making (Alba and Marmorstein, 1987; Einhorn and Hogarth, 1975, 1981; Tversky, 1969, 1972; Simon, 1955; Svenson, 1979). Moreover, most decisions are contextual decisions and are made with respect to a reference point rather than following a clearly defined sequence from problem recognition to purchase behavior (Kahneman and Tversky, 1979, 1984; Thaler, 1985, 1998).

Several eminent researchers such as Bettman (1993), Hoch and Loewenstein (1991), Holbrook and Hirschman (1982), and Loewenstein (1996), have critiqued the purely cognitive view and the computer metaphor of the mainstream paradigm. These researchers have pointed to affect as a key motivational construct that must be considered in addition to 'cold' information processing. Most importantly, researchers have distinguished between two distinct types of communications: informational/cognitive and transformational/affective (Puto and Wells, 1984; Batra and Ray, 1986; Holbrook and Batra, 1987).

Finally, interpretive approaches to consumer behavior have contrasted the focus on functional attributes prevalent in the information processing paradigm with an experiential view of consumer behavior that focuses on the symbolic, hedonic and aesthetic nature of consumption (Holbrook and Hirschman, 1982). Interpretive researchers have also critiqued the mechanistic step-by-step view of the information-processing paradigm; they view consumer responses and experiences, emerging from the life context of the consumer (Mick and Buhl, 1992), as dynamic and to a large degree as unconscious (Thompson et al., 1989).

These three key critiques of information processing and choice have provided new research directions and have explored phenomena that did not fall into the traditional information-processing subject matter. Yet, while both BDT and the research on mood and affect have relaxed some of the assumptions – speaking of 'bounded rationality' or the 'motivational value' of affect – both approaches still subscribe to the core paradigmatic assumptions. In other words, BDT and research on mood and affect primarily specify the conditions under which bounded rationality (instead of normative rationality) and affective effects (instead of cognitive ones) apply but they do not propose alternative assumptions or processes (Shiv and Fedorikhin, 1999). Moreover, none of the three approaches has provided a broad and comprehensive alternative paradigm to information processing that incorporates these critiques. Conceptually, the interpretive approaches come closest to providing a broad alternative. However, in practice, interpretive research has focused on a narrow range of research phenomena such as art and cultural consumption and has not provided a viable alternative for explaining most marketing phenomena.

Most importantly, none of the alternative approaches to the mainstream marketing paradigm of information processing and choice takes into consideration the latest view in cognitive science – the major discipline for studying how the human mind works. In cognitive science, which brings together evolutionary biology, cognitive psychology, philosophy of mind and artificial intelligence, an evolutionary perspective is considered to be essential for understanding the mind. However, an evolutionary view stands in sharp contrast to the assumptions of the mainstream marketing paradigm of information processing and choice.

COGNITIVE SCIENCE AS AN ALTERNATIVE

The difference between the traditional information processing paradigm used in marketing and the cognitive science view can be illustrated by examining the behavior of a non-human species: a cockroach. Let us take a look at escape behavior of a cockroach and how this behavior might be explained first by the information-processing paradigm and then by a cognitive scientist committed to an evolutionary perspective.

Ritzmann (1993) has pointed out that the cockroach is extremely skillful in its escape behavior. For example, the cockroach senses the wind disturbances caused by the motion of an attacking predator. It is able to distinguish winds caused by predators from normal air currents and breezes. When it initiates an escape motion, it does not simply run at random. Instead, it takes into account its own initial orientation, the presence of obstacles (for example, walls), the degree of illumination, the direction of the wind and many other variables.

In the spirit of information processing and choice, one might be tempted to explain the cockroach's behavior by trying to model a vast database of explicitly stored knowledge that the cockroach constantly accesses and retrieves to guide behavior. Such a database would include choice rules or heuristics such as: if you are being attacked, don't run into the wall. A change in light intensity is dangerous. Gentle breezes are okay, and so on and on. However, as Dreyfus (1991) noted, such a model would require vast amounts of explicitly coded and stored knowledge (Dreyfus estimates the database to include several volumes) and an information search across the databases might not produce real-time bodily responses because the combination of input parameters (that is, initial body orientation, the distance and the orientation of obstacles, degree of illumination, the wind direction) is huge and likely to be different from occasion to occasion.

Instead, it is more parsimonious and accurate to view the 'mind' of the cockroach from an evolutionary perspective. That is, the cockroach has certain body parts that are specialized toward the detection of specific local cues in its environment and the cockroach's perceptual system detects these cues without any complex computing mechanism. Moreover, the perceptual system is connected with a motor system that produces appropriate behavior. For example, the cockroach has two antenna-like structures called cerci, which are covered with hairs sensitive to detect wind direction and velocity. Escape motions are activated only if the wind is accelerating at 0.6 m/s^2 or more. The interval between sensing and response is very short: 58 milliseconds for a stationary roach and 14 milliseconds for a walking roach. The initial response is a turn that takes between 20 and 30 milliseconds. As this example illustrates, the cockroach, like any organism, is sensitized to the environmental aspects of its own environmental niche, that is, ecosystem.

Indeed, what applies to the cockroach seems to apply to the baseball player as well. Rather than modeling the baseball player's catching behavior as anticipating the continuing trajectory of the ball by actively 'computing' it, it is more parsimonious to assume that he is attuned to his particular environment and thus perceives it and behaves (runs) in such a way that the acceleration of the tangent of elevation of gaze from him to the ball is kept at zero (Clark, 1997). From an evolutionary point of view, the key difference between a cockroach and a baseball player is that they have evolved through a different series of responses relative to their *own ecosystem*. Interestingly, focusing on the organism–ecosystem relation rather than data storage and central information processing, the field of artificial intelligence has been extremely successful over the past ten years in designing mobile robots – including a highly functioning humanoid robot that performs complex perceptual and behavioral tasks (Brooks, 1994).

In sum, cognitive science replaces the notion of computed goals and tasks, the universality of symbolic calculations, and the notion of disembodied cognition with the idea of context- and environment-dependent behavior, specialized response systems and environmentally embedded cognition. Finally, rather than merely focusing on fully or partially rational behavior and functional attributes, the evolutionary framework focuses on experiences that arise out of the responses of specialized, stimuli-specific brain structures.

EMBODIED COGNITION, AFFORDANCES AND MODULARITY: A NEW VIEW OF CONSUMER COGNITION

We now explore how the evolutionary perspective may be useful as a framework for consumer cognition and consumer behavior. Later in the chapter, we will use the framework to propose a theory of consumer experiences that addresses how experiences arise, how they can be described and how consumers respond to them. Three theoretical constructs are critical: embodied cognition (Clark, 1997; Lakoff and Johnson, 1999; Varela et al., 1997), affordances (Gibson, 1966, 1979), and mind modularity (Fodor, 1983; Pinker, 1997; Plotkin, 1998).

Embodied Cognition

Embodied cognition is environmentally embedded cognition that results from our direct, physical responses when we interact with our environments (Clark, 1997). Cognitions are thus not just reflections of our external reality (that is, representations), but they are also shaped by bodily experiences. Embodied cognition is reflected in what Lakoff and Johnson have called primary metaphors, that is, universal, or at least widespread, conceptualizations that we use to judge and reason about abstract concepts (Lakoff and Johnson, 1999, p. 45). For example, the metaphor of 'warmth' in understanding the concept of affection can be traced to early childhood; each time parents show affection toward a newborn baby by touching and holding it, the baby's body temperature rises due to the body contact. Thus, a neural firing occurs between the part of the brain that senses the increase in body temperature and the part of the brain that deals with the understanding of the concept of affection (Narayanan, 1997). As a result, associations are automatically built up between the two domains without any conscious reasoning. Later in life, we are able to separate the conceptual domains of warmth and affection; however, the formed neural link continues to exist. These persisting associations form the basis for expressions like 'a warm intention' or 'a cold person'. In sum, people are evolutionarily predisposed to acquire primary metaphors and the acquisition of primary metaphors is one example of embodied cognition.

While primary metaphors are evolutionarily determined, Lakoff and Johnson argue that there is also a secondary level of metaphors that can be understood only within a cultural context. For example, a lyric from a pop song that says 'they were speeding on a highway of love' is an example of a secondary metaphor that is understood only within a certain cultural context. This duality of metaphors – primary, which are evolutionarily determined, and secondary, which are culturally determined – is important for the theory of consumer experiences that we will propose later on in this chapter.

Affordances

How does the embodied mind perceive the world? Gibson's (1966, 1979) answer is by exploiting *affordances*. He defines an affordance as an opportunity for use, intervention, and interaction with some object: 'The affordances of the environment are what it offers to the animal . . . To perceive an object, an event, or a person is to perceive what they afford.' So, perception is rooted in tracking these opportunities for action that are presented to the perceiver by some local cues in the environment. For example, to a human a wooden chair affords sitting, but to a woodpecker it affords something quite different. Organisms do not require an inferential process to perceive these affordances; rather, they perceive affordances directly. Evolutionary theory explains why this is the case; namely, the same environmental cues are perceived differently by different organisms because these cues play different roles in their respective ecosystems. As with metaphors, we can easily imagine a 'secondary' level at which additional perceptions of chairs exist that are culturally determined or learned and thus affected by inferential processes. For example, differentiating the Barcelona chair designed by Mies van der Rohe from a Biedermeier chair requires cultural knowledge and perhaps even education in art history. Gibson's point is not that cultural perceptions of chairs do not exist, but simply that there are some perceptions that are non-inferential. From the theoretical perspective advocated by Gibson, such inferential attributes of chairs, however, are quite peripheral and largely irrelevant.

As part of the theory of consumer experiences that we propose later, we will claim that typical marketing stimuli such as advertisements, packages, products, logos, retail spaces and websites all contain affordances that consumers can pick up and use to perceive and evaluate those stimuli. According to the embodied nature of consumer cognitions, they respond to these stimuli on two levels – a primary (that is, a pre-conscious, direct-perception) level at which they perceive the affordances directly, and a secondary (that is, conscious-reasoning) level at which they draw inferences.

Modularity of the Mind

Dewey (1922, 1925), describing organism–environment interactions that make up the human experience, has claimed that human experience is at once composed of the following experiences: bodily, social, intellectual and emotional. Similarly, according to a number of cognitive scientists (Pinker, 1997; Plotkin, 1998; Fodor, 1983), the human mind has a modular structure. The idea of modular structure of the mind goes hand in hand with the evolutionary claim against the mind as central processor. A module is a special purpose, mostly autonomous computational system, and it solves a very restricted class of problems (Fodor, 1983). Modules are innate and are an evolutionary adaptation (Pinker, 1997; Plotkin, 1998). Strong evidence for this modular view comes from patients with brain impairments. Typically, damage to one part of the brain inhibits some specific cognitive abilities but not others (see Pinker, 1997 for discussion).

How many mind modules are there? Unfortunately, there is no consensus among cognitive scientists about the exact number. Fodor (1983) assumes massive mind modularity. In contrast, Pinker has identified four rather general modules that correspond to a large degree to the types of human experiences postulated by Dewey: sensory perception, feelings and emotions, creativity and reasoning, and social relations. (In contrast to Dewey, Pinker does not list a 'bodily' module; however he added a 'sensory' module.) We believe that the precise number of modules should not be a major concern for marketers. Moreover, it is quite possible that Pinker's (1997) modules (compared to Fodor's) are simply higher-order mental modules that are part of interrelated brain structures. Therefore, in the theory of experiences that we present in the next section, we take Pinker and Dewey's broad perspective as a starting point and propose five modules that are particularly relevant to describe and explain marketing phenomena.

A THEORY OF CONSUMER EXPERIENCES

Based on this framework, we propose a theory of consumer experiences. The theory consists of three key theoretical constructs: (1) experiential modules; (2) primary vs. secondary experiences; and (3) the hierarchy of experiential modules.

First, the theory distinguishes five types of experiential modules. Experiential modules are input devices that are specialized for certain kinds of perceptual input that give rise to certain internal experiences. They are: (1) a sensory module that is shaped by and responds to sensory information contained in marketing stimuli; (2) an affective module that is shaped by and responds to affective information contained in marketing stimuli; (3) an intellectual module that is specialized for appeals to consumers' intellect and is engaged creatively; (4) a bodily module that reacts to and deals with information that affects consumers' bodily actions; and (5) a social module that reacts to and deals with information that relates consumers to their kin, sex and broader social context.

Table 11.1   A theory of consumer experiences

	Experiential Modules				
	Sensory	Affective	Intellectual	Bodily	Social
Primary Level	Spectral colors and primary shapes (e.g., geons)	Stimuli that trigger primary emotions	Syllogisms and thought schemas		Kinship
Secondary Level	Complex colors and shapes; aesthetics	Stimuli that trigger complex emotions	Stimuli that stimulate problem solving and creativity	Lifestyles	

Secondly, in line with Lakoff and Johnson's distinction between primary and secondary perceptions, we propose that there is a primary and secondary level at which each experience arises (see Table 11.1). The primary level consists of evolutionarily determined, direct responses to the affordances in the environment. That is, we posit that some experiences arise from the direct perception of certain affordances, contained in marketing stimuli such as product design, packaging, communications, websites and so on.

The third theoretical construct of our theory relates to what we call 'hierarchy of modules'. This notion is comparable to the hierarchy-of-effects model in advertising (Strong, 1925), which may be viewed as a specific application of step-by-step processing. Traditional hierarchy-of-effects models claim that exposure to advertising resulting in persuasion goes through certain steps ranging from awareness and comprehension to attitude formation and purchase intention. The theory of consumer experiences proposes that there is a hierarchy of responses across different modules. Specifically, the sensory, affective, bodily modules are engaged faster than the intellectual and social modules because the former modules possess evolutionary primacy. Evidence for evolutionary primacy exists in the form of neurological research that shows that the centers for sensory (the thalamus), muscular and affective (limbic system and amygdala) structure are located at evolutionarily older and lower structures of the nervous system than the modules for thought and relational information, which are located in the neocortex (Damasio, 1994; Goleman, 1995; LeDoux, 1993).

As Table 11.1 shows, at the primary level, visual attributes of certain colors and shapes trigger the sensory module; facial displays of universal primary emotions (for example, a smile) trigger the affective module; syllogisms, some thought schemas and violations of expectations trigger the intellectual module; stimuli that result in arousal and/or pain trigger bodily modules; and references to kin (mother, father, sister, brother) trigger the social module.

Let us consider a real-life marketing example as an illustration – the New Beetle. The sensory reaction of attracting attention, the affective reaction to the New Beetle as 'warm', 'friendly' or 'cute', and the bodily tendency to 'want to hug it' may be driven directly by the similarity of the car's physical features with those of other 'attention getting', 'warm' and 'huggable' objects (such as babies). Thus, the physical design seems to contain a set of affordances that result in perceptions and experiences without any inferential processes.

The secondary level consists of a conscious step-by-step process of perception, encoding, storage and retrieval that results in the respective experiences. For example, seeing the new Beetle prompts retrieval of the image of the old Beetle, and fond memories that result in nostalgia. We believe that such processes can be explained well by various theories within the traditional marketing paradigm, and such inferential explanations have been presented for the affective module. However, secondary-level inferential processes have been somewhat neglected for the sensory, bodily and social modules. Yet, it is easy to see how theories on color, shape or typeface processing may be constructed for the sensory module; how inferential theories about textures, product touch and explorations may be constructed for the bodily module; and what form inferential theories about social-category perceptions of products might take.

On the secondary level, the major difference between our theory and the traditional marketing literature is our focus on experiential rather than functional attributes. For example, basic sensory elements such as certain colors and shapes can be used to form different aesthetic styles (for example, minimalism vs. ornamentalism, realism vs. abstraction, dynamic vs. static, loud/strong vs. quiet/weak) and themes (for example, messages that communicate content and meaning about a brand; for example: names, slogans, jingles, symbols) (Schmitt and Simonson, 1997). Reaction to styles and themes requires time, pre-existing knowledge and conscious effort; this can include knowledge that the consumer accumulates through repetitive interaction with the product. Another example: on the secondary level of the affective module, consumers may have reactions that result in complex emotions like jealousy or nostalgia (as is the case in Beetle ads). The secondary level of the intellectual module concerns problem solving (for example, figuring out how a new product operates by reading the manual and relying on existing knowledge) and creativity. Secondary bodily experiences may include perceptions of one's body in terms of perceptions of body type as 'athletic' (that is, mesomorph), 'fat' (that is, endomorph), or 'skinny' (that is, ectomorph) (for example, Portnoy, 1993; Spillman and Everington, 1989). Finally, secondary social experiences are related to an individual's role in a broader social context.

EMPIRICAL RESEARCH

As with any other theory, an empirical research program must be initiated that tests the theory of consumer experiences that we developed in the context of an evolutionary paradigm. Therefore, research programs need to be initiated that test the different aspects of the theory. This needs to be done in several ways.

1. Evidence for the types of experiences and their discriminant validity must be provided. This can be achieved by constructing scales that tap into the five different experiences, by examining their factor structure and intercorrelations with pertinent external measures. Such tests should be conducted with different marketing stimuli. That is, consumers should be asked to rate various advertisements, logos, packages, retail spaces and websites on measures that tap into the five modules. Brakus and Schmitt (2000) have constructed a scale in line with these criteria, and the scale has been shown to be reliable and valid for TV ads, print ads and logos. Moreover, Dubé

and Le Bel (1999) have shown that pleasure is a multi-dimensional experiential construct tapping all the five modules proposed by our theory (however, depending on the type of stimuli, Dube and Le Bel's research revealed at times a combined sensory-affective type of pleasure).

2. The claim that the two levels are distinct and engage different processes (direct perception vs. inference making) must be tested. Measuring differential reactions to stimuli across different levels can do this. Respondents should be able to recognize stimuli more easily and quickly on the primary, evolutionarily determined direct-perception level than on the secondary, inferential level. Moreover, there should be greater interpersonal consistency at the primary level than the secondary level, and responses should be affected less by exposure time. Such evidence has been provided in several experiments for sensory, affective and intellectual modules (Brakus and Schmitt, 2000).

3. Evidence that supports the 'hierarchy of modules' claims must be provided. If the sensory, affective and bodily modules possess evolutionary primacy, then respondents should take less time to evaluate stimuli that trigger these modules compared to the intellectual and social modules, and this effect should occur at the primary level. Brakus and Schmitt (2000) have provided evidence for this claim in an experiment, comparing sensory, affective and intellectual modules. Moreover, Zajonc (1980) has shown that affect precedes cognitive responses, a finding corroborated by Pham et al. (1999).

4. Finally, empirical support should be provided for the usefulness of the strategic matrix that is part of the theory. This can be done through cases of successful applications and by developing strategic planning tools in line with the matrix. The authors have developed such tools, which are currently being tested in terms of their ecological validity and usefulness in several client projects by a major advertising agency. In addition, researchers should develop specific research tools, in line with the research methodologies proposed by Zaltman (1997), which will examine how managers make strategic decisions about their customers' experiences.

At the same time, our framework and theory of consumer experiences could have a positive impact on traditional research areas, even on those that may seem to be remote from its core, such as the areas of gender-related consumption patterns, discrete choice models, satisfaction and game theory. For example, as Saad and Gill (2000) have shown, the effect of gender on various consumer-related behaviors that has been traditionally investigated under 'social role theory' or 'socialization process' can be re-examined within the evolutionary framework. Regarding choice modeling, in addition to estimating choice models that account for latent brand attributes (Chintagunta, 1994; Elrod, 1988) or unique brand attributes (Elrod and Keane, 1994; Erdem, 1996), researchers should model the differential impact that experiential and functional attributes have on choice, variety seeking and habit persistence. Similarly, our theory – and the research resulting from it – also has the potential of complementing comparison-based models of satisfaction (Anderson and Sullivan, 1993; Oliver, 1980) with a view that shows that the experience of satisfaction is influenced by experiential cues in the consumption situation in addition to functional product performance relative to a pre-satisfaction standard or expectation. Finally, signaling research in game theory (Tellis, 1986) may benefit from exploring the

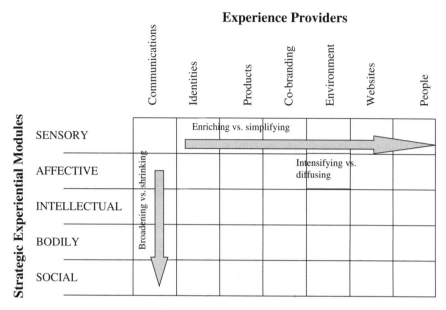

Figure 11.1   Strategic issues in the management of consumer experiences

possibility of signaling high quality through the appropriate choice of experiential attributes rather than high price – a notion that one might use to explain the recent strategy pursued by Apple Inc., which no longer uses a premium price strategy but does focus heavily on the customer experience.

STRATEGIC ISSUES

The theory of experiences is not relevant only for addressing specific research issues; it is equally pertinent to broader strategic marketing management issues. The key strategic marketing issues of the theory of consumer experiences are depicted in the matrix shown in Figure 11.1. The figure shows the types of experiences – termed 'strategic experiential modules' – in the rows and, in the columns, what we call 'the experience providers' – communications, identities (names, logos and signage), product design, co-branding, buying environments, websites and people. 'Experience providers' are the key implementation devices for creating marketing experiences. Given the embodied nature of cognitions, experience providers contain affordances to which consumers react by engaging experiential modules (that is, sensory, affective, intellectual, bodily, and/or social modules). At a general level, that is, the level that is appropriate for most strategic decisions, experience providers include communications (for example, advertising, PR materials, brochures), visual and verbal identity (for example, brand names, logos), product presence (for example, design and packaging), co-branding (that is, the presence of another company's logo or visual identity), retail environments, websites and people (for example, the uniform, the voice).

As the figure shows, there are three key strategic issues.

- Intensity. The intensity issue ('Intensifying vs. Diffusing') concerns individual grid cells. Should the specific experience provided in a given experience provider be experientially enhanced or diffused? For example, Hallmark Cards uses its greeting cards products and advertisements to induce an affective experience. The question is: what is the right level of intensity to induce the experience?
- Breadth. The breadth issue ('Enriching vs. Simplifying') concerns the management across the experience providers. Should the organization enrich a given experience by adding additional experience providers that provide the same experience, or simplify the experience by concentrating it into certain experience providers? For Hallmark, this decision may include the consideration of whether or not the firm should open 'experiential retail spaces' (as Nike and Starbucks have done), perhaps of the 'affective variety', in addition to its more functional selling spaces.
- Depth. The depth issue ('Broadening vs. Shrinking') concerns the management across strategic experiential modules: should the organization target only one single experiential module or should it target several modules at the same time? That is, should Hallmark use primarily symbolism that appeals to the affective module or perhaps consider additional symbolism to appeal to the intellectual module or to social modules?

The two-dimensional matrix shown in Figure 11.1 can be expanded easily to include a third dimension that may be strategically useful, depending on a firm's marketing strategy. For example, a firm operating on a global scale may add an additional country dimension and examine whether the same or different experiences should be provided in different country markets. Another dimension may be different target segments, thus resulting in experiential segmentation. Finally, a service firm may consider different steps in the service process (for example, before the flight, in-flight, after the flight in the airline industry) to target experiences at different steps in the extended service experience.

CONCLUSION

This chapter was guided by two objectives. First, we aimed to present an alternative to the traditional marketing paradigm of information processing and choice in the form of an evolutionary framework that takes into account recent work in cognitive science. The framework is guided by three assumptions: the mind that processes marketing stimuli must be thought of as 'embodied', it responds to 'affordances' and it is 'modular'. Second, to illustrate the usefulness of the new framework for the field of marketing, we presented an empirically testable theory of consumer experiences. The theory includes five types of experiential modules, two experiential levels at which modular effects occur, a hierarchy of modular responses and a strategic matrix that marketing practitioners will find useful for planning customer experiences. As part of the theory, we provided specific empirical predictions and preliminary evidence in support of these predictions. Due to the broad and ambitious nature of the framework and theory, additional systematic research programs are needed to examine the theoretical and applied aspects of the framework and theory.

Through the framework and theory presented here, we hope to provide an impetus to move beyond the mainstream marketing paradigm and consider alternative approaches. As we discussed, the current marketing paradigm often fails to explain some of the most interesting initiatives in applied marketing today (such as the cases alluded to in the beginning of the chapter). Moreover, the traditional paradigm of information processing and choice also imposes a set of restricting assumptions that have already been critiqued by alternative research streams. Finally, the paradigm as such has discouraged researchers from exploring the exciting phenomena that exist at the sensory, spontaneous-affective and social level – phenomena that are critical for achieving a complete theoretical and practical picture of marketing.

REFERENCES

Alba, Joseph W. and Howard Marmorstein (1987), 'The effects of frequency knowledge on consumer decision making', *Journal of Consumer Research*, **14**(June), 14–26.

Alba, Joseph W., Howard Marmorstein and Amikva Chattopadhyay (1992), 'Transitions in preference over time: the effects of memory on message persuasiveness', *Journal of Marketing Research*, **29**(November), 406–16.

Anderson, Eugene W. and Mary W. Sullivan (1993), 'The antecedents and consequences of customer satisfaction for firms', *Marketing Science*, **12**(Spring), 125–43.

Barkow, Jerome H., Leda Cosmides and John Tooby (eds) (1992), *The Adapted Mind: Evolutionary Psychology and the Generation of Culture*, New York: Oxford University Press.

Batra, Rajeev and Michael L. Ray (1986), 'Affective responses mediating acceptance of advertising', *Journal of Consumer Research*, **13**(March), 234–49.

Bettman, James R. (1979), *An Information Processing Theory of Consumer Choice*, Reading, MA: Addison-Wesley.

Bettman, James R. (1993), 'The decision maker who came in from the cold', in Leigh McAlister and Michael L. Rothschild (eds), *Advances in Consumer Research*, **20**, Provo, UT: Association for Consumer Research.

Bettman, James R., Eric J. Johnson and John W. Payne (1991), 'Consumer decision making', in Thomas S. Robertson and Harold H. Kassarjian (eds), *Handbook of Consumer Behavior*, Englewood Cliffs, NJ: Prentice-Hall.

Bourdieu, Pierre (1990), *The Logic of Practice*, Cambridge: Polity Press.

Brakus, J.J. and Bernd Schmitt (2000), 'Empirical tests of theory of consumer experience', working paper, Columbia University.

Brooks, R. (1994), 'Coherent behavior from many adaptive processes', in Dave Cliff et al. (eds), *From Animals to Animats 3: Proceedings of the Third International Conference on Simulation of Adaptive Behavior*, Cambridge, MA: MIT Press.

Carpenter, Gregory S., Rashi Glazer and Kent Nakamoto (1994), 'Meaningful brands from meaningless differentiation: the dependence on irrelevant attributes', *Journal of Marketing Research*, **31**(August), 339–50.

Chintagunta, Pradeep (1994), 'Heterogeneous logit model implications for brand positioning', *Journal of Marketing Research*, **31**(May), 304–11.

Clark, Andy (1997), *Being There: Putting Brain, Body, and World Together Again*, Cambridge, MA: MIT Press.

Cohen, Joel B. and Charles S. Areni (1991), 'Affect and consumer behavior', in Thomas S. Robertson and Harold H. Kassarjian (eds), *Handbook of Consumer Behavior*, Englewood Cliffs, NJ: Prentice-Hall.

Damasio, Antonio (1994), *Descartes' Error: Emotion, Reason, and the Human Brain*, New York: Grosset/Putnam.

Dewey, John (1922), *Human Nature and Conduct*, New York: The Modern Library.

Dewey, John (1925), *Experience and Nature*, revised edition, New York: Dover.

Dreyfus, Hubert L. (1991), *Being-in-the-World: A Commentary on Heidegger's Being and Time, Division I*, Cambridge, MA: MIT Press.

Dubé, Laurette and Jordan L. Le Bel (1999), 'Are all pleasures the same? An empirical test of unitary and differentiated views of pleasure', working paper, McGill University.

Einhorn, Hillel J. (1971), 'Use of nonlinear, noncompensatory models as a function of task and amount of information', *Organizational Behavior and Human Performance*, **6**, 1–27.

Einhorn, Hillel J. and Robin M. Hogarth (1975), 'Unit weighting schemes for decision making', *Organizational Behavior and Human Performance*, **13**, 171–92.

Einhorn, Hillel J. and Robin M. Hogarth (1981), 'Behavioral decision theory: processes of judgment and choice', *Annual Review of Psychology*, **32**, 53–88.

Elrod, Terry (1988), 'Choice map: inferring a product market from observed choice behavior', *Marketing Science*, **7**(Winter), 21–40.

Elrod, Terry and Michael P. Keane (1994), 'A factor-analytic model for representing the market structure in panel data', *Journal of Marketing Research*, **32**(February), 1–16.

Engel, James F., Roger D. Blackwell and Paul W. Miniard (1990), *Consumer Behavior*, 6th edn, Chicago, IL: Dryden Press.

Erdem, Tulin (1996), 'A dynamic analysis of marketing structure based on panel data', *Marketing Science*, **15**(Winter), 359–78.

Fishbein, Martin and Icek Ajzen (1975), *Belief, Attitude, Intention and Behavior: An Introduction to Theory and Research*, Reading, MA: Addison-Wesley.

Fodor, Jerry (1983), *The Modularity of Mind*, Cambridge, MA: Bradford Books and MIT Press.

Gibson, James J. (1966), *The Senses Considered as Perceptual Systems*, Boston, MA: Houghton Mifflin.

Gibson, James J. (1979), *The Ecological Approach to Visual Perception*, Boston, MA: Houghton Mifflin.

Goleman, Daniel (1995), *Emotional Intelligence*, New York: Bantam.

Harman, Gilbert (ed.) (1993), *Conceptions of the Mind: Essays in Honor of George A. Miller*, Hillsdale, NJ: Erlbaum.

Holbrook, Morris B. and Rajeev Batra (1987), 'Assessing the role of emotions as mediators of consumer responses to advertising', *Journal of Consumer Research*, **14**(June), 404–20.

Holbrook, Morris B. and Elizabeth C. Hirschman (1982), 'The experiential aspects of consumption: consumer fantasies, feelings, and fun', *Journal of Consumer Research*, **9**(September), 132–40.

Hoch, Stephen J. and George F. Loewenstein (1991), 'Time-inconsistent preferences and consumer self-control', *Journal of Consumer Research*, **17**(March), 492–507.

Howard, John A. (1977), *Consumer Behavior: Application of Theory*, New York: McGraw-Hill.

Howard, John A. and Jagdish N. Sheth (1969), *The Theory of Buyer Behavior*, New York: Wiley.

Johar, Gita V., Kamel Jedidi and Jacob Jacoby (1997), 'A varying-parameter model of on-line brand evaluations', *Journal of Consumer Research*, **24**(September), 232–47.

Johnson, Eric J. and John W. Payne (1985), 'Effort and accuracy in choice', *Management Science*, **31**(April), 395–414.

Kahneman, Daniel and Amos Tversky (1979), 'Prospect theory: an analysis of decision under risk', *Econometrica*, **47**, 263–91.

Kahneman, Daniel and Amos Tversky (1984), 'Choices, values, frames', *American Psychologist*, **39**, 341–50.

Kotler, Philip (1997), *Marketing Management: Analysis, Planning, Implementation, and Control*, 9th edn, Upper Saddle River, NJ: Prentice-Hall.

Kuhn, Thomas S. (1996), *The Structure of Scientific Revolutions*, 3rd edn, Chicago, IL: University of Chicago Press.

Lakoff, George and Mark Johnson (1999), *Philosophy in the Flesh*, New York: Basic Books.

LeDoux, Joseph (1993), 'Emotional memory systems in the brain', *Behavioral Brain Research*, **58**(December), 69–79.

Loewenstein, George F. (1996), 'Out of control: visceral influences on behavior', *Organizational Behavior and Human Decision Processes*, **65**(March), 272–92.

Mick, David Glen and Claus Buhl (1992), 'A meaning-based model of advertising experiences', *Journal of Consumer Research*, **19**(December), 317–38.

Mitchell, Andrew (1983), 'Cognitive processes initiated by exposure to advertising', in Richard J. Harris (ed.), *Information Processing Research in Advertising*, Hillsdale, NJ: Erlbaum.

Narayanan, S. (1997), 'Embodiment in language understanding: sensory-motor representations for metaphoric reasoning about event descriptions', doctoral dissertation, Department of Computer Science, University of California, Berkeley.

Newell, Allen and Herbert A. Simon (1972), *Human Problem Solving*, Englewood Cliffs, NJ: Prentice-Hall.

Oliver, Richard L. (1980), 'A cognitive model of antecedents and consequences of satisfaction decisions', *Journal of Marketing Research*, **17**(November), 460–69.

Olshavsky, Richard W. and Donald H. Granbois (1979), 'Consumer decision making: fact or fiction?', *Journal of Consumer Research*, **6**(September), 93–100.

Payne, John W. (1976), 'Task complexity and contingent processing in decision making: an information search and protocol analysis', *Organizational Behavior and Human Performance*, **16**, 366–87.

Pham, Michel Tuan, Joel B. Cohen, John W. Pracejus and G. David Hughes (1999), 'Affect monitoring and stimulus evaluation as alternative valuation pathways', manuscript under editorial review.

Pinker, Steven (1997), *How the Mind Works*, New York: Norton.

Plotkin, Henry (1998), *Evolution in Mind: An Introduction to Evolutionary Psychology*, Cambridge, MA: Harvard University Press.

Porter, Michael E. (1985), *Competitive Advantage: Creating and Sustaining Superior Performance*, New York: Free Press; London: Collier Macmillan.

Portnoy, Enid J. (1993), 'The impact of body type on perceptions of attractiveness by older individuals', *Communication Reports*, **6**(Summer), 101–8.

Puto, Christopher P. and W.D. Wells (1984), 'Informational and transformational advertising: the differential effects of time', in *Advances in Consumer Research*, **11**, pp. 638–43, Provo, UT: Association for Consumer Research.

Ritzmann, Roy E. (1993), 'The neural organization of cockroach escape and its role in context-dependent orientation', in Randall D. Beer et al. (eds), *Biological Neural Networks in Invertebrate Neuroethology and Robotics*, Boston, MA: Academic Press.

Saad, Gad and Tripat Gill (2000), 'Applications of evolutionary psychology in marketing', *Psychology and Marketing* (forthcoming).

Schmitt, Bernd and Alex Simonson (1997), *Marketing Aesthetics*, New York: The Free Press.

Shiv, Baba and Alexander Fedorikhin (1999), 'Heart and mind in conflict: the interplay of affect and cognition in consumer decision making', *Journal of Consumer Research*, **26**(December), 278–92.

Simon, Herbert A. (1955), 'A behavioral model of rational choice', *Quarterly Journal of Economics*, **69**, 99–118.

Simonson, Itamar and Stephen M. Nowlis (2000), 'The role of explanations and need for uniqueness in consumer decision making: unconventional choices based on reasons', *Journal of Consumer Research*, **27**(June), 49–68.

Spillman, Diana M. and Caroline Everington (1989), 'Somatotypes revisited: have the media changed our perception of the female body image?', *Psychological Reports*, **64**(June, part 1), 887–90.

Strong, Edward K. (1925), *The Psychology of Selling*, New York: McGraw-Hill.

Svenson, Ola (1979), 'Process descriptions of decision making', *Organizational Behavior and Human Performance*, **23**, 86–112.

Tellis, Gerard J. (1986), 'Beyond the many faces of price: an integration of pricing strategies', *Journal of Marketing*, **50**(October), 146–60.

Thaler, Richard (1985), 'Mental accounting and consumer choice', *Marketing Science*, **4**(Summer), 199–213.

Thaler, Richard (1998), 'Mental accounting matters', *Journal of Behavioral Decision Making*, **12**, 183–206.

Thompson, Craig J., William B. Locander and Howard R. Pollio (1989), 'Putting consumer experience back into consumer research: the philosophy and method of existential-phenomenology', *Journal of Consumer Research*, **16**(September), 133–46.

Tversky, Amos (1969), 'Intransitivity of preferences', *Psychological Review*, **76**, 31–48.

Tversky, Amos (1972), 'Elimination by aspects: a theory of choice', *Psychological Review*, **79**, 281–99.

Varela, Francisco J., Evan Thompson and Eleanor Rosch (1997), *The Embodied Mind: Cognitive Science and Human Experience*, Cambridge, MA: MIT Press.

Zajonc, R.B. (1980), 'Feeling and thinking: preferences need no inferences', *American Psychologist*, **35**(February), 151–75.

Zaltman, Gerald (1997), 'Rethinking marketing research: putting people back in', *Journal of Marketing Research*, **34**(November), 424–37.

PART IV

Empirical studies and scales for brand and experience management

In this part, the authors present and analyze recent empirical research and scale development in the areas of brand and experience management.

Ferraro, Chartrand and Fitzsimons examine the results of a variety of empirical research that provides insight into the ways that incidental brand exposure influences consumers without their awareness, intent or control.

Brakus, Schmitt and Zhang present the results of an experiment measuring how experiential attributes – such as color, shapes and affective cues – are processed, and how they affect consumer judgments, in comparison to the processing of functional attributes.

Zarantonello reviews consumer-based brand scales developed in marketing and consumer behavior literature, categorizing and analyzing each scale, and identifying the progressive shift from cognitive to relational to experiential scales for brands.

Sood and Zhang address the role of brand naming in branding strategies, presenting research studies on the effects of naming strategies on adult and child consumers, naming strategies with varied stimuli, and naming strategies applied to brand extensions.

12. The effects of incidental brand exposure on consumption

Rosellina Ferraro, Tanya L. Chartrand and Gavan J. Fitzsimons

Brand names and logos are pervasive in the everyday environment. They are under our feet at the supermarket, they serve as props in our favorite TV shows, they are visible on the side of the city bus driving by, and they are displayed on the clothing our friends wear. These are just a few examples of ways in which people are constantly and consistently exposed to brands in the course of their daily activities. Sometimes these brand displays are able to grab people's attention. Other times, however, this brand exposure is not the focal point of their attention, and as a result, people may or may not be aware that they have been exposed to brands in these contexts. Yet, even if people are unaware of the brand exposure, these brands may still be processed and have effects on subsequent attitudes and behaviors. This chapter focuses on the ways in which everyday brand exposure influences consumers without their awareness, intent or control, and explores how this non-conscious process occurs.

We refer to these types of brand exposures as *incidental brand exposure*. More formally, an incidental brand exposure refers to automatic processing of visual brand information while conscious attention is directed elsewhere. In this chapter we present evidence from research in both marketing and social psychology that supports the notion that incidental brand exposure can affect consumer behavior. This is a critical area to explore for both theoretical and practical reasons. Firms believe in the power of incidental exposure. For example, they are investing with increased frequency and monetary resources in product placement. Brands are increasingly appearing as central props in TV programs, Hollywood films and music videos (Posnock, 2004). Firms have turned to this method because its stealth nature allows it to be more innocuous than traditional print and television advertising, and can thus potentially influence perceivers without their attempts to avoid or counterargue the message. The brand appears as a realistic part of the scene, and as a result, consumers are not guarding against its potential persuasive power as they would with more typical advertising appeals (Friestad and Wright, 1994). Additionally, brands in these placements generally do not take center stage and so may not garner viewers' direct attention. Therefore, it is possible that their influence may be operating non-consciously.

Is this type of incidental brand exposure worth the expense? In other words, does it work? Interest in showing the effects of incidental exposure to brands has been ongoing since the 1950s when James Vicary claimed to have successfully used subliminal exposure (that is, stimuli presented below the threshold of conscious awareness) to increase consumption of products. Vicary claimed to have increased the sales of popcorn and Coke at a movie theater in New Jersey by exposing viewers to the words 'EAT POPCORN' and 'DRINK COKE' during a film at a speed too fast to be consciously noticed. It was later discovered that Vicary had fabricated his data. Since that time, numerous studies have failed to show an effect of subliminal persuasion on consumption behavior (see Greenwald et al., 1991; Moore, 1982; Trappey, 1996).

This research would suggest that incidental exposure to brands may have little to no effect on preferences and behavior. However, this prior research focused on subliminal persuasion, which requires subliminal perception and a change in attitudes or behavior, a fairly complex process. Incidental brand exposure, by contrast, may change behavior through a much simpler, more direct route when the brands are familiar to the consumer. Indeed, recent research in marketing and social psychology suggests that attitudes, choice and behavior can be influenced as a function of incidental brand exposure. In recent years, there has been an increase in research examining conditions under which visual stimuli, presented above or below conscious awareness thresholds, go on to affect attitudes and behavior without conscious awareness or intent. Epley et al. (1999) review research indicating that subliminally presented stimuli can be perceived non-consciously and that such non-consciously processed stimuli can then go on to affect high-level cognitive processes. We review some of that research below and also provide evidence for these effects when the stimuli are presented above conscious awareness but their subsequent influence is not recognized by the individual exposed to the stimuli.

THE BRAND–BEHAVIOR RELATIONSHIP

The most successful brands are those that have created strong associations between the brand and positive images and concepts (for example, Hallmark and caring, Volvo and safety). Firms spend millions of dollars developing and reinforcing these associations. Further, research by Aaker and colleagues (for example, Aaker, 1997; Aaker et al., 2001; Aaker et al., 2004) indicates that consumers attribute human personality characteristics to brands, characteristics that arise from the associations created by marketers. Aaker (1997) proposed a framework to identify and measure five key characteristics of brands: sincerity, ruggedness, sophistication, excitement and competence. These perceptions of personality characteristics are prevalent across cultures (Aaker et al., 2001). Not only do consumers identify these characteristics, they also respond to brands as if they possessed these humanlike characteristics. Aaker et al. (2004) showed that consumers felt more commitment to brands that were perceived as sincere than to brands perceived as exciting. But they responded more negatively to transgressions by the sincere brands, suggesting that consumers had developed links between these brands and expectations of responsibility and reliability.

Brand knowledge, including these associations, is stored in memory, resulting in the existence of an overarching brand knowledge structure that links all of its relevant brand associations. Research in automaticity has provided evidence that knowledge structures and their corresponding associations can be activated, and, once activated, influence subsequent judgments and behaviors to be in line with the activated concepts. This suggests that brand knowledge structures, like other knowledge structures, can be activated and hence influence judgments and behaviors corresponding to the activated associations. The automaticity literature indicates that such activation may occur via three routes that invoke the cognitive, evaluative and motivational systems, respectively (see Bargh, 1997; Bargh and Chartrand, 1999). Which route is in play determines the nature of the subsequent influence.

Cognitive Route

Within a brand context, the cognitive route of influence involves semantic activation of associations to the brand name (Anderson and Bower, 1973). As a result, preferences and subsequent behavior are influenced such that they are guided by these activated associations. This activation is a purely cognitive process. An example of a cognitive process can be found in Shapiro et al. (1997), who provide evidence that incidental exposure to an ad increases the likelihood that the product depicted in that ad will be included in a consideration set. The authors asked participants to read an article in the center column of what presumably was a magazine page on the computer screen. Participants believed that they would be tested on their memory and comprehension of the article. In the experimental condition, the target ads were placed outside of participants' focal view in the left column of the screen. No ads were shown in the control condition. The findings indicate that this peripheral placement of the ad resulted in an increased inclusion of the product in the consideration set even though participants did not process the ad attentively and did not recollect ever having seen it.

Evaluative Route

Evaluations, including global judgments as to whether an object is good or bad, were traditionally assumed to be made consciously and intentionally. In fact, models of attitude formation and of the evaluative process hold that one weighs the positive and negative features of the attitude object and with intention and deliberation makes a decision about how one feels about it. However, prodded by Zajonc's (1980) famous challenge to this position – that 'preferences need no inferences' – a substantial body of evidence has accumulated that one's evaluations often become activated directly, without one needing to think about them, or even be aware that one has just classified the attitude object as good or bad. Instead, just the mere presence of the attitude object is sufficient to cause the corresponding evaluation. The mere exposure phenomenon is an example of such an evaluative route affecting preferences. Zajonc (1968) showed that mere exposure to a novel stimulus is a sufficient condition for generating increased liking for that stimulus. In one of Zajonc's initial studies, he exposed participants to Chinese characters, varying the frequency of exposure. Participants were later shown the same characters and asked to indicate how 'good' they thought the meaning of the character to be. Zajonc found that as the frequency of exposure increased, so too did the favorable evaluations, although the marginal increase with each subsequent exposure began to decrease after approximately 12 exposures. Many studies since then have replicated this effect (for a review see Bornstein, 1989). Effects of mere exposure have been found when participants are aware as well as unaware that stimuli have been presented (Bornstein et al., 1987; Kunst-Wilson and Zajonc, 1980). However, the effects appear more potent when people are unaware of having been exposed to the stimuli (Bornstein, 1989). Thus, conscious awareness of the stimuli is not necessary to attain the positive effects of repeated exposure. Generally, the mere exposure research has involved exposure to novel stimuli such as Chinese ideographs, polynomials, unfamiliar words or unfamiliar faces.

Janiszewski (1988, 1990, 1993) examined mere exposure in the consumption domain, specifically focusing on incidental processing of fictitious brand name information. Janiszewski defined incidental exposure as exposure devoid of any intentional effort to process the brand information. In his studies, participants were given a study instrument meant to resemble a real newspaper. Participants were asked to read an article with the target brand advertisement presented peripherally to that article. The results across this stream of research indicate that incidental exposure to a brand name resulted in more favorable evaluations of that brand. This effect was enhanced when the presented stimuli matched the relative lateralized processing strength of the brain (that is, an incidental pictoral exposure will have a greater impact if presented in the left (versus right) peripheral visual field).

Can mere exposure influence choice? Ferraro et al. (forthcoming) examined whether repeated exposure to known stimuli, the Dasani brand, could extend beyond positive evaluation to actual choice behavior. Given that consumers are repeatedly exposed to the same brands in their daily interactions with others, the authors hypothesized that incidental repeated exposure to other consumers using a given brand could lead to increased choice of that brand. Further, they hypothesized that the type of person that comes to be associated with using that brand moderates the frequency of exposure effect. The authors presented participants with 20 photos of undergraduate students engaged in everyday activities such as waiting for the bus or eating lunch. They manipulated whether zero, four or 12 of these photos contained a Dasani bottled water near the focal individual, such that it appeared that the focal individual had chosen that brand.

After viewing the photos, the authors told participants that as a 'thank you' for their participation in the study they would receive a bottle of water and they were given a choice of four brands, including Dasani. The results indicated that choice of Dasani increased with the number of exposures to the brand in the photos. However, this effect was limited to only those participants who were not aware that they had been exposed to the Dasani in the photos. The authors further showed that associating a brand and a type of user can moderate this frequency of exposure effect.

Motivational Route

The third method through which incidental brand exposure may influence behavior is goal priming. Goals are desired end-states and thus motivational in nature. By their very definition, it seems a necessary condition that goals be consciously available and that behavior is consciously directed to achieving those goals. However, Bargh (1990) proposed that goal activation and pursuit could occur without conscious awareness and intention. The repeated activation and pursuit of goals in specific environmental contexts can lead to their automatization, resulting in the possibility that environmental features could activate goals and their subsequent pursuit without conscious awareness or intent.

Just as with intentional goal activation, once a goal has been non-consciously activated, the individual will pursue actions that allow him or her to move towards achieving that goal. However, the individual will not have any awareness that the goal was activated or that he or she took actions to achieve that goal. In one of the early papers showing non-conscious goal priming, Chartrand and Bargh (1996) asked participants to complete a scrambled sentence task as a means of supraliminally priming one group with an impression formation goal and one group with a memorization goal. In an ostensibly unrelated second study, participants then read 24 behavioral statements that described behaviors in four different trait categories. Participants primed with the impression formation goal recalled more behaviors than those primed with the memorization goal, replicating earlier findings using explicit experimenter instructions to memorize or form an impression. Further, they showed more organization of the material in memory. Importantly, the participants did not realize that they had the goal or that it was driving their information processing.

Bargh et al. (2001) showed that goals can be activated without conscious awareness and operate to effectively guide behavior. In one study, participants were given a high performance goal or no goal using a word search puzzle. Participants were asked to locate 13 explicitly provided words. Six of the words were neutral and did not vary across conditions. In the high performance goal condition, the seven remaining words were related to the concept of high performance (for example, succeed, achieve). In the neutral priming condition, these seven words were neutral in nature (for example, ranch, carpet). The authors measured performance using three additional word search puzzles, for which participants were not given the list of words to look for. As predicted, participants in the high performance goal condition found a greater number of words compared to the participants in the neutral priming condition.

In study 2, Bargh et al. (2001) primed the goal of cooperation versus no goal. In addition, the authors manipulated whether participants were given an explicit cooperation goal or not. Two participants completed the study at the same time. The cooperation goal was primed using a scrambled sentence task. In this task, participants were asked to create 4-word sentences from sets of five words. In the cooperation goal condition, 10 of the 30 sets contained words related to cooperation. In the no-goal condition, all 30 word sets were neutral with respect to cooperation. Participants then completed a resource-dilemma task in which they could harvest from a common resource pool that had to be replenished periodically (that is, fishing from a lake with a limited number of fish). The dependent measure was the amount of resource returned. After the scrambled sentence task, participants read the instructions for the resource task. The conscious cooperation goal participants were then given additional instructions stating that it was important that both participants cooperate and were told to set themselves the following goal, 'I intend to cooperate as much as possible.' Both the priming and the conscious goal conditions produced cooperative behavior. There was greater cooperation when participants were given the explicit conscious goal to cooperate. Importantly, participants in the no-conscious goal condition showed an increase in cooperation due to goal priming just as did participants in the conscious-goal condition.

It is important to distinguish between goal priming and semantic activation. Semantic activation does not have motivational qualities, while non-conscious goal pursuit does. Once a goal has been activated it persists over time until the individual achieves that goal. Motivational states increase in strength over time, and goal-directed individuals will persist in spite of obstacles or interruptions (Atkinson and Birch, 1970). Semantic activation of concepts, on the other hand, is a cognitive state and decreases in strength over time. Therefore, semantic activation dissipates in a relatively short period. Evidence for this comes from inserting a delay between the priming task and the relevant dependent measures.

In order to test this, Bargh et al. (2001) examined the effects of priming a high performance goal with and without a delay between the priming task and measurement of the dependent variable. A high performance goal or no goal was activated using word-search puzzles. The delay manipulation involved asking participants to draw their family tree. Two dependent variables were used; one perceptual and one behavioral in nature. For the perceptual measure, participants were asked to read a behavioral description of a target person (Donald), designed to be ambiguous with regard to whether Donald is a high achiever. The description included high performance, goal-related behaviors that could be understood as evidence of an achieving nature or as due to situational pressures; for example studying all night could be interpreted as evidence of an achieving nature or as evidence that Donald had not studied much previously. Participants were asked to rate Donald on six traits; half of these pertained to the degree to which Donald was a high achiever and the other three were achievement-irrelevant filler items. The behavioral measure consisted of three word-search puzzles. For the impression formation measures, goal primed participants rated Donald higher than did the neutral primed participants. Ratings of Donald were lower in the delay condition for the goal primed participants. The ratings did not differ across delay conditions for the neutral primed participants. In contrast, performance on the word-search task increased for goal primed participants after a delay. In the no-delay condition, performance was higher for goal primed participants than for neutral primed participants. With the delay, performance was significantly enhanced for the goal primed participants, while performance did not differ for the neutral primed participants. These results suggest that the perceptual effects of priming decayed over time, whereas the motivational effects increased over time.

Since brands are an integral feature of the environment and because they involve developed associations, they too can activate goals. Fitzsimons et al. (2008) showed that brands with certain associations can activate goals related to those associations. They specifically examined the association of Apple Computers and creativity. Apple Computers has diligently worked to create associations for its brand that reflect creativity, innovation and ingenuity. The authors hypothesized that exposure to the Apple logo would activate the associated construct of creativity and would trigger the goal to be creative. As a result, participants would exhibit greater creativity in a subsequent task. The authors subliminally primed participants with the Apple Computers logo, the IBM logo, or a neutral pattern. The IBM brand was used because a pretest confirmed that although it does not have an association with creativity, it is generally viewed positively.

Creativity was measured using an alternative uses task, a standard measure of creativity (for example, Eisenberger et al., 1998; Glover and Gary, 1976). In this task, participants were asked to list as many alternative uses as they could come up with for a brick (for example, as a hammer). Participants primed with the Apple logo came up with more uses for the brick than did either the control group or the IBM group. In addition, those uses were rated by a set of judges as more creative than either the control group or the IBM group. These measures did not differ across the control and IBM groups.

Importantly, participants did not express awareness of what was presented during the subliminal priming task or awareness that their behavior had been influenced.

To show that this process was goal priming and not trait or stereotype priming, the authors conducted another study that was identical in nature to the study just described but included a delay between the priming task and the brick uses measure. The authors found that the participants primed with the Apple logo showed greater creativity than did either the control or the IBM group in the no-delay condition, but importantly, this difference was enhanced in the delay condition. This suggests that more than just semantic activation occurred as the effect persisted beyond the delay period; in other words, a creativity goal was activated.

As further evidence of the ability of brands to prime goals, the authors conducted an additional study showing that the need to fulfill the goal dissipated after progress was made towards achieving that goal via another outlet. The authors primed participants with either the Disney Channel brand logo or the E! Channel brand logo. A pretest indicated that although the Disney and E! channels are rated equally positively, the Disney Channel is perceived as honest, while the E! Channel is perceived as neutral in the honesty dimension. In this study, participants were supraliminally primed using a brand logo rating task. Participants were asked to rate various fonts and colors of television channel logos, with the Disney or E! channel logos comprising 25 per cent of the logos rated. The other logos did not differ across conditions. Participants were given an opportunity to fulfill the honesty goal by responding to a goal progress question related to honesty. The control group was not asked a goal-progress question. The distinction between the low- and high-progress conditions was that the question in the low-progress condition referred to thinking about changes one could make to become more honest, whereas the question in the high-progress question referred to thinking about behaviors that actually show they are an honest person. All participants then completed a social desirability measure as the measure of honesty. Disney-primed participants scored higher in honesty than did the E!-primed participants in the low and control conditions. However, in the high-progress condition, the Disney-primed participants did not differ from the E!-primed participants. This suggests that in the high-progress condition, participants were given the opportunity to satisfy their honesty goal and hence did not need to exhibit honesty on the social desirability measure.

As a further example of a brand's ability to activate goals, Chartrand et al. (forthcoming) used subliminal exposure to activate prestige or value goals using prestige- or value-oriented retail brands. The authors subliminally exposed participants to names of upscale (Tiffany, Neiman Marcus and Nordstrom) or value (Wal-Mart, Kmart and Dollar Store) retailers. Participants were then presented with two different options of socks and microwaves, of which one option was a prestige option and the other a value option. The socks were Nike socks sold for $5.25 a pair (prestige option) or Hanes socks sold for $6 for two pairs (value option). The microwave options were a Haier microwave for $69 (value option) or a Sharp microwave for $99 (prestige option). Participants were asked to indicate their relative preference for the two options on a 1–7 scale anchored by 'strong preference for [the value option]' and 'strong preference for [the prestige option]'. For both products, participants expressed stronger relative preference for the value option when they had been primed with the valued-oriented brands than when primed with the prestige brands. Importantly, none of the participants made the connection linking the priming task to the choice task.

CONCLUSIONS

Summary

The research presented in this chapter provides strong evidence for the ability of brands to activate evaluations, semantic associations, and goals. Incidental exposure to brands led to increased choice of that brand and greater relative preference for the brand. For example, incidental repeated exposure to the Dasani brand led to increased choice of that brand. Subliminal exposure to prestige brands led to increased preference for prestige product options. The various effects reported above also reflect the variance in the nature of the exposure itself. The various effects occurred whether the brand exposure was subliminal or supraliminal in nature, suggesting that these influences operate whether or not the exposure is available for conscious processing. This suggests that even if consumers are not consciously aware that they have seen the brand, it still can influence them. In sum, the evidence to date suggests that incidental exposure to brands can lead to changes in preferences, choices and behaviors.

Implications

The ability of brands to influence preferences and behaviors via everyday exposures implies that people are more affected by brands in the environment than initially thought. This influence works at a non-conscious level, and by that we mean that even if the brand is processed consciously, its effects are not consciously known or intended. The effects do not arise from conscious consideration of brand information, but from processes that occur without conscious knowledge or intent. As a result, exposure to brands in our everyday context, outside of direct advertising attempts, can have a big influence on behavior. For example, we may not realize that being exposed to someone walking by carrying a can of Coke can impact our choice for that product. And, consumers' ability to protect themselves from such influences is limited.

From a practical perspective, firms must understand and control the automatic associations people have of their brands. Clearly, these associations are relevant when consumers make choices after conscious consideration of brand information. Importantly, as this research shows, these associations are also relevant when consumers do not know they are processing that brand information. Firms must work to create and continuously reinforce the specific image that they wish their product to have. Consideration of these associations must go well beyond simple positive versus negative. Take two brands, one of which has a positive, creative image, and one which has a positive, hyper-athletic image. Both generate equally positive associations, but the creative brand will activate a desire to be more creative, a goal that can be satisfied by a wide variety of consumers in a wide variety of contexts. A goal to be hyper-athletic by contrast, may be very difficult to satisfy for most consumers. Thus, incidental exposure and even use of these two brands may lead one consumer to be positive and satisfied while the other consumer starts positive and becomes increasingly dissatisfied, all outside his or her awareness (see Chartrand (2008) for a discussion of potentially negative effects of 'mystery moods', or affective states individuals cannot attribute to a particular cause).

Another implication of this research is that incidental exposure may be just as power-ful, if not more so, than traditional advertising. Traditional advertising works by inform-ing and reinforcing, but it is subject to avoidance and counter-argumentation by the perceiver. Thus, it is not surprising to see increases in spending on alternative marketing tactics, such as product placement or guerilla marketing. These tactics place the brand in seemingly real contexts. In these instances, there is limited possibility that the perceiver will act to limit the brand's influence potential.

Future Research

One critical aspect of the influence of incidental brand exposure is that people are not aware of exposure to the brand. An interesting question to consider is what might occur when people are aware of the brand and of its potential influence over them. Imagine you leave a cafe in which another customer is using an Apple computer. As you are leaving you are asked what type of computer the other patron was using, and are able to report that it was an Apple computer. But had you not been asked it is unlikely that you would have consciously processed the fact that another patron was using an Apple computer. Had you walked out without being asked a question, would you find yourself more cre-ative, analogous to the true non-conscious exposure in Fitzsimons et al. (2008), or would you perhaps consciously 'correct' for any potential influence another patron's laptop selection might have upon you?

The effects of incidental exposure may be more potent when there is a complete lack of conscious awareness, as conscious awareness may stimulate conscious correction processes if people are aware that the brand exposure might affect their choice in specific ways (Wegener and Petty, 1995; Wilson and Brekke, 1994). In mere exposure studies, increased liking tends to attenuate after a relatively small number of exposures when par-ticipants are aware of the stimulus but not under subliminal exposure, suggesting that some type of correction is occurring (Bornstein, 1989). Janiszewski (1993) also suggests that consumers will be most susceptible to the influence of familiarity with a brand whenever they do not actively use recognition or frequency information to discount its influence.

The effects reported here have not been examined in the long term. In many situations where we might be exposed to a brand, there is no immediate outlet to buy that brand. So, from a practical perspective, knowing how long these effects last is critical. Evidence suggests that semantic activation effects are short-lived as activation dissipates. However, there is evidence that mere exposure effects can last for some time after the exposure. Murphy and Zajonc (1993) and Winkielman et al. (1997) provide evidence that affective response to stimuli presented in an earlier block of materials persisted and was difficult to override with stimuli presented in a later block of materials. If semantic activation can affect preferences in the immediate term, these changes in preferences may persist and can potentially last until the appropriate situation arises for the corresponding behavior to occur. We also know that goals persist until they are fulfilled or displaced. This suggests that goals that have been activated by brands can last for some time as they wait to be fulfilled and, as a result, can potentially carry over until the purchase situation arises. Therefore, it is important to formally hypothesize and examine the extent to which these effects might last.

Finally an important avenue to explore is what occurs when a brand's associations are negative. For example, as attitudes towards smoking have changed, people's associations for brands such as Marlboro may have become very negative. Will incidental exposure to the Marlboro brand lead to increased preference for the brand as mere exposure indicates, or would the effects be consistent with the negative associations with that brand or smoking in general? Further, some brands with positive associations could be linked to negative goals. For instance, a high end brand such as Mercedes may have positive associations but may also be linked to goals which are perceived negatively by society, such as materialism. In these situations there appears to be a conflict between the semantic activation of the concept and the activation of the goal. What would happen in this instance? Does the motivational influence of the goal override the cognitive influence of the concept?

There is a great deal of future research to be done exploring these interesting and important issues involving behavioral effects of incidental brand exposure.

REFERENCES

Aaker, Jennifer (1997), 'Dimensions of brand personality', *Journal of Marketing Research*, **34**, 347–57.

Aaker, Jennifer, V. Benet-Martinez and J. Garolera (2001), 'Consumption symbols as carriers of culture: a study of Japanese and Spanish brand personality constructs', *Journal of Personality and Social Psychology*, **81**, 492–508.

Aaker, Jennifer, Susan Fournier and Adam Brasel (2004), 'When good brands do bad', *Journal of Consumer Research*, **31** (1), 1–16.

Anderson, John R. and Gordon H. Bower (1973), *Human Associative Memory*, Washington, DC: Winston.

Atkinson, J.W. and D. Birch (1970), *The Dynamics of Action*, New York: Wiley.

Bargh, John A. (1990), 'Auto-motives: preconscious determinants of social interaction', in E. Higgins and R.M. Sorrentino (eds), *Handbook of Motivation and Cognition: Foundations of Social Behavior, vol. 2*, New York: Guilford Press, pp. 93–130.

Bargh, John A. (1997), 'The automaticity of everyday life', in R.S. Wyer, Jr. (ed.), *The Automaticity of Everyday Life: Advances in Social Cognition*, vol. 10, Mahwah, NJ: Erlbaum, pp. 1–61.

Bargh, John, A. and Tanya L. Chartrand (1999), 'The unbearable automaticity of being', *American Psychologist*, **54**, 462–79.

Bargh, John. A., Peter M. Gollwitzer, Annette Lee-Chai, Kimberly Barndollar and Roman Trotschel (2001), 'The automated will: nonconscious activation and pursuit of behavioral goals', *Journal of Personality and Social Psychology*, **81**, 1014–27.

Bornstein, Robert F. (1989), 'Exposure and affect: overview and meta-analysis of research, 1968–1987', *Psychological Bulletin*, **106**(2), 265–89.

Bornstein, Robert F., Dean R. Leone and Donna J. Galley (1987), 'The generalizability of subliminal mere exposure effects: influence of stimuli perceived without awareness on social behavior', *Journal of Personality and Social Psychology*, **53**(6), 1070–79.

Chartrand, Tanya L. and John A. Bargh (1996), 'Automatic activation of impression formation and memorization goals: nonconscious goal priming reproduces effects of explicit task instructions', *Journal of Personality and Social Psychology*, **71**, 464–78.

Chartrand, Tanya L. (2008), 'Mystery moods and perplexing performance: consequences of succeeding and failing at a nonconscious goal', unpublished manuscript, Duke University, Durham, NC.

Chartrand, Tanya L., Joel Huber, Baba Shiv and Robin J. Tanner (forthcoming), 'Nonconscious goals and consumer choices', *Journal of Consumer Research*.

Eisenberger, R., S. Armeli and J. Pretz (1998), 'Can the promise of reward increase creativity', *Journal of Personality and Social Psychology*, **74**(3), 704–14.

Epley, Nicholas, Kenneth Savitsky and Robert A. Kachelski (1999), 'What every skeptic should know about subliminal persuasion', *Skeptical Inquirer*, September/October, pp. 40–45, 58.

Ferraro, Rosellina, James R. Bettman and Tanya L. Chartrand (forthcoming), 'The power of strangers: the effect of incidental consumer–brand encounters on brand choice', *Journal of Consumer Research*.

Fitzsimons, Grainne M., Tanya L. Chartrand, and Gavan J. Fitzsimons (2008), 'Automatic effects of brand exposure on behavior: how Apple makes you "think different"', *Journal of Consumer Research*, **35**(1), 21–35.

Friestad, Marian and Peter Wright (1994), 'The persuasion knowledge model: how people cope with persuasion attempts', *Journal of Consumer Research*, **21**(June) 1–31.

Glover, J.A. and A.L. Gary (1976), 'Procedures to increase some aspects of creativity', *Journal of Applied Behavior Analysis*, **9**(1), 79–84.

Greenwald, A.G., E.R. Spangenberg, A.R. Pratkanis and J. Eskenazi (1991), 'Double-blind tests of subliminal self-help audiotapes', *Psychological Science*, **2**, 119–22.

Janiszewski, Chris (1988), 'Preconscious processing effects: the independence of attitude formation and conscious thought', *Journal of Consumer Research*, **15**(2), 199–209.

Janiszewski, Chris (1990), 'The influence of nonattended material on the processing of advertising claims', *Journal of Marketing Research*, **27**(3), 263–78.

Janiszewski, Chris (1993), 'Preattentive mere exposure effects', *Journal of Consumer Research*, **20**, 376–92.

Kunst-Wilson, William Raft and Robert B. Zajonc (1980), 'Affective discrimination of stimuli that cannot be recognized', *Science*, **207**(1 February), 557–8.

Moore, Timothy E. (1982), 'Subliminal advertising: what you see is what you get', *Journal of Marketing*, **46**(2), 38–47.

Murphy, Sheila T. and Robert B. Zajonc (1993), 'Affect, cognition, and awareness: affective priming with optimal and suboptimal stimulus exposures', *Journal of Personality and Social Psychology*, **64**(5), 723–39.

Posnock, Susan T. (2004), 'It can control Madison Avenue', *American Demographics*, **26**(1), 28–33.

Shapiro, Stewart, Deborah J. MacInnis and Susan E. Heckler (1997), 'The effects of incidental ad exposure on the formation of consideration sets', *Journal of Consumer Research*, **24**, 94–104.

Trappey, C. (1996), 'A meta-analysis of consumer choice and subliminal advertising', *Psychology and Marketing*, **13**, 517–30.

Wegener, Duane T. and Richard E. Petty (1995), 'Flexible correction processes in social judgment: the role of naïve theories in corrections for perceived bias', *Journal of Personality and Social Psychology*, **68**(1), 36–51.

Wilson, Timothy D. and Nancy Brekke (1994), 'Mental contamination and mental correction: unwanted influences on judgments and evaluations', *Psychological Bulletin*, **116**(1), 117–42.

Winkielman, Piotr, Robert B. Zajonc and Norbert Schwarz (1997), 'Subliminal affective priming resists attributional interventions', *Cognition and Emotion*, **11**(4), 433–65.

Zajonc, Robert B. (1968), 'Attitudinal effects of mere exposure', *Journal of Personality and Social Psychology Monographs*, **9**(2), 1–27.

Zajonc, Robert B. (1980), 'Feeling and thinking: preferences need no inferences', *American Psychologist*, **35**(2), 151–75.

13. Experiential attributes and consumer judgments

J. Joško Brakus, Bernd H. Schmitt and Shi Zhang

Traditionally, marketers have focused on functional and meaningful product differentiation and have shown that such differentiation is important because consumers engage in a deliberate reasoning process (Chernev, 2001; Shafir et al., 1993; Simonson, 1989). However, nowadays products in many categories are functionally highly similar, and it is difficult for consumers to differentiate products based on functional attributes. An alternative way of differentiating is to emphasize non-functional product characteristics or certain aspects of the judgment context.

For example, the VW New Beetle brand has used unique colors and shapes very prominently. Apple Computers has used a smiley face that appeared on the screen of computers when they were powered up as well as translucent colors to differentiate, for example, its iMac and iPod lines from competitive products. In addition, Apple Computers has integrated the colors and shapes of the product design with the design of its websites and the so-called AppleStores. Similar approaches focusing on colors, shapes or affective stimuli have been used for other global brands as well and for local brands in all sorts of product categories, including commodities like water and salt.

Here we refer to such attributes, which have emerged in marketing as key differentiators, as 'experiential attributes' (Schmitt, 1999). Specifically, experiential attributes consist of non-verbal stimuli that include sensory cues such as colors (Bellizzi et al., 1983; Bellizzi and Hite, 1992; Degeratu et al., 2000; Gorn et al., 1997; Meyers-Levy and Peracchio, 1995) and shapes (Veryzer and Hutchinson, 1998) as well as affective cues such as mascots that may appear on products, packaging or contextually as part of ads (Holbrook and Hirschman, 1982; Keller, 1987). Experiential attributes are also used in logos (Henderson et al., 2003), and as part of the judgment context, for example, as backgrounds on websites (Mandel and Johnson, 2002) and in shopping environments (Spies et al., 1997).

Unlike functional attributes, experiential attributes are not utilitarian (Zeithaml, 1988). Instead, experiential attributes may result in positive 'feelings and experiences' (Schwarz and Clore, 1996; Winkielman et al., 2003). Yet, how exactly do consumers process experiential attributes? How can consumers use them to reach a decision among alternatives? Moreover, are there different ways of processing experiential attributes? In this chapter, we examine how experiential attributes are processed and how they are of value in consumer decision-making. We distinguish two ways of processing experiential features: deliberate processing, which is similar to the way functional attributes are processed, and fluent processing, which occurs without much deliberation. We identify judgment contexts in which consumers process experiential attributes deliberately or fluently, and show how consumers' judgments are affected by these contexts.

HOW DO CONSUMERS PROCESS EXPERIENTIAL ATTRIBUTES?

Deliberate processing is reason-based and often inferential (Broniarczyk and Alba, 1994; Brown and Carpenter, 2000; Carpenter et al., 1994; Shafir et al., 1993; Simonson, 1989). It occurs step by step and is goal-directed (Chernev, 2001; Fischer et al., 1999).

Deliberate processing may also occur for experiential attributes. For example, consumers can engage in inferential reasoning when they judge whether the color 'red' is the right color for the product or when they reason why a company may have put an affective symbol such as a 'smiley' face on the product. Such deliberate processing for experiential attributes is similar to the process that occurs on a regular basis for functional attributes or for so-called 'trivial' attributes (Brown and Carpenter, 2000; Carpenter et al., 1994).

However, experiential attributes may also be processed by circumventing deliberation. To account for such processing in judgment and choice contexts, especially for feelings and experiences, the concept of 'processing fluency' has been introduced (Schwarz and Clore, 1996; Winkielman et al., 2003). Highly fluent processing of an experiential attribute occurs when a consumer spontaneously gets an impression of the stimulus and responds to it in a direct and immediate way without consciously labeling the stimulus as a specific attribute (Dubé et al., 2003). Fluent processes are involved, for example, in spontaneous visual categorization and discrimination (Grunert, 1996; Schneider and Shiffrin, 1977; Tulving and Schacter, 1990). Fluent processes also occur when people engage in simple congruency matching tasks (Kelley and Jacoby, 1998; Roediger, 1990), for example when individuals discriminate one stimulus type from another (for example, color from shape) or when they distinguish one stimulus category from another (for example, visually presented experiential stimuli from textually presented functional information) (Edell and Staelin, 1983; Houston et al., 1987; Shepard, 1967). Fluent processing of stimuli results in more positive judgments (Schwarz, 2004; Winkielman et al., 2003). Fluency effects have also been obtained in consumer research; it has been shown that fluency affects the generation of category-exemplars, the formation of consideration sets and brand choice as well as judgments (Lee, 2002; Lee and Labroo, 2004; Shapiro, 1999).

Given the previous research and findings, we assume that functional attributes are always processed deliberately. However, processing of experiential attributes may occur deliberately or fluently, and we suggest that there are two factors that determine whether experiential attributes are processed deliberately or fluently. The first factor relates to the set of alternatives, specifically the nature of the functional attributes that are part of the product description: whether they are diagnostic or not (Shafir et al., 1993; Simonson, 1989). The second factor relates to the judgment context (the environment in which the judgment takes place), specifically the type of contextual cues that can prime experiential attributes: whether they are of a matching or non-matching stimulus type (Schmitt, 1994). We now examine different sets of alternatives and contexts to formulate hypotheses about how they may affect judgments about experiential attributes.

HYPOTHESES DEVELOPMENT

First, consider a situation in which there are only functional attributes – alternatives are not differentiated by experiential attribute, that is, a sensory attribute such as color and shape or an affective attribute such as a smiley face. This is a standard situation that has been used in many prior marketing studies. We use this situation to establish a benchmark or control condition. Based on prior research, consumers in this situation should engage in deliberate reasoning to determine which alternative is superior. Moreover, the context should be irrelevant: for context to act as a prime and affect evaluations, it is necessary that the contextual cue is perceptually or conceptually related to the stimulus to be judged (Winkielman et al., 2003). Since this is not the case here, the deliberate processing of the functional attributes should take place irrespective of the judgment context. Thus, we predict:

H1: When consumers judge two functional alternatives, consumers will focus on determining which alternative is superior and evaluate the dominating alternative more positively than the dominated alternative, irrespective of contextual cues.

Next, consider product alternatives differentiated on both functional and experiential attributes. A consumer faces such a situation when there are products in the marketplace that contain important functional features as well as experiential features (for example, a technology product like an Apple computer that delivers functional value but also prominently features experiential attributes).

If the judgment context is experiential, then the contextual experiential cues can serve as primes for the experiential attributes of the alternatives and affect judgments about them. Taking the experiential contextual cues into account, consumers can deliberately infer that the experiential attributes presented visually – in addition to functional attributes – may provide value to them. This inferential process is similar to that investigated for functionally trivial attributes presented verbally where consumers can infer value from the presence of such attributes (Brown and Carpenter, 2000; Carpenter et al., 1994). Moreover, the value provided by the visually presented experiential attributes should be independent of their type (for example, whether they are an attractive color or a smiley face) because of the mere fact that once experiential attributes are present in addition to functional attributes, consumers will infer that there is some value in these experiential attributes beyond the value that exists in the textually-presented functional attributes. In other words, the experiential attribute can make up for functional inferiority of a product.

However, if the judgment context, for example, the shopping environment or a website, is non-experiential, then, as in the prior situation, the functionally dominant alternative will be preferred because it will be seen as the superior product based on consumers' reasoning about functional attributes. Therefore we predict the following interaction:

H2a: When consumers judge two alternatives such that one alternative dominates the other alternative on functional attributes, but the functionally inferior alternative is differentiated with either a sensory or an affective attribute, consumers evaluate equally either alternative in the presence of experiential (sensory or affective) cues in the judgment context;

H2b: However, consumers evaluate the functionally dominating alternative more positively than the dominated alternative in a non-experiential context.

Finally, consider a situation in which experiential attributes and functional attributes are both present but the functional attributes are not diagnostic (that is, functional attributes have the same values for all alternatives). A consumer faces such a situation when products are comparable in functionality but possess an attractive experiential attribute. In this situation, functional and experiential value cannot be compared, as in the previous case. Most likely, therefore, the experiential context will draw consumers' attention to the experiential attributes of the alternatives, and consumers will engage in a spontaneous, simple visual categorization and matching of the experiential contextual cue with the experiential product attributes. This process will be a fluent one and result in positive evaluations (Schwarz, 2004; Winkielman et al., 2003). Thus, if the judgment context includes a certain sensory cue (for example, a specific color), consumers will most likely look for and notice when the cue matches with another sensory attribute of the same type (that is, another color). On the other hand, if consumers encounter an affective contextual cue (for example, a heart), they will most likely notice a matching affective attribute (for example, a smiley face). However, if there is no prime, that is, the judgment context is non-experiential, consumers will engage in deliberate processing of the functional attributes (as in the situation described first). Yet the deliberate processing of these functional attributes will make it hard for them to render a judgment: both alternatives are equally good. Thus, there will be no difference in consumers' evaluations of the alternatives in a non-experiential context in this situation.

H3: When consumers judge two functionally equally good alternatives and one of the alternatives is differentiated with a sensory attribute and the other alternative is differentiated with an affective attribute then:

H3a: Consumers evaluate the alternative with the sensory attribute more positively than the alternative with the affective attribute in the presence of sensory cue in the judgment context;

H3b: Consumers evaluate the alternative with the affective attribute more positively than the alternative with the sensory attribute in the presence of affective cue in the judgment context; however,

H3c: There is no difference in consumers' evaluations of the two alternatives in a non-experiential judgment context.

Next, we test our predictions in an experiment.

EXPERIMENT

Method

Overview
We constructed four judgment situations to test our hypotheses. In judgment situation 1, the benchmark to test H1, we asked respondents to evaluate two standard black computer

diskettes; one diskette was clearly superior to the other. The task was performed three times in three different contexts, which were defined by a banner ad in which we systematically manipulated one visual element to create a sensory, an affective, and finally a non-experiential context.

In judgment situation 2, we asked respondents to evaluate two computer diskettes; one diskette was functionally dominant, but the functionally inferior diskette was differentiated with a sensory attribute. The task was again performed for all three contexts. It was used to test H2.

Judgment situation 3 was similar to judgment situation 2 with the exception that the functionally inferior diskette was differentiated with an affective attribute. Again, the evaluation task was performed in three different contexts. It was also used to test H2; however for a different stimulus (affective rather than sensory).

Finally, in judgment situation 4, where we tested H3, we asked respondents to evaluate, in three contexts, two functionally equally good computer diskettes, but one of them was differentiated with a sensory attribute and the other was differentiated with an affective attribute.

Design

A 4 (judgment situation with two alternatives: functionally dominant vs. functionally dominated, functionally dominant vs. sensory, functionally dominant vs. affective, affective vs. sensory) $\times$ 3 (contextual cue contained in the banner ad: sensory, affective, non-experiential) $\times$ 2 (the two stimulus alternatives in each judgment situation) design was employed. Judgment situation was a between-subjects factor and the other factors were manipulated within-subjects. The dependent measure was likelihood of choosing each alternative on a seven-point scale (1 = 'definitely no,' 7 = 'definitely yes').

Stimuli

Three kinds of computer diskettes were created: the 'functional' diskette (that is, the regular black diskette), the 'sensory' diskette which had a transparent bright green color (sensory product attribute) instead of the standard black color, and the 'affective' diskette, which was a standard black diskette with a smiley face (affective product attribute) on it. Each diskette was described with five functional attributes. The values of the two critical functional attributes for the dominant alternative were 2HD (double high density) and 95 per cent magnetically shielded, whereas for the dominated alternative they were HD (single high density) and 90 per cent magnetically shielded. The values of the remaining attributes were the same for both alternatives (capacity 1.44 MB, IBM compatible, formatted). The attributes were presented on a sheet of paper attached to the diskette.

We pre-tested functional dominance by exposing 26 college students to a hypothetical choice situation where we asked them to choose between two standard black diskettes. Twenty-three of them picked the dominant diskette, $\chi^2(1) = 15.38, p < .01$.

We also conducted another pre-test to make sure that respondents perceived the sensory and the affective alternatives as equally attractive in the absence of functional attributes. Thirty-eight college students were randomly assigned to two groups, in which participants saw a 'prototype' of a diskette, either the sensory one or the affective one, and were asked to rate the attractiveness of the 'prototype product' on a seven-point scale (1 = 'not attractive at all', 7 = 'extremely attractive'). The sensory diskette received a rating of 4.89 and the affective diskette was 4.30, and the difference was not significant, $t(36) = 1.07, p > .28$.

Four different judgment situations were created, each of which consisted of two alternatives: A and B. In judgment situation 1, A and B were both standard functional black diskettes and A dominated B on the listed functional attributes. In judgment situation 2, A was the functional diskette and B was the sensory diskette and A dominated B on the listed functional attributes. In judgment situation 3, A was the functional diskette and B was the affective diskette and again A dominated B. And finally, in judgment situation 4, A was the sensory diskette and B was the affective diskette and A and B were equally attractive in terms of the listed functional attributes.

Participants and procedure
Ninety-eight college students, different from the ones who participated in the pre-tests, were randomly assigned to one of the four judgment situations. Participants were told that they would see some products and website banners. The specific instructions were:

> We would like to know your opinion about some products. As you can see, you have received a prototype of two computer diskettes. One prototype is marked 'Diskette A' and another is marked 'Diskette B'. For each prototype we also list the features that each prototype diskette has – density, percentage of magnetic shielding, whether the diskette is formatted or not, compatibility, and capacity. We are thinking about advertising these diskettes on a commercial web site and we have three banners in mind for the websites.

At this point, participants were given a color printout of each of the three website banners, one at a time, each being separately labeled as 'Banner 1' (or '2' or '3'). After seeing a banner, and before seeing the next banner, participants were asked to indicate the likelihood of choosing diskette 'A' as well as diskette 'B' on seven-point scales (1 = 'definitely not choose it', 7 = 'definitely choose it'). This rating process was repeated three times, and participants provided a total of six choice likelihood ratings. The order of presentation of banners was counterbalanced across participants.

The banner had the wording 'Welcome to the dot in .com', with the letter 'o' in the word 'dot' differently represented for sensory (a solid circle in orange color; the sensory contextual cue), affective (a heart; the affective contextual cue) and non-experiential (a normal lower case letter 'o') banner. We pre-tested whether the sensory and the affective banner were of the appropriate stimulus type (that is whether they were perceived in fact as 'sensory' and 'affective' banners). To do so, we showed a color printout of the sensory and of the affective banner to 26 college students, and asked them to rate each banner on six bipolar seven-point scales. The scales measuring sensory impact were 'this banner does not try/tries to have sensory appeal', 'this banner tries/does not try to engage my senses', and 'this banner is/is not focused on sensory appeal'. The affective scales were: 'this banner tries/does not try to appeal to feelings', 'this banner does not try/tries to be affective', and 'this banner tries/does not try to be emotional'. The appropriate items were reversely coded and a composite sensory (alpha = 0.69) and affective (alpha = 0.74) rating was computed. On the sensory composite scale, the mean rating for the sensory banner was 5.41 compared to a mean rating of 3.44 for the affective banner, $t(25) = 10.96, p < .0001$. Conversely, on the affective composite scale, the mean rating for the affective banner was 5.85 compared to 4.40 for the sensory banner, $t(25) = 10.04, p < .0001$.

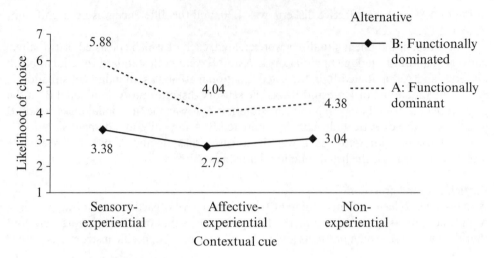

Figure 13.1   Alternative by contextual cue interaction: judgment situation 1 (benchmark)

Results

A $4 \times 3 \times 2$ mixed ANOVA performed on the choice likelihood ratings revealed a main effect of banners containing contextual information, $F(2, 180) = 21.26, p < .0001$, and a main effect of choice alternative, $F(1, 90) = 34.61, p < .0001$. The analysis also revealed a two-way interaction of judgment situation by alternative, $F(3, 90) = 3.53, p < .02$, and an interaction of alternative by contextual cue: $F(2, 180) = 6.46, p < .001$.

Importantly, the ANOVA revealed a significant three-way interaction, $F(6, 180) = 10.77, p < .0001$, indicating different likelihood of choice patterns for the alternatives across the four situations. Separate 2 (alternative) $\times$ 3 (banners containing contextual cues) ANOVAs on choice likelihood ratings were performed for each situation, the results of which are shown in Figures 13.1 to 13.4. Below, M stands for the mean likelihood of choice, the first index stands for alternative (A or B, see Figures 13.1 to 13.4), and the second index stands for the contextual cue contained in the banner (sensory, affective, non-experiential).

In benchmark situation 1 (Figure 13.1), the ANOVA revealed a main effect of alternative, indicating that respondents preferred alternative A ($M_A = 4.76$) over B ($M_B = 3.06$), $F(1, 23) = 20.99, p < .001$. This result was consistent with the manipulation of having A dominate B in situation 1 and supported our benchmark prediction (H1). In support of that prediction, the likelihood of choosing the functionally dominant alternative, alternative A in this case, was greater than the likelihood of choosing the functionally dominated alternative, alternative B in this case, irrespective of the type of the contextual cue: $M_{Asense} = 5.88 > M_{Bsense} = 3.38, t(23) = 6.19, p < .001; M_{Aaffect} = 4.04 > M_{Baffect} = 2.75, t(23) = 2.67, p < .02$; and $M_{Anonexperiential} = 4.38 > M_{Bnonexperiential} = 3.04, t(23) = 2.37, p < .03$.

In situation 2 (Figure 13.2), the ANOVA revealed a main effect of contextual cue contained in a banner, $F(2, 44) = 5.42, p < .008$, the main effect of alternative, $F(1, 22) = 4.10, p < .06$, and an interaction of contextual cue by alternative, $F(2, 44) = 6.81, p < .003$. When sensory contextual cue was used, choice likelihood ratings were similar for the

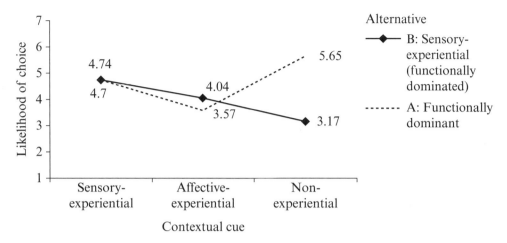

Figure 13.2   Alternative by contextual cue interaction: judgment situation 2

alternatives, $M_{\text{Asense}} = 4.70$, $M_{\text{Bsense}} = 4.74$, $t(22) = 0.07$, NS. Similar results were observed when the affective contextual cue was used, $M_{\text{Aaffect}} = 3.57$, $M_{\text{Baffect}} = 4.04$, $t(22) = 0.81$, NS. Hence, either contextual experiential cue, sensory or affective, primed either experiential product attribute, sensory or affective, and managed to offset the functional inferiority of the dominated alternative that was also differentiated with an experiential attribute. Therefore, H2a was supported. However, when the non-experiential contextual cue was used, the ratings were significantly higher for the functionally dominant alternative A than for functionally dominated alternative B, $M_{\text{Anonexperiential}} = 5.65 > M_{\text{Bnonexperiential}} = 3.17$, $t(22) = 4.18$, $p < .001$, because the respondents used the diagnostic information contained in functional attributes as the evaluation criterion, as was predicted by H2b.

As expected, the results for situation 3 (Figure 13.3) were analogous to those in situation 2. Again, the main effect of contextual cue was significant, $F(2, 44) = 5.28$, $p < .009$. The main effect of alternative was also significant, $F(1, 22) = 8.94$, $p < .007$. Importantly, the interaction of contextual cue by alternative was significant, $F(2, 44) = 12.48$, $p < .001$. When provided with the sensory contextual cue, respondents were equally likely to choose the functionally dominant diskette and the affective diskette, $M_{\text{Asense}} = 4.74$ versus $M_{\text{Bsense}} = 4.22$, $t(22) < 1$, NS. Similar results were obtained for the functionally dominant diskette and the affective diskette when respondents were provided with the affective contextual cue, $M_{\text{Aaffect}} = 3.26$ versus $M_{\text{Baffect}} = 4.09$, $t(22) = 1.53$, NS. However, respondents strongly preferred the functionally dominant alternative to the affective diskette in the non-experiential context, $M_{\text{Anonexperiential}} = 5.48$ versus $M_{\text{Bnonexperiential}} = 2.78$, $t(22) = 7.31$, $p < .001$. Thus, the effect confirming H2 was replicated with a different stimulus pair.

Finally, in situation 4 (Figure 13.4) where respondents had to judge the sensory (A) and affective (B) diskettes, which had equally attractive functional attributes, the results revealed a marginal main effect of alternative (in favor of the affective diskette), $M_A = 4.0 < M_B = 4.43$, $F(1, 24) = 3.21$, $p < .09$, and a significant interaction of contextual cue by alternative, $F(2, 46) = 15.15$, $p < .001$. When the respondents were exposed to the sensory contextual cue, they indicated a much higher likelihood of choosing the sensory diskette

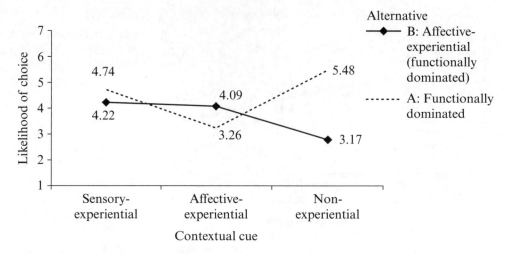

Figure 13.3   Alternative by contextual cue interaction: judgment situation 3

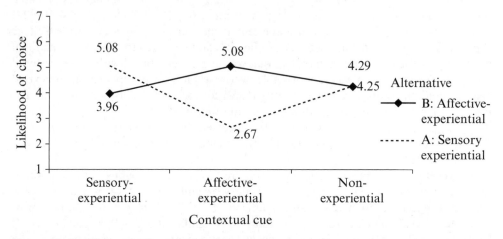

Figure 13.4   Alternative by contextual cue interaction: judgment situation 4

than the affective diskette, $M_{\text{Asense}} = 5.08 > M_{\text{Bsense}} = 3.96$, $t(23) = 2.41$, $p < .03$, as was predicted by H3a. In contrast, when the affective contextual cue was used, respondents' ratings were significantly higher for the affective than for the sensory diskette, $M_{\text{Aaffect}} = 2.67 < M_{\text{Baffect}} = 5.08$, $t(23) = 8.21$, $p < .001$, as was predicted by H3b. Finally, in the non-experiential context, no significant differences were observed, $M_{\text{Anonexperiential}} = 4.29$ versus $M_{\text{Bnonexperiential}} = 4.25$, $t(23) < 1$, NS, which means that the respondents based their judgment on functional product attributes in the absence of experiential contextual cues, and were equally likely to choose either alternative, because they were equally good on functional attributes, as was predicted by H3c.

Another way of testing the differential impact of experiential contextual information on consumers' judgments can be presented by analyzing the results across judgment situations (Figures 13.1 to 13.4). Below, M stands for the mean likelihood of choice, the first index stands for alternative (A or B, see Figures 13.1 to 13.4), the second index stands for the judgment situation (1 or 2 or 3 or 4, see Figures 13.1 to 13.4), and the third index denotes the contextual cue (sensory, affective, non-experiential). For example, when we compare the likelihood of choice between the functionally dominated alternative in situation 1 (alternative B; functional alternative with no experiential attribute) and the sensory alternative in situation 2 (alternative B) (see Figures 13.1 and 13.2), and these alternatives were *equally good functionally*, we see that in the sensory context respondents had greater likelihood of choosing the sensory alternative, $M_{B2sense} = 4.74$, over the functional alternative, $M_{B1sense} = 3.38$, $t(45) = 2.89$, $p < .01$. The same is true in the affective context: the likelihood of choice for the sensory alternative was $M_{B2affect} = 4.04$ and for the functional it was $M_{B1affect} = 2.75$, $t(45) = 2.45$, $p < .02$. The effect disappeared in the non-experiential context: $M_{B1nonexperiential} = 3.04$ for the functional vs. $M_{B2nonexperiential} = 3.17$ for the sensory alternative, $t(45) = 0.28$, NS, which we would expect since the two products did not differ on functional attributes.

A similar pattern of results can be obtained by comparing situations 1 and 3. This time we compare the functionally inferior alternative in situation 1 (alternative B; functional alternative with no experiential attribute) and the affective alternative in situation 3 (alternative B). Note again that these two alternatives were *equally good functionally*. In the sensory context the likelihood of choosing the affective alternative, $M_{B3sense} = 4.22$, was marginally greater than the likelihood of choosing the functional alternative, $M_{B1sense} = 3.38$, $t(45) = 1.65$, $p = .1$. In the affective context the likelihood of choosing the affective alternative was $M_{B3affect} = 4.09$; it was significantly greater than the likelihood of choosing the functional alternative $M_{B1affect} = 2.75$, $t(45) = 2.43$, $p < .02$. Similar to the previous comparison, in the non-experiential context the effect disappeared again: $M_{B1nonexperiential} = 3.04$ for the functional alternative vs. $M_{B3nonexperiential} = 2.78$ for the affective one, $t(45) = 0.56$, NS.

We can separate the influence of the sensory context from the affective context on judgment, as we previously did in situation 4, when we compare situations 1 and 4. This time we first compare the inferior functional alternative from situation 1 (alternative B; functional alternative with no experiential attribute) to the sensory (A) and then to the affective alternative (B) in situation 4. Again, in all these comparisons we examine alternatives that were *equally good functionally*. In the sensory context the likelihood of choosing the sensory alternative was $M_{A4sense} = 5.08$ and the likelihood of choosing the functional alternative was $M_{B1sense} = 3.38$. The difference between the two is significant, $t(46) = 3.64$, $p < .001$, because the sensory context increases the likelihood of choosing the sensory alternative. However, the likelihood of choosing the affective alternative and the functional alternative in the sensory context was the same: $M_{B4sense} = 3.96$ vs. $M_{B1sense} = 3.38$, $t(46) = 1.28$, NS. The results were exactly the opposite in the affective context. Basically, there was no difference in the likelihood of choosing between the functional and the sensory alternatives: $M_{B1affect} = 2.75$ vs. $M_{A4affect} = 2.67$, $t(46) = 0.20$, NS. However, the likelihood of choosing the affective alternative was greater than the likelihood of choosing the functional alternative in the congruent affective context: $M_{B4affect} = 5.08$ vs. $M_{B1affect} = 2.75$, $t(46) = 5.00$, $p < .001$. Finally, in the non-experiential context these differences in the likelihood were significant: $M_{B1nonexperiential} = 3.04$ for the functional vs. $M_{A4nonexperiential} = 4.29$ for the sensory alternative, $t(46) = 2.43$, $p < .02$, and

$M_{B1nonexperiential}$ = 3.04 for the functional vs. $M_{B4nonexperiential}$ = 4.25 for the affective alternative, $t(46)$ = 2.34, $p < .03$. This result indicates that the sensory and the affective alternatives were more attractive than the purely functional alternative.

Finally, although functional attributes were not the focus of the present study, it is interesting to note that functional attributes were negatively affected by the set of alternatives under experiential priming conditions. When we examine the data for functional alternatives in Figures 13.1 to 13.4 across situations, we note that in the same judgment context the same functional alternative (that is, the dominating alternative without an experiential attribute) was consistently evaluated worse when it was evaluated in a set of mixed alternatives (that is, against a dominated experiential alternative) than when it was evaluated in a set of purely functional alternatives (that is, against the dominated functional alternative). Specifically, in the mixed-alternatives sets (situations 2 and 3; Figures 13.2 and 13.3), in the sensory context, the means for the dominating functional alternative were $M_{A2sense}$ = 4.70 and $M_{A3sense}$ = 4.74 respectively, compared to the mean of $M_{A1sense}$ = 5.88 in the set of purely functional alternatives (situation 1; Figure 13.1), $F(1, 90) = 6.84$, $p < .02$. Similarly, in the sets of mixed alternatives (situations 2 and 3; Figures 13.2 and 13.3), in the affective judgment condition, the means of the dominating functional alternative were $M_{A2affect}$ = 3.57 and $M_{A3affect}$ = 3.26 compared to the mean of $M_{A1affect}$ = 4.04 in situation 1 (Figure 13.1), $F(1, 90) = 1.96$, NS. While this effect was non-significant ($p < .2$), it did occur in the expected direction. However, the functional dominance appears to be stronger in mixed-alternatives sets (situations 2 and 3; Figures 13.2 and 13.3) relative to the set of purely functional alternatives (situation 1; Figure 13.1) in non-experiential judgment contexts, $M_{A2nonexperiential}$ = 5.65 and $M_{A3nonexperiential}$ = 5.48 vs. $M_{A1nonexperiential}$ = 4.38, $F(1, 90) = 7.20$, $p < .01$.

Discussion

The results of our study strongly indicate that experiential attributes affect consumer judgments. As many products in today's marketplace are highly similar functionally and therefore difficult to differentiate on a functional basis, there is an alternative way to differentiate products: using experiential attributes and experiential contexts to affect consumer judgments and evaluations.

Specifically, when the products to be judged had functional attributes only, consumers evaluated the product with the functionally dominant attributes more favorably than the one with dominated attributes, irrespective of context. However, in situations in which both functional and experiential attributes were present, the experiential attribute (sensory or affective) was able to make up for the functional inferiority of the experiential alternative, when the judgment context included an experiential cue (sensory or affective). Finally, when functional and experiential attributes were both present but the functional attributes were not diagnostic, the alternative that was evaluated most positively was the one that matched the stimulus-specific context. That is, an alternative with a sensory attribute was most positively evaluated in a sensory judgment context, whereas an alternative with an affective attribute was most positively evaluated in an affective judgment context.

The results of the study indicate the operation of different processes in different situations. Unlike functional attributes which are processed deliberately, experiential attributes demonstrate processing flexibility and can be processed deliberately or fluently. Deliberate processing of experiential attributes occurs when consumers decide whether experiential attributes can offer value in addition to the value that functional attributes provide (as in situations 2 and 3). Fluent processing occurs when functional information is non-diagnostic and therefore cannot provide value for decision-making. Under such circumstances (as in situation 4), experiential contextual cues draw consumers' attention to the experiential attributes of the alternatives, and consumers spontaneously engage in a visual categorization process to match the experiential contextual cue with an experiential attribute of the same type. In other words, judgment context may be used either as a reason to justify the presence of experiential features, or it may be used to prime a specific category of experiential attributes that matches the judgment context.

The experiential stimuli used in our studies (for example, colored diskettes) are reminiscent of what have been called 'trivial' attributes in marketing research such as 'alpine class down fill' (for down jackets) or 'Brazilian high-altitude roasting process' (for coffee) (Carpenter et al., 1994; Brown and Carpenter, 2000). Trivial attributes are traditionally considered to be irrelevant features and to contribute little to product functionality; yet it has been found that they contribute value despite their lack of functionality (Carpenter et al., 1994). However, there are some critical differences between trivial attributes and experiential attributes. First, trivial attributes in previous research have been presented exclusively in verbal or textual form (Carpenter et al., 1994; Brown and Carpenter, 2000). In contrast, experiential attributes are mostly non-verbal visual stimuli. More importantly, trivial attributes *imply* functionality. For example 'alpine class down fill' suggests greater warmth protection and 'Brazilian high-altitude roasting' implies better taste (Carpenter et al., 1994). Thus consumers confer value to them through an inferential process based on this implied functionality. Experiential attributes, however, do not imply functionality. It is not clear why a diskette of a particular color, or with a smiley face on it, should be better on any functional dimension than a diskette with a different color or without a smiley face. Consumers thus cannot use experiential attributes to draw inferences about functionality. However, they can use experiential attributes to derive meaning or value that makes up for functional inferiority. For example, an attractive color or a smiley face can be seen as valuable as a functional attribute because it adds appropriate aesthetical or emotional appeal to the product.

One important issue for future research concerns the degree to which experiential and functional approaches are transferable across markets and cultures and to what degree they are culture-dependent. For example, it may be the case that experiential attributes are universal in their appeal and effect when they are processed fluently. However, when they are processed deliberately, personal and cultural meanings may influence their appeal and effectiveness. Another issue of future research concerns how experiential attributes affect choice. We suggest that experiential attributes be incorporated into choice models to determine how their presence affects choice probabilities. That is, in addition to estimating choice models that account for latent brand attributes (Chintagunta, 1994; Elrod, 1988) or unique brand attributes (Erdem, 1996), researchers should model the differential impact that experiential and functional attributes have on consumer brand choices, thus paving the way for experiential choice models (Degeratu et al., 2000).

From an applied marketing perspective, the present chapter explains, in part, the success of the recent product launches such as the Apple iMac and iPod, and the VW New

Beetle discussed earlier. Based on our research, an experiential approach can increase the likelihood of choosing a brand, especially when consumers perceive both the experiential attributes (for example, the color and design of Apple products) and the presentation context (the website and stores) as attractive and interrelated. Therefore companies should incorporate experiential approaches into marketing strategy to differentiate their products. This requires, first, that managers select those sensory or affective attributes that enhance the value of a product in the most effective way. Moreover, managers should be sensitive to the importance of the context in which the product is placed. That is, certain shopping environments, websites, and the design of certain communications can be beneficial or detrimental to product success (Buchanan et al., 1999). Most importantly, experiential marketing requires an integrated approach that gets the consumer to view the product, its packaging, its shopping environment, as well as websites and communications, as one consistent whole (Schmitt, 1999; Schmitt, 2003).

REFERENCES

Bellizzi, J.A. and R.E. Hite (1992), 'Environmental color, consumer feelings, and purchase likelihood', *Psychology and Marketing*, **9**(5), 347–63.

Bellizzi, J.A., A.E. Crowley and R.W. Hasty (1983), 'The effects of color in store design', *Journal of Retailing*, **59**(1), 21–43.

Broniarczyk, S.M. and J.W. Alba (1994), 'The role of consumers' intuitions in inference making', *Journal of Consumer Research*, **21**(December), 393–407.

Brown, C.L. and G.S. Carpenter (2000), 'Why is the trivial important? A reasons-based account for the effects of trivial attributes on choice', *Journal of Consumer Research*, **26**(March), 372–85.

Buchanan, L., C.J. Simmons and B.A. Bickart (1999), 'Brand equity dilution: retailer display and context brand effects', *Journal of Marketing Research*, **36**(August), 345–55.

Carpenter, G.S., R. Glazer and K. Nakamoto (1994), 'Meaningful brands from meaningless differentiation: the dependence on irrelevant attributes', *Journal of Marketing Research*, **31**(August), 339–50.

Chernev, A. (2001), 'The impact of common features on consumer preferences: a case of confirmatory reasoning', *Journal of Consumer Research*, **27**(March), 475–88.

Chintagunta, P. (1994), 'Heterogeneous logit model implications for brand positioning', *Journal of Marketing Research*, **31**(May), 304–11.

Degeratu, A.M., A. Rangaswamy and J. Wu (2000), 'Consumer choice behavior in online and traditional supermarkets: the effects of brand name, price, and other search attributes', *International Journal of Research in Marketing*, **17**(1), 55–78.

Dubé, L., M.-C. Cervellon and H. Jingyuan (2003), 'Should consumers' attitudes be reduced to their affective and cognitive bases? Validation of a hierarchical model', *International Journal of Research in Marketing*, **20**(3), 259–72.

Edell, J.A. and R. Staelin (1983), 'The information processing of pictures in print advertisements', *Journal of Consumer Research*, **10**(June), 45–60.

Elrod, T. (1988), 'Choice map: inferring a product market from observed choice behavior', *Marketing Science*, **7**(Winter), 21–40.

Erdem, T. (1996), 'A dynamic analysis of market structure based on panel data', *Marketing Science*, **15**(Winter), 359–78.

Fischer, G.W., Z. Carmon, D. Ariely and G. Zauberman (1999), 'Goal-based construction of preference: task goals and the prominence effect', *Management Science*, **45**(August), 1057–75.

Gorn, G.J., A. Chattopadhyay, T. Yi and D.W. Dahl (1997), 'Effects of color as an executional cue in advertising: they are in the shade', *Management Science*, **43**(October), 1387–400.

Grunert, K.G. (1996), 'Automatic and strategic processes in advertising effects', *Journal of Marketing*, **60**(October), 88–101.

Henderson, P.W., J.A. Cote, S.M. Leong and B. Schmitt (2003), 'Building strong brands in Asia: selecting the visual components of image to maximize brand strength', *International Journal of Research in Marketing*, **20**(4), 297–313.

Holbrook, M.B. and E.C. Hirschman (1982), 'The experiential aspects of consumption: consumer fantasies, feelings, and fun', *Journal of Consumer Research*, **9**(September), 132–40.

Houston, M.J., T.L. Childers and S.E. Heckler (1987), 'Picture-word consistency and the elaborative processing of advertisements', *Journal of Marketing Research*, **24**(November), 359–69.

Keller, K.L. (1987), 'Memory factors in advertising: the effects of advertising retrieval cues on brand evaluations', *Journal of Consumer Research*, **14**(December), 316–33.

Kelley, C.M. and L.L. Jacoby (1998), 'Subjective reports and process dissociation: fluency, knowing, and feeling', *Acta Psychologica*, **98**(April), 127–40.

Lee, A. (2002), 'Effects of implicit memory on memory-based versus stimulus-based brand choice', *Journal of Marketing Research*, **39**(November), 440–54.

Lee, A. and A.A. Labroo (2004), 'The effect of conceptual and perceptual fluency on brand evaluation', *Journal of Marketing Research*, **41**(May), 151–65.

Mandel, N. and E.J. Johnson (2002), 'When web pages influence choice: effects of visual primes on experts and novices', *Journal of Consumer Research*, **29**(September), 235–45.

Meyers-Levy, J. and L.A. Peracchio (1995), 'How the use of color in advertising affects attitudes: the influence of processing motivation and cognitive demands', *Journal of Consumer Research*, **22**(September), 121–38.

Roediger, H.L. (1990), 'Implicit memory: retention without remembering', *American Psychologist*, **45**(September), 1043–56.

Schmitt, B.H. (1994), 'Contextual priming of visual information in advertisements', *Psychology and Marketing*, **11**(1), 1–14.

Schmitt, B.H. (1999), *Experiential Marketing*, New York: Free Press.

Schmitt, B.H. (2003), *Customer Experience Management*, Hoboken, NJ: Wiley.

Schneider, W. and R.M. Shiffrin (1977), 'Controlled and automatic human information processing: I. Detection, search, and attention', *Psychological Review*, **84**(1), 1–66.

Schwarz, N. (2004), 'Meta-cognitive experiences in consumer judgment and decision making', *Journal of Consumer Psychology*, **14**(4), 332–48.

Schwarz, N. and G.L. Clore (1996), 'Feelings and phenomenal experiences', in E.T. Higgins and A.W. Kruglanski (eds), *Social Psychology: Handbook of Basic Principles*, New York: Guilford Press, pp. 433–65.

Shafir, E., I. Simonson and A. Tversky (1993), 'Reason-based choice', *Cognition*, **49**(October–November), 11–36.

Shapiro, S. (1999), 'When an ad's influence is beyond our conscious control: perceptual and conceptual fluency effects caused by incidental ad exposure', *Journal of Consumer Research*, **26**(June), 16–36.

Shepard, R.N. (1967), 'Recognition memory for words, sentences and pictures', *Journal of Verbal Learning and Verbal Behavior*, **6**, 156–63.

Simonson, I. (1989), 'Choice based on reasons: the case of attraction and compromise effects', *Journal of Consumer Research*, **16**(September), 158–74.

Spies, K., F. Hesse and K. Loesch (1997), 'Store atmosphere, mood, and purchasing behavior', *International Journal of Research in Marketing*, **14**(1), 1–17.

Tulving, E. and D.L. Schacter (1990), 'Priming and human memory', *Science*, **247**(January), 301–6.

Veryzer, R.W., Jr. and J.W. Hutchinson (1998), 'The influence of unity and prototypicality on aesthetic responses to new product designs', *Journal of Consumer Research*, **24**(March), 374–94.

Winkielman, P., N. Schwarz, T.A. Fazendeiro and R. Reber (2003), 'The hedonic marking of processing fluency: implications for evaluative judgment', in J. Musch and K.C. Klauer (eds), *The Psychology of Evaluation: Affective Processes in Cognition and Emotion*, Mahwah, NJ: Erlbaum, pp. 189–217.

Zeithaml, V.A. (1988), 'Consumer perceptions of price, quality and value: a means–end model and synthesis of evidence', *Journal of Marketing*, **52**, 2–22.

14.   A literature review of consumer-based brand scales

Lia Zarantonello

INTRODUCTION

Measurement cannot be disregarded in brand management, as it is an integral part of the process of planning, implementing, and evaluating brand strategies (Keller, 2003). Although branding has become a common practice and a well-established discipline since the 1980s, measurement of one or more aspects related to brands started only in 1990. Since then, a significant amount of attention has been paid to the concept and measurement of brand equity, which is considered the most important content to capture the value held by a brand for a specific target of consumers (Aaker, 1991; Keller, 1993, 2003). Over the last decade, scholars have developed measures aimed at capturing other dimensions of brands that were not comprised in the brand equity construct.

The purpose of the chapter is to review the brand scales that have been proposed in marketing and consumer behavior literature, and that have been conceived from a consumer perspective. Basically, scales are 'instruments that are collections of items combined into a composite score, and intended to reveal levels of theoretical variables not readily observable by direct means' (DeVellis, 2003, pp. 8–9), and allow scholars to reach at least two objectives: on the one hand, they help to understand constructs better and to develop theoretical frameworks; on the other hand, they constitute instruments that measure such constructs, in all their dimensions. Therefore, the review conducted here is useful for both practitioners and academicians. The former group might discover the existence of scales, different from brand equity, that can be employed in the management of their brands. The latter group may find information on areas that should be considered by future research.

To address this objective, the chapter is organized as follows. Before starting the review, I describe the criteria that were followed in order to identify and categorize the scales. After that, all the scales are presented. For each of them, a definition of the construct that the scale intends to measure will first be given. Secondly, the scale considered will be presented with reference to its structure (for example, number of factors), its items (for example, number and quality of the items), and the technique used it to rate it (for example, Likert or semantic differential scales). This will be followed by a description of the development and/or validation process, and an overview on the studies that originated from each scale after it was proposed in literature. In most cases, the description of the scale is enriched with comments on scale weaknesses or critical areas that should be improved. Finally, implications emerging from the literature review are discussed.

LITERATURE SEARCH AND CATEGORIZATION

The chapter reviews 12 published measurement scales that are related to brands and consumers. Journals from which the scales were drawn include *Advances in Consumer Research*, the *International Journal of Market Research*, the *Journal of Advertising Research*, the *Journal of Brand Management*, the *Journal of Business Research*, the *Journal of Consumer Psychology*, the *Journal of Consumer Research*, the *Journal of Marketing Research*, the *Journal of Marketing*, the *Journal of Product and Brand Management*, the *Journal of Sport Management*, and the *Service Industries Journal*. Scales considered cover the time period from 1996 to 2007. This was not an a priori condition, as journals published before 1996 were consulted as well, but no scales were found. As mentioned above, brand scales started to appear in literature only in the 1990s.

In order to identify the measurement scales to include in the literature review, three criteria were followed by the author. The first criterion established that the subject of the scale had to be the brand. This led to the exclusion of many scales whose primary focus was something different from the brand. For example, the literature is filled with scales that measure one facet of consumer behavior, from consumer involvement (Zaichkowsky, 1985) to consumer materialism (Richins and Dawson, 1992) to consumer desire for unique products (Lynn and Harris, 1997).

According to the second criterion, brand scales had to be conceived from a consumer perspective. Again, several scales had to be excluded. In the case of brand equity, for example, measures that view it from a company or a financial perspective (for example, Simon and Sullivan, 1993) were omitted from the analysis; only consumer-based ones were taken into account.

The third criterion referred to the methodology used to develop the scale. To be considered, scales had to be developed in accordance to traditional and well-established procedures of scale development (Churchill, 1979; but also Nunnally and Bernstein, 1994; DeVellis, 2003). According to Churchill's guidelines, researchers should first specify the domain of the construct (first step) and generate items which capture such domain (second step). They should then collect data and purify the measure (third and fourth steps), and iterate these steps until they obtain a satisfying outcome. New data should also be collected (fifth step), in order to assess both scale reliability and construct validity (sixth and seventh steps). At this point, researchers may develop norms (eighth step). Churchill's framework was later improved, thanks to contributions that applied structural equation modeling to the scale validation process (for example, Anderson and Gerbing, 1988; Fornell and Larcker, 1981; Bagozzi and Yi, 1988).

The scales that resulted from these operations are reported in Table 14.1. Once identified, the 12 scales were carefully analyzed. This analysis led to the identification of three groups of scales on the basis of their conception of both the consumer and the brand. The first group includes scales that rely on a traditional, cognitive approach to the consumer. The peculiarity of this approach is to focus on individuals' internal mental processes, the learning process, attitudes, the role of memory, and the decision-making process (Solomon, 2004). Scales included in this group are aimed at measuring brand equity; consumers' perceptions in specific fields such as sports, luxury, and non-durable goods; children's attitudes towards the brands; and consumers' tendency to use brand names in their decision-making process.

Table 14.1 Overview of the scales considered

Citation	Scale Purpose	Scale Structure	Samples/Studies	Validation process	Subsequent Research
Brand Parity Scale (Muncy, 1996).	To measure how much brands of non-durable goods are perceived as similar.	One factor with five items to be rated on a five-point Likert scale.	Pretests with student samples. Main study with 985 actual consumers.	No validity tests.	Iyer and Muncy (2005).
Brand Personality Scale (Aaker, 1997).	To measure the set of human characteristics associated with a brand.	Five factors, 15 facets, and 42 items to be rated on a five-point Likert scale.	Two pretests with 16 and 25 respondents each. Main study with 631 actual consumers; test-retest sample of 81 actual consumers. Confirmatory study with 250 actual consumers.	Tests of content validity. Convergent validity tested via exploratory factor analysis.	Among others: Siguaw et al. (1999); Aaker et al. (2001); Alvarez-Ortiz and Harris (2002); Wysong et al. (2002); Supphelen and Gronhaug (2003); Venable et al. (2005); Ekinci and Hosany (2006); Lentz et al. (2006); Okazaki (2006); Opoku et al. (2006); van Rekom et al. (2006).
Brand Attitude Scale for Children (Pecheux and Derbaix, 1999)	To measure children's attitude towards brands.	Two factors with seven items to be rated on a four-point Likert scale. The scale developed is in French.	Pretests with mothers, teachers and children. First data collection with 155 children. Second data collection with 149 children. Test-retest study with 198 children. Validity study with 53 children.	Tests of content validity. Test of construct validity (i.e., convergent and discriminant) via multitrait-multimethod matrix. Test of discriminant validity (AVE and confidence interval around correlation estimates).	Pecheux and Derbaix (2002).
Multidimensional Brand Equity Scale (Yoo and Donthu, 2001)	To measure consumer-based brand equity.	Three factors with 10 items to be rated on a five-point Likert scale. Scale was developed both in English and Korean.	Pilot study with 414 students. Main study with 1530 students.	Tests of content and convergent validity. Construct validity partially tested.	Washburn and Plank (2002); Kim and Kim (2004); Atilgan et al. (2005); Pappu et al. (2005).

Scale	Purpose	Structure	Studies	Validity tests	Sources
Brand Community Integration Scale (McAlexander et al., 2002)	To measure consumers' integration in a band community.	Three factors with 13 items (of which two are not reported for privacy reasons).	Pretest with participants to a brandfest. Pretest study completed by 453 participants; post-test study by 259.	Test of content validity. Test of convergent validity (AVE). Chi-square test. ANOVA.	McAlexander et al. (2003). Algesheimer et al. and Herrmann (2005). Quinn and Devasagayam (2005).
Brand Dependence Scale (Bristow et al., 2002)	To measure the tendency of consumers to use brand names in their decision-making process.	One factor with seven items to be rated on a six-point Likert scale.	Pretest with 40 students. Main study with 208 students.	Tests of content validity. Test of convergent and discriminant validity via exploratory factor analysis. Test of predictive validity was questionable.	—
Brand Trust Scale (Delgado-Ballester et al., 2003; Delgado-Ballester, 2004)	To measure the level of trust a consumer has in a brand.	Two factors with four items each to be rated on a five-point-Likert scale.	Pretests with six consumers and five experts. Main study with 272 actual consumers. Validation study with 127 actual consumers.	Tests of content, convergent (AVE and indicator's loadings analysis) and discriminant validity (confidence interval around factor correlation estimates, chi-square test, and AVE).	Delgado-Ballester and Mununera-Alemán (2005).
Centrality of Visual Product Aesthetics Scale (Bloch et al., 2003)	To measure the importance that visual aesthetics holds for a consumer.	One factor with 11 items to be rated on a five-point Likert scale.	Pretests with four experts, five marketing faculty/students, and four judges. Main study with 318 actual consumers. Confirmatory study with 136 consumers. Five validity studies with 108, 53, 190, and 165 students, and 62 experts each.	Tests of content validity. Test of convergent validity (examination of item reliabilities). Lagrangian multiplier tests. Tests of discriminant validity (chi-square test and AVE). Test of construct validity.	—

Table 14.1 (continued)

Citation	Scale Purpose	Scale Structure	Samples/Studies	Validation process	Subsequent Research
Brand Luxury Index Scale (Vigneron and Johnson, 2004)	To measure how much a brand is perceived as luxurious.	Five factors with 20 items to be rated on a seven-point semantic differential scale.	Pretests with 12 managers, 25 students, and 77 experts. Main study with 884 students. Reliability study with 186 students. Validity studies with 1322 students in total (186 + 463 + 331 + 342).	Tests of content, predictive, and nomological validity. Construct validity (i.e., convergent and discriminant) tested via multitrait-multimethod matrix.	–
Emotional Attachment Scale (Thomson et al., 2005)	To measure how much consumers are emotionally attached to brands.	Three factors with 10 items to be rated on a seven-point Likert scale.	Pretest with 68 students. Main study with 120 students. Reliability study with 65 students. Two validity studies with 184 and 179 students each.	Tests of content, convergent, and predictive validity. Discriminant tested via exploratory factor analysis.	–
Team Brand Association Scale in Professional Sports (Ross et al., 2006)	To measure consumers' associations on professional sport team brands.	Eleven factors with 41 items to be rated on a seven-point Likert scale.	Pretest with 40 students. Main study with 367 students. Face validity study with three experts. Validity study with 447 students.	Test of content validity. Tests of convergent and discriminant validity (indicator's loadings analysis, residuals matrix, confidence interval around the correlation estimates, and AVE). Test of criterion-related validity.	–
Brand Experience Scale (Zarantonello et al., 2007)	To measure experiences generated by brands.	Three factors with 12 items to be rated on a seven-point Likert scale.	Pretests with experts, 30 students, and 68 students. Main study with 293 students. Confirmatory study with 193 students.	Tests of content validity.	

Table 14.2   The output of the scale categorization process

Group	Scales
Cognitive	<ul><li>Multidimensional Brand Equity Scale</li><li>Team Brand Association Scale in Professional Sports</li><li>Brand Luxury Index Scale</li><li>Brand Parity Scale</li><li>Brand Attitude Scale for Children</li><li>Brand Dependence Scale</li></ul>
Relational	<ul><li>Brand Personality Scale</li><li>Brand Trust Scale</li><li>Emotional Attachment Scale</li><li>Brand Community Integration Scale</li></ul>
Experiential	<ul><li>Centrality of Visual Product Aesthetics Scale</li><li>Brand Experience Scale</li></ul>

The second group comprises scales that are founded on a more recent and innovative approach definable as 'relational' (Fournier, 1998). In this perspective, the brand is viewed as an active partner rather than a passive object; it is believed to be animated and to have its own personality. As a consequence, the relationships between consumers and brands are treated as relationships between individuals. In fact, the scales belonging to this group consider such dimensions as the personality of brands, the amount of trust consumers put in brands, and consumers' emotional attachment to brands, as well as the relationship between consumers and brand communities.

The last group includes scales that originated from the experiential view of consumer behavior, developed in the 1980s (Holbrook and Hirschman, 1982; Hirschman and Holbrook, 1982) and recently established in the field of branding (for example, Schmitt, 1999, 2003; Smith and Wheeler, 2002). According to this perspective, consumers are not mere rational decision-makers. They are driven by emotions in many circumstances of their life. Moreover, aspects such as aesthetics, hedonic responses, leisure, creativity and fantasies, neglected by the traditional view of consumer behavior, play an important role in consumers' activities. There are two instruments that have been developed to measure one or more of these aspects. One is focused on the impact that a specific brand expression (that is, the product) has on consumers. The other one starts from a broader, holistic view of consumers' experience, and attempts to measure in all its dimensions.

The three groups that were identified, as well as the scales composing each of them, are summarized in Table 14.2.

COGNITIVE SCALES

Multidimensional Brand Equity Scale

Since Farquhar's definition of brand equity as 'the "added value" with which a given brand endows a product' (Farquhar, 1989, p. 24), other scholars have given their definition of that concept (for example, Aaker, 1991; Keller, 2003). The lack of agreement of what brand equity is has resulted in a variety of methods and techniques to measure it. Yoo and Donthu (2001) were the first to develop a consumer-based brand equity scale by following a rigorous procedure. They conducted studies in two countries simultaneously (the US and South Korea), thus obtaining a measure which was not only reliable, valid, parsimonious, and generalizable across products, but also generalizable across cultures.

More specifically, Yoo and Donthu's Multidimensional Brand Equity (MBE) scale is composed of 10 items grouped into three factors. The first factor includes three items on brand loyalty, which is considered exclusively in its attitudinal nature. The second factor contains two items on consumers' perceptions of the quality of a brand in comparison with other brands, and is aimed at measuring brand quality as perceived by consumers. In the third factor there are five items, three on brand awareness and the remaining two on brand associations. Whereas the former are referred to consumers' ability to recognize a brand, the latter concern the ability to think of a brand and its characteristics. A Korean version of the scale is also available.

1. Brand loyalty
   – I consider myself to be loyal to X
   – X would be my first choice
   – I would not buy another brand if X is available at the store
2. Perceived brand quality
   – The likely quality of X is extremely high
   – The likelihood that X would be functional is very high
3. Brand awareness/associations
   – I can recognize X among other competing brands
   – I am aware of X
   – Some characteristics of X come to my mind quickly
   – I can quickly recall the symbol or logo of X
   – I have difficulty in imaging X in my mind

The first step in developing the MBE scale consisted in generating the set of items on brand equity and selecting the brands to administer. A literature review produced a set of 48 items, which was reduced to 22 after a content validity check. A list of 12 brands from three product categories (that is, athletic shoes, camera film and color television sets) was identified by following some criteria, such as that brands had to be available in both the US and Korea.

A pilot study was then conducted, in order to purify the set of items. At this stage, a Korean version of the scale was prepared thanks to the help of two bilingual experts. A sample of 414 university students (196 Americans and 218 Koreans) effectively completed the questionnaire (in English or Korean), by rating the items on a five-point Likert scale anchored at 1 = 'Strongly disagree' and 5 = 'Strongly agree'. On the basis of Cronbach's alpha coefficients, the number of items retained was 17.

A sample of 1530 students (577 Americans, 320 Korean Americans, and 633 Koreans) effectively participated in the main study, whose objective was to identify the final set of items. Again, the questionnaire was available in both English and Korean. Respondents rated the items on a five-point Likert scale; in addition to brand equity, items on brand attitude and purchase intention, product category involvement and experience, and brand purchase experience were included in the questionnaire for validity purposes.

Data collected were analyzed on three levels: an individual analysis (to evaluate commonalities across samples); a multi-group analysis (to test factorial invariance across samples); and a pooled analysis (to identify culture-free universal dimensions in the pooled sample). The individual analysis resulted in removing three items with poor reliability and in identifying three factors instead of the expected four, as brand awareness and brand associations items loaded on the same factor. This emerged from exploratory factor analyses, and was supported by confirmatory factor analyses performed through LISREL 8. The multi-group analysis led to removing four more items, and showed that the resulting 10-item solution was invariant across samples. Further evidence of the universality of the 10 items was provided by the last level of analysis.

Finally, scale validity was tested. Construct validity was tested by comparing the MBE scale with two constructs, that is, purchase intention and brand attitude. High correlations between the MBE and the other measures were obtained, thus proving the predictive validity of the scale. However, no specific test of discriminant validity was provided. To test convergent validity, a unidimensional measure – called 'Overall Brand Equity' (OBE) – was developed by the researchers. The initial set of 18 items was reduced to four, after multi-step examinations.

1. It makes sense to buy X instead of any other brand, even if they are the same
2. Even if another brand has the same features as X, I would prefer to buy X
3. If there is another brand as good as X, I prefer to buy X
4. If another brand is not different from X in any way, it seems smarter to purchase X

High correlations between the two measures supported the convergent validity of the MBE scale.

An earlier version of Yoo and Donthu's scale (1997), almost identical to the one just described, was validated by Washburn and Plank (2002). As underlined by these two researchers, the MBE scale represents only a first step towards the development of a universally accepted brand equity scale, as it needs further improvement and refinement. In particular, what they question about the MBE scale is that it does not distinguish between brand awareness and brand associations, whereas these two dimensions are conceptualized as distinct in literature (for example, Aaker, 1991; Keller, 2003). Moving from this major limitation, Pappu et al. (2005) tried to develop an improved consumer-based brand equity scale, by generating items that covered aspects of brand associations (for example, organizational associations and brand personality traits) that were not considered in previous research. In addition, they involved probabilistic samples of consumers.

Despite the criticism made of Yoo and Donthu's work, applications of their brand equity scale can be found in literature. This is the case of Atilgan et al.'s (2005) work, where they used the MBE scale to explore causal relationships between brand equity and its four components in the beverage industry. One more example is the work of Kim and Kim (2004), who adapted the MBE scale to the restaurant industry and used it to investigate the brand equity effects on the performance of fast-food chains.

Team Brand Association Scale in Professional Sports

Brand perceptions in general, and brand associations in particular, cannot be measured without relating them to a specific market segment, product category, or even a brand (Low and Lamb Jr., 2000). As a consequence, brand association scales with standard items cannot be found in literature. Recently, a brand association scale has been developed in the area of sport management by Ross et al. (2006), in order to evaluate consumers' thoughts and ideas on professional sport team brands.

This scale, called Team Brand Association Scale (TBAS), is composed of 41 items grouped into 11 factors. Most of them are referred to the sport team itself, as they consider aspects as brand visual identity, team rivals and history, organizational attributes, non-player personnel, team success and play. The remaining dimensions are focused on both the stadium and consumers, with reference to the consumption of food/beverages at the stadium, relationships with other fans, and commitment to the team.

1. Brand mark
   - The symbol of the team
   - The team's logo
   - The team colors
2. Rivalry
   - Beating the team's main rival
   - The team's biggest opponent
   - The team's conference
3. Concessions
   - Eating a specific food at the stadium/arena
   - Eating at the stadium/arena
   - Concessions at the stadium/arena
   - Consuming beverages at the stadium/arena
4. Social interaction
   - Other fans of the team
   - Going to games with my friends
5. Team history
   - A specific era in the team's history
   - Game-winning plays in the team's history
   - Championship the team has won
   - The most recent championship the team won
   - The success of the team in the past
6. Commitment
   - Being a fan of the team since childhood
   - Regularly following the team
7. Organizational attribute
   - An organization committed to its fans
   - A team loyal to its fans
   - The team giving back to the community
8. Non-player personnel
   - The head coach

  – A current coach on the team
  – Excellent coaches
  – The team's management
  – Owners of the team
9. Stadium community
  – The area surrounding the stadium/arena
  – The community surrounding the stadium/arena
  – The location of the stadium/arena
  – The city that the team is from
  – What stadium/arena the team plays its home games in
  – The team's home stadium/arena
  – Unique characteristics of the team's stadium/arena
10. Team success
  – A winning team
  – The performance of the team
  – Quality players
  – The quality of the team
  – A great team
11. Team play
  – How the team scores its points
  – Specific team characteristics

To develop the TBAS, Ross et al. implemented a four-stage research design. In the first stage, a free thought listing technique was used and the initial items for the scale were identified. A small sample of university students participated in the study, by writing down thoughts on their favorite team. A content analysis of such thoughts allowed the researchers to formulate 70 items.

In the second stage, a sample of 367 students indicated to which extent each association came to their mind when thinking of their favorite sport team. Responses were measured on a seven-point Likert scale, which ranged from 1 = 'Never' to 7 = 'Always'. Exploratory factor analysis was carried out using the Comprehensive Exploratory Factor Analysis (CEFA) program and the maximum likelihood method with oblique rotation. A 10-factor solution resulted on the basis of several criteria (that is, Kaiser criterion, scree test, RMSEA, parallel analysis, extent of interpretability).

In the third stage, a panel of experts was asked to review scale items and structure. According to the feedback provided, a few changes were made to the TBAS: the number of items was reduced from 50 to 41; one factor ('characteristics of sport') was renamed ('rivalry'); and one factor ('consumption experience') was divided into two factors ('social interaction' and 'concessions').

In the last stage, a sample of 447 students rated the final set of items on a seven-point Likert scale. A confirmatory factor analysis with LISREL 8.54 was performed, and the resulting goodness-of-fit indexes were acceptable in all cases. Validity tests were conducted as well. Criterion-related validity was assessed by including items from Gladden and Funk's (2002) Team Association Model in the questionnaire, and by correlating the two measures. Whereas the TBAS exhibited criterion-related validity, some problems emerged in convergent and discriminant validity tests. The residual matrix, useful for convergent validity (Bagozzi and Yi, 1988), revealed that two factors ('social interaction' and 'commitment') contained items with unacceptable residual values. According to Fornell and Larcker's (1981) criteria, two factors lacked discriminant validity: for 'team play' and 'commitment' the squared correlation was higher than the average variance extracted.

In conclusion, the TBAS can be used to measure most consumers' associations related to a professional sport team brand effectively. However, it is clear that the scale needs further improvements, especially in three of its eleven factors ('social interaction', 'commitment', and 'team play'). Scale length should also be considered, in the light of the fact that shorter scales are more manageable and easier to administer than longer ones.

Brand Luxury Index Scale

Another scale measuring consumers' perceptions is that proposed by Vigneron and Johnson (2004) with regard to luxury brands. Moving from the assumptions that brands may be luxurious and not luxurious, and that luxury brands themselves may be associated with different levels of luxuriousness, they found that a scale measuring these differences could be of particular use.

Vigneron and Johnson's scale consists of five factors, some of which refer to non-personal-oriented perceptions and some others to personal-oriented perceptions. In particular, 'conspicuousness', 'uniqueness', and 'quality' each reflect a distinctive trait of luxury brands. 'Hedonism' and 'extended self' are centered on consumers' responses to luxury brands, and move from the assumption that luxury brands are an inestimable source of symbolic meanings and emotional benefits. Each of the 20 items is measured on a seven-point semantic differential scale.

1. Conspicuousness
   - Conspicuous/noticeable
   - Popular/elitist
   - Affordable/extremely expensive
   - For wealthy/for well-off
2. Uniqueness
   - Fairly exclusive/very exclusive
   - Precious/valuable
   - Rare/uncommon
   - Unique/unusual
3. Quality
   - Crafted/manufactured
   - Up-market/luxurious
   - Best quality/good quality
   - Sophisticated/original
   - Superior/better
4. Hedonism
   - Exquisite/tasteful
   - Attractive/glamorous

– Stunning/memorable
5. Extended self
   – Leading/influential
   – Very powerful/fairly powerful
   – Rewarding/pleasing
   – Successful/well regarded

The Brand Luxury Index (BLI) originated from a theoretical framework outlined by the researchers on the basis of a literature review. This signifies that the five dimensions of the brand luxury construct had been identified by Vigneron and Johnson before developing the scale, and that the scale was a means of testing the hypothesized model. The development of the BLI scale took place in Australia, and non-probabilistic samples of Australian respondents were involved throughout the process.

First of all, items were generated and brands were selected. A set of 157 bipolar adjectives was created through a literature review, followed by qualitative interviews with managers, and focus groups with university students. A panel of experts was asked to review the items, in order to reduce the set of items (from 157 to 30) and assure item content validity. At the same time, a pool of brands was chosen according to their awareness and potential luxury image with targeted respondents.

Secondly, a sample of 884 students rated how much each item described the brands provided on a seven-point semantic differential scale. An exploratory factor analysis, using principal component analysis and varimax rotation, was run. It followed a confirmatory factor analysis, performed through the AMOS 5 maximum likelihood method. After removing eight items, the resulting goodness-of-fit indexes were acceptable. A two-week test-retest reliability study was also conducted, in order to assess scale internal consistency over time. A sample of 176 students was involved, and new brands were administered. Data analysis revealed that two items had low test-retest correlations, and therefore they were dropped from the scale. The revised scale was submitted to a new confirmatory factor analysis, and the indexes obtained were satisfying.

Lastly, several studies were conducted to test different types of scale validity. Further evidence of content validity was provided by a second content validity check, whose procedure was similar to that used by Zaichkowsky (1985). Instead of experts, a sample of 186 students was involved in the study this time. Predictive validity was assessed as well, by using a single-item scale on perceived luxury as a criterion. Two distinct samples of students were employed, for a total of 463 respondents. With reference to nomological validity, it was demonstrated that the BLI scale was strongly and positively correlated with five luxury-related scales, that is, a measure of materialistic attitudes (Moschis and Churchill, 1978), a fashion involvement factor (Tigert et al., 1976), an enduring involvement scale (Higie and Feick, 1988), a money-prestige scale (Yamauchi and Templer, 1982), and a price-prestige scale (Lichtenstein et al., 1993). A sample of 331 respondents was used this time. Finally, the construct validity of the scale was tested through Campbell and Fiske's (1959) multitrait-multimethod matrix method. A new data collection was thus realized, with 342 students rating items on Likert, Staple and semantic differential scales. The three requirements suggested by Campbell and Fiske were completely satisfied.

Brand Parity Scale

One more scale dealing with consumers' perceptions can be found in marketing and consumer behavior literature: Muncy's (1996) scale on brand parity, which is intended to measure consumers' perceptions of non-durable goods. Brand parity is defined by the author as 'the overall perception held by consumers that the differences between the major brand alternatives in a product category are small' (Muncy, 1996, p. 411), and is therefore negatively correlated to product differentiation. The development of such a scale is justified by the fact that consumers are increasingly viewing products as similar to each other, whereas marketing practitioners need to follow the diktat of product differentiation in order to gain a competitive edge.

The brand parity scale is extremely short, as it is composed of five items. The first two items express the same concept, with the difference that one is positively worded and one is negatively worded. Similarly, the last two items convey an identical meaning though their style and form are different. Price is mentioned in item number 3.

1. I can't think of many differences between the major brands of X
2. To me, there are big differences in the various brands of X
3. The only difference between the major brands of X is the price
4. X is X; most brands are basically the same
5. All major brands of X are basically alike

Before starting to develop the scale, three constructs of particular interest were selected (that is, cognitive brand loyalty, price sensitivity, and perceived utility of marketplace information) and a relationship between each of them and brand parity was hypothesized.

The first stage of the scale development process consisted in generating the initial set of items. To do that, a pretest with 29 university students and a literature review were first conducted. Then, the resulting eight items were administered to a sample of 93 students, thanks to which the measure was purified and the number of items was reduced to five. A similar procedure was followed to develop a measure of the three other constructs considered.

In the second stage of the research, three versions of the questionnaire were prepared and mailed to a sample of 1200 actual consumers. Each version contained one of the three product categories investigated (that is, laundry detergent, shampoo and toothpaste), plus the set of 18 items (five on brand parity, five on brand loyalty, four on price sensitivity, and four on information utility); items had to be evaluated on a five-point Likert scale. A total of 985 questionnaires returned to the researcher, with a response rate of 82 per cent. From data analysis it emerged that the brand parity scale – as well as the three other measures – was reliable. Structural equation analysis performed through LISREL 7 provided evidence of the hypothesized relationships between brand parity and the other three constructs: brand parity was demonstrated to be negatively correlated to brand loyalty and information utility, and positively correlated to perceived price.

The major criticism that can be leveled at Muncy's scale is that the procedure followed to develop it is rather simplified. For example, no experts were involved in any stage of the research. Moreover, it is not clear how the scale unidimensionality was established and there is no evidence of the different types of scale validity.

Even so, applications of the scale have appeared in later literature. In particular, Iyer and Muncy (2005) used it to investigate further the relationship between brand parity and brand loyalty. Their study, in which non-durable goods were replaced by services from the overnight delivery-service industry, showed that brand parity moderated the effects of consumer satisfaction and perceived quality on brand loyalty.

Brand Attitude Scale for Children

In addition to consumers' perceptions – whose measurement was the objective of the last three scales described – marketing scholars and practitioners have paid great attention to consumers' attitudes towards the brand. Brand attitudes have usually been studied in research on advertising effects, where respondents were exposed to specific stimuli such as TV commercials, and their attitudes towards the brand were measured with reference to such stimuli (see, among others, Batra and Athola, 1990; Batra and Ray, 1986; Batra and Stayman, 1990; Batra and Stephens, 1994). Although evidence of their reliability and/or validity was generally provided, most of these measures were not developed following a rigorous procedure. One exception is Pecheux and Derbaix's (1999) scale, built in accordance with Churchill's (1979) and directed towards the measurement of brand attitudes apart from advertising. Their focus, instead of adults, is on children of 8–12 years old, given their increasing importance as both actual and future consumers.

Pecheux and Derbaix's scale is extremely simple, due to the particular market segment to which it is addressed. It is composed of seven items, four of which reflect the hedonic nature of attitudes, and the remaining three are related to the utilitarian nature of attitudes. All of them are short and positively worded, and are measured on a four-point Likert scale. The scale was originally written in French, as it was developed in Belgium. An English translation is provided by the authors.

1.   Hédonique (Hedonic)
     – J'aime beaucoup (I like it very much)
     – J'aime ça (I like it)
     – C'est genial (It is great/brilliant)
     – C'est gai (It is cheerful/fun)
2.   Utilitariste (Utilitarian)
     – C'est utile (It is useful)
     – C'est pratique (It is practical or handy)
     – Ça ne sert à rien (It is useless)

The scale development process started with an exploratory phase, which consisted in reviewing the extant literature and conducting three pilot studies (four focus groups with mothers and teachers; an interpretative study with 13 children; and in-depth interviews with 49 children). The output was a set of 18 items and a list of the brands most known by children, that is, Coca-Cola, Cote d'Or, Kellogg's, and Nike.

To purify the measure, two data collections were realized. In the first, a sample of 155 rated the items for two brands of their choice, using a four-point Likert scale where 1 = 'Definitely disagree', 2 = 'Disagree', 3 = 'Agree', and 4 = 'Definitely agree'. On the basis of the analyses performed (that is, exploratory factor analysis, Cronbach's alpha coefficients, and cluster analysis), five items were dropped from the scale. In the second data collection, a sample of 149 children judged the 13 remaining items on a four-point Likert scale. The analyses performed (that is, exploratory factor analysis and Cronbach's alpha coefficients) led the researchers to remove four items, as they had low loadings or were redundant.

The third and fourth data collections were aimed at assessing test-retest reliability, as well as convergent and discriminant validity. A sample of 198 children participated effectively in the two data collections, with the latter taking place two weeks after the former. On both occasions, the questionnaires administered included the nine items on brand attitudes plus others on a related construct (that is, involvement in a product category); all to be rated using two answer formats (four-point Likert and Semantic Differential scales). Data collected were first submitted to a test-retest analysis, from which it emerged that two items had to be removed. A confirmatory factor analysis using LISREL 8 was thus carried out, in order to test the two-factor, seven-item solution. Good goodness-of-fit indexes were obtained for both collections and answer formats. Next, the multitrait-multimethod matrix (Campbell and Fiske, 1959) was created by making use of the involvement construct, and the convergent and discriminant validity of the brand attitude scale were demonstrated. Further evidence of discriminant validity was provided by a confidence interval around the estimated factor correlations and average variance extracted computation for each factor (Fornell and Larcker, 1981).

One final data collection was realized in order to test the criterion-related validity of the scale. A sample of 53 children rated the items on brand attitude, plus others on their intentions to ask for a brand. New brands from three product categories (sport shoes, video games and chocolates) were surveyed. Results showed a positive correlation between the two measures.

In sum, Pecheux and Derbaix's scale appears to be a valid instrument to measure children's attitudes towards brands. However, its applications should be limited to Belgium or other French-speaking countries in Europe which share a similar culture. On the other hand, the English version of the scale should be submitted to further analysis before being used. Even though the bidimensional nature of consumers' attitudes was demonstrated by research conducted in the US, the seven items developed and validated in French may not be suited to investigate the attitudes of English or American children.

Brand Dependence Scale

The last measure described in this cognitive section is the Brand Dependence Scale (BDS) developed by Bristow et al. (2002). The purpose here is to assess the weight of brand names in consumers' decisions or, more precisely, to measure the tendency of people to use brand names in the decision-making process. As underlined by the researchers, in fact, the scale should be considered as a measure of tendency rather than attitude, as it tries to capture consumers' 'behavior toward purchasing the product rather than affect about the product itself' (Bristow et al., 2002, p. 347).

The BDS includes seven items; all of them are lengthy yet understandable, and have to be rated on a six-point Likert scale. In the second, third and sixth item, brand dependence is investigated by mentioning a single brand name. In the first, fourth, fifth and seventh item, alternative and competing brand names are indicated as well.

1. When it comes to buying X, I rely on brand names to help me choose among alternative products
2. I would be more likely to purchase X that had a well-known brand name
3. Brand name would play a significant role in my decision of which X to purchase
4. When faced with deciding among two or more brands of X, I depend on the brand name of each product to help me make a choice
5. If faced with choosing between two X with similar features, I would select the better known brand name
6. The brand name of X is important to me when deciding which product to purchase
7. Regardless of what features a competing brand of X may offer, I would buy the brand of X that I most trust

The initial set of items was generated through a literature review, discussions among researchers, and interviews with consumers. A sample of 40 college students judged their content validity, leaving seven items for the next phase.

After that, a questionnaire including items about brand dependence, and another construct (brand disparity) was administered to a sample of 208 students. They were asked to express their agreement or disagreement with each sentence for two product categories (personal computers and pairs of jeans), using a six-point Likert scale where 1 = 'Strongly disagree', 2 = 'Disagree', 3 = 'Slightly disagree', 4 = 'Slightly agree', 5 = 'Agree', and 6 = 'Strongly agree'. Items on brand disparity were drawn from Muncy's scale described previously.

Data collected were thus submitted to an exploratory factor analysis (principal component analysis with varimax rotation), from which two factors emerged clearly: one corresponding to brand dependence, one to brand disparity. The reliability of the scale was assessed through Cronbach's alpha coefficients, and all the values obtained were satisfying. This was sufficient, according to the researchers, to claim scale convergent and discriminant validity. New analyses were performed to test the construct validity of the scale, and a positive correlation between brand disparity and brand dependence was found.

In general, it seems that the analyses conducted by Bristow et al. do not provide an adequate evidence of scale validity. Apart from content validity, in fact, the other types of validity should be faced more deeply. Convergent and discriminant validity were tested only via an exploratory factor analysis, which is not considered as sufficient in literature. Moreover, it is not clear why all but one of the items from Muncy's scale were used; no explanation is given on this point.

RELATIONAL SCALES

Brand Personality Scale

The idea that brands, like humans, have a personality emerged in the 1960s. However, a reliable, valid and generalizable scale to measure it was proposed by Aaker (1997) only at the end of the 1990s. Although brand personality is defined as 'the set of human characteristics associated with a brand' (Aaker, 1997, p. 347) and thus is conceptually similar to human personality, it differs from the latter in how it is formed. Whereas human personality traits are deduced from elements such as individuals' behavior, attitudes and beliefs; brand personality traits are the result of any direct or indirect contact between the consumer and the brand.

Similarly to human personality scales, which consist of five dimensions (that is, extroversion, agreeableness, conscientiousness, emotional stability and openness), the brand personality scale is composed of five factors. 'Sincerity', 'excitement' and 'competence' cover aspects taken into account by human personality scales as well. 'Sophistication' and 'ruggedness' have no equivalent. Each brand personality factor includes a series of traits, which are summarized by one or more facets. In total, there are 42 traits and 15 facets.

1. Sincerity
   – Down-to-earth (down-to-earth, family-oriented, small-town)
   – Honest (honest, sincere, real)
   – Wholesome (wholesome, original)
   – Cheerful (cheerful, sentimental, friendly)
2. Excitement
   – Daring (daring, trendy, exciting)
   – Spirited (spirited, cool, young)
   – Imaginative (imaginative, unique)
   – Up-to-date (up-to-date, independent, contemporary)
3. Competence
   – Reliable (reliable, hard-working, secure)
   – Intelligent (intelligent, technical, corporate)
   – Successful (successful, leader, confident)
4. Sophistication
   – Upper class (upper class, glamorous, good-looking)
   – Charming (charming, feminine, smooth)
5. Ruggedness
   – Outdoorsy (outdoorsy, masculine, western)
   – Tough (tough, rugged)

The process of developing the brand personality scale consisted of several phases. In the first instance, personality traits were generated by reviewing both psychology and marketing literature, and by conducting an exploratory study with 16 respondents. The output was a set of 309 non-redundant items. A sample of 25 respondents was then asked to rate how descriptive the personality traits were of brands in general, using a seven-point Likert scale. Only traits with an average rating of six were retained, for a total of 114. In addition to item generation, the first phase involved the selection of brands. A total of 37 brands from different product categories were taken from the 1992 EquiTrend study, and divided into four groups. A version of the questionnaire was prepared for each group.

Next, a probabilistic sample of 1200 respondents was mailed a questionnaire and asked to rate the 114 personality traits on a five-point Likert scale. In total, 631 questionnaires returned to the researcher (a 55 per cent return rate). From an exploratory factor analysis (principal components analysis with varimax rotation) there emerged a five-factor solution on the basis of criteria such as the scree plot and the level of variance explained.

Four traits with low loadings were removed. Further exploratory factor analyses were run on four sub-samples (that is, males vs. females, young vs. older respondents), and similar results were obtained. A facet identification phase was also conducted, in order to find the traits that best represented each dimension. An exploratory factor analysis was run within each factor, and a total of 15 facets were identified. A clustering procedure was thus followed to determine the most representative traits for each facet.

The objective of the next phase was to test scale reliability. A sub-sample of 200 respondents was randomly selected from the original sample and was mailed a questionnaire two months after the first data collection. The test-retest sample consisted of 81 subjects (a 41 per cent return rate). On the basis of test-retest correlations, three traits were dropped from the scale. Cronbach's alpha coefficients were also calculated for each factor, and all were satisfactory.

The final study was conducted in order to confirm the scale structure, using an independent sample of respondents and a new list of brands. A total of 20 brands from 10 product categories was identified from the 1992 EquiTrend study, and divided into two groups. A probabilistic sample of 250 respondents was mailed the new questionnaire, and 180 of them returned the questionnaire to the researchers (a 72 per cent return rate). A confirmatory factor analysis (generalized least squares) was thus performed, and good fit indexes were obtained. To support convergent validity an exploratory factor analysis was conducted, and a solution similar to the previous one emerged.

What is arguable about this scale is the methodology followed in the last part of its development process. In fact, no specific tests were performed to assess the discriminant or the predictive validity of the scale. In addition, the proof given to support the convergent validity (that is, an exploratory factor analysis) was not sufficient.

Although questioned by a few (Azoulay and Kapferer, 2003), the brand personality scale counts numerous developments and applications in literature. The cross-cultural generalizability of Aaker's scale was verified by Aaker et al. (2001) in a later research. Two cultures were taken into account, that is, the Japanese and the Spanish. Results revealed that Japan and the US shared four out of five dimensions ('sincerity', 'excitement', 'competence' and 'sophistication'), whereas Spain and the US shared three dimensions ('sincerity', 'excitement' and 'sophistication'). Culture-specific dimensions were found in Japan ('peacefulness') as well as in Spain ('peacefulness' and 'passion').

Further evidence that the brand personality scale is not generalizable across cultures has been provided by several other researchers. Among others, Alvarez-Ortiz and Harris (2002) tested the scale in Mexico, finding that the five-dimension solution did not fit the data well and that a sixth culture-specific dimension ('gender') existed. Supphelen and Grønhaug (2003) tested the brand personality scale in Russia, and noticed that the resulting factors were only in part similar to Aaker's (that is, 'successful and contemporary', 'sincerity', 'excitement', 'sophistication' and 'ruggedness').

Another noteworthy study is that of Lentz et al. (2006), who developed a brand modernity scale starting from Aaker's scale. In fact, these authors focused on a trait (that is, up-to-date) that was included in the brand personality scale but that, according to their opinion, deserved more attention. Providing that a brand can be defined as modern when 'it represents a recent trend and/or lifestyle of the target group, and is communicated by means of innovative communication' (Lentz et al., 2006, p. 147), they developed and validated a scale that tries to capture this aspect.

Several other studies on brand personality can be found in literature. Some of them are focused on the construct of brand personality, its antecedents and consequences (for example, Wysong et al., 2002). Some others, instead, test the applicability of the brand personality scale to a specific context. The fields to which the scale has been applied are as diverse as tourism destinations (Ekinci and Hosany, 2006), corporate branding (for example van Rekom et al., 2006), websites (for example, Okazaki, 2006; Opoku et al., 2006), non-profit organizations (Venable et al., 2005), and restaurants (for example, Siguaw et al., 1999).

Brand Trust Scale

A first important element that distinguishes relationships in general, and relationships between consumers and brands in particular, is the level of trust between the subjects. Consumers' trust in brands, therefore, is an element that cannot be omitted or ignored in a relational perspective. Delgado-Ballester et al. (2003; see also Delgado-Ballester, 2004) proposed a Brand Trust Scale (BTS) that measures how much a brand is considered trust-worthy, given that brand trust is 'the confident expectations of the brand's reliability and intentions in situations entailing risk to consumer' (Delgado-Ballester et al., 2003, p. 37).

The BTS is composed of two dimensions (brand reliability and brand intentions) of four items each. The first dimension results from consumers' perceptions that the brand satisfies their needs, and represents a starting point for developing trust. The second dimension, instead, reflects consumers' beliefs that the brand will hold their interests if negative events with the product occur. All items are positively worded and are measured on a five-point Likert scale.

1. Brand reliability
    – X meets my expectations
    – I feel confident in X
    – X never disappoints me
    – X guarantees satisfaction
2. Brand intentions
    – X would be honest and sincere in addressing my concerns
    – I could rely on X to solve the problem
    – X would make any effort to satisfy me
    – X would compensate me in some way for the problem with the product

The initial set of items was generated through a literature review, in-depth interviews with six consumers, and five experts' evaluations. The outcome was a set of 13 items.

The BTS scale was administered, via telephone interviews, to a random sample of consumers. Respondents were asked to think of a deodorant they had used recently and to rate the items with that brand in mind, using a five-point Likert scale. A total of 272 questionnaires were collected, and divided randomly into two equal parts. Analyses (that is, correlations and principal component analysis) of the first half of the sample led the researchers to remove one item and to identify a bidimensional factor structure.

Analyses (that is, confirmatory models in LISREL 8.3) of the second half of the sample supported the solution previously obtained, although four items had to be dropped from the scale. This half of the sample was also used to assess the internal consistency of the scale, as well as its validity. Convergent validity was tested according to Anderson and Gerbing's (1988) and Bagozzi and Yi's (1988) recommendations, whereas discriminant validity was tested by following the procedures provided by Anderson and Gerbing (1988) and Fornell and Larcker (1981).

In order to test the construct validity of the scale, a new study was conducted. The BTS was administered by telephone to a random sample of 127 consumers, who were asked to think of a brand of shampoo and then to rate the items. A confirmatory factor analysis was run, and the goodness-of-fit indexes obtained were acceptable. In addition to the BTS, the questionnaire included items on brand overall satisfaction and brand loyalty. From the analyses it emerged that brand trust was positively correlated with both measures.

In conclusion, what is questionable about this scale is that it was developed and validated through a single data collection (although probabilistic and split in two parts, the sample was one). Literature on scale development (for example, Churchill, 1979), in fact, suggests that the items that are being tested should be submitted to several samples of respondents. Similarly, the number of product categories that were surveyed by Delgado-Ballester et al. was too restricted. By administering a larger number of brands, the researchers might have improved the generalizability of the scale across product categories.

A shorter version of the scale was later developed by Delgado-Ballester and Mununera-Alemán (2005), in order to investigate the relationship between brand trust and brand equity. It was found that brand trust was positively associated with brand loyalty, which in turn was positively related to brand equity.

Emotional Attachment Scale

In addition to brand trust, the relationship between consumers and brands can be described in terms of consumers' emotional attachment to brands. The Emotional Attachment (EA) scale was proposed by Thomson et al. (2005) and intended to measure the strength of such an attachment. Or, in other words, the 'emotional-laden target-specific bond between a person and a specific object', that is, the brand (Thomson et al., 2005, pp. 77–8). The interest towards this topic stems from psychology: attachment theory has demonstrated that an individual's attachment to an object *latu sensu* (for example, a person, an animal, a place) is a strong predictor of his or her behavior in relation to that object.

The EA scale consists of 10 items, grouped into three dimensions. The first dimension refers to consumers' feelings of warmth towards the brand. The second dimension contains items that indicate a deeper and more intense attachment to the brand. The third dimension includes items regarding consumers' feelings of closeness to the brand. Items are composed of an adjective, and are measured on a seven-point Likert scale.

1. Affection
    – Affectionate
    – Friendly
    – Loved
    – Peaceful

2. Passion
    - Passionate
    - Delighted
    - Captivated
3. Connection
    - Connected
    - Bonded
    - Attached

In total, five studies were conducted by Thomson et al. to develop the EA scale. In study 1, a set of 39 items was created after reviewing the psychology literature on attachment. Next, 68 university students were asked to think of a brand to which they were emotionally attached, to rate the items using a seven-point Likert scale, and to specify any other emotion that described their feelings towards the brand. From the resulting set of 49 items, the researchers removed those with a mean rating inferior to 4 and those considered as 'non-emotional' by two independent judges.

In study 2, a sample of 120 students was asked to identify a brand to which they were emotionally attached and to rate the 35 items on a seven-point Likert scale. Items with low mean ratings and limited variance were dropped, as well as others not judged by over 10 per cent of respondents. An exploratory factor analysis with oblique rotation was performed. The outcome was a three-factor solution with 10 items (only those with a loading greater than .5 were retained). Correlations between dimensions were significant, and Cronbach's alpha coefficient for the scale was acceptable.

The purpose of study 3 was to test the internal consistency of the scale, as well as its dimensional structure. Sixty-five students were asked to think of a brand of their choice and to rate the 10-item scale by keeping that brand in mind. Cronbach's alpha coefficient for the scale was calculated, and confirmatory factor analyses were run using structural equation modeling. The model that fit the data better assumed three first-order correlated factors ('affection', 'passion' and 'connection') loading on a second-order factor (the EA construct).

Study 4 was designed to assess the convergent validity of the scale. To that end, 184 students were asked to identify a brand to which they had either a weak or strong emotional attachment, and to rate the items using a seven-point Likert scale. In addition to the EA scale, the questionnaire included four measures of attachment behaviors (proximity maintenance, emotional security, safe haven and separation distress) developed in psychology (Hazan and Shaver, 1994; Hazan and Zeifman, 1999) and adapted to the brand context. Cronbach's alpha coefficients were calculated for all measures, and the scores were high in all cases. Analyses through structural equation modeling revealed that the EA scale was significantly related to each of the four attachment behaviors.

The last study was aimed at assessing both discriminant and predictive validity. A random, non-student sample of 179 respondents was asked to identify a brand to which they were strongly, moderately, or weakly emotionally attached, and then to rate the items. The questionnaire included the EA scale as well as other measures drawn from literature, that is, brand attitude (Batra and Stayman, 1990), satisfaction (Mano and Oliver, 1993), involvement (Zaichkowsky, 1985), brand loyalty (Sirgy et al., 1991), and willingness to pay a premium price. Discriminant validity was tested by comparing the EA scale with brand attitude, satisfaction and involvement measures. An exploratory factor analysis with oblique rotation was run, and provided evidence that the EA scale was distinct from the others, as its three dimensions loaded on a single factor. Predictive validity was assessed by relating the EA scale to brand loyalty and willingness to pay a premium price. From structural equation modeling there emerged a positive correlation between the EA scale and the other measures.

In sum, the only issue that can be raised about the development and validation of the EA scale regards its discriminant validity, which was demonstrated through an exploratory factor analysis. Additional analyses could have been performed.

Brand Community Integration Scale

One further scale proposed here which measures the strength of consumers' relationships is that of McAlexander et al. (2002). The purpose of their work was to understand the nature, building process, and implications of a brand community. To that end, they first conducted ethnographic fieldwork in two brand communities (Harley Davidson and Jeep), then quantitative analysis in only one of them (Jeep). A Brand Community Integration (BCI) scale was thus developed, in order to measure consumers' relationships inside a brand community and to triangulate qualitative findings.

The BCI scale consists of four factors corresponding to the entities with which consumers develop relationships. The first dimension is referred to consumers' feelings towards the product owned. The second dimension is focused on the bond with the brand, and contains similar items to those listed in brand loyalty measures (an individual who belongs to a brand community is particularly loyal to that brand). Two additional items are included in this dimension, but are not reported by the researchers as they are aimed at investigating specific-brand values and associations of the company that sponsored the research. The third dimension examines consumers' feelings towards the organization that sponsored the event. The fourth dimension concerns the relationship between the consumer and other consumers of the same product.

1. Product
   - I love my X vehicle
   - My X vehicle is one of my favorite possessions
   - My X vehicle is fun to drive
2. Brand
   - If I were to replace my X vehicle, I would buy another X
   - X is of the highest quality
   - X is the ultimate sport-utility vehicle
3. Company
   - The X division understands my needs
   - The X division cares about my opinions
4. Other owners
   - I have met wonderful people because of my X
   - I feel a sense of kinship with other X owners
   - I have an interest in a club for X owners

The development of the BCI scale originated from the model elaborated by the researchers on the basis of their ethnographic fieldwork. Such a model established that brand communities were characterized by four customer-centric relationships, and thus provided a hypothesis about the dimensions that composed the brand community construct. To develop the items, ethnographic findings were supported by a review of the extant literature and a pretest study. The outcome was a set of 16 items.

The main study was structured as a one-group pre-test/post-test quasi-experimental design (Cook and Campbell, 1979) of the impact of the brandfest considered, that is, the National Camp Jeep event. The same questionnaire was administered twice (that is, before and after the event) and the same instructions were given on both occasions (to rate the items using a five-point Likert scale anchored at 1 = 'Strongly disagree' and 5 = 'Strongly agree'). Five weeks prior to the event, all pre-registered participants were mailed the questionnaire, and 453 of them were returned to the researchers (a 40 per cent return rate). Three weeks after the event, the respondents who had returned the questionnaire were mailed another questionnaire; a total of 259 questionnaires were sent back to the researchers (a 57 per cent return rate).

Several data analyses were then performed. A confirmatory factor analysis using LISREL 8 was conducted in order to test the hypothesized four-factor model. After removing three items, the model exhibited an acceptable fit. Reliability and average variance extracted were calculated for each factor by following both Gerbing and Anderson's (1988) and Fornell and Larcker's (1981) procedures. Evidence that each dimension (that is, 'product', 'brand', 'company' and 'other owner') was distinct from the others and reflected a single higher-order construct (that is, brand community integration) was provided by testing a second-order model.

Finally, the BCI scale was used to understand the impact of the brandfest on consumers' attitudes towards the event. Two types of tests – structural equation and repeated measure analysis – were performed, by comparing pre- and post-event scores for each component of the BCI scale and for the composite measure of brand community integration. Results revealed that the brandfest had a significant, positive impact on consumers who had a less favorable attitude before the event.

The BCI has been well received in literature, as testified by several publications that have appeared. McAlexander et al. (2003) developed a revised version of the scale with reference to the gaming industry and used it to investigate the relationships between brand community integration and brand loyalty. Quinn and Devasagayam (2005) adapted the BCI scale to the context of ethnic marketing and studied the relationship between ethnicity and membership of a brand community. The BCI scale also has the merit of having encouraged other authors to develop scales pertaining to brand community. An example is the scale created by Algesheimer et al. (2005), which is intended to measure the individual's identification with a specific brand community.

EXPERIENTIAL SCALES

Centrality of Visual Product Aesthetics Scale

In the light of the increasing importance of aesthetics in consumers' lives (for example, Postrel, 2003), Bloch et al. (2003) developed a Centrality of Visual Product Aesthetics

(CVPA) scale in order to measure the importance of the visual aspect of products in consumers' experiences. CVPA is defined as 'the overall level of significance that visual aesthetics holds for a particular consumer in his/her relationships with products' (Bloch et al., 2003, p. 552), and is described as a general consumer trait. It can range from zero (when individuals have no artistic or aesthetic sensibility) to high levels (when purchase, usage and consumption activities are dominated by aesthetics).

More specifically, the CVPA scale is composed of 11 items grouped into three dimensions. The first dimension refers to the value that consumers attach to products as means of enhancing the quality of their life or society in general. The second dimension concerns the individuals' ability to recognize, classify and evaluate product designs. The last dimension concerns the individuals' responses to design objects, given that these are capable of generating intense responses (either positive or negative). All items are measured on a five-point Likert scale.

1. Value
   – Owning products that have superior designs makes me feel good about myself
   – I enjoy seeing displays of products that have superior designs
   – A product's design is a source of pleasure for me
   – Beautiful product designs make our world a better place to live
2. Acumen
   – Being able to see subtle differences in product designs is one skill that I have developed over time
   – I see things in a product's design that other people tend to pass over
   – I have the ability to imagine how a product will fit in with designs of other things I already own
   – I have a pretty good idea of what makes one product look better than its competitors
3. Response
   – Sometimes the way a product looks seems to reach out and grab me
   – If a product's design really 'speaks' to me, I feel that I must buy it
   – When I see a product that has a really great design, I feel a strong urge to buy it

The CVPA scale development process consisted of eight phases. In the first phase the set of items was generated through a literature review, in-depth interviews with experts, and evaluations by marketing faculty or students. The outcome was a set of 34 items organized into four semantic groups ('value of design', 'acumen', 'level of response' and 'design determinancy').

In the second phase, a random sample of 1050 consumers was mailed a questionnaire, and a usable response was returned by 318 of them (a 30 per cent return rate). The task was to rate the items listed on a five-point Likert scale. Data analyses (item-to-total correlations and principal component analysis) led the researchers to drop 17 items from the scale. The final solution was a 15-item scale with three dimensions.

In the third phase, the scale was administered by mail to a random sample of 520 consumers, with usable responses from 136 of them (a 26 per cent return rate). A series of confirmatory factor analyses through EQS led to the removal of four additional items, and showed that the model with the best fit was unidimensional. The internal consistency of the scale was tested through Cronbach's coefficient alpha and average variance extracted (Fornell and Larcker, 1981).

In the fourth phase, a sample of 108 university students rated the CVPA items plus others from four related constructs, that is, Style of Processing Scale (Childers et al., 1985), Desire for Unique Consumer Products Scale (Lynn and Harris, 1997), and two factors from the scale on consumer materialism (Richins and Dawson, 1992). The discriminant validity of the scale was tested by following Fornell and Larcker's (1981) and Anderson and Gerbing's (1988) guidelines. Data from studies 3 and 4 were then combined to test the construct validity of the scale. In study 3 respondents indicated, among a list of 30, the products for which the visual aspect mattered. Analyses showed that high numbers of products marked corresponded to higher scores reported in study 4. Two other measures (Style of Processing Scale and Desire for Unique Consumer Products) behaved similarly.

In the fifth phase, a sample of 53 students rated the CVPA scale on social desirability (Paulhus, 1993). A low correlation between the two measures proved that the CVPA scale was not subjected to social desirability bias.

In the sixth phase, a know-group validation test was conducted. A questionnaire containing the scale was mailed to a sample of 250 experts, and usable responses were obtained by 62 of them (a 25 per cent return rate). Data collected were compared with those from studies 1 and 2. The mean for the scale was significantly higher for experts than for the general population.

In the seventh phase, a sample of 190 students participated in a study to test if CVPA levels influence consumers' reactions to products with a different aesthetic quality. After viewing the pictures of two toasters (with high/low quality), respondents completed a questionnaire with the CVPA scale and other questions. From data analysis it emerged that high and low CVPA consumers showed significantly different reactions in terms of aesthetic appraisal of the product, attitude towards the product, and purchase intention.

In the last phase, a total of 165 students participated in a study to test if CVPA levels influence the importance attributed to aesthetics in making purchases. This time, the product employed as stimulus was a bathroom scale, and the method used was a conjoint analysis. While some hypothesized relationships (that is, increased power, memory and warranty resulted in higher purchase intention), some others did not (that is, high aesthetic quality corresponded to higher purchase intention but not vice versa).

Brand Experience Scale

The final scale pertaining to consumers' experiences that has been developed in literature is that of Zarantonello et al. (2007). The Brand Experience Scale measures consumers' experiences generated by brands, given that 'consumer experiences with a brand arise when consumers are exposed to brands and pay attention to the experiential aspects of brands' executions'. In addition to studies from consumer research and marketing, the theoretical foundation for this scale was provided by the theory of mind modularity (Fodor, 1983; Pinker, 1997; Plotkin, 1998; Tooby and Cosmides, 2000) and Dewey's experience categorization (Dewey, 1922).

Specifically, the scale consists of four factors of three items each. The first factor concerns the impact that brands have on consumers' five senses. The second factor concerns the wide range of affective responses (for example, feelings and sentiments) that can be generated by brands. The third factor focuses on the ability of brands to induce consumers to think and, in the last analysis, to assume an open and creative attitude. The fourth factor regards the behavioral nature of experience, and includes items on bodily experiences, lifestyles and actions. Most items are positively worded and a few are negatively worded; similarly, most items are written in the impersonal form and a few in the personal form.

1. Sensory Items
   – I find this brand interesting in a sensory way
   – This brand makes a strong impression on my visual sense or other senses
   – This brand does not appeal to my senses
2. Affective Items
   – This brand induces feelings and sentiments
   – I do not have strong emotions for this brand
   – This brand is an emotional brand
3. Intellectual Items
   – This brand stimulates my curiosity and problem solving
   – I engage in a lot of thinking when I encounter this brand
   – This brand does not make me think
4. Bodily Items
   – I engage in physical actions and behaviors when I use this brand
   – This brand results in bodily experiences
   – This brand is not action oriented

The scale development process started with an item generation phase. An extensive literature review was undertaken, and a panel of consumer researchers and experience consultants screened the initial set of items. The set of 125 items was administered – in the form of a questionnaire – to a sample of 30 students, who rated to what extent each item described their experiences with the brand in general. The output was a set of 83 items organized into five groups ('sense', 'feel', 'think', 'act' and 'relate').

At the same time, the list of brands was identified. A sample of 68 students provided names of brands marketed in an experiential/non-experiential fashion. A total of 21 brands (16 of which were experiential and five non-experiential) resulted from this assessment. The 21 brands were split into five groups, with one non-experiential brand being included in all of them to test the internal consistency of the scale. Different versions of the questionnaire were prepared for each group.

A sample of 293 students participated in the main study, whose task was to rate the 83 brands by referring to the brands listed and using a seven-point Likert scale. Data collected were factor-analyzed (principal component analysis with varimax rotation). A four-factor solution resulted, and items with high loading were retained for a total of 19 items). Cronbach's coefficient alphas were acceptable in all cases, and the mean score for the 21 brands that had been defined as 'experiential' was higher than those defined as 'non-experiential'.

A sample of 193 students participated in a subsequent study aimed at confirming the structure of the brand experience that previously emerged. A shorter version of the scale was used and a new list of brands was administered. Confirmatory factor analyses revealed that the goodness-of-fit indexes of the four-factor model were acceptable.

The scale development reported is not completed, as the scale is currently being tested in its divergent and predictive validity. Subsequent studies aim at demonstrating that brand experience is conceptually different from other constructs (that is, brand personality), and that it influences dimensions such as brand loyalty and consumer satisfaction.

CONCLUSION

In this chapter a literature review of measurement scales related to brands and consumers was carried out in order to understand which brand dimensions have been investigated and how they have been measured. The review is not expected to be exhaustive or complete; rather, it is exploratory and intended to provide an initial analysis of the state of the art of brand scales conceived from a consumer perspective. Literature revealed 12 scales that were developed by following rigorous, scientific methodologies. Sources different from those consulted here might be considered by future reviews so as to carry out an improved and extended analysis.

Despite these limitations, some important points emerged in this review. While all 12 scales are consumer-based, the analysis revealed that they were founded on three frameworks: cognitive, relational and experiential. The theoretical shift from a cognitive to a relational to an experiential framework reflects the progressively greater importance attached to consumers' inner aspects. Scales that were classified as belonging to a cognitive approach measure one or more dimensions strongly connected to brands, such as brand equity and attitudes towards the brand. Scales classified as based on a relational approach are focused on the consumer/brand relationship, and they consequently consider aspects such as consumers' emotional attachment to brands or consumers' level of trust in brands. Scales that were labeled as experiential are instead centered on consumers *tout court*, as they take into account consumers' experiences in some or all of their dimensions.

While most of the scales reviewed utilized cognitive and relational approaches, only a few contributions utilized experiential perspectives. Future research should concentrate on this latter approach for at least two reasons. Firstly, it is the most recent and least studied, and thus requires further investigation to understand the construct of experience better. Secondly, it constitutes an area of interest for both academicians, who need empirical evidence to support theoretical constructs, and professionals, for whom experience is the cutting edge in differentiating their brand from competing ones.

From a managerial point of view, the analysis conducted has highlighted that brand equity is not the only dimension that describes the value consumers attach to brands. In fact, other dimensions such as brand personality, brand trust and brand experience can improve our understanding of why brands are appealing and relevant to consumers. Measuring these dimensions allows managers to have a more complete view of the value of their brand and its strength on the market. For example, experiential scales could be used to discriminate between brands that have the same equity (for example, brand awareness and brand associations) but that are still perceived as different by consumers. By using such scales, managers could capture that part of value that is not included in brand equity.

REFERENCES

Aaker, David A. (1991), *Managing Brand Equity*, New York: The Free Press.
Aaker, Jennifer L. (1997), 'Dimensions of brand personality', *Journal of Marketing Research*, **34**(3), 342–52.
Aaker, Jennifer L., Verónica Benet-Martínez and Jordi Garolera (2001), 'Consumption symbols as carriers of culture: a study of Japanese and Spanish brand personality constructs', *Journal of Personality and Social Psychology*, **81**(3), 492–508.
Algesheimer, René, Utpal M. Dholakia and Andreas Herrmann (2005), 'The social influence of brand community: evidence from European car clubs', *Journal of Marketing*, **69**(3), 19–34.
Alvarez-Ortiz, Cecilia and Judy Harris (2002), 'Assessing the structure of brand personality among global and local Mexican brands', *American Marketing Association*, Conference Proceedings, **13**, 263–4.
Anderson, James C. and David W. Gerbing (1988), 'Structural equation modeling in practice: a review and recommended two-step approach', *Psychological Bulletin*, **103**(3), 411–23.
Atilgan, Eda, Serkan Aksoy and Serkan Akinci (2005), 'Determinants of the brand equity: a verification approach in the beverage industry in Turkey', *Marketing Intelligence and Planning*, **23**(2/3), 237–48.
Azoulay, Audrey and Jean-Noël Kapferer (2003), 'Do brand personality scales really measure brand personality?', *Journal of Brand Management*, **11**(2), 143–55.
Bagozzi, Richard P. and Youjae Yi (1988), 'On the evaluation of structural equation models', *Journal of the Academy of Marketing Science*, **16**(1), 74–94.
Batra, Rajeev and Olli T. Athola (1990), 'The measurement and role of utilitarian and hedonic attitudes', *Marketing Letters*, **2**(2), 159–70.
Batra, Rajeev and Michael L. Ray (1986), 'Affective responses mediating acceptance of advertising', *Journal of Consumer Research*, **13**(2), 234–49.
Batra, Rajeev and Douglas M. Stayman (1990), 'The role of mood in advertising effectiveness', *Journal of Consumer Research*, **17**(2), 203–14.
Batra, Rajeev and Debra Stephens (1994), 'Attitudinal effects of ad-evoked model and emotions: the moderating role of motivation', *Psychology and Marketing*, **11**(3), 199–13.
Bloch, Peter H., Frédéric F. Brunel and Todd J. Arnold (2003), 'Individual differences in the centrality of visual product aesthetics: concept and measurement', *Journal of Consumer Research*, **29**(4), 551–65.
Bristow, Dennis N., Kenneth C. Schneider and Drue K. Schuler (2002), 'The brand dependence scale: measuring consumers' use of brand name to differentiate among product alternatives', *Journal of Product and Brand Management*, **11**(6/7), 343–56.
Campbell, Donald T. and Donald W. Fiske (1959), 'Convergent and discriminant validation by the multitrait-multimethod matrix', *Psychological Bulletin*, **56**(2), 81–101.
Childers, Terry L., Michael J. Houston and Susan E. Heckler (1985), 'Measurement of individual differences in visual versus verbal information processing', *Journal of Consumer Research*, **12**(2), 125–34.
Churchill Jr., Gilbert A. (1979), 'A paradigm for developing better measures of marketing constructs', *Journal of Marketing Research*, **16**(February), 64–73.
Cook, Thomas D. and Donald T. Campbell (1979), *Quasi Experimentation*, Boston, MA: Houghton Mifflin.
Delgado-Ballester, Elena (2004), 'Applicability of a brand trust scale across product categories: a multigroup invariance analysis', *European Journal of Marketing*, **38**(5/6), 573–92.
Delgado-Ballester, Elena and Jose L. Munuera-Alemán (2005), 'Does brand trust matter to brand equity?', *Journal of Product & Brand Management*, **14**(3), 187–96.
Delgado-Ballester, Elena, Jose L. Munuera-Alemán and Marí J. Yagüe-Guillén (2003), 'Development and validation of a brand trust scale', *International Journal of Market Research*, **45**(1), 35–53.
DeVellis, Robert F. (2003), *Scale Development: Theory and Applications*, 2nd edn, Thousand Oaks, CA: Sage.
Dewey, John (1922), *Human Nature and Conduct*, New York: The Modern Library.

Ekinci, Yuksel and Sameer Hosany (2006), 'Destination personality: an application of brand personality to tourism destinations', *Journal of Travel Research*, **45**(2), 127–39.

Farquhar, Peter H. (1989), 'Managing brand equity', *Marketing Research*, **1**(3), 24–33.

Fodor, Jerry (1983), *The Modularity of Mind*, Cambridge, MA: Bradford Books, The MIT Press.

Fornell, Claes and David F. Larcker (1981), 'Evaluating structural equation models with unobservable variable and measurement error', *Journal of Marketing Research*, **18**(1), 39–50.

Fournier, Susan (1998), 'Consumers and their brands: developing relationship theory in consumer research', *Journal of Consumer Research*, **24**(4), 343–73.

Gerbing, David W. and James C. Anderson (1988), 'An updated paradigm for scale development incorporating unidimensionality and its assessment', *Journal of Marketing Research*, **25**(2), 186–92.

Gladden, James M. and Daniel C. Funk (2002), 'Developing an understanding of brand associations in team sport: empirical evidence from consumers of professional sports', *Journal of Sport Management*, **16**(1), 54–81.

Hazan, C. and D. Zeifman (1999), 'Pair bonds as attachments', in Jude Cassidy and Phillip R. Shaver (eds), *Handbook of Attachment: Theory, Research, and Clinical Applications*, New York: Guilford Press, pp. 336–54.

Hazan, Cindy and Phillip R. Shaver (1994), 'Attachment as an organizational framework for research on close relationships', *Psychological Inquiry*, **5**(1), 1–22.

Higie, Robin A. and Lawrence F. Feick (1988), 'Enduring involvement: conceptual and methodological issues', in Thomas K. Srull (ed.), *Advances in Consumer Research*, Vol. 16, Provo, UT: Association for Consumer Research, pp. 690–96.

Hirschman, Elizabeth C. and Morris B. Holbrook (1982), 'Hedonic consumption: emerging concepts, methods and prepositions', *Journal of Marketing*, **46**(3), 92–101.

Holbrook, Morris B. and Elizabeth C. Hirschman (1982), 'The experiential aspects of consumption: consumer fantasies, feelings, and fun', *Journal of Consumer Research*, **9**(2), 132–40.

Iyer, Rajesh and James A. Muncy (2005), 'The role of brand parity in developing loyal customers', *Journal of Advertising Research*, **45**(2), 222–28.

Keller, Kevin L. (1993), 'Conceptualizing, measuring, and managing customer-based brand equity', *Journal of Marketing*, **57**(1), 1–22.

Keller, Kevin L. (2003), *Strategic Brand Management: Building, Measuring, and Managing Brand Equity*, 2nd edn, Upper Saddle River, NJ: Prentice Hall.

Kim, Woo G. and Hong-Bumm Kim (2004), 'Measuring customer-based restaurant brand equity: investigating the relationship between brand equity and firms' performance', *Cornell Hotel and Restaurant Administration Quarterly*, **45**(2), 115–31.

Lentz, Patrick, Christine Sauermann and Hartmut H. Holzmüller (2006), 'Brand modernity: scale development and implications for brand management', *American Marketing Association*, Conference Proceedings, **17**, 147.

Lichtenstein, Donald R., Nancy M. Ridgway and Richard G. Netemeyer (1993), 'Price perceptions and consumer shopping behavior: a field study', *Journal of Marketing Research*, **30**(2), 234–45.

Low, George S. and Charles W. Lamb Jr. (2000), 'The measurement and dimensionality of brand associations', *Journal of Product and Brand Management*, **9**(6), 350–68.

Lynn, Michael and Judy Harris (1997), 'The desire for unique consumer products: a new individual differences scale', *Psychology and Marketing*, **14**(6), 601–6.

Mano, Haim and Richard L. Oliver (1993), 'Assessing the dimensionality and structure of the consumption experience: evaluation, feeling and satisfaction', *Journal of Consumer Research*, **20**(3), 451–66.

McAlexander, James H., Stephen K. Kim and Scott D. Roberts (2003), 'Loyalty: the influence of satisfaction and brand community integration', *Journal of Marketing Theory & Practice*, **11**(4), 1–11.

McAlexander, James H., John W. Schouten and Harold F. Koenig (2002), 'Building brand community', *Journal of Marketing*, **66**(1), 38–54.

Moschis, George P. and Gilbert A. Churchill Jr. (1978), 'Consumer socialization: a theoretical and empirical analysis', *Journal of Marketing Research*, **15**(4), 599–609.

Muncy, James A. (1996), 'Measuring perceived brand parity', in Kim P. Corfman and John G. Lynch Jr (eds), *Advances in Consumer Research*, Vol. 23, Provo, UT: Association for Consumer Research, pp. 411–17.

Muniz, Albert M. and Thomas C. O'Guinn (2001), 'Brand community', *Journal of Consumer Research*, **27**(4), 412–32.

Nunnally, Jim C. and Ira H. Bernstein (1994), *Psychometric Theory*, 3rd edn, New York: McGraw-Hill.

Okazaki, Shintaro (2006), 'Excitement or sophistication? A preliminary exploration of online brand personality', *International Marketing Review*, **23**(3), 279–303.

Opoku, Robert, Russell Abratt and Leyland Pitt (2006), 'Communicating brand personality: are the websites doing the talking for the top South African business schools?', *Journal of Brand Management*, **14**(1/2), 20–39.

Pappu, Ravi, Pascale G. Quester and Ray W. Cooksey (2005), 'Consumer-based brand equity: improving the measurement – empirical evidence', *Journal of Product and Brand Management*, **14**(2/3), 143–54.

Paulhus, Delroy L. (1993), 'The balanced inventory of desirable responding', Reference Manual, BIDR, Version 6, Department of Psychology, University of British Columbia, Vancouver, Canada.

Pecheux, Claude and Christian Derbaix (1999), 'Children and attitude toward the brand: a new measurement scale', *Journal of Advertising Research*, **39**(4), 19–27.

Pecheux, Claude and Christian Derbaix (2002), 'Children's reactions to advertising communication: multiple methods, moderating variables and construct validity issues', in Susan M. Broniarczyk and Kent Nakamoto (eds), *Advances in Consumer Research*, Vol. 29, Valdosta, GA: Association for Consumer Research, pp. 531–8.

Pinker, Steven (1997), *How The Mind Works*, New York: Norton.

Plotkin, Henry (1998), *Evolution in Mind: An Introduction to Evolutionary Psychology*, Cambridge, MA: Harvard University Press.

Postrel, Virginia (2003), *The Substance of Style: How the Rise of Aesthetic Value is Remarking Commerce, Culture & Consciousness*, New York: HarperCollins Publishers.

Quinn, Michael and Raj Devasagayam (2005), 'Building brand community among ethnic diaspora in the USA: strategic implications for marketers', *Journal of Brand Management*, **13**(2), 101–14.

Richins, Marsha L. and Scott Dawson (1992), 'A consumer values orientation for materialism and its measurement: scale development and validation', *Journal of Consumer Research*, **19**(3), 303–16.

Ross, Stephen T., Jeffrey D. James and Patrick Vargas (2006), 'Development of a scale to measure team brand associations in professional sport', *Journal of Sport Management*, **20**(2), 260–79.

Schmitt, Bernd H. (1999), *Experiential Marketing: How to Get Customers to Sense, Feel, Think, Act, and Relate to Your Company and Brands*, New York: The Free Press.

Schmitt, Bernd H. (2003), *Customer Experience Management: A Revolutionary Approach to Connecting with Your Customers*, Hoboken, NJ: John Wiley & Sons.

Siguaw, Judy A., Anna Mattila and Jon R. Austin (1999), 'The brand-personality scale', *Cornell Hotel and Restaurant Administration Quarterly*, **40**(3), 48–55.

Simon, Carol J. and Mary W. Sullivan (1993), 'The measurement and determinants of brand equity: a financial approach', *Marketing Science*, **12**(1), 28–52.

Sirgy, Joseph M., Gita S. Johar, Coskun A. Samli and Claudius B. Claiborne (1991), 'Self-congruity versus functional congruity: predictors of consumer behavior', *Journal of the Academy of Marketing Science*, **19**(4), 363–75.

Smith, Shaun and Joe Wheeler (2002), *Managing the Customer Experience: Turning Customers Into Advocates*, London: Prentice Hall.

Solomon, Michael R. (2004), *Consumer Behavior: Buying, Having, and Being*, 6th edn, Upper Saddler River, NJ: Pearson Education Inc.

Supphelen, Magne and Kjell Grønhaug (2003), 'Building foreign brand personalities in Russia: the moderating effect of consumer ethnocentrism', *International Journal of Advertising*, **22**(2), 203–26.

Thomson, Matthew, Deborah J. MacInnis and Whan C. Park (2005), 'The ties that bind: measuring the strength of consumers' emotional attachments to brands', *Journal of Consumer Psychology*, **15**(1), 77–91.

Tigert, Douglas J., Lawrence J. Ring and Charles W. King (1976), 'Fashion involvement and buying behavior: a methodological study', in Beverlee B. Anderson (ed.), *Advances in Consumer Research*, Vol. 3, Cincinnati, Ohio: Association for Consumer Research, pp. 46–52.

Tooby, John and Leda Cosmides (2000), *Evolutionary Psychology: Foundational Papers*, Cambridge, MA: MIT Press.

van Rekom, Johan, Gabriele Jacobs, Peeter W.J. Verlegh and Klement Podnar (2006), 'Capturing the essence of a corporate brand personality: a western brand in Eastern Europe', *Journal of Brand Management*, **14**(1/2), 114–24.

Venable, Beverly T., Gregory M. Rose, Victoria D. Bush and Faye W. Gilbert (2005), 'The role of brand personality in charitable giving: an assessment and validation', *Journal of the Academy of Marketing Science*, **33**(3), 295–312.

Vigneron, Franck and Lester W. Johnson (2004), 'Measuring perceptions of brand luxury', *Journal of Brand Management*, **11**(6), 484–506.

Washburn, Judith H. and Richard E. Plank (2002), 'Measuring brand equity: an evaluation of a consumer-based brand equity scale', *Journal of Marketing Theory and Practice*, **10**(1), 46–62.

Wysong, Scott, Jim Munch and Susan Kleiser (2002), 'An investigation into the brand personality construct, its antecedents, and its consequences', *American Marketing Association*, Conference Proceedings, **13**, 512–18.

Yamauchi, Kent T. and Donald I. Templer (1982), 'The development of a money attitude scale', *Journal of Personality Assessment*, **46**(5), 522–28.

Yoo, Boonghee and Naveen Donthu (1997), 'Developing and validating a consumer-based overall brand equity scale for Americans and Koreans: an extension of Aaker's and Keller's conceptualizations', paper presented at the 1997 AMA Summer Educators Conference, Chicago, IL.

Yoo, Boonghee and Naveen Donthu (2001), 'Developing and validating a multidimensional consumer-based brand equity scale', *Journal of Business Research*, **52**(1), 1–14.

Zaichkowsky, Judith L. (1985), 'Measuring the involvement construct', *Journal of Consumer Research*, **12**(3), 341–52.

Zarantonello, Lia, Bernd H. Schmitt and Josko J. Brakus (2007), 'Development of the brand experience scale', *Advances in Consumer Research*, Vol. 34, forthcoming.

15.   The role of brand naming in branding strategies: insights and opportunities

Sanjay Sood and Shi Zhang

INTRODUCTION: THE FOCUS OF TRADITIONAL BRANDING RESEARCH

The branding strategy for a firm reflects the number and nature of common or distinctive brand elements applied to the different products sold by the firm. The often asked important questions include which brand elements can be applied to which products and what is the nature of new and existing brand elements that are to be applied to new products.

One critical area that intersects several such brand elements is the research on brand extension. Past traditional research has revealed that successful brand extensions occur when the parent brand is seen as having favorable associations and there is a perception of fit between the parent brand and the extension product.

There are many bases of fit: product-related attributes and benefits, as well as non-product-related attributes and benefits related to common usage situations or user types. In general, the findings point to the generalization that brand extensions are evaluated more favorably when perceived 'fit' is higher than when perceived fit is lower. Category similarity defined in terms of feature overlap is often used as the basis for fit judgments. For example, near extension categories that are physically similar to the parent brand category are evaluated more positively than far extension categories that are physically dissimilar to the parent brand category.

A number of recent studies have explored situations in which the main effect of near extension being evaluated more favorably than far extensions can be significantly moderated. Park et al. (1991) showed that perceived fit can also be determined by brand concept consistency. In addition, Broniarczyk and Alba (1994) showed that perceived fit can be judged on the basis of a salient association that connects the parent brand to the extension.

THE EFFECTS OF NAMING STRATEGIES

In the traditional model, the extensions studied were named by simply adding the parent brand to a new product in the extension category, for example, Froot Loops lollipops. According to the categorization model used in the traditional approach (Boush and Loken, 1991), when consumers evaluate an extension with a parent branding strategy cues they base judgments on the similarity between the parent brand category and the extension category; evaluations are favorable (unfavorable) in similar (dissimilar) extension categories. More recent brand extension research has begun to investigate the impact of naming strategies that go beyond parent branding strategies. This research extends the traditional model by pairing the parent brand name with other cues that can be used to evaluate the extension.

In this chapter we will review research on the effects of sub-branding, co-branding, ingredient branding, and endorsement branding strategies on extension evaluations. Sub-branding involves a pairing of the parent brand name with an individual name that is not another brand. For example, Courtyard by Marriott and Apple iPod are two forms of a sub-branding strategy that differ in the order of the parent brand name and individual name components. Sub-branding is perhaps the most popular form of naming strategy in practice.

In contrast, co-branding, ingredient branding and endorsement branding involve a pairing of the parent brand name with a second brand name that is well known to consumers. For example, a Visa credit card that earns American Airlines frequent flier miles is a co-branded product; a Dell personal computer with Intel Inside is an example of an ingredient branded product; and Levi's Dockers is an endorsement branded product. One important difference between these dual branded strategies is the perceived contribution of each brand to the success or failure of the new product. The two brands (for example Visa and American Airlines) are typically perceived to contribute more or less equally in a co-branded strategy; the ingredient brand (for example Intel) is less of a contributor to success; and the endorsing brand (for example Levi's) has the least direct connection to the extension.

From a theoretical perspective, these brand naming variations can be conceptualized in terms of varying the salience of the parent brand name. In the traditional brand extension paradigm, only the parent brand name is used as a basis for judgment when evaluating the extension. Branding strategies such as sub-branding add another cue (either an individual brand name component or another brand name altogether) which determines how the parent brand name will be used in judging the extension. In this chapter we will review several findings and present some new research that suggests that there may be much more flexibility in terms of brand extension possibilities than previously considered in the traditional model.

We begin by detailing recent research that has identified several interesting findings related to the effectiveness of a sub-branding strategy. This research builds on the traditional brand extension model by examining person factors, category factors, and the effects of sub-branding on parent brand dilution. We conclude by reviewing research on strategies that involve two brand names jointly present on one new product.

A. PERSON FACTORS: CHILDREN VS. ADULTS

One particular approach is to examine individual differences in extension evaluations. In particular, the traditional model of brand extension evaluations did not consider the effects of age. Zhang and Sood (2002) showed that extension evaluations depend on the age of the respondent as well as the naming strategy.

In a series of experiments, Zhang and Sood showed that children usually do not use category similarity as a criterion when evaluating extensions, while adults do, as shown in

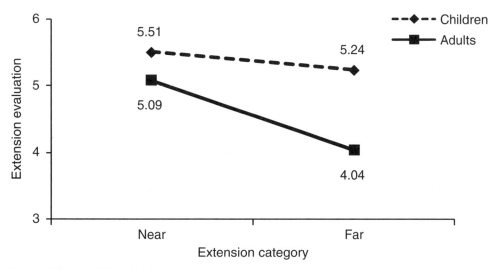

Source: Zhang and Sood (2002).

Figure 15.1 Perceived category fit and extension evaluation

Figure 15.1. They suggested that while children are capable of explicitly judging category similarity, they do not do so when evaluating extensions where the similarity judgment task is implicit. To test this idea, they conducted an experiment in which half of the children were cued to make similarity judgments prior to extension evaluations, and the other half were not cued. To rule out the possibility that differences between children's and adults' judgments stem from differences in involvement in the judgment process, they also included a measure of involvement. Similarly, to rule out the possibility that there were unique category effects effectively, they also used a range of product categories. They hypothesized that when children are cued, deep cues such as category similarity would be made salient at the time of evaluation, and children would use deep cues and rate near extensions more favorably than far extensions. In contrast, they predicted that, when children were not cued, they would not use deep cues and they would rate near and far extensions equivalently. Indeed, the findings supported the hypotheses, as shown in Figure 15.2. This pattern of results showed that children possess the ability to make use of deep cues, although they do not spontaneously use this ability if the judgment task only implicitly requires them to do so.

Next, the authors focused on the processes children use to arrive at extension evaluations in the absence of deep cues. The authors reasoned that if it is indeed true that children rely more on surface cues than on deep cues, then children should be more sensitive to surface manipulations than adults. They predicted that children would be more likely than adults to base their evaluations on surface cues such as visual characteristics (for example product color, shape, size), brand names (for example strong vs. weak names), and brand name characteristics (for example rhyming vs. non-rhyming names).

This prediction was tested using one of these surface cues (rhyming vs. non-rhyming names) largely because past research has accumulated strong evidence that linguistic perceptual similarities in stimuli are salient for children. They expected and found that

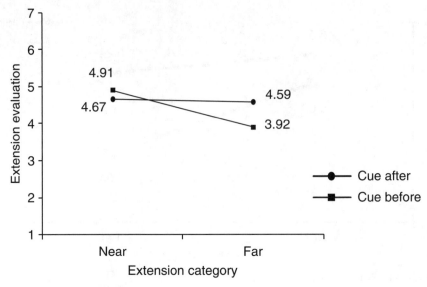

Source: Zhang and Sood (2002).

Figure 15.2   Extension evaluation by category fit and cue timing

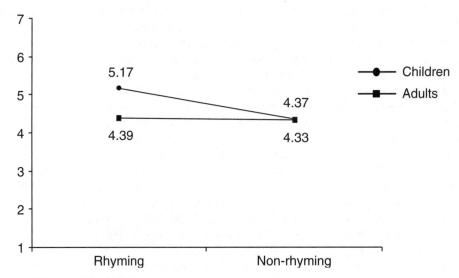

Source: Zhang and Sood (2002).

Figure 15.3   Extension evaluation by brand name characteristic and age

children relied more on surface characteristics of extension names and preferred extensions with rhyming names to extensions with non-rhyming names, regardless of category similarity. In contrast, the adult participants relied more on deep characteristics of extension category similarity and prefer near extensions to far extensions, regardless of name characteristics (see Figure 15.3).

Zhang and Sood's studies have shown that children and adults evaluate brand extensions differently with respect to the use of deep and surface cues. Adults use deep features such as category similarity while children tend to use surface features such as brand names and name characteristics as a basis for extension evaluations. The research is one of the first demonstrations of age as an important moderator of brand extension evaluations. It identifies important aspects of the underlying processes that are different for children and adults in brand extension evaluations.

B. EXTENSION CATEGORY FACTORS: EXPERIENTIAL PRODUCTS

When can brand name characteristics also influence adult consumer judgment of brand extension evaluations? To answer this question, Sood and Dreze (2006) explored a new frontier of research on experiential products as extension categories. The authors reasoned that the usual brand extension evaluation process involves products that are tangible with a list of attributes. However, the extension categories can also be entities that are intangible or more experiential. For example, movie sequels are new extensions that in general require consumer experience in order to be able to best evaluate the new product, relative to a new brand of toothpaste. Because consumers lack a basis of judgment in experiential products, they would tend to rely on the name itself to deduce information about the content (for example the sequel). Thus, changing the extension product category to experiential products created an ideal and realistic situation in which naming can potentially affect adult consumer extension evaluations.

Sood and Dreze's research diverges from past brand extension research in that they predict that, when the products being extended are experiential and intangible in nature (such as movies), dissimilar extensions will be preferred to similar extensions. They base the predictions on the notion that experiential attributes have a different basis for evaluation compared to tangible attributes. According to the categorization model, assimilation with the parent brand improves evaluations when extensions are similar because the activated parent brand associations, typically search attributes such as cavity protection for Crest, are favorable in similar extension contexts such as mouthwash (Keller, 1993). For movie sequels, the parent brand associations that come to mind are likely to be experiential attributes such as the original movie's storyline, its genre, and memorable scenes. These attributes are typically featured in movie trailers and television ads; hence they should be relatively easy to recall.

In contrast to physical goods, the authors suggest that experiential attributes are subject to satiation. In the context of movies, attributes such as the storyline and genre tend to satiate such that consumers prefer to experience something different in the sequel; hence dissimilarity is preferred to similarity. Although high similarity provides a closer connection to the original film, in experiential contexts this process of assimilation is more likely to result in satiation and may therefore lower sequel evaluations. For example, if the original movie is an action/adventure film, consumers may be more attracted to a sequel that also includes a new genre such as a romance relative to a sequel that simply continues the previous theme.

This contrast between tangible goods and intangible goods was used as the basis for the investigation of sub-branding hypotheses.

Table 15.1   Stimuli used

Original movie title	Numbered title	Phrased title	Sequel's similarity
			Near (similar)
Daredevil	Daredevil 2	Daredevil: Taking to the Streets	Action
			Far (dissimilar)
Daredevil	Daredevil 2	Daredevil: Taking to the Streets	Action plus romance

Source: Sood and Dreze (2006).

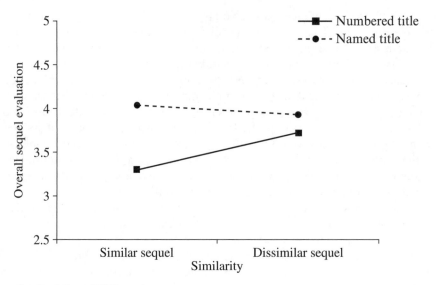

Source: Sood and Dreze (2006).

Figure 15.4   Sequel evaluation by similarity and title strategy

Given that the effects of satiation in experiential goods settings are well established in psychology and consumer behavior, the authors suggest that although not commonly considered in extension research, satiation can provide some insight to brand extensions in experiential categories. Using stimuli as shown in Table 15.1, the authors found what they predicted: dissimilar extension categories are rated more favorably than similar categories, as shown in Figure 15.4.

The authors suggest that the title strategy for sequels affects the degree of assimilation of the sequel and consequently influences the likelihood of satiation with the sequel's storyline. Similar to a 'parent-name-only' branding strategy, a numbered sequel title (for example, *Daredevil 2*) relies heavily on knowledge of the original movie (*Daredevil*) as a basis for evaluations of the sequel. In contrast, a named sequel title (*Daredevil: Taking it to the Streets*) relies less heavily on the original movie as a basis for evaluations because the added part of the name cues novelty in the plot. In addition, the extra phrase may help

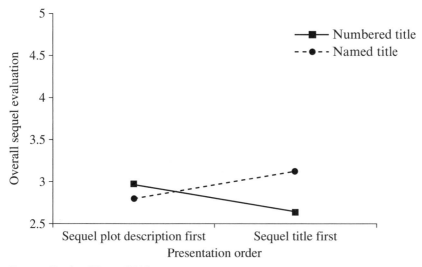

Source: Sood and Dreze (2006).

Figure 15.5 Sequel evaluation by presentation order and title strategy

to sub-type the sequel as potentially offering a different experience than the original. If numbered sequels are more likely to be assimilated with the original movie and subject to satiation than named sequels, then perceived similarity should significantly affect numbered sequels but not named sequels.

If assimilation is the mechanism underlying movie sequel evaluations, the authors further suggested that evaluations would be influenced by the presentation order of information. Specifically, the sequel title is the key piece of information that leads to assimilation. If the sequel title is provided before the plot description, then the parent movie category should be activated to a greater extent when the sequel is numbered (vs. named), leading to a greater degree of assimilation. If the sequel title is provided after the plot description, however, then the parent movie activation is equalized across naming strategies, and evaluations of numbered sequels should more closely resemble named sequels. In summary, assimilation is more likely when a numbered title is provided before the description relative to when a numbered title is provided after the description. In contrast, named sequels should not be as subject to assimilation and therefore order of presentation. Indeed, experimental results support their hypotheses, as shown in Figure 15.5.

Finally, the authors provided empirical support for their findings using real data from the Internet Movie Database (www.imdb.com). Visitors to this website are invited to provide their own ratings to movies that they have seen. These visitors typically rate the sequel and provide comments on why a particular film was good or bad.

The database included over 400 sequels, including every sequel that had been launched up to the year 2000. In total, the database contained over four million ratings of sequels. As shown in Figure 15.6, the proposed hypotheses were shown to emerge in the ratings data such that dissimilar sequels were rated higher than similar sequels and numbered sequels were rated lower than named sequels.

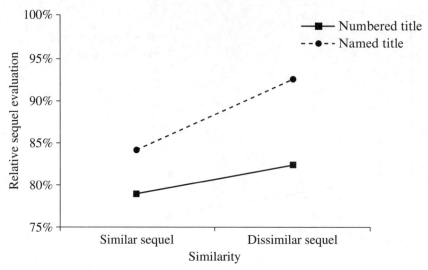

Source: Sood and Keller (2008).

Figure 15.6   IMDB movie rating by similarity and title strategy

An interesting and critical brand element that these studies focused on is sub-typed brand name. In a branding context, sub-typing has been associated with sub-branded extensions. Sub-branding is a form of brand extension that combines a parent brand name with an individual name to form the name of a brand extension (for example, *Courtyard by Marriott*). Research suggests that extensions which include the parent brand name only (*Marriott*) are more likely to be assimilated with parent brand knowledge structure while sub-branded extensions (*Courtyard by Marriott*) are more likely to be sub-typed as distinct from the parent brand (Milberg et al., 1997). Movie sequel names belong to this type of sub-branding extensions evaluations, in which the naming itself and how it is constructed can significantly affect consumer evaluations of the extension categories.

A third area of sub-branding research examines the effects of branding strategies on feedback effects to the parent brand, commonly referred to as dilution effects. That is, we are often as concerned with how evaluations of the parent brand may change as with the success or failure of an extension.

C. DILUTION EFFECTS

Sood and Keller (2008) examined how sub-branding may influence the effects of product experience on extension evaluations and parent brand dilution. The authors reasoned that sub-branding may have an impact on evaluations because the semantic meaning of the individual name component can help to position the extension in its new category.

This positioning effect is most pronounced in dissimilar categories because parent brand knowledge is not considered to be relevant for the extension when the categories do not have physical similarity. For example, consider if Tropicana were to introduce a new type

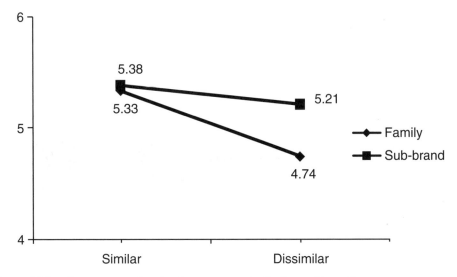

Figure 15.7   Extension evaluation by category similarity and branding strategy

of cola. This brand extension may receive low ratings because the knowledge that comes to mind for Tropicana is not favorable in the context of a cola. However, if the extension used a sub-branding strategy such as Quencher by Tropicana, the individual name could help divert attention away from the parent brand and help to position the extension more favorably. The authors examined this positioning prediction in the context of a taste test. Respondents were provided with direct experience regarding the success or failure of the extension via product trial. An extreme prediction would therefore be that branding strategy would not have any effect at all on evaluations because, in contrast to the vast majority of previous branding research, in this case consumers could try the product.

In contrast, the authors predicted that the typical branding effect would emerge and that sub-branding would provide a positioning benefit in dissimilar categories. This positioning effect of sub-branding was tested using an experimental design that included two parent brand replicates, Tropicana and Pepsi, extended to two categories, juice and cola. The individual components of the sub-brand names were selected to be meaningful in the extension categories; Quencher in cola and Sunburst in juice. Finally, in order to examine dilution effects, respondents either tasted a beverage that tasted good (for example, real Pepsi or Tropicana) or bad (for example, diluted Pepsi or Tropicana).

The authors found support for the positioning hypothesis, as shown in Figure 15.7. Note that these results are particularly striking because branding effects persisted even when consumers were allowed to experience the product. Specifically, Tropicana juice was rated higher than Pepsi juice and Pepsi cola was rated higher than Tropicana cola, even though respondents drank exactly the same drink!

The finding that a sub-branding strategy influences evaluations even when consumers have experience with the product suggests that branding strategy may also moderate dilution effects. Dilution effects occur when consumers use extension evaluations to update their evaluations of the parent brand. We have outlined the process of how dilution effects may be moderated by branding strategy in Figure 15.8.

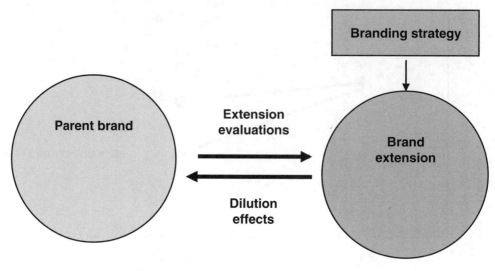

Source: Sood and Keller (2008).

Figure 15.8   Model of the impact of branding strategy on dilution effects

The authors reasoned that if the individual component in the sub-brand name reduces the reliance on the parent brand name as a cue on which to base extension evaluations, then the parent brand should also be somewhat shielded from the effects of parent brand dilution. In other words, the sub-brand name may signal to consumers that the extension is intentionally different from the parent brand.

The authors examined this prediction by giving respondents direct experience with the product again, but this time the drinks were pretested to be unfavorable. As shown in Figure 15.9, sub-branding shielded the parent brand from dilution effects.

In summary, sub-branding research has revealed several important and interesting effects. First, the meaningfulness of the individual component of the sub-brand name has a large effect on evaluations. For children, rhyming names had a greater impact than category similarity. In movies, a numbering strategy did not provide any new information about the sequel, hence evaluations were lower. In terms of parent brand dilution, a meaningful sub-brand name shielded the parent brand name from unwanted feedback effects.

We now turn our attention to the effects of naming strategies with two well-known brands. In contrast to sub-branding, the effect of two brand names depends upon the perceived connection between each brand and the new product.

D. NAMING STRATEGIES WITH TWO BRANDS: CO-BRANDING INGREDIENT BRANDING, AND ENDORSEMENT BRANDING

Recent research has also investigated the effects of branding strategies when two brand names are present. In this case, consumers must judge the consistency between the brand names themselves and between the brand names and the extension category. In addition,

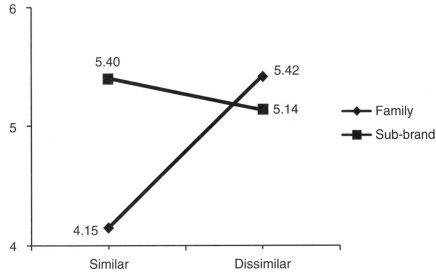

Source: Sood and Zhang (2008).

Figure 15.9 *Impact of brand extension category similiarity and branding strategy upon parent brand dilution*

there is an issue of how consumers may perceive each brand's relative contribution to the success or failure of the product.

Co-branding involves a pairing of the parent brand name with another well-known parent brand name such that both brands share roughly equal responsibility for creating the extension. Park et al. (1996) showed that the order of the co-brands determines extension evaluations. For example, a co-branded extension named Godiva cake mix by Slimfast was perceived to be relatively rich in flavor whereas a co-branded extension named Slimfast cake mix by Godiva was perceived to be relatively low in calories.

Ingredient branding involves a pairing of two parent brand names such that one brand bears primary responsibility for creating the product while the other brand offers an expertise or specialization on a specific attribute. Desai and Keller (2002) found that co-branded ingredients (for example, Tide with Irish Spring scented bath soap) led to higher evaluations of dissimilar line extensions, whereas self-branded ingredients (for example, Tide with its own EverFresh scented bath soap) led to higher evaluations of similar line extensions.

Endorsement branding may be considered a weaker form of pairing two brands because the endorsing brand often plays a much more secondary role relative to the endorsed brand. As a result, attention is directed towards the endorsed brand to a much greater extent than in co-branding or ingredient branding strategies. In general, there are explicit and implicit endorsement strategies. For example, Levi Strauss launched the Dockers brand with an explicit endorsement strategy. In the introductory period, the Levi's brand was present alongside the Dockers brand in the television advertising campaign. Over time, however, the Levi's name was dropped from the primary marketing activities and the brand became Dockers. The endorsing brand may therefore serve as a risk reduction mechanism until the endorsed brand becomes more familiar to consumers. Endorsement branding may also be conceptualized as an implicit strategy in the form of brand partnerships and sponsorships. For example, Mountain Dew's sponsorship of the X-Games represents an implicit endorsement of Mountain Dew for the X-Games. In this case, both brands benefit from this type of complementary relationship because there is synergy in regards to the target market for both the X-Games and Mountain Dew.

Sood and Zhang (2008) examined this latter type of implicit endorsement relationship in the context of children. The authors reasoned that for adults an endorsement strategy works on a rational basis where the endorsing brand either plays a risk reduction role or a complementary role as described above. As children develop into adults, they become exposed to a myriad of endorsement strategies and begin to develop a set of rules for evaluating these relationships between multiple brands. The evaluation process is likely to become more sophisticated as children transition from early stages of childhood to the later stages of childhood. In particular, the authors were interested in an affective-oriented endorsement strategy that pairs two well-liked brands together without defining a more rational basis for the relationship.

In the experiment the authors presented a set of younger children (for example, aged 7 to 9) and older children (for example, aged 10 to 12) with a choice between various candies, cookies and cereals. In the control condition, the children were presented with a choice between one item alone (for example, a package of M&Ms) or two items together (for example, a Hershey bar and a package of bubble gum). In the affective endorsement condition, the lone item was paired with another brand on the package (for example, M&Ms with Barbie). The hypothesis was that in the control condition, both younger and older children would prefer to have two candies rather than one. In the affective endorsement condition, younger children would be more likely than older children to prefer the affective endorsement because they have not developed decision strategies that evaluate what benefit the second brand has to offer. As shown in Figure 15.10, this prediction was supported.

Although older children were not influenced by the affective endorsement, the authors examined other factors that did influence older children. The authors speculated that older children may be susceptible to social endorsements, specifically what brands their friends may prefer. The second study was designed to test this social endorsement prediction. The control condition was as before, providing younger and older children with a choice between either one item alone or two items together. The social endorsement condition presented the same choice options, however the lone item was identified as the option that most of their classmates preferred. The prediction was that the older children would be influenced by the social endorsement, as they are in the stage of development where social relationships are quite salient. Younger children, however, have not yet matured and would continue to prefer two items over the lone item. As shown in Figure 15.11, this prediction was supported.

DISCUSSION

In this chapter we have reviewed recent research on brand naming that builds on the traditional brand extension model. In contrast to the traditional model where the parent

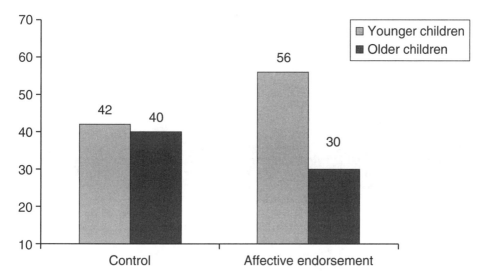

Source: Sood and Zhang (2008).

Figure 15.10 Item evaluation by affective endorsement and age

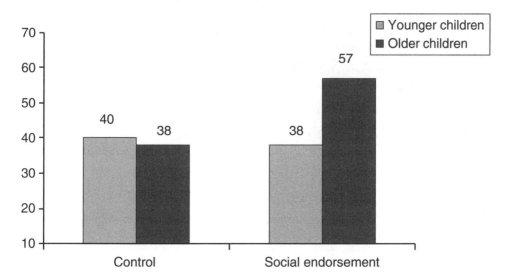

Source: Sood and Zhang (2008).

Figure 15.11 Item evaluation by social endorsement and age

brand name is the primary basis of judgment, brand naming strategies introduce another cue to be used in evaluations. How this added cue is interpreted will depend upon person factors, category factors and the meaningfulness of that cue in the context of the evaluation.

REFERENCES

Aaker, David A. and Kevin Lane Keller (1990), 'Consumer evaluations of brand extensions', *Journal of Marketing*, **54**(January), 27–41.

Boush, David M. and Barbara Loken (1991), 'A process tracing study of brand extension evaluations', *Journal of Marketing Research*, **28**(February), 16–28.

Broniarczyk, Susan M. and Joseph W. Alba (1994), 'The importance of the brand in brand extension', *Journal of Marketing Research*, **31**(May), 214–28.

Desai, Kalpesh K. and Kevin L. Keller (2002), 'The effects of ingredient branding strategies on host brand extendibility', *Journal of Marketing*, **66**(1), January, 73–93.

Gurhan-Canli, Zeynep and Durairaj Maheshwaran (1998), 'The effects of extensions on brand name dilution and enhancement', *Journal of Marketing Research*, **35**(November), 464–73.

Keller, Kevin Lane (1993), 'Conceptualizing, measuring, and managing customer-based brand equity', *Journal of Marketing*, **57**(March), 1–22.

Keller, Kevin Lane (1998), *Strategic Brand Management*, Upper Saddle River, NJ: Prentice-Hall.

Keller, Kevin Lane and David A. Aaker (1992), 'The effects of sequential introduction of brand extensions', *Journal of Marketing Research*, **29**(February), 35–50.

Loken, Barbara and Deborah Roedder John (1993), 'Diluting brand beliefs: when do brand extensions have a negative impact?', *Journal of Marketing*, **57**(July), 71–84.

Milberg, Sandra J., C. Whan Park and Michael S. McCarthy (1997), 'Managing negative feedback effects associated with brand extensions: the impact of alternative branding strategies', *Journal of Consumer Psychology*, **6**(2), 119–40.

Park, C. Whan, Sandra Milberg and Robert Lawson (1991), 'Evaluation of brand extensions: the role of product level similarity and brand concept consistency', *Journal of Consumer Research*, **18**(September), 185–93.

Park, C. Whan, Sung Youl Jun and Allan D. Shorker (1996), 'Composite branding alliances: an investigation of extension and feedback effects', *Journal of Marketing Research*, **33**(November), 453–66.

Sood, Sanjay and Xavier Dreze (2006), 'Brand extensions of experiential goods: movie sequel evaluations', *Journal of Consumer Research*, **28**(June), 129–41.

Sood, Sanjay and Kevin Lane Keller (2008), 'The effects of branding strategies and product experience on brand evaluations', working paper, University of California, Los Angeles, USA.

Sood, Sanjay and Shi Zhang (2008), 'Children's evaluation of brand endorsements', working paper, University of California, Los Angeles, USA.

Zhang, Shi and Sanjay Sood (2002), '"Deep" and "surface" cues: brand extension evaluations by children and adults', *Journal of Consumer Research*, **28**(June), 129–41.

PART V

Practitioner perspectives

In this part, a practitioner perspective on brand and experience management is provided by authors engaged in the management of global brands. Their focus is on the practical, managerial and organizational requirements of effective brand and experience management.

Seddon, Executive Vice President of branding agency Milward Brown Optimor, assesses a variety of approaches to brand valuation, with insights and recommendations for how to maximize financial returns from brand strategy.

Roth, Chief Marketing Officer of branding agency Landor Associates, examines the challenges of managing a global consumer brand, and presents best practices and tools from case studies of work done with BP and Panasonic.

Nakai, of Japanese communications firm ADK, identifies ten of the most overlooked barriers to successful branding and presents lessons for organizational practices and leadership decisions which can avert these sources of potential failure.

Rogers, Director of the Center on Global Brand Leadership, examines the recent shift of brand management practice into non-consumer industries, and provides best practices for management of B2B corporate brands, illustrated by the successful branding of business software provider SAP.

16. Returns on brand investments: maximizing financial returns from brand strategy

Joanna Seddon

A fundamental shift is taking place in attitudes towards brands and marketing. The traditional view that brands are 'hot air' and marketing a cost, is still very much alive. As McDonald (2002) tells us, 'CFOs see their marketing colleagues as slippery, evasive, and unaccountable.' Recent research among CEOs has found that over a quarter of them still consider marketing an expense. However, the majority do not, choosing instead to focus on branding as a major investment.

Behind this lies an evolution in the structure of business in the US as well as around the world. The move from manufacturing to a service- and information-based economy has been accompanied by a dramatic rebalancing of corporate assets. In the old manufacturing world, corporate value was tangible value – the value contained in property, plant and equipment. These things were relatively easy to measure. This was the world for which the current accounting and financial valuation standards were created (mostly in the 1950s). They made sense until quite recently. As late as 1980, 80 per cent of the value of the Fortune 500 list of companies was represented by tangible assets. Since then, change has happened fast. Intangible assets grew to overtake tangibles as a proportion of shareholder value around 1990. They now account for over 70 per cent of the value of the Fortune 500, trending upwards (see Figure 16.1).

This change has drawn the attention of accountants and financiers. They have struggled to develop new accounting rules to tackle the problem of measuring intangibles (with varying degrees of success, discussed later in this chapter). For most companies, the most important intangible asset is the brand. Brand is estimated to represent around a third of the total value of US and European corporations, less for those in Asia-Pacific.

However, to manage the brand as a financial asset requires an understanding of how the brand creates value. For this we need to define the brand in a way that makes sense financially. From a financial standpoint, the brand has two components: identity and reputation. Simply put,

Brand = Identity + Reputation

Here, identity is considered to be a clear and simple 'mark', with concrete and legally defensible attributes. Reputation consists of the psychological benefits resulting from a particular set of associations in the mind of customers. These differentiate it from competitors and create a promise of future performance, which constitutes the reputation of the business.

Market Capitalization of the S&P 500 (Index 100 = book value of equity)
1978–2010E

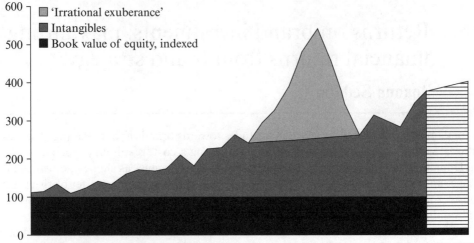

Source: S&P; Bloomberg; Milward Brown Optimor analysis.

Figure 16.1   Intangible assets account for a growing proportion of shareholder value

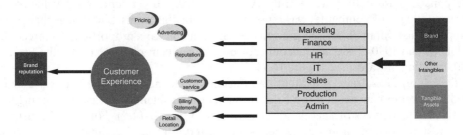

Source: ©Millward Brown Optimor Analysis 2006.

Figure 16.2   Brand as both cause and effect

The brand is created and managed through the customer experience – the points at which the company interacts with customers and potential customers. These points of interaction include traditional marketing activities (including both visual and verbal communications) and all the products and operations of the business. But the brand acquires a power and existence of its own. It establishes a non-rational hold over the buying behavior of the customer. This creates a pact between the customer and the company, which guarantees a flow of future sales and profits. The unique power of the brand lies in its ability to transfer customer loyalty across products, services and categories. The brand can be separated from the products and operations of the company and franchised and licensed to third parties for use in new situations (see Figure 16.2).

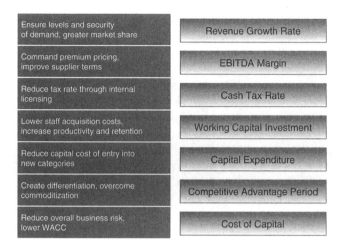

Figure 16.3   Brand impacts key value drivers

From a financial point of view, the brand creates value primarily, but by no means solely, through its influence on customer buying decisions. Brand can impact a company's financials up and down the value chain, influencing supply as well as demand. Figure 16.3 illustrates some of the ways in which brand affects seven of the key financial drivers of a company (see Figure 16.3).

Most brand valuation and measurement focuses on the first two value drivers: revenues and margins. However, brand also impacts business in other less obvious ways, which should also be taken into account when measuring its effectiveness.

MAJOR AREAS OF BRAND FINANCIAL IMPACT

1. *Revenues*: Brand has a direct impact on sales through its role in driving the customer purchase decision. Brand influences both the original decision to buy a product or service, and the decision to keep on buying and become a loyal customer. By creating a bond with loyal customers, brand increases the security of future revenue streams. By increasing preference for a company's products or services, brand helps to grow market share.
2. *Margins*: Brand can make it possible for a company to achieve higher margins for its products, by charging higher prices. Even in categories where it is difficult to obtain a price premium, for example mobile telephony, brand can have a positive impact on margins. By increasing customer loyalty, brand reduces churn and leads to lower customer acquisition costs. Brand loyal or 'bonded' customers are always the most profitable (see Figure 16.4).
3. *Tax rate*: There is potential for some global companies to consolidate brand ownership and control through creation of brand holding companies and internal licensing systems. Companies such as Nestlé, Shell and Vodafone have all have done this.

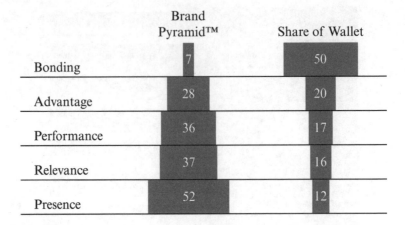

Source: Millward Brown Analysis: BrandZ data 1998–2005.

Figure 16.4   Bonded customers are the most profitable

4. *Working capital*: Brand can reduce employee costs. Studies have shown that companies with strong brands, such as Microsoft and Goldman Sachs, can hire more easily from the top business schools and for lower salaries. Brand can also help a company achieve better payment terms both with its suppliers and customers. A company with a strong brand may be able to pay its suppliers later, and get its customers to pay earlier, than a company with a weaker brand, leading to lower receivables and higher payables.
5. *Capital expenditure*: Companies with strong brands have the option to minimize investment costs and risks when extending into new areas, by licensing the brand to a third party, and receiving a risk-free stream of royalty rates – pure profit. An example is Gap, whose rapid expansion of stores has been entirely due to brand licensing.
6. *Competitive advantage period*: Brand can prolong periods of competitive advantage. By creating a bond with customers, a strong brand creates a barrier for entry. Customers are reluctant to switch to new players, making it difficult for them to gain market share, even when their products and services are of equal or higher quality.
7. *Cost of capital*: A strong brand can reduce a corporation's cost of capital. Studies have shown that companies with strong brands such as Toyota, or owners of a portfolio of strong brands, such as Procter & Gamble, are able to obtain additional basis points on their bond prices, and command higher credit ratings than companies with similar financial profiles but weaker brands.

The importance of brand will continue to increase with the growth of globalization and the advent of a 'flat world'. In a global economy, all other things rapidly become equal. Standards of education and training are equalizing. Innovations can be quickly copied. Advantages in cost structure and business models are temporary. Brand becomes the only sustainable source of future differentiation.

BRAND VALUATION METHODOLOGIES

There are five or six distinctly different methodologies for valuing brands. These can be roughly divided into three categories: Back of the envelope, Internal, and Flawed/incomplete approaches.

'Back of the Envelope' Brand Valuation Approaches

Some brand valuation methods are focused on just putting a value on a brand at a given point in time. They provide no insight into the sources of brand value, nor guidance on how to manage the brand. These valuation methods are typically geared towards transactions such as mergers and acquisitions, brand securitization, or licensing deals (internal or external). They are also often used for the purpose of reporting brands on balance sheets, as required by accounting rules. These methods are static in nature, and are relatively unsophisticated.

These approaches value brands from a financial market perspective. Key metrics used for valuing the brand are taken from third party examples, using publicly available data. They are based on the assumption that it is possible to find sufficient information on comparable transactions to deduce parameters to apply to the brand being valued.

There are two valuation approaches which fall into this category: the market-based method and the royalty relief method.

Market-based valuations

This method consists of taking disclosed brand values for comparable brands and applying those to the brand being valued. A more sophisticated approach consists of using brand valuation multiples. If there are transactions available that actually disclose a specific value for the brand, one can then calculate a multiple for that transaction – say brand value per dollar of revenue or brand value per dollar of earnings before income tax and dearness allowance (EBITDA), and then apply that multiple to the brand being valued.

The problem with the system of comparables is that relevant data is often not available. Further, in most cases, available transactions do not specifically disclose brand values but just overall enterprise values. It then becomes necessary to estimate what portion of the enterprise value is related to the brand being valued and then to apply a multiple to that value. This is particularly difficult in cases where a company operates with more than one brand and in more than one country. Without access to internal data, value cannot be accurately attributed to a brand.

In the end, it often turns out that the only validation of the available data is that it resulted in a transaction, that is that it was accepted as fair by both sides. For these reasons, the multiple approach is generally used as a secondary methodology, to test and validate the results obtained from other brand valuation methods, just as one would check a company valuation against market valuation multiples of comparable companies.

Royalty relief

The royalty relief method arrives at the value of a brand by calculating the value of the future royalty payments that a company would need to pay a third party to license the brand, if it did not own the brand itself. A royalty rate is applied to forecast future sales. The stream of brand royalties is then discounted back to a net present value.

The problem then becomes how to determine what would be the correct royalty fee levels for the brand, especially in the case when the brand to be valued is not already licensed out. Here, the most common approach is to look at licensing deals for comparable brands. Licensing databases with information on past transactions are available for this purpose.

This approach is market-based in that the valuation is based on what the market would be willing to pay for a license to the brand. For this reason, this approach is often favored by accounting firms, since market value is an accepted test of a fair valuation by most accounting standards.

The problem with this approach is that the brand licensing market lacks transparency and sophistication. The first comparable was usually established by rule of thumb. Comparables reflect the balance of power between particular licensors and licensees at the time of negotiation rather than the intrinsic value of the brand. As a result, valuations based on royalty relief calculations tend to undervalue the brand and favor the licensee over the licensor, as there is no business-related basis for justifying royalty rates.

Flawed or Incomplete Brand Valuation Methodologies

Certain brand valuation approaches are fundamentally flawed in their logic. The main issue is that they only look at one aspect of brand value. When used in isolation, these methods fail the most basic test of any valuation method: that it should be conceptually sound. However, when used in conjunction with other methods, they can provide a useful check and throw additional light on specific sources of brand value.

Three such approaches are in common usage: the cost-based approach, the premium price method, and the brand equity approach.

Cost-based approaches

The idea is that a brand can be valued as the sum of the marketing and advertising costs incurred to build the brand, or of the replacement cost if the brand had to be built from scratch today.

This approach has two major flaws. First, it assumes that future value can be related to past costs, which is not necessarily the case. Spending has never been a guaranteed way to build value. There are numerous examples of companies who have spent millions or even billions on advertising without creating a strong brand.

The most extreme cases occurred during the dot.com boom. In 2000, Internet businesses are estimated to have spent over $3 billion on TV and sponsorships. Today, most of these brands have disappeared. Perhaps the best-known is example is Pets.com, the on-line petfood delivery business, which spent over $47.5 million in advertising in two years, including a $2 million Super bowl spot featuring its famous sock puppet, before collapsing in November 2000. Other dot.coms committed themselves to multi-year stadium sponsorships, which they then had to renege on, amid extreme embarrassment. Webvan, an online grocery delivery service, undertook a three-year sponsorship of the San Francisco ballpark, at a cost of several million dollars. This included putting Webvan stickers on the stadium's 43 000 cup holders (which had to be peeled off soon after when the company went bust). Other stadiums had to be ignominiously renamed. These included not only the Houston Astro's Enron field, a $100 million, 30-year deal (the sponsorship has been resold, back to an old economy brand and the stadium renamed Minute Maid), but also the New England Patriots CMGI stadium (a 15-year, $114 million sponsorship) and the Baltimore Ravens' PSINet Stadium.

More traditional businesses have also paid out huge sums on advertising without producing commensurate results. SBC and Bell South paid out over $4 billion dollars advertising on Cingular to little purpose – the brand did not create a strong bond with consumers and at the time of writing, will soon be replaced by AT&T. The second fallacy of this approach is that it presupposes that brands are built only through investment in advertising, whereas the brand is the result of many different types of investments: not only advertising and marketing, but also R&D and product design, and every aspect of the customer experience. Starbucks and Google are two companies which have created valuable brands, without significant investment in marketing. Starbucks' advertising spend runs at less than 1 per cent of revenues ($76 million during the calendar year 2004–2005). The brand has been built almost wholly by investment in the experience. Google's advertising investment was one tenth that of AOL and MSN during 2003–2006. During the same period, Google emerged as the world's third most valuable brand, as a result of a compelling product experience, in combination with a brilliant PR strategy.

Cost-based approaches can be helpful as a 'rule of thumb' for allocating ownership when more than one party has invested in marketing a brand. However, even in these cases, measurement of the comparative effectiveness of their marketing initiatives needs to be taken into account.

Price premium
The idea behind the price premium method is that a brand creates value by enabling its owner to charge a premium price for the products sold under that brand name. The method then consists of estimating that price premium based on a study of non-branded products in the category, or of market research on price sensitivity and purchase behavior. A brand price premium is then calculated and applied to estimates of future sales volumes, and brand cashflows are calculated and then discounted to arrive at a brand value.

The fundamental flaw of this approach is the initial hypothesis that brands create value only by enabling a price premium. In reality, brands create value in a given category by any superior combination of a price premium and a volume premium. In the case of a high-end fashion brand such as Louis Vuitton, there is a very high price premium, offset by a negative volume premium: there are more unbranded suitcases sold than Vuitton luggage. In the case of discount brands such as Wal-Mart, for instance, it is exactly the opposite: there is a negative price premium more than offset by a positive volume premium. For both of these types of brands, the premium price approach would fail to provide an accurate valuation.

In some highly commoditized categories, brand owners may feel that a price premium is the most meaningful measure of brand health. Hewlett Packard, for example, utilizes the price premium approach. However, it must be recognized that this is only part of the answer. Unless price premium is used in combination with an approach that also takes volume into consideration, it will provide an inaccurate reflection of brand value.

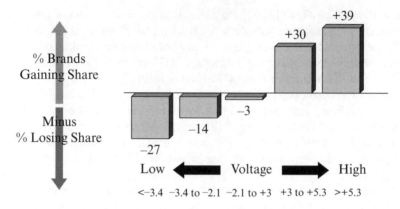

Source: Millward Brown Analysis: BrandZ data 1998–2005.

Figure 16.5   Voltage validated by market share analysis

Brand equity 'valuation' approaches

Some methods attempt to calculate a brand value without any connection to the financials of the business they are considering. Underlying this is confusion over the exact meaning of the words 'brand value'. This phrase is sometimes used as if it were interchangeable with the term 'brand equity'. Brand equity is itself a rather vague and imprecise term. It is most generally used to denote a brand proposition and set of attributes, intended to differentiate a company's products and services from competitors and create a bond with its customers.

Market research companies have developed different techniques for measuring brand equity. Some of these focus on brand attributes and personality, others consider the customers' relationship with the brand. An example of the attribute-based approach is Y&R's Brand Asset Valuator. This measures the strength of brand perceptions along four dimensions: Differentiation, Relevance, Esteem and Knowledge. BAV also evaluates Brand Image using a mix of 48 'image' and 'personality' attributes. Millward Brown's Brand Dynamics methodology measures a brand's success in converting the customers of its products into loyal or 'bonded' customers. It recognizes that in all markets, a small number of consumers account for a large proportion of sales. Loyal customers are more valuable to a brand than occasional customers. The Brand Dynamics Pyramid measures the stages through which a customer relationship develops, and quantifies the brand's success in creating loyalty. The Brand Signature identifies a brand's strengths and weaknesses at each level. Brand Voltage, a summary of signature, is a leading indicator of share (see Figure 16.5).

Similar frameworks based on 'the customer funnel' are also used by some management consulting companies, such as McKinsey. Another way to build economic use valuation models without a link to business financials is through correlation of brand metrics with stock performance, the method preferred by CoreBrand. The idea here is to find out how much of the company's market capitalization can be accounted for by brand-related factors: the approach is purely external, includes no business valuation, and has very poor granularity.

All of these brand equity approaches only provide part of the answer. Market research is an important component of any brand valuation methodology that seeks to understand how brand drives value. However, on its own, the answers provided by research stop at abstract attributes, such as 'image', 'consideration' and 'loyalty'. A hard financial component must be added to determine the financial value of the brand.

Of these research methodologies, the 'pyramid' or 'customer funnel' approaches, which measure customer relationships, are best adapted to brand valuation. Attempts have been made to link image-based approaches to business financials, with little success. The most serious of these, Brand Economics, a joint venture of Young & Rubicam and the EVA consultants Stern Stewart, met with little success.

Internal or 'Economic Use' Brand Valuation Methodologies

The preferred method for valuing brands is the economic use approach. If properly implemented, economic use brand valuation combines the best elements of the financial market approaches (hard financial numbers) with the advantages of the brand equity-based approaches (research-based measurement of customer attitudes towards brands). Economic use brand valuation can provide both a robust financial value for the brand and an understanding of how brand creates value in the business. This helps identify the actions taken that grow the value which a brand adds to the business. Brand valuation ceases to be just a brand measurement tool and becomes a brand management tool. The starting point for any application of the economic use method is to calculate the economic value of a brand to the current owner, in its current use.

The approach used is also used by accountants and analysts for valuing a business. Underlying the brand valuation is a business valuation model, which can take one of several commonly used approaches such as Discounted cash flow, Economic value added, and Economic profit.

There are four components to brand valuation:

- Segmentation
- Financial forecasting
- Brand driver analysis
- Brand risk analysis

For the analysis to be accurate, it should be 'bottom-up'. A preliminary step is to segment the business into relevant components of value. Depending on the nature of the business, the segmentation may consider customer segments, products, channels and geography. The objective is to drill down to the level at which the brand behaves differently. The brand valuation analysis is then conducted for each segment.

Three pieces of analysis are involved. First, financial forecasts are obtained, either from the company or from outside sources, and used to calculate the future cashflows for each segment. The second step is to isolate the portion of the cashflows which can be attributed to the brand from overall cashflows. A 'brand driver analysis' is employed to understand the contribution brand makes to driving revenue and profits. The analysis addresses two key questions: 'What are the drivers of the customer purchase decision?' and 'What role does brand play in that decision?' The reasoning is that the customer decision to purchase drives 100 per cent of demand (if no money changes hands, there are no cash flows). The output of the brand driver analysis is a determination of what portion of that 100 per cent can be attributed to the impact of brand, as opposed to everything else that happens in the business (product, pricing, distribution, customer service and so forth).

In a third step, the portion of future cashflows that has been identified as having been created by the brand is then discounted to obtain a net present value, taking into account the risk associated with the brand. The concept is that brand may be more or less risky than the business as a whole. Generally the brand carries more risk. The total value of the brand is the sum of the value in each segment.

All firms employing the economic use method for brand valuation use similar approaches to financial forecasting. The models have to be conceptually similar in order to meet basic principles of valuation and conform to accounting standards. However, the ways in which these models are applied can be significantly different.

Simply put, the major differences depend on whether the purpose of the valuation is financial or strategic.

The older practitioners, such as Interbrand and Brand Finance, take a primarily financial approach to brand valuation. Brand valuation is seen as the preserve of the accountants and firmly divorced from strategy. The objective is to obtain a financial number for the brand. The focus is consequently on the financial inputs to the valuation. The non-financial inputs (the brand driver analysis and brand risk analysis) tend to be derived in a fashion that is often qualitative, and at worst, cavalier. The outputs from this type of valuation may meet the needs of finance professionals for compliance or royalty rate determination or of management for benchmark metrics, but are of little use for running the business.

The newer approach to brand valuation, used by Millward Brown Optimor and some other consulting firms, is more strategic. The view is that brand valuation should not be just about a number. It should be a strategic tool for brand and marketing management. Properly applied, the brand valuation approach can be used not just to measure the current value that brand contributes to a business, but also to identify the strategies and actions that the company can take to grow that value. This view has major implications for how the valuation is conducted. You can only identify how to grow brand value if you have a sound understanding of how that value is created. This means that the non-financial inputs to the model have to be as rigorous as the financial inputs. This 'share-holder value-added' approach to brand valuation utilizes quantitative market research in addition to financial and industry data. Market research is used to identify the macro and micro drivers of the brand experience and quantify the importance of each factor in driving the customer purchase decision. Statistical analysis is used to determine the brand's impact on each factor.

The Millward Brown BrandZ and Brand Dynamics brand equity tools are particularly well adapted to this process. These tools measure the drivers of the customer purchase decision and determine the success of the brand in converting its consumers to 'bonded' or brand loyal users. Brand effectiveness can be measured absolutely, as a percentage of the purchase decision, and relatively, by comparing the brand's success in creating a bond with its customers with competitor and category norms (see Figure 16.6). Studies on the BrandZ data, tracked since 1998, have shown that a brand's success in converting customers to the 'bonded' stage is directly correlated to both sales and margins.

A similar approach is taken to the determination of brand risk. A rigorous bench-marking of brand strength against competitors provides a wealth of information for brand

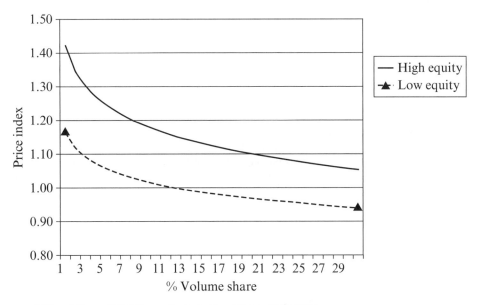

Source: Millward Brown R&D Group Analysis: BrandZ data 1998–2005.

Figure 16.6 Strongly bonded brands command both higher price points and larger market shares

strategy and brand measurement purposes, as well as feeding into the determination of a brand discount rate. This type of brand valuation can be used not only to measure the current financial value of the brand, but also to model 'what if scenarios' to determine what strategy will add most value to the business and track results on an ongoing basis.

The overall conclusion is that while the more quantitative economic use valuation represents best practices, which brand valuation method is most appropriate for you depends on the application for which you wish to use it. As they say, it is 'horses for courses'.

Strategic applications of brand valuation include: brand performance measurement, brand positioning and communications strategy, brand architecture and portfolio management, brand experience and customer touch point optimization, brand innovation and brand expansion, marketing investment allocation, and the ongoing tracking of brand and marketing ROI. The application of brand valuation to these issues requires a best practices economic use model, one that combines financial data, quantitative customer research data, and competitor data.

BRAND PERFORMANCE MEASUREMENT

Before making any major decisions about brand strategy, it is customary to conduct an initial brand audit, or assessment of the current state of the brand. This enables the company to understand the brand's strengths, weaknesses and leverage points in the context of competitors' strategy. However, there is no systematic framework for evaluating the brand – the information is compiled and conclusions made in a subjective fashion. This process relies on the brand consultant or brand manager's judgment and expertise.

Emerging best practices include not only a qualitative assessment of brand perceptions but also a quantitative analysis of brand performance. This approach utilizes the same data. The difference is the use of more robust, quantitative inputs, and a financial component.

The advantage of this approach is that it allows the state of the brand to be measured on hard financial as well as softer metrics. Most importantly, it sets up a model of how brand creates value in the business. This becomes the foundation for brand strategy development. It provides a framework for idea generation, and a dynamic model which can be used to test the financial impact of alternative brand strategy and investment options.

BRAND ARCHITECTURE AND BRAND PORTFOLIO MANAGEMENT

Brand architecture is one of the most powerful applications of the brand valuation model. Decisions about brand architecture can have major business consequences. Brand architecture impacts marketing investment levels and effectiveness, the clarity and impact of the offering, and, above all, customer loyalty and purchase behavior. The wrong brand architecture decision can lead to significant customer loss and decline in market share.

Especially in the aftermath of an acquisition, brand architecture decisions are difficult to make. The issues are emotional and political. The CEO of the acquired brand will almost always claim that changing the name will lead to loss of sales. Sometimes this is very true, sometimes not true at all, and, most often, partly true.

Brand valuation can help to raise the debate to a more objective level, by putting facts and figures around brand architecture issues. The first step is to conduct an economic use valuation of the brands in question. This establishes the current strength and effectiveness of each brand. Alternative brand architecture scenarios can then be developed and run through the brand valuation model. The objective is to identify the solution which will generate most future revenues, profits and value for the business, taking into account the different levels of investment that each option will require.

The case of Conoco-Phillips illustrates the application of brand valuation to solve difficult and strategically critical brand architecture problems. As a result of a merger, this leading energy sector company found itself with a brand portfolio of six market-facing gasoline brands. The situation was fraught with complexity, including costly overlap of brands in several regions, inefficient use of the refining pipeline, anxious wholesalers demanding to know whether their retail locations would need rebranding, and strong emotional ties to certain brands at the senior leadership level. The approach taken was to value each brand at a regional/state level, and to create a model that allowed different portfolio scenarios to be evaluated financially. This model included not only the effects of brand equity, but also the impact of tangible operational factors, such as the cost of rebranding a gas station, the marketing spend required to support rebranding, and the potential volume loss due to loyalties to brands that would be changed. The analysis resulted in a streamlined brand portfolio with greater brand focus on a regional basis, resulting in significant operational efficiencies – reduced spend on marketing, and on branding and physical materials for retail gas stations. The analysis also identified a number of inefficient retail gasoline assets in certain regions, which resulted in the sale of those assets, further strengthening the overall portfolio.

Brand valuation can also be applied to the rationalization of brand portfolios, in situations where a much larger number of brands need to be evaluated. In this situation, a lighter approach is appropriate, which includes running the different brands through a financial filter.

BRAND EXPERIENCE AND CUSTOMER TOUCHPOINT OPTIMIZATION

Brand valuation tools can also be used to analyze brand performance at key touchpoints and prioritize investment at the customer level. The brand value analysis identifies the levers which drive the customer purchase decision, determines which are the most important, and measures how well the brand is performing on each. This makes it possible to identify the customer touchpoints that really matter and recommend the types of investment required for each. This approach is valuable both for consumer products brands (where the focus will be on the impacts of different elements of the marketing mix) and for retail, services, and B2B brands, where the major drivers of customer decision-making may not be related to marketing.

In industries such as telecommunications, retail banking, fast-food, and travel and hospitality, non-marketing factors produce, on average, five times the number of impressions on customers as marketing factors. The customer's view of a retail banking brand is more likely to be affected by the behavior of customer service people, in the branch or on the phone, or by the ease-of-use of Internet banking services, than by advertising. The way to improve brand performance may be to invest in employee training, IT, or branch facilities. Until deficiencies are corrected, investment in these areas is likely to produce higher returns than investment in marketing.

The brand valuation model allows different investment options to be compared and prioritized according to expected returns. For example, will a hotel gain greater financial results from improving the quality of the beds or the reception area or by building a spa? Should an airline focus on providing a better experience at check in, offer more leg room, or better flight entertainment? Investment options may include environment, employees, products and services in addition to, or instead of, marketing.

BRAND INNOVATION AND BRAND EXPANSION

In addition to identifying and quantifying opportunities within the existing business, brand valuation creates a framework and model that can be applied to new opportunities and new situations. These include both new product development and the expansion of existing offers into new categories and new geographical markets.

Companies are rarely short of ideas – the challenge is how to select the right one and implement it in a way that will be successful. The brand valuation framework can be used to compare the valuation creation potential of different ideas and then determine the best way to take them to market. Questions that can be answered include: which innovation idea has the greatest revenue and profit potential? What are the risks involved and how can they be minimized? How should the new product be branded? Can an existing brand be used, or would it be better to create a new one, or license a brand from a third party? How should the new brand go to market? What positioning should be used? How should it be priced? How much should be invested behind it? The outcome is a case for brand development.

This approach is being adopted by major producers of consumer packaged goods, such as Cadbury and Coca-Cola, as well as innovation and venture capital-backed start-ups.

MARKETING BUDGET ALLOCATION AND OPTIMIZATION

The brand value concept provides the key to solving one of the major marketing issues of the day – how to optimize the effectiveness of marketing budgets. On its own, the brand valuation tool is sufficient to address the 'big picture' marketing issues. The data provides a comparison of value creation potential across brands, businesses and markets. This makes it possible to answer such questions as:

- Why spend on marketing as compared to investing in product development, sales force or discounting on price? Would companies such as GM and Dell have done better to dedicate a larger portion of their resources to brand investment instead of price promotion?
- How should marketing budgets be allocated across brands, businesses and geographical markets?
- At a brand level, which customer segments should be the primary targets of marketing investment? Which phases of the buying cycle? Should the focus be on acquiring customers or retaining customers?

Traditional marketing mix ROI measurement and optimization models use econometrics. These statistical models, though complicated to implement, are founded on a simple idea: correlating past spend on different marketing activities against the sales that resulted. In the best cases, they can provide a very granular and valuable picture of the sales impact of different investments. There is nothing else available that provides such detail on what happened when we spent a dollar on TV versus a dollar on print advertising, Internet, and whatever other relevant items data is available for.

However, these models have several disadvantages. First, they require a large amount of data, including sales and marketing investment for each item of the mix, on a weekly basis, over a period of several years, to deliver robust results. In some categories (notably consumer packaged goods) and some countries (primarily the US and UK), this data may be readily available. In others, it may not be, and modeling becomes a challenge. Secondly, marketing mix models only measure short-term effects. Further, simulations and market allocation models only work for the immediate future, assuming no changes in market conditions.

The solution lies in combining the brand valuation and the marketing mix models. This is a three-way process which involves measuring: the impact of marketing investment on short-term sales, the impact of marketing investments on the brand, and the impact of brand on sales and longer-term value creation.

BIBLIOGRAPHY

Bullen, Halsey and Regina Cafini (2006), 'Accounting standards regarding intellectual assets', *Seminar Creation, Recognition and Valuation of Intellectual Assets*, United Nations, Department of Economic & Social Affairs, July.

'BCBG Max Azria Picks up $53 million', *IpFrontline*, December, 2004.

Davies, Roy (2006), 'Who's who in Bowie bonds', www.exeter.ac.uk, July.

Deloitte Touche Tohmatsu (2007), 'IAS Plus International Accounting Standards: IFRS 3', <http://www.iasplus.com/standard/ifrs 03.htm>.

Die Tank AG (2004), 'Imarken Bewertung', *Absatzwirtschaft*, Verlagsgruppe Handelsblatt GmbH.

Financial Accounting Standards Board (2007), 'Summary of Statement No. 142' <http://www.fasb.org/st/summary/stsum142.shtml>.

License Magazine study (2005), 'Li©ense! 2005 Industry Annual Report', *License Magazine*, October.

Lightspeed Research (2004), Lightspeed integrated marketing study conducted for Advertising Age, October 2003.

McDonald, M. (2002), 'Key elements of world class marketing', Cranfield School of Management.

'Securitising intellectual property: intangible opportunities', *The Economist*, June 17, 2006.

Wan Lixin (2006), 'Branding: The next step', *China International Business*, February.

17.   The challenge of the global brand

Hayes Roth

'We're a global brand.'

How many times, in how many boardrooms around the world, has this claim been made over the past 30 years? In the 1970s it was almost always more vision than fact, with only a handful of companies able to cite concrete evidence of such status – arguably Coca-Cola, Pepsi and Pan American Airways; maybe Colgate-Palmolive, IBM and Shell – and even these (with the possible exception of Pan Am) could essentially point only to 'Western' markets as their domain. Whole continents were still off-limits politically and culturally to American and Western European brands.

In the 1980s, it was primarily global hope-to-be's who were beginning to stake ground for the future while struggling to figure out how to actually get there. Cool start-ups and aggressively reinvented brands in fashion, technology and transportation – Nike, Microsoft, Sony, Apple, British Airways, Honda – began to push frontiers and establish brand reputations far in excess of their actual market footprint.

By the 1990s, as the walls between East and West crumbled, the race for global brand domination was on. It became the 'decade of the brand' and everyone had to have one. Never mind that the so-called brand was as ethereal as vaporware or as disappointing as the mostly forgotten, ill-conceived, fundamentally flawed online experiments of the late 1990s (remember the Pets.com sock puppet?).

Today, global brands aren't a marketer's fantasy. They are highly valued, tangible corporate assets that require immense investment and infrastructures to manage, build and quantify. And they come from everywhere. Eight of the top 100 global brands ranked by a Millward Brown Optimor Study in 2006 are not American, and 14 of them did not even exist 25 years ago.[1] Perhaps most telling of all, the fourth most valuable brand ranked in this study is China Mobile.

This is a big, powerful club. But to rightfully belong takes far more than size and recognition. Large, successful, truly global brands are about something more than footprint and distribution – they are about a commonly understood, relevantly differentiating idea that transcends borders, cultures and geographies. We see them when we travel, we read about them in the world's financial publications and we measure them on valuation lists of all kinds. But what does it take to create the kind of idea that is at the center of a strong brand? And how do mere mortals build them from the inside out, extend them across borders, reinvent them to remain fresh and relevant . . . and then build them some more?

The answer begins with a simpler question: Why create a global brand at all?

Kevin Keller, respected professor and author of *Strategic Brand Management*, outlines the rationale succinctly. Global brands give companies competitive advantages, such as:

- economies of scale in production and distribution
- lower marketing costs
- power and scope
- consistency in brand image
- ability to leverage good ideas quickly and efficiently
- uniformity of marketing practices[2]

There are two other, perhaps even more pressing drivers of global brand expansion: the first being the Internet. Though it's clearly too soon to fully gauge the Internet's full impact on business and society in the decades to come, it is obvious that this transcendent medium has profoundly changed our perspective on both.

The second driver is the rapid growth of global travel for business and tourism, particularly since 2003. Its relevance can be felt in every major airport in the world, as these hubs become modern-day international bazaars catering to visitors of every language, geography and culture. Both Boeing and Airbus are gambling heavily on this growth market with major new aircraft designed for long-distance, high-volume travel. The projection that China will become the largest exporter of tourists by 2008 ensures that this is a low-odds bet.

The influence these factors have on how companies and organizations of all sizes perceive and market their brands is extensive and demanding. It is no longer prudent to develop a brand identity or name for even a regionally driven product or business without considering its cross-cultural implications. This usually means registering a logo and tagline internationally, a laborious process but one essential to any business thinking about its future. On the Internet, traditional marketing territories are irrelevant – the brand goes where the customer takes it. As Douglas Holt, John Quelch, and Earl Taylor write:

> The rise of global culture doesn't mean that consumers share all the same tastes or values. Rather, global brands allow people to participate in a shared conversation, drawing on shared symbols. Like entertainment, sports, or politicians, global brands have become the *lingua franca* for consumers all over the world.[3]

Global availability does not equal global branding. Being able to access a specialty product in China from a computer terminal in Spain does not qualify a brand as global, nor does having a product appear concurrently on shelves in Jakarta and Rome. A true brand represents a consistent set of associations and attributes that are recognizable to a relevant target audience of sufficient size and quality to sustain a viable, growing business. A global brand must do this on an international scale, delivering a reliable core promise while remaining relevant to diverse audiences.

Though some well-established corporations have been known to launch a product concurrently across the globe, such tactics are rare. Product and service launches from even the largest corporations tend to roll out regionally, and start-up organizations almost never embark as global brands. Messrs Hewlett and Packard were unlikely to have been contemplating world domination from the garage on Addison Avenue as they built their fledgling business. Even the ubiquitous Starbucks was first a local coffeehouse. Most new ideas begin by serving either a niche market with a highly relevant idea, or a broad market with a highly differentiated offering. Both take time and considerable energy to establish successfully on a large scale.

So how are global brands created? Is there a formula for success? A set of simple rules, perhaps, from which others may learn and prosper? Or is it more like the path of the salmon, an instinctual and desperate struggle to move upstream against all odds until finally arriving at the 'high water' from which to propagate?

Not surprisingly, the answer is elusive and varied. At Landor Associates, we have had the great privilege to work with visionary leaders across almost every industry and product category. Over time we have noted some branding truths as well as the inevitable exceptions. As always, the case can best be made through example. Here are the stories of two great companies that took very different paths to building a global brand: BP and Panasonic.

It has been our experience that the most successful brand initiatives are driven from the top down. The CEO and team incite bold leadership, informed by a deep understanding of the organization's multiple constituents, both internal and external. Then the brand is constructed around a clearly defined core idea and communicated through a cohesive arsenal of marketing tools that relay a consistent message at every point of consumer contact. Examples abound – FedEx, GE, Apple – but one of the most remarkable in recent years is BP. BP is a classic story of what Landor (and *Fortune* magazine) defines as a 'breakaway brand'.[4] BP has not only reinvented its own brand but has also managed to surpass its category in striking and measurable ways in the process.

STARTING AT THE TOP

The BP story has become for many a textbook example of a successful corporate brand transformation on a global scale, and for some very good reasons. First, it began with a clear vision by a strong leader, Lord John Browne, who wanted to forge a new kind of company around the merger of several well-established brands, chief among them British Petroleum, Amoco, Castrol, and bits and pieces of major oil and gas companies such as Mobil and Arco. By committing publicly to a broader purpose for his company, Browne charted a course for effecting the necessary internal change to accomplish and reinforce it, then telegraphed this mission dramatically through breakthrough branding and marketing communications. Like all good visions, it was a serious stretch for the organization. Lord Browne and his team did not set out to be merely one of the best petroleum companies in the world – they wanted BP to be one of the best *companies* in the world, period.

This meant moving from being primarily a refiner of hydrocarbons to a provider of complete energy solutions; from being focused purely on performance and the bottom line to addressing bottom- *and* top-line growth; from being driven largely by its traditional physical asset base to using knowledge and innovation to create future value *beyond petroleum*.

To accomplish this also meant that BP needed to evolve from a multinational corporation to a diverse global citizen organized around an enduring set of brand principles. With BP's upstream and downstream markets spanning over 100 countries, the leadership challenge was to find a common purpose and voice that could resonate meaningfully and credibly across multiple audiences while differentiating the brand from its competitors.

Through work with Ogilvy & Mather and Landor, the 'beyond petroleum' concept became much more than an ad line. As a symbol of the new strategy for the organization, it became a mantra that championed both a vision and a promise for its future.

INTEGRATING THE BRAND PROMISE

Advertising-driven promises are all too frequently broken. Lord Browne and his team set out to make the 'beyond petroleum' concept an integral part of corporate culture. Its promise therefore needed to be made clear and approachable to all employees in words that would resonate in their daily lives at BP, wherever in the world they served their company and its customers. It had to mean something important to BPers everywhere – especially those who were relatively new to the company. The brand idea informed a Brand Driver™ platform, which defined what the brand stood for and what it aspired to be in the future (see Figure 17.1). It served as a foundation for a series of internal and external initiatives, keeping them focused on delivering the brand promise to customers.

From this brand idea came the now-famous helios logo, the evocative representation of the 'beyond petroleum' brand idea. Symbolizing energy (the sun) and environmental sensitivity (green) in a stylized, sunflower motif, it has been given broad and exciting interpretation across every aspect of BP's brand expression. In short, it was an unexpected solution to a complex design challenge. It signaled BP leadership's determination to be differentiated while maintaining focus on its overarching mission to be a leading energy solutions provider and a good global citizen.

Great design can serve as an inspiring banner when properly presented and explained. The BP logo had aesthetic and symbolic appeal, but it was essentially an empty vessel – it would become what BP chose to make of it, which was quite a lot. BP understood that to deliver its 'beyond petroleum' promise to customers, employees needed to understand how the promise applied to their daily jobs. Wisely, BP began its transformation from the inside, creating a series of tools including websites, CDs, brand movies, newsletters and all manner of company-branded tokens that emphasized not only the excitement of the new logo but, more critically, the idea behind it. Indeed, it was the *story* of the brand and its promise that BP focused on telling.

Brand champion workshops were organized to train the trainers, generating ownership among individuals who then evangelized the mission to others. In all, more than 1400 brand champions were trained in 19 countries over the initial two months following the launch. This was viral marketing at its best – from the inside. The effort was also measured, revealing that by the ninth month post-launch, 97 per cent of all BP employees were aware of the new identity and its 'beyond petroleum' promise.[5]

Awareness and action, of course, are two different things. BP leadership knew that to engage the hearts and minds of employees over the long term, the brand transformation would have to be about more than flag waving. The result was the creation of the Helios Awards Program. Every year this program honors those employees who have contributed to the company and their respective communities through actions judged to be 'on brand': progressive, innovative, performance-oriented and green. In this way leadership communicates that 'beyond petroleum' should be a way of life at BP, not just this year's ad slogan.

**Brand Driver
Platform**

Landor

VERBAL BRAND DRIVER *"Beyond Petroleum"*

BRAND PROMISE At the core of BP is an unshakable commitment to human progress. We aim for radical openness: we will be the magnet for people who want to change the world with new ideas, by delivering a performance standard that challenges the world's best companies.

BELIEFS *Progressive* – transforming the way we do business
Innovative – delivering breakthrough solutions
Performance – setting world class standards
Green – demonstrating environmental leadership

VISUAL BRAND DRIVER™   *typography*

automobile   activity

furniture   *mood (green)*   object

animal   drink

BP Brand Driver™ Platform   architechture

Source: Developed by Landor. Reprinted with permission.

Figure 17.1   BP Brand Driver^{TM} Platform

PUTTING THE BRAND TO WORK

It's all fine and good to tell a great story but, in the end, deeds count more than words. BP chose its initial actions carefully. Early on, it committed publicly to reducing greenhouse emissions by 10 per cent by 2010, the equivalent of taking 18 million cars off the road. It initiated partnerships with leading auto manufacturers in the pursuit of more efficient engines and practical alternative fuels. BP quickly became one of the world's largest producers of solar panels and solar power, and the second largest provider of natural gas. In the summer of 2005, the company announced an $8 billion investment program in alternative energy.

These actions have been well noted by the public. BP was voted Britain's Most Admired Company and Lord Browne its Most Admired Leader by *Management Today* shortly after its brand launch in 2002. This was the first time in the awards' history that one company received both top accolades. The admiration for BP continues around the world. *Fortune* magazine has similarly ranked BP a Most Admired Company, and in 2005 BP was ranked a Most Respected Company by the *Financial Times*, coming in at seventh.[6]

These were among the many clear indicators that BP was achieving its goal of being one of the world's great companies. But did this positive thinking have any impact on its bottom line? That, too, has been impressive – retail sales at convenience stores increased 23 per cent within one year of the rebranding effort.[7] Overall sales and sales of lubricants and fuels steadily increased between 5 and 10 per cent above market growth through 2004.[8] By 2005, BP reported serving over 13 million customers per day. Profits have been exceptional – at $91.3 billion in 2005 – and have enabled BP to fund new initiatives that will drive its future business.[9]

Retail represents less than 15 per cent of BP's business worldwide. BP is first and foremost an upstream energy developer and supplier in a highly commoditized category, subject to immense global trade and economic factors. Can effective branding truly impact corporate brand value in such an industrialized segment? *Fortune* magazine thought so, recognizing BP as one the 10 most improved brands from 2001 to 2005 in terms of brand equity value. As quantified by Young & Rubicam's BrandAsset® Valuator research, the world's oldest and largest brand database, in conjunction with Stern Stewart's Economic Value Added analytics, the value of BP's intangible assets (which include its brand) increased by more than $7 billion during this time period, while the intangible assets of its larger energy rivals declined in value.[10]

What does BP itself think of all this as it surveys its global brand universe? To quote its advertising tagline, 'It's a start'. Like any good company, BP is focused on the considerable challenges of fully delivering its brand promise around the world. Large-scale transitions are by nature fraught with difficulties, but how an organization meets those challenges determines the ultimate success of its brand and business. BP is clearly committed to its brand promise. Lord Browne himself said:

> In a global market place, branding is crucially important in attracting customers and business. It is not just a matter of a few gasoline stations or the logo on pole signs. It is about the identity of the company, and the values that underpin everything that you do and every relationship that you have.[11]

That's the textbook approach to building a global brand.

It goes without saying that not every company operates the same way. Top-down, charismatic leadership expedites global branding programs, but such an approach may not be culturally appropriate for some companies. Building a global brand requires navigating a political, and often emotional, minefield inside mostly large, labyrinthine organizations. Even under the best of circumstances, it is never a tidy process.

Occasionally, the impetus for brand transformation begins at the regional level. Market forces and local leadership become a dynamic catalyst for change, and a region can become a model for the rest of the organization. Navigating political tides and conflicting priorities across geographies and within divisions is risky. But it can work, with great vision, bold determination, and huge measures of patience. This is what happened to the Panasonic brand. The momentum for managing Panasonic as a global brand came from the North American division of Matsushita Electric Industrial. After nearly 10 years of effort, it is still very much a work in progress.

STARTING AT THE REGIONAL LEVEL

Panasonic's path for building its global brand can be traced back to 1997, when Matsushita Electronics Corporation of America (MECA) called Landor's New York office asking for help in understanding its customer base and their perceptions of its Panasonic brand. Although Panasonic has been a household name for decades across much of the planet, few people are aware that Panasonic is actually but one brand in the portfolio of Matsushita Electric Industrial Company, one of Japan's largest and most respected corporations.

Founded by Konosuke Matsushita (see Figure 17.4), a remarkable innovator who began making headlamps for bicycles in 1923, Matsushita is today the world's biggest and most successful consumer electronics maker. Matsushita Group contains over 380 companies, including technology megabrands such as Panasonic, National and JVC. In the 1990s, the Japanese giant even owned Universal Studios for a period of time.

Today Panasonic's parent has $81 billion in sales of plasma TVs, stereos, camcorders, DVD players, cameras, computers, copiers and a breadth of home products ranging from microwaves and refrigerators to women's shavers. It is a company on the move, yet Matsushita is virtually unknown to the general public outside Japan. The Panasonic brand, on the other hand, is almost ubiquitous, visible wherever electronic goods are sold in every corner of the world. Unfortunately, as Landor's research in the mid-1990s bore out, the Panasonic brand was known all too well and loved by all too few.

In the 1990s, Matsushita was driven largely by its manufacturing divisions. Each was quite independent in its own marketing arena, and little cohesive effort was devoted to identifying or targeting core customer needs. Though slogans proclaiming 'The Customer Comes First' abounded on office walls, in truth, the attitude of 'If we build it, they will come' pervaded. It was all about producing good, highly functional products, generally unexceptional but for being extremely well made.

Moreover, 'branding' was a word used only in connection with where to put a logo in an ad or brochure. The size, color and dimensions of the Panasonic visual identity were largely a matter of personal taste . . . or lack thereof. The promise of its brand was never discussed. Although this approach mirrored that of the company worldwide, in the US, the sheer cacophony of communications from different marketing activities produced acute message overload. Panasonic notoriously spent less than its competitors in advertising and promotional dollars, so the net effect of this marketing scattershot was to further erode any definable value in the Panasonic brand.

Yet this was the company that pioneered the DVD, the SD memory chip, and the lithium ion rechargeable battery. In truth, it should have been anything but a weak brand!

AN HONEST ASSESSMENT

Panasonic had established a pattern of trying to be everything to everybody – offering consumer electronic products of every type and style across consumer, professional and industrial segments alike. As a result, it failed to establish a clear position to any of its constituents. Its diffuse approach was further reflected in the more than 20 different advertising taglines in use around the world (see Figure 17.2). One in particular surfaced frequently and perhaps best expressed its almost apologetic approach to innovation and leadership: 'Panasonic – Just slightly ahead of our time'. Ironically, internal frustration over this somewhat modest tagline helped stimulate a hunger for change.

In 1997 a core team of marketers at the Secaucus, New Jersey, headquarters for Matsushita Electronics Corporation of America (MECA) began in earnest to evaluate the equities and liabilities of the Panasonic brand. At the time, MECA was responsible for the marketing and selling of all Matsushita products in North America. It asked Landor to conduct a robust evaluation of the Panasonic brand. This was the first time that Panasonic (and Matsushita) had undertaken a truly comprehensive brand analysis among its core customers. Both qualitative and quantitative in method, the research took place over a six-month period in 1998 and encompassed consumer, professional and industrial customer segments.

The results were revealing. Though fundamentally strong, the Panasonic brand was losing its distinctiveness and trailing Sony on virtually all critical metrics. Importantly, it was perceived as offering good quality, but it lacked a strong emotional tie with its customers. Across the board, people (especially younger audiences) saw Panasonic as simply behind the times, a brand with little (and declining) differentiation. The implication was clear: if Panasonic did not address the needs of younger audiences, the brand would forever be cast as 'not for me'.

There were positive findings as well. Although arch-rival Sony was perceived as prestigious and cool, it was also seen as unapproachable, arrogant and over-priced. This was an illuminating crack in the Sony armor, presenting an opportunity that Panasonic's marketing team was quick to grasp. For years Panasonic management had chafed in the shadow of this media-darling brand, frustrated that Sony was getting the spotlight while Panasonic received little attention for making breakthrough – and unbreakable – products that delivered real customer value day in and day out.

Interestingly, consumers viewed Panasonic as an American brand despite its Japanese heritage and as warm, friendly and unpretentious. Three key attributes with the potential to differentiate Panasonic also emerged: 'solutions focused', 'having progressive ideas' and

What's New
by
Panasonic

Panasonic
POWER TOOLS

Panasonic !
Batteries - Create A New World

Panasonic
Broadcast

Inconsistent Panasonic branding

Source: Reprinted with permission of Panasonic.

Figure 17.2   Inconsistent Panasonic logos

being able to 'enhance human experience'. From these foundations a great brand could be rebuilt.

Landor concluded that Panasonic should begin to speak with a single voice in North America – compellingly and consistently wherever consumers experienced the brand. As part of this effort, it was time to develop a corporate tagline that communicated a differentiating position based on customer insight: a solutions-focused, customer-friendly brand offering easy-to-use, innovative products, backed by good customer support.

REDEFINING THE PANASONIC BRAND

In 1999 the regional Panasonic marketing team, led by Bob Greenberg and Tom Murano, marshaled resources and support for a full-blown repositioning of the Panasonic brand. Landor's New York office was asked to develop a process for crafting a formal brand positioning incorporating the research insights, with the goal of creating a new, universal tagline and, ultimately, overall brand expression. It was the first time anyone in Matsushita's then 65-year history had ever hired a brand consulting firm.

Landor recommended an approach that it had been developing: the Brand Driver™ Workshop. Designed to build inclusive participation – and responsibility – into the brand development process, it provides an engaging, participatory forum for the exchange of ideas and insights. Panasonic was asked to invite 15 to 20 of its most senior marketing and business team leaders from North America for a full-day offsite session. Also invited were senior advertising and online agency partners from Grey Worldwide and other vendors.

The point of the work session was to get everyone who had their hands on the Panasonic brand to hammer out a set of ownable, differentiating and customer-relevant attributes. Putting the team in the same room for a day would shortcut a lengthy buy-in process later and foster ownership of the final brand idea. The resulting output was assimilated by Landor and crafted into three or four brand concepts and positioning strategies for collective review.

On 21 June, 2001, an all-day Brand Driver session with Panasonic's key marketing representatives and partner agencies was held in Secaucus, New Jersey. All hands were on deck: rivals, colleagues, partner agencies – people whose fates entwined, though many had never met. As Landor had requested, the full spectrum of Matsushita's North American businesses and core suppliers engaged in a series of interactive exercises. These were designed first to deconstruct the Panasonic brand, then collectively to identify the emotional, functional, competitive and future-facing characteristics that would be most ownable, differentiating and relevant to Panasonic customers over the long term.

The work session concluded that Panasonic needed to keep, lose or add the personality attributes shown in Table 17.1

A filtering exercise performed by the group further narrowed the focus to those attributes deemed most relevant and differentiating. From this, Landor believed the richest opportunity lay in the following themes:

- expertise from the ground up; inside-out expertise
- breadth of offerings coupled with heritage of providing value-rich features

Table 17.1   Panasonic brand attributes

KEEP	LOSE	ADD
Reliable	Slow	Modern
Relationship-builders	Apologetic	Expert
Good value	Cautious	Authority
Life-enhancing	Out-dated	Improving
High quality	Boring	Energetic
Customer-focused	Not a leader	Smart
Global	Poor service	Solutions
Friendly	Ease of repair	Innovative

Source: Created by Landor. Reprinted with permission.

- arbiter of what is good and valuable
- commitment to being in touch with customer needs
- passion for creating advanced products that work

Out of this pool of ideas, a Brand Driver soon emerged that immediately intrigued Panasonic management and was ultimately embraced. It was built on the thinking of founder K. Matsushita, who once said: 'Better service for the customer is for the good of the public, and this is the true purpose of enterprise.' The Verbal Brand Driver and statement of brand purpose was, as a result, relatively simple and clear:

PRAGMATIC VISIONARIES

For over 75 years, Panasonic has set the standards for excellence in electronics. It is our passion for perfection – our tenacity in applying our unparalleled expertise to creating innovative products and services that surprise and delight our customers – that sets us apart. We are pragmatic visionaries, driven to always exceed expectations and add relevant value to our customers at work and play.

FROM BRAND DRIVER™ TO BRAND ACTION

From this strong, forward-thinking platform, a dramatic brand revival was staged in North America. Immediate next steps included the development of a new tagline to replace 'Just slightly ahead of our time'. After several weeks of collaborative work with Grey Worldwide, the Landor naming team presented 'ideas for life' as one of 10 recommended finalists.

Panasonic's marketing leaders decided to test the finalists internally to pick a favorite, and 'ideas for life' emerged as the clear choice. After confirming that the tagline would clear both legal and cultural hurdles around the world, the stage was set for the next phase of the project, which was to create a new look and feel for the brand's visual representation across all its communications. This, too, Landor was charged to accomplish, but with several notable restrictions mandated by Matsushita headquarters in Japan:

- The core Panasonic logotype (Helvetica Black) could not be altered; the heritage brand typography must remain intact
- Panasonic Blue must remain the primary color of the brand expression
- This rebranding effort was to remain strictly confined to the North American region

Landor's designers embraced the first two criteria enthusiastically. The bold, no-nonsense look of the classic Panasonic brand typography was both appropriate for the brand and its new North American positioning and also built on years of equity that it had earned the world over. Landor designers also began to explore an extended secondary color palette around the tagline itself to add new life to the signature without detracting from its core equities in blue. The team believed it critical to build the 'ideas for life' promise into the Panasonic signature in a wholly integrated and visually dramatic way. This ultimately resulted in the now nearly ubiquitous blue signature band (or 'ribbon') found in Panasonic's marketing communications across North America and in selected markets around the world (see Figure 17.4).

As this exciting new look for the brand began to evolve and take shape internally, management's enthusiasm for the new brand positioning and visual look and feel gained momentum. Greenberg and Murano became active evangelists to managers across the continent, advocating not only the benefits of a new, unified look for Panasonic but also the critical importance of the brand idea behind it. They began to use 'ideas for life' as a mantra: its dual meaning of 'new ideas for everyday life' and 'products that last for a lifetime' became a filter for how Panasonic should think about its customers' needs and the products it should develop.

The marketing team also recognized the necessity for a cohesive, well-communicated launch of the brand concept within the regional organization. This initiative could not be viewed as simply another corporate slogan or ad campaign. 'Ideas for life' and all it represented had to be understood as being bigger than anything previously contemplated within Panasonic. It was about being a leadership brand with a distinct point of view. When it came time to launch the new brand in the fall of 2002, Panasonic was poised for significant change.

Launch day started with a voice mail greeting for every employee from actor Christian Slater, Panasonic's new advertising spokesperson. Then came an online message from the chairman and CEO of MECA, Hideaki 'Don' Iwatani, explaining the new identity system and its significance. At the Secaucus headquarters, staff were greeted by outdoor banners, corridor posters and hastily repainted hallways dramatically featuring the new brand look and signature. This carried through to showcasing *Wall Street Journal* and *New York Times* ads running that week and continuing throughout the year. The cafeteria came alive with displays of new products that exemplified the 'Ideas for Life' concept – demonstrating not only what the organization said, but also what it *did* (see Figure 17.3).

Panasonic ideas for life

Source: Signature created by Landor. Reprinted with permission of Panasonic.

Figure 17.3 Panasonic's bold new signature connects the brand to its promise

NEW RESPECT FOR THE BRAND

This day marked the beginning of an attitudinal shift within the North American division. Previously hard divisions between segments and product lines began to soften, and the power of a unified brand voice became increasingly clear. Never a big marketing spender, Panasonic leadership started to realize the obvious efficiencies and marketing advantages gained when all communications speak from a common perspective. Other early indicators of its impact were equally exciting. A leading telecommunications provider called some nine months after the launch and asked Panasonic to partner with it on a major co-branding opportunity. As a Panasonic spokesperson commented, 'This never would have happened with the 'old' Panasonic.' Clearly something fresh and exciting was afoot.

But what was the reaction in Japan to the excitement in the States? It could perhaps best be summarized as cautious interest. There was soon little doubt that the momentum building behind 'ideas for life' in the US represented an opportunity for Panasonic worldwide, but there was extreme concern about whether this strategy would be equally appropriate elsewhere, particularly in Japan.

At first, the North American branding team was asked to conform to a frustrating series of additional guideline details regarding nuances, such as the proximity of the Panasonic name to the tagline. Long discussions ensued about how 'Panasonic ideas for life' should be presented: horizontally, as a 'read through', or vertically stacked to match the existing standards. Each of these hurdles was dealt with patiently and successfully, but they pointed to a larger issue: parent and region did not share the same vision for the Panasonic brand.

Then, in an exciting shift, Matsushita headquarters asked Landor's Tokyo office to create a set of global brand guidelines. They were to govern the use of the 'ideas for life' brand signature and visual representation around the world. This seemed promising to all concerned. It was a chance to formally codify the breakthrough concept and design thinking behind 'ideas for life' and share it with the rest of the organization.

But the end result of this Japan-led project proved disappointing and frustrating for the US team. While the North American partners presented their successful branding system as an example of effective, customer-focused thinking, the rest of Panasonic essentially adopted the 'ideas for life' tagline – but none of its meaning or graphic distinctiveness. The brand idea that had become a guidepost in the US was lost. Moreover, its visual representation was essentially discarded; Japan launched an alternative look, and the rest of the world was left to fend for itself.

Such dichotomy rarely works well in branding, though culturally it reflected Matsushita's long (and traditionally successful) heritage of allowing independent geographies and divisions to market as they saw fit, with few requirements for brand consistency. As the months wore on, it was tacitly if not overtly agreed that each region could go its own way for the most part, so long as 'ideas for life' was adopted as the universal tagline for the organization. This alone, it was felt, represented a major step forward and marked about as much global enforcement as was warranted.

Nonetheless there was growing curiosity about developments in North America in other areas of the company. Greenberg and Murano received frequent invitations to tell their branding story to Panasonic marketing and business leaders from other regions, such as South America and EMEA (Europe, the Middle East and Africa). As Greenberg noted in his speech to the *Economist* Marketing Roundtable in New York in March 2003:

> If we succeed, it is critical we all understand that Panasonic's 'ideas for life' concept is not just an advertising campaign. It is not the latest management slogan for success. It is much more than that. It is a true brand idea: a simple, compelling articulation of our founder's vision. K. Matsushita was a pragmatic visionary. He sought to create innovative, practical products to improve our everyday lives.

His language carried a compelling message throughout the organization. Still more powerful was the mounting evidence that the Panasonic brand in the US was no longer perceived as the 'good old reliable' brand second to Sony. In fact, in part as a reflection of the apparent transformation taking place at Panasonic North America, the organization was asked to deliver the keynote speech at the January 2004 Consumer Electronics Show in Las Vegas, the biggest, most prestigious electronics convention in the world. Panasonic and its 'ideas for life' positioning had arrived – literally – on the world stage.

A NEW ADVOCATE FOR CHANGE

As this perceptual shift gained momentum, Panasonic needed an executive advocate to leverage the new brand idea into dramatic sales success. A new chairman and CEO, Yoshihiko 'Yoshi' Yamada, took the helm of the North American region in June 2004 and set an aggressive course for change. He immediately began restructuring the workforce, going so far as to officially change its name from Matsushita Electronics Corporation of America to Panasonic Corporation of North America, in recognition of the brand its customers valued most.

The CEO's stated goal has been to shift the corporate culture from a sales-driven company to a market maker within three years. In just over a year, Yamada instituted a 360-degree integrated marketing program, a much higher advertising investment, a new PR offensive and media tactics, fresh employee communications, and a new focus on extreme customer satisfaction.

Yamada also made it clear that he supported the 'ideas for life' brand platform. He asked his managers to explore innovative ways of building the brand beyond traditional media and marketing thinking. Moreover, he instructed the US Panasonic team to focus on a core product area as the vanguard for demonstrating Panasonic's leadership. Plasma TV was the chosen product, and he charged them to make Panasonic the number 1 selling brand of plasma TVs in America in that same year.

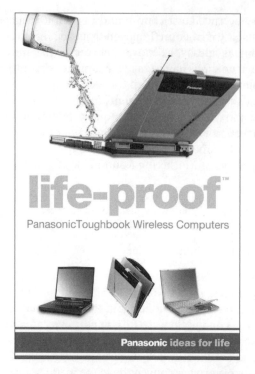
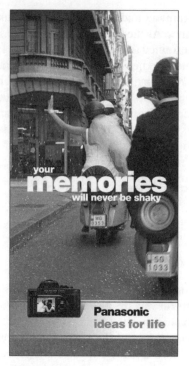

Above – The new Panasonic brand idea expressed in its "Ideas for Life" ad campaign.

Left – Konosuke Matsushita, founder of Matsushita Electric Industrial Company.

Source: All advertisements reproduced with permission of Panasonic.

Figure 17.4   The new Panasonic brand idea expressed in its 'Ideas for Life' campaign

Yamada understood that the equity accrued to the top brand in such a visible and hotly contested category would add luster to the entire Panasonic product line. He was determined to achieve this challenging goal, and by the end of 2005 the North American group had met his sales objectives: Panasonic was hailed as the leading plasma TV manufacturer by consumer and trade publications alike. Praised for their performance, features and value, Panasonic plasma TVs continue to lead all brands in worldwide unit and revenue market share for the category. They also dominate *Consumer Reports*' rankings, taking the top three spots for high-definition TVs and earning the Quick Pick designation.[12]

A SECOND CHANCE

In December 2005, Matsushita's marketing team in Japan contacted Panasonic North America and Landor – to discuss a global branding initiative. It was a watershed moment for all concerned and, it was hoped, represented the culmination of years of effort. This was, at last, a chance to develop a common point of view about the Panasonic brand that could transcend geographies and cultures.

In ensuing discussions with the Panasonic Brand Marketing Group, the Landor team made it clear that for a global brand initiative to be successful, input from senior leadership around the world would be required. Previous attempts to build uniformity behind the 'ideas for life' brand initiative had stumbled for lack of involvement by regional managers and open, cross-border dialogue. Anyone who scanned the multiple Panasonic websites around the world could see the problem. They all signed off with 'Panasonic', and they all featured the words 'ideas for life' somewhere; yet none beyond the US site integrated the *idea* behind the tagline into communications.

The Landor team, itself comprised of an international collection of senior consultants from Singapore, Hong Kong, New York, Tokyo and London (whose collective nationalities included Germany, Japan, India, South Africa, and the US), set up a series of extended Brand Driver workshops in Asia, the US and Europe to reassess and collectively redefine the Panasonic Brand Driver. The purpose of these work sessions differed from the first round. It was agreed that the conceptual thinking behind 'ideas for life' was relevant and differentiated to customers, and visionary and motivating to employees; it was not to be discarded. The goal was to add dimension and validation to the current brand concept. It was hoped that fresh input from around the world would deepen and reinforce the 'ideas for life' concept through a fuller articulation of the brand promise in diverse categories, geographies and cultures.

And this is where the saga ends . . . for now. The Brand Driver workshops have been completed and initial recommendations prepared. What happens next is an open question. As with all significant effort, the project's success remains wholly dependent on its champions. Unfortunately, change is never easy or clean. Despite our best intentions, some things never get off the ground. As Professor Erich Joachimsthaler writes,

> Because humans generally resist change, because people feel justified confidence in knowing their own country's competition and consumers, any suggestion otherwise is threatening. To ensure that teams overcome such reluctance, a brand champion must be in charge.[13]

Fortunately, the Panasonic brand has always had its champions, most recently in Bob Greenberg and Tom Murano. They have passionately and consistently nurtured and advocated for the power of the Panasonic brand. In any global initiative, idea champions are critical to success. At their instigation, Panasonic North America put itself on the line many years ago and has remained there, year in and year out. Landor's overall experience would argue that global brands only succeed with corporate management's stamp of approval. But in this case, a lone region took the initiative, learned through trial, and helped transform a 75-year-old company and industry – when many would have given up long ago.

Murano asked, 'In building an enduring technology business, are we better served going to market with a dozen small brands – or as a well-integrated, strongly rationalized and focused organizational brand?' Greenberg, Murano and the organization they serve appear to have made their choice. Despite following an unconventional path to global brand management, Matsushita and its flagship Panasonic brand have recognized the opportunities and benefits inherent in global alignment. The next few years will determine whether they have the courage, vision and skill to seize the opportunity that lies before them – to make Panasonic the truly global, leadership brand it so clearly deserves to be.

LESSONS LEARNED

Building a Global Brand

Start at the top
Large corporations are very resistant to change without a dramatic business imperative (for example, a major new competitive threat, an industry sea change, new management, mergers, acquisitions or divestitures). Changing a company from the division level up is particularly challenging and generally requires extensive sell-in and reselling to address the 'not-invented-here' response of factions and silos common in most large organizations. The most successful corporate revitalizations tend to take shape from the top down.

Question orthodoxy, stick to vision
BP senior management set a strategic goal for the company that defied category convention and demanded tangible change throughout its organization. Panasonic North America infused energy into a me-too brand by taking the initiative in its region, sticking to its vision, and evangelizing results. Adhering to a visionary strategy and ignoring naysayers are key to implementing large-scale change.

Anticipate resistance and manage it
Managing expectations within an organization and across cooperative partnerships during times of extreme change can be highly challenging and require considerable hands-on effort. The strong collaboration between Ogilvy & Mather, Landor and BP helped create communications that were direct extensions of the BP brand. The likelihood of success is heightened significantly through a collaborative process. Invite input, integrate output, and provide continuous and candid feedback. To foil territorial tendencies, include internal teams and key external suppliers. Keep partners in all relevant meetings to minimize back-channeling.

Meet face-to-face

Landor's US team made an unfortunate mistake in not pushing for direct, face-to-face involvement with its Tokyo team in the first re-branding initiative. Communicating exclusively by phone, email and video conferencing can allow misunderstanding to creep in when the stakes are high and client agendas are not aligned.

Choose partners who've done it before

Global branding is a complex undertaking that demands direct, personal commitment, an open and patient mind, cultural sensitivity, and experienced people and processes to manage on an ongoing basis. Don't try this with amateurs!

Managing a Global Brand

Aim for consistency, not rigid standardization

Establishing a brand successfully across geographies and cultures is less about rules and more about fundamental understanding of the brand idea. Every culture has its own codes and nuances that must be respected. Local managers must have the flexibility to adapt to and take advantage of opportunities in their region while simultaneously expressing the core spirit of the brand.

Focus on the customer, not the ad campaign

Advertising a brand idea without delivering it day in and day out is a recipe for failure. Shape a brand through products, communications and interaction with customers. Starbucks spends virtually nothing on traditional advertising, yet it has established a premium brand in a commoditized category. It built a dominant global brand by focusing on its customers: delivering a premium product and a consistent, regionally sensitive brand experience around the globe.

Engage your employees

The best way to deliver a consistent, branded experience is to internally align an organization around its Brand Driver™. BP's persistence in deeply engaging its employees with its brand continues to inspire a brand-led business. Like all great brands, BP is built on high principles and customer-centered attitudes that are reinforced and rewarded by the organization.

WHAT IS A BRAND DRIVER™ PLATFORM?

The Brand Driver™ platform is Landor's unique approach to brand definition and positioning. It defines what a brand stands for today and what it aspires to be in the future. It provides a frame of reference for a company's offer and determines how to bring its goods to market. It positions a brand in the marketplace and drives strategic and creative expression.

The success of a brand is determined in large part by its relevance to target consumers and its differentiation from competitors. If a brand does not tap into consumer needs, it will not sell, nor will it be able to command effective margins unless it establishes a point of difference from competitors. A Brand Driver platform gives a brand vision and focus by defining its relevant differentiation.

A Brand Driver platform is a driver of change, used to pinpoint unique and ownable brand attributes that can spur growth. As a result, each platform carries implications for clients' businesses, surfacing strategic imperatives to help them execute their vision. The more unique and differentiated a brand, the more stringent its imperatives will be. Landor's Brand Driver platform comprises four mutually reinforcing components: a Statement of Relevant Differentiation, a Visual Brand Driver, a Verbal Brand Driver and Brand Beliefs. Together, they portray a brand in both visual and verbal terms.

Statement of Relevant Differentiation

The Statement of Relevant Differentiation defines, in verbal terms, the core value of a brand and delineates a unique and ownable brand vision. It identifies a frame of reference for the brand, a core brand claim, reasons to believe in that claim and the benefits it gives to customers.

Visual Brand Driver

A structured grid of nine categories of images, this is a visual representation of the Brand Driver Platform. Often the Visual Brand Driver reveals surprising nuances about a brand's personality that may not be evident in verbal expression, and it is frequently used to compare current and future visions of a single brand or a brand and its competitors. The Visual Brand Driver adds another layer of understanding to a brand and is an effective means of communicating a brand's positioning to multiple audiences.

Verbal Brand Driver

The Verbal Brand Driver encapsulates the unique and ownable aspects of a brand in a short, compelling statement. It is an emblematic catchphrase that conjures up a powerful, memorable insight. Created by a team of strategists and designers, it is evocative and tangible, inspiring visual imagery and design.

Brand Beliefs

Brand Beliefs articulate the core and enduring beliefs of a company and drive its behavior at every point of contact. They describe how a company should go to market, deliver its offerings, and respond to new situations. In contrast to the statement of relevant differentiation, which may need to be modified over time, beliefs should stay with a company for the long term. They should resonate with employees and guide interactions with customers at each point of contact.

NOTES

1. The BrandZ top 100 brands ranking, as determined by Millward Brown Optimor and Euromonitor International, was published in a special report for the *Financial Times* (3 April 2006).
2. Kevin Lane Keller, *Strategic Brand Management: Building, Measuring, and Managing Brand Equity*, Upper Saddle River, NJ: Pearson Education, 2003, p. 683.
3. Douglas Holt, John Quelch and Earl Taylor, 'How global brands compete', *Harvard Business Review*, September 2004.
4. From 2001 to 2005, a period when most oil and petroleum companies were losing profits and public favor, BP was recognized for its ability to outperform its competitors as one of the top 'Breakaway Brands' in *Fortune* magazine's salute to the ten brands that most dramatically increased their value; Al Ehrbar, 'Breakaway brands: How ten companies, making products from drills to waffles, took good brands and made them much, much better', *Fortune*, 31 October 2005, pp. 153–70.
5. The new BP brand was launched on 24 July, 2000. Employee surveys conducted by an independent firm completed shortly after the launch found that 97 per cent of employees were aware of the new brand, 76 per cent were favorable to the new brand, 80 per cent were aware of the four brand values, 77 per cent believed it was credible for BP to go 'beyond petroleum', and 90 per cent said that the company was going in the right direction; data provided by BP.
6. 'Britian's most admired companies: Double first', *Management Today*, 18 December 2002; 'Special report: The world's most respected companies', *Financial Times*, 18 November 2005.
7. *Wall Street Journal*, July 2002.
8. Sales data tracked by BP (2004).
9. BP's 2005 annual report: 'Making energy more: Annual report and accounts 2005'.
10. BrandEconomics analysis conducted for the 2005 Breakaway Brands study; see Al Ehrbar, 'Breakaway brands: How ten companies, making products from drills to waffles, took good brands and made them much, much better', *Fortune*, 31 October 2005, pp. 153–70.
11. *Chicago Business Journal*, 3 April 2000.
12. Panasonic continues to lead all brands in worldwide unit and revenue market share for the plasma TV category with 26 per cent market share and the No. 1 position in Japan, China and North America; Greg Tarr, 'Panasonic leads global PDP market', *Twice*, twice.com/article/CA6310730.html, accessed 22 June 2006. Panasonic models have also topped *Consumer Reports*' plasma TV ratings over 2005 and the first half of 2006. Four of the top five high-definition models belong to Panasonic; *Consumer Reports*, 'Ratings: Plasma TVs', consumerreports.org/cro/electronics-computers/tvs/plasma-tvs/reports/ratings/ratings/index.htm (accessed 22 June 2006).
13. Erich Joachimsthaler, 'The lure of global branding', *Harvard Business Review*, Nov/Dec 1999.

18. Why does branding fail? Ten barriers to branding

Noriyuki Nakai

While much has been argued regarding the strength of the brand and the commitment it brings to the customer, an overlooked area in the field of brand management is the barriers managers face when undertaking a branding strategy. Accordingly, this chapter surveys ten of the most common causes of a brand's failure, and the important lessons that can be learned from them.

BARRIER 1: LACK OF ORGANIZATIONAL COMMITMENT

The first of these reasons for failure is the lack of organizational commitment. For example, let us take an example of a company that is looking to develop a cutting edge, innovative personal computer brand. It will have to accordingly determine the specifications, design, price, communications, sales channels, production processes, customer services and other key elements that together make the customer feel that it is 'innovative'. A failure on any dimension signals an overall brand failure.

A brand is not just an identifier but is something substantial which creates a particular experience for the customer. Branding, the process to create this experience, must involve by nature a variety of professionals. With a brand manager at the center, technical, manufacturing, research, sales, advertising, promotion, customer service, legal, finance, human resources and other professionals have to work seamlessly together to create the unique brand experiences. In essence, branding is not just a brand manager's job but a process of integrating various professional functions led by the brand manager.

Today's corporations have a complex structure of functions meticulously divided by boundaries. Every department, division or group is managed by professionals in each field, the so-called vertical division structure. This structure has effectively worked to enhance the specialized knowledge in an organization and has contributed to efficient management. But from the viewpoint of branding, it sometimes can be a serious barrier.

Too often, the barrier is intensified by conflicting interests or egos of each division. A technical manager may feel that the new technology is the central selling point. An advertising manager may simply be interested in winning an award using a striking advertising idea. A promotion manager may want to sell the brand with a deep discount coupon which will instantly increase sales. This forces the brand manager to spend an enormous amount of time persuading everyone rationally and emotionally, until a unanimous compromise is reached.

It is not hard to imagine how many times this kind of negotiation happens. Ironically, such negotiations often sacrifice productivity to get things done. Hence, a vast amount of effort is spent on the 'exploration of insights' with internal stakeholders, leaving the consumer behind. For many firms, except truly brand-oriented ones, this is the reality we face.

Every division has its own culture, style, motivation, responsibility – and egos. With this sort of corporate environment, the vitally important aspect in the branding process is to integrate various professionals toward the brand vision. In this sense, branding is not just a matter of marketing but also a matter of organizational dynamics management.

Now you sit at a table with your staff for a kick-off meeting of a branding project. Remember, before you start, to ask yourself whether all the members are on the same page. If the answer is no, the meeting will be a waste of your time. You must go back a step and get them on board. If necessary, make some time to share the vision and the objective, to convince the head of each division, or higher officers, why they should seamlessly collaborate for the sake of branding. Even if the answer is yes, a lot of other challenges await you besides marketing issues. I will discuss these challenges in later sections.

In essence, branding starts before marketing and goes beyond marketing. If you face such a problem, what will help you is not a marketing or brand management text but one on organizational management, or even better, an autobiography of a politician.

Lesson 1: If you are handling a brand, you are in charge of organizational management, too.

BARRIER 2: LACK OF MANAGERIAL COMMITMENT

Your firm suffers commoditization of the product. Parity in product performance causes fierce price wars and heavy expenditures for 'push' activities. What is the problem? The answer is clear: a lack of brand power. Accordingly, you, as marketing director, make a proposal to top management to start a brand enhancement project with needed investment. The answer, as you had expected, is negative. The top executive says, 'What we need is sales, not a brand. Just make a good product and sell it.'

Surprisingly, the top executive usually speaks at a board meeting about the importance of a brand as an intangible asset for the firm, whether it is a product or corporate brand. He surely understands the importance of a brand to the firm in theory, but does not believe it in reality. To his mind, branding is too abstract to invest in and therefore an unrealistic consideration as regards generating earnings. He firmly believes that only superior products and a strong sales force can make money. If you have never encountered this type of top management, you are lucky.

Here lies the real difficulty. The fundamental problem was that the lack of brand power caused poor sales. A soluble problem, so it seems. Then you propose to start a branding project. But at this point the top executive suddenly turns negative. No, there is no money to invest. He agrees with the branding project in his head, but disagrees with it in his heart. Thus, the argument goes round and round to reach nowhere.

Since branding is a cross-functional process of various professionals, it involves a number of people, time and costs, either direct or indirect. Without a clear decision and true commitment from management, people will not move to embrace branding, and sufficient time and money will not be allocated. For corporate branding, the brand manager is the CEO. He must align all the functions – strategy development, marketing, finance, R&D, human resources, production, logistics, distribution and others – with a shared brand vision.

Before setting up a branding project, you must convince top management that branding is about selling. It requires investing the people, money and time to sustain the growth that will come in the future. Remember, we suffer from commoditization. A subtle differentiation in product attributes will be written off sooner or later, as history indicates. The only solution is to create a sustainable brand that consistently and continually stages an enjoyable experience for the customer.

Lesson 2: Get the management on board, otherwise the project will die sooner or later.

BARRIER 3: LACK OF EMPOWERMENT

One of the most remarkable characteristics of branding is that everyone thinks they can do it, using their feelings, intuition and common sense. Unlike technology, finance or legal specialties, branding does not seem to require special knowledge that frightens the layman. Hence everyone, particularly corporate executives, cannot resist meddling in the details of the planning. This sometimes makes a branding project stray off course.

Suppose you develop an advertising plan with an ad agency and present it to the board for final approval. The presentation covers the objective, target and strategy, and all the board members have no objection. When it comes to the advertising slogan, however, the CEO starts giving his opinion based simply on his own 'feeling'. What is worse, another executive insists that the character featured in the ads should be Sharon Stone and not Michelle Pfeiffer. Suddenly, the elaborately designed communication plan starts collapsing. If you are a brand manager, you must have experienced this kind of disruption, perhaps something similar to this.

It is the executive's responsibility to make a strategic decision from a bird's eye view. But it is not their job to express their feelings on the details of the brand design. The problem that sometimes occurs is that the detailed branding elements are altered, based on such a 'backseat driver's' suggestions, resulting in an incoherent brand design. Once the strategy is confirmed with management, execution must be fully orchestrated by the brand manager.

Branding is the strategic accumulation of the details – specs, design, shape, color, touch, size, name, package design, slogan, ad copy, visual, music, character and so on. In fact, every detail of the brand's touchpoints virtually determines the consumer's sense and feel for the brand. The color, for example, which seems only a small detail from the strategic point of view, may play the most critical role for the brand and signify the essence of the brand.

You may think it is important to have an objective opinion from people outside the team and you are right. But in that case, you should listen to the consumer rather than the executives who are not the target. Be prepared to convince management by listening to the consumer first. It is the consumer who pays money for the brand.

Lesson 3: You must be empowered to manage the brand's execution. Convince the management to bet on your team.

BARRIER 4: LACK OF ENTHUSIASM

It is said that branding ideas should be developed at the intersection of consumer needs and a firm's resources. Analysis, strategic planning and systematic execution of the strategy are all important. But another important requirement rarely pointed out is the passion and enthusiasm of the individual who drives branding.

Ultimately, branding is about moving people – internal staff, suppliers, top management, outside partners and other stakeholders. Since none of them are under the brand manager's direct control, you cannot order them to do anything, yet you still have to influence them to move toward branding. In this circumstance, it is quite naive to assume that theory or logic alone can motivate people.

Today, modern medical technology can 'manage' existing life to some extent, but cannot create it. Similarly, modern branding theory can manage an existing brand to some extent, but cannot create it. Although we don't yet know what created life, we are sure that what created a brand was the passion, aspiration or imagination of an enthusiastic individual or group.

It does not seem that all of today's power brands were born from strategic planning. Steve Jobs (Apple), Phil Knight (Nike), and Bill Gates (Microsoft) only did what they were really excited about and willing to take risks on; none of them, I believe, 'strategically' planned from the start to develop a brand that would conquer the global market. What created these brands was passion, persistence, patience and even prejudice; namely, the 4Ps of branding.

Everyone knows that every decision involves risks. We can manage risk using the sophisticated techniques taught in business school, but taking a risk is essentially a gamble. Just like an entrepreneur, someone must be willing to bet on the brand. In many organizations, everyone cries for the need of branding, but no one starts doing it. This situation typically shows the lack of an enthusiastic driver of the brand.

The success of branding largely depends on the performance of the person who integrates the team. A branding leader must behave like an enthusiastic entrepreneur, taking a risk, teaming up the right people, sharing the vision and motivating them to collaborate. When you start a branding project, ask yourself if you are passionate and enthusiastic enough and if you are convinced that the project will succeed. If the answer is no, find the right person instead of you.

Lesson 4: A brand is born from enthusiasm embraced by a proper strategic environment.

BARRIER 5: LACK OF INSIGHT

The base of brand leadership, as we discussed, is passion and enthusiasm. But I am not such a spiritualist as to believe that everything will go well with only passion and enthusiasm. In fact, a countless number of branding projects fail every day, even when led by extraordinarily passionate and enthusiastic managers.

Suppose you, as a brand manager, brief the team on a new brand strategy. 'There is a substantial need for a beverage that tastes good, yet contains no calories. So develop a brand to meet these needs.' What waits for you is the response, 'I don't think so.'

R&D people may say, 'according to our tremendous research in the past, there is no evidence to support this product formulation.' Or laboratory people may say 'according to our studies, a non-calorie claim gives a negative impression on perceived taste. So even if the real taste is good, the product may fail.' Or the top management may say, 'We have already tried this in the past. It failed. The consumer doesn't want that kind of product.' They believe that they know the consumer better than you, which may be true.

The product must sell, which means there must be a large group of people who will pay money for it. If everyone on your team is convinced that customers will pay for it, then the team will find less reason to resist. Thus, the foundation of brand leadership starts with the fact that you know the consumer better than any other person. You should have insights into the consumer behavior.

When asked about consumer insights, some managers may simply describe them as 'those in their 20s–30s who want to buy this product as . . .' or others, a little more sophisticated, may say 'frustrated office-workers aged 20–30 in urban areas potentially desire such an enjoyable experience as . . .' This is not an insight but your 'wish'. Gaining consumer insight does not mean simply describing a hypothetical consumer need or behavior in support of your product.

In customer insight, the key question is 'why?' The objective of insight research is to find why the consumer behaves as they do. If you find the hidden, true reason, then your power of persuasion will be significantly enhanced and the odds for success increased. Thus, a branding leader should get close to the real consumer. The very reason that the team will go with your direction is that you know the consumer, who will determine the success of the brand.

Lesson 5: Those who spend money on the brand are number 1. Those who understand their motivations are the strongest brand leaders.

BARRIER 6: LACK OF FOCUS

You must have heard the terms segmentation and concentration. They refer to clearly defining the target and strategically allocating business resources to the segment. This kind of strategic focus is clearly a good idea. But this is the toughest challenge to execute in branding.

Suppose you handle a beer brand that tastes smooth and mild. Sales of the brand are stable but the potential is limited to a small segment: mild beer lovers, most of whom are light drinkers. Knowing that heavy drinking is concentrated among dry beer drinkers, you may be tempted to sell your brand in that segment, by repositioning it, by changing the taste, packaging and advertising in the process. This is the beginning of the end.

Do you believe that a brand established as a mild tasting beer can sell in the dry beer drinker segment? I'm quite sure your answer is no. But, in reality, it is surprising that a lot of good 'niche' brands try to expand into bigger markets, only to find that they fail and lose their original brand franchise too. As a result, the poor brand dies of 'Chasing the Big Trophy' syndrome.

Why does this happen? It is because every manager is under strong sales pressure and so, naturally, is inclined to increase short-term sales, not recognizing that they are jeopardizing the long-term sustainable sales generated from the brand asset. To them, the 'segmentation of the market' sounds like the 'limitation of sales potential'. Sales people and, in particular, top management who are directly responsible for sales are quite reluctant to give up the potential they feel they are able to achieve.

Strategy by definition means an allocation of limited resources. This means one must abandon some aspects of existing potential when developing strategy. Also, as frequently pointed out, marketing strategy starts from the segmentation of the target. Now that we cannot make friends with everyone – as we all fully understand from our experiences – it is important to our survival that we distinguish who we should become friends with and who we should ignore. The problem is that, when it comes to marketing decisions, we are inclined to try to make friends with everyone, which jeopardizes the existence of our brands.

Before making a decision on segmentation, look at the person near you who unexpectedly became a general manager. A specialist is always stronger than a generalist in any given field. Forcing a specialist to do a generalist's job impairs the specialist's strength and leaves him suffering. A strong niche brand is like a capable specialist in the organization. Allot it to keep its focus, and it will perform well.

Lesson 6: Those who run after two hares will catch neither – a strategy is a decision to abandon something.

BARRIER 7: LACK OF PATIENCE

Rome was not built in a day. Neither was any power brand. It takes a significant amount of time from the development of the brand to the establishment of a customer franchise. A brand gradually grows into an image in the consumer's mind through a sequence of experiences. Therefore, throughout the brand development process, the brand must continue to behave consistently. A small inconsistent experience may instantly destroy what has been accumulated over time.

Suppose you launched a new product or service yesterday with high aspirations to build a sustainable brand. Also suppose, however, that today's sales do not look good. Under strong pressure from management or sales, the easiest response is to use 'push' tactics such as a discount promotion or a premium give-away campaign. The use of pure 'push' tactics however is akin to the use of drugs; you feel better for a moment, but will suffer soon. You then begin to depend on such tactics. This vicious circle eventually kills the brand and eliminates your original quest to develop a brand that assures sustainable sales.

The second easiest measure to undertake in the face of slow sales is to change the brand design – the taste (of the product), the package design, the brand slogan or the advertising – under the guise of improvement. But you have to ask yourself if you really need to change one of these. If you are convinced that the 'who' (target) and the 'what' (experience offered to the customer) are mismatched, then you have reason enough to make changes. You are faced with a strategic failure and which cannot be recovered through the use of tactics anyway. But if they are not mismatched, you should remain patient and examine the identity of the brand.

Identity is not necessarily the name or a visual symbol but anything that symbolizes what customers think is most important about the brand; that is, the slogan, tonality of communications, the taste of the product, touch, sound, scent, style, behavior and other elements. For Apple Inc., the product design is the identity of the brand and reflects the brand promise of 'creative experience'. So, what is the identity of your brand? Is the slogan or tonality of communications essential for your brand? What about other aspects of your product or service? If they do not serve as the brand identity, do not hesitate to improve these aspects to accommodate changes in market trends. But the essential aspects of the brand's identity must remain consistent.

Branding is an investment involving risk and time. You spend money today expecting a return after several years. The golden rule of investment is to have a long-term perspective. Before thinking about changing something, remember the fact that all strong brands have remained consistent in essence and identity over time. And the owners of these brands have been patient.

Lesson 7: Once you place a bet, stick with it. Changing the cards halfway means that you bet on nothing.

BARRIER 8: LACK OF FRAMEWORK

The spectacular biblical project to build the Tower of Babel failed due to a lack of a common framework in communication. Workers started speaking in different languages and could no longer communicate with each other. The project ran aground, and the workers dispersed to different places on Earth. This is quite similar to what usually goes on in our offices today. The only difference is that we do nothing to challenge God. What we are doing is just branding.

When you use the very simple, easy and popular term 'brand concept development', for example, does your team share the exact same meaning? Does your team conjure up the image of what they are going to develop? Some may confuse the term with the benefits of the product. Or others may think it is a reference to the personality of the brand. Another example of potential misunderstanding: what is the difference between 'brand essence' and 'brand core'? What about 'brand experience' and 'brand benefit'?

One of the most serious and frequent problems is the confusion of brand and product. Some may think branding means putting a name on a product and promoting it. For them, a brand is no more than a name on a product. In managing the brand, however, we need to imagine an invisible person who markets a set of products. To attract the customer, he expresses his character and behaves accordingly, using all the signals: the product, package, price, customer service, advertising, reputation (if controllable) and others. What we promote is 'him', not the product per se, which is just one of these signals from 'him'. We cannot hope that our team will work together effectively if some of the team are focused on developing a product with a given name and others are focused on developing a brand.

It may sound too fundamental or even primitive, but this kind of confusion sometimes leads to a serious disruption in branding. When we work with outside partners, in particular, we should be more careful about this issue because each organization has its own culture and terminology. Even if exactly the same words are used, they may mean different things in different organizations.

Before starting your project, you should thoroughly discuss the objective (what to develop) and framework (how to develop it) at the beginning. Then define each step in the terms of its concrete output, using some examples if possible. Even with these efforts, confusion will occur without exception. At that time, fix the problem. It's your job. If there is never confusion, the team does not need you.

Lesson 8: Make sure that everyone in the team speaks the same language. Brand Communication starts within the team.

BARRIER 9: LACK OF SUBSTANCE

The highlight of branding is brand slogan development. 'Sheer Driving Pleasure'. 'Just Do It'. 'Think Different'. These statements clearly articulate the promises of what the customer's experience of the brand will be and at the same time connote the way the brand will deliver the promise. That is why they appeal so strikingly to the heart of the consumer. Unfortunately, however, we see many brand statements that say something but mean nothing.

Those working on these brands no doubt have spent a lot of time in research, strategic planning and product development. They must have discussed the vision of the brand enthusiastically and finally come up with the essence of the brand that needs to be shared with and by everyone – internally and externally. Unfortunately, what often happens in the final stage of brand development is the writing of hopelessly boring words in beautifully designed typeface.

For example, you might have seen a lot of brand statements using the word 'new'. For example, a 'new life', a 'new era', a 'new style' and the like. Such phrases stop further thought. Once this word enters your mind, you think no further as to how you might appeal to the heart of the consumer. We, as consumers, only care what the brand promises us, and we don't care if it is 'new'. If what the brand does for us is unique and original, we feel it is new. As such, being new is just the result of the consumer perception that is created in response to the stimuli from your brand.

What matters is to define what the consumer gets from the brand in a unique and original way. For the Virgin group, whose business is heavily diversified among music stores, beverages, airlines, and so on, it is difficult to describe the essence of their offering. The consistent way they go about business is described as iconoclastic. That's it. Although there is no beautifully crafted plaque with the word 'iconoclasm' engraved on it hanging in the CEO's office, the company behaves or at least looks like there is. This is important.

When it comes to branding, actions must match words. A brand must reflect its word. In other words, a brand statement should suggest, motivate or at least imply to stakeholders what the brand offers and how it behaves. If the stakeholders understand the brand's constitution in the form of an unwritten law, there is no need for a brand statement. Before paying big money to a branding consultancy to develop a beautiful brand logo and statement, create the substance with which to deliver the actual brand experience to the customer.

Lesson 9: Actions, not words.

BARRIER 10: LACK OF AN IDEA

In the last stage of brand planning, you and the team come up with the final proposal that clearly defines the vision, objective and strategies to be used: the target, product design, key benefits, communications, channels, price and so forth. There is no flaw in your logic and the proposal looks perfect. Now, all you have to do is execute the plan. But why don't you take a little time to think about the 'idea' behind your plan. What do you really want to do?

In day-to-day business, we sometimes find a beautifully designed blueprint for a brand but without an idea. It is important, needless to say, to define the vision and objectives in terms of sales, profits or market share. It is important, too, to explain how the product performs, who the target is, and what the rational and emotional benefits are. These, however, are not the branding idea. The branding idea is about how you would entertain the consumer. It is a simple answer to the questions, 'What truly delights the customer about this brand?' and, most importantly, 'What excites you and your team?' If you cannot answer these questions at once, you should rethink your plan – before moving on to execution.

In many cases, if you have a product to sell, you are strongly inclined to raise it to a brand by wrapping it in additional benefits and values. You then pick up the numbers from some research data and say 'there is a need for these benefits'. Or when creating a positioning map, you find a vacant area and say, 'here is an opportunity'. But wait. This strategy may look plausible enough to convince your boss, who hardly has the opportunity to actually come into contact with the consumer. But in fact, the strategy is fabricated in your mind only and rings no bell among the consumers.

It may be easy to convince yourself and the decision-makers, but you can't fool the consumer. You must adopt a strategy that prevents you from misleading yourself. Even if the branding strategy makes total sense to you, it still may not have a powerful brand idea. Drop it unless you get excited. Although this argument may sound theoretical, many instances around us indicate that branding ideas with no excitement will fail. Why? Because ideas that do not excite you cannot excite the customer.

In an earlier section, I said a brand manager must be enthusiastic and should even be prejudiced in favor of the brand. But this is true only when you believe in it from your heart. Don't be deceived by your own strategy. If it is a branding idea worth investing your own money in, go for it. Otherwise, stop and think it over.

Lesson 10: Tell in a word why the customer will be delighted. That's the brand idea to focus on.

CONCLUSION

Branding is the process of creating a unique experience of the brand that the consumer can enjoy at every touchpoint: the product, the package design, the service, the advertising, the promotions, the publicity, the website, the reputation and other touchpoints. It's about moving people by aligning all the necessary functions in the organization with the brand vision. It's not about simply communicating the benefits of a brand or creating an image of a product or service. We now know that the most fundamental driver of branding is leadership – like any other business project.

A brand manager must involve various professionals who are needed to create the considerable touchpoints of the brand and to form an integrated team that works seamlessly. Obtain true commitment from top management and the requisite delegation authority to manage the project, in order to overcome organizational obstacles. Show your enthusiasm to the team; it is your passion that will fuel it. Acquire insights into the consumer; people will trust the person who knows the customer best. Share a thinking framework to guide the team; the team needs to know what and how to think about the brand.

When your team comes up with an idea, stop for a moment. If it does not really excite you, it will not excite the consumer, even if it strategically makes sense. In developing a brand, you must be patient. A brand crystallizes in the consumer mind through a vast accumulation of experiences over time. So once you have decided on a brand positioning, remain focused. Don't try to sell the brand to everyone in spite of the pressure for sales expansion. You cannot be loved by everyone. Finally, remember the ultimate objective of branding is to realize the promise to the customer through the organization's actions. Make sure that the brand statement works as a compass for all the stakeholders, not just as a decoration in the CEO's office.

Unfortunately, as a communication executive, I have experienced so many branding failures, some of which were my fault and others perhaps not. Looking back to these failures, I feel most of them were not the result of marketing factors but rather the result of managerial factors, which may seem too elementary or even too anachronistic to point out in branding texts. Many such texts tend to ignore the fact that branding heavily involves organizational/human dynamics. But we should first think about how we manage organizational/human dynamics for branding. In this sense, managing organizational intelligence/creativity is the most critical issue to be addressed. For marketers, failing before marketing is a total waste of time. We would rather our failure be in the marketing stage at the very least, so that failure can guide our success in the future.

19. Building a B2B corporate brand[1]

David L. Rogers

In the 1990s and first decade of the 21st century, the practice of brand management expanded into new types of business organizations. Previously, branding was a common practice in companies that sold to large markets of end-consumers – B2C branding. The principles of brand management arose from the marketing of fast-moving consumer goods and then expanded into other consumer goods (for example, durables such as automotives) and into services. Branding concepts and frameworks were used to develop both product brands (Kitkat, Cadillac, Macintosh) and corporate brands for the companies selling those products (Nestlé, General Motors, Apple Computers).

In the 1990s, however, brand management began to be utilized by companies selling to business customers as well – B2B branding. These brands were being marketed not to mass-market consumers purchasing fast-moving packaged goods, but to business managers responsible for the financial return on (often substantial) purchasing investments. Many such B2B companies had grown up with a strong product and engineering-focused culture that did not always embrace the market-focused orientation of brand management. The global scale of many B2B companies posed additional challenges for the integration and consistency expected of traditional brand management.

Are B2B brands necessary? An early assumption was that brands did not matter in B2B markets, only price and product innovation. The customer was expected to be less emotional and much more analytical in their purchasing decisions. But highly visible and widely-admired brands have assumed market leadership in a wide variety of B2B categories: technology (IBM), manufacturing (Boeing), information (Dow Jones), financial services (Goldman Sachs), consulting (McKinsey), as well as in highly diversified B2B companies (GE).

The experience of these and other successful B2B corporate brands reveals a variety of lessons for B2B brand management.

WHY BRAND B2B?

Brands do matter in B2B markets, especially for companies whose business offers are complex and whole-solutions-focused, as opposed to companies selling simple discrete products (for example agricultural products) or services (for example traditional telephony) that are easily commoditized. The absence of exact product or service parity in industries like enterprise software or aerospace engineering creates opportunities for brands to add value.

B2B corporate brands create value by serving multiple constituencies. Like many consumer brands, B2B brands typically must appeal to multiple parties in a purchasing chain:

instead of child and parent (for a consumer product), this chain may include a specialized purchaser (from an equipment procurement office), their boss, and even the CEO, if the product is high-profile enough. Additional important constituencies for a B2B corporate brand include: investors, internal employees, business press, and other key influencers.

HOW TO BRAND B2B?

The basic principles for managing B2B corporate brands are the same as for consumer brands. The brand needs to be built around a positioning, or 'brand promise', that is simple and clear, is relevant to the brand's customers, and is aligned with the company's business strategy.

The brand needs a clear naming architecture that links different products, services, and divisions to the company's master brand and reflects how closely linked these divisions, and their customers, are.

The brand needs to be consistently communicated across all communication channels. This requires integration of marketing communications on a scale that can be quite challenging for global corporate brands. The many communications touchpoints that need to be integrated include: logo, taglines, worldwide advertising, websites, events and trade shows, and customer service interactions.

WHO BRANDS B2B?

Building a strong corporate brand requires leadership from the top. For B2B companies, there is often the added challenge of an internal culture that has not historically been focused on a customer- or market-focused perspective. In this case, it may be helpful to bring in an outside partner or to place managers who are newer to the company in a leading role for brand management; their fresh perspective can help B2B companies see how their brand may be perceived outside of their own walls.

Building a strong corporate brand requires everyone to be involved. Organizational alignment is key. Leaders must communicate the brand vision internally throughout the company. Rather than taking a 'brand police' approach, brand managers should provide tools and resources that will make it easier for every division of the company to align with brand standards than to continue to communicate in an unintegrated fashion.

B2B BRANDS CHANGE

Corporate brands must reflect the business strategies of their companies; this is no less true for B2B companies than B2C. But business strategies change over time. A B2B company may move into new categories, form new alliances, or acquire or spin-off new divisions. The company's constituents and customer segments may change. So the corporate brand needs to be flexible in a way that a single product brand might not need to be. It needs to be able to retain its core brand promise while adapting to an evolving business strategy.

SAP: BUILDING A GLOBAL B2B BRAND

The Center on Global Brand Leadership at Columbia Business School has worked with a variety of businesses to address key strategic issues in building and managing their brands. One of the Center's leading sponsors and strategic partners has been SAP, the global manufacturer of enterprise software for businesses worldwide.

Between 2000 and 2005, a major global initiative at SAP was undertaken to build the corporate brand. During this period, market perceptions of the brand shifted from significantly hampering the company's performance to bolstering significant year-over-year growth worldwide. Independent measurements of SAP's brand value showed a growth of nearly $3 billion.

The story of how SAP's corporate brand was rebuilt in this time period is instructive for many other B2B companies seeking to build strong corporate brands. It is particularly relevant because SAP faced a variety of challenges common to B2B companies seeking to build strong brands.

Before its rebranding initiative, SAP suffered from inconsistent and ineffective communications. The perception of the brand was worse than the reality of what the company offered in terms of product quality and innovation. SAP is a large global company; before 2000, it had a very decentralized communications structure, which could only be partly changed in its reorganization. SAP was steeped in an engineering-driven history and culture, to which a consumer-marketing or brand focus was quite alien. And yet, with leadership from the top, and effective brand management processes, a broad organizational re-alignment around the brand was undertaken that led to impressive financial results.

THE CHALLENGE FOR SAP

At the start of 2000, Hasso Plattner and Henning Kagermann, co-CEOs of software giant SAP AG, realized their firm needed new direction for its brand. SAP's global messaging – from advertising, to logo, to website – was sprawling, inconsistent, and confusing. In the hot new marketplace of the Internet, SAP was seen as being left behind. The buzz in the press was not on SAP.

The reality of SAP was much more impressive than its perceptions. The German-based company, founded in 1972, was already the leading enterprise software provider in every major market, with sales in more than 50 countries worldwide. SAP was the world's largest enterprise software company and the world's third-largest independent software supplier overall, with 12 500 customers and 25 000 software installations, predominantly within large companies.

SAP had a long history of market success, based on innovative product development. Founded by five engineers from IBM, SAP fostered an organizational culture that was highly product-driven. Its first product in 1972 was a real-time data processing software which was later named R/1. By the end of the decade, examination of SAP's IBM database and dialog control systems led to the birth of its big next-generation product, SAP R/2. In the 1990s, a new product using the client-server model and the uniform appearance of graphical interfaces was developed. It was named R/3. By its 25th anniversary in

Source: SAP Global Marketing, images provided by the company to the author.

Figure 19.1   Local SAP advertising, 1999–2000

1997, the company employed nearly 13 000 people, with foreign sales accounting for the majority of customers. In 1998, SAP was listed on the New York Stock Exchange for the first time. As the company grew, SAP's reputation was built on its products and its heritage of market leadership and reliability.

By contrast, branding and marketing had never been a strong focus of the company's culture. Sales people and other employees spoke in complex jargon that often confused outsiders. Marketing had grown into a decentralized function, organized at the country level. Multiple advertising agencies produced independent local campaigns with inconsistent company and product messaging, and advertising was extremely product-focused (see Figure 19.1). Inside and outside of the company, there was no consistent way to answer the question, 'What does SAP do?'

WEAK PERCEPTIONS AND BRAND IMAGE

In 2000, marketing fell under the board area of Hasso Plattner. It had become clear to him that strong marketing and brand management were key to maintaining the company's

Source: SAP Global Marketing, images provided by the company to the author.

Figure 19.2   Multiple SAP logos

position in the marketplace. SAP was perceived as a latecomer to the Internet. The marketplace had changed drastically; SAP found itself fighting for share with new 'best-of-breed' Internet vendors such as I2 and Siebel. The Internet had led to a wave of hot new products, and companies of all sizes were entering the market looking for enterprise software. *The Wall Street Journal* wrote: 'SAP was late to recognize the e-commerce boom, even as the Internet was transforming every aspect of its business.' *BusinessWeek* asked, 'What's sapping SAP? . . . It has been left out of a flurry of deals.'

It was in the face of this pressure that the company's new Internet-enabled suite of products, mySAP.com, was launched. The new product suite was strong. But there was concern that the company itself was viewed as passé. In light of hot new competitive products, this perception was so feared, that the decision was made to replace the corporate brand altogether with the new product brand. It was believed that this would be a strong signal to the market that the company was part of the Internet Generation. A sweeping overhaul in 1999 led to the replacement of the SAP logo with the new mySAP.com logo on the company's website, brochures, product packaging, vehicles and signage. By allowing a new product line to stand for the entire company, this change put SAP's own brand equity at risk. It also caused confusion. When the world looked for the SAP company website, viewers were redirected to www.mySAP.com. Instead of finding SAP, the corporation, they found themselves at what appeared to be a product website.

SAP also faced other branding problems. Its logo appeared in a profusion of variations across the world (see Figure 19.2). Branding taglines were similarly numerous and

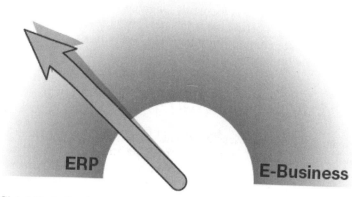

ERP   E-Business

Source: SAP Global Marketing, images provided by the company to the author.

Figure 19.5   The 'SAP-ometer'

an e-business player. 'For the last year, the "SAP-ometer" had been swinging wildly,' said Homlish, 'from the old image of the enterprise provider, to the new "Internet-friendly" image of mySAP.com. I didn't want another wild swing in the brand. If we were going to change the perception, it would need to be evolutionary, not revolutionary. We needed a credible brand promise' (see Figure 19.5).

Homlish looked to center the SAP brand promise around the company's proven strengths. These strengths became obvious through customer feedback. 'When I spoke with customer executives, I saw a common theme,' recalled Homlish. 'SAP was considered a mission-critical part of almost every great company on the planet.' The brand promise selected was that SAP turns businesses into best-run businesses. A tagline was needed to convey this promise. However, given Homlish's concern about sudden changes in the brand, it was decided that the new tagline would evolve through three distinct stages.

The tagline would begin with a positioning that had much in common with the Internet image of 1999. The three stages planned for the tagline were:

- The Best-Run e-Businesses Run mySAP.com
- The Best-Run e-Businesses Run SAP
- The Best-Run Businesses Run SAP

This evolutionary approach, which took place over 18 months, enabled the SAP positioning to be relevant over time, evolve as the business changed, and stay true to SAP's core.

The tagline was just the first of several elements of the brand identity that needed to change. SAP's brand architecture was redesigned to give the SAP brand its own identity. The logo for mySAP.com, with its bright multi-colored lettering (more reminiscent of mass consumer brands such as eBay and Yahoo! than a B2B firm) was pared down to a simple white 'SAP' on blue backdrop. The new brand architecture clearly placed the SAP brand as the master brand, with the product sub-brands (mySAP CRM, etc.) sitting under it (see Figures 19.6 and 19.7).

Source: SAP Global Marketing, images provided by the company to the author.

Figure 19.3   'The City of e' campaign

constantly shifting, from 'We Can Change Your Business Perspective' (1997) to 'A Better Return on Information' (1997–1998) to 'The City of e' (1999) to 'The Time of New Management' (2000) to 'You Can. It Does.' (2000) (see Figure 19.3). Advertising campaigns in different markets resulted in inconsistent positioning for the company. The company was represented on the Internet by one global website, more than 30 local country sites, and numerous subsidiary company sites – with a total of 9000 web pages with no consistent governance, design or content creation across them (see Figure 19.4). The result was a weak and unclear brand promise. The challenge, as Plattner identified it, was how to transform SAP from a product-driven company into a market-driven company. To rebuild the SAP brand, he would need to change the mindset of the entire organization.

THE GLOBAL MARKETING OFFICE

Plattner began by radically changing the way marketing was led and organized within the company. In picking a leader for the new marketing mission, he broke several taboos: going outside the company, outside the software industry, and outside Germany. He hired an American, Martin Homlish, from Sony, to serve as SAP's new Global Chief Marketing Officer. Many were surprised by the appointment of Homlish, the man who launched the hit Sony Playstation, to lead marketing at a traditional B2B company. But Plattner was looking for a new vision.

At a board meeting in the Spring of 2000, Plattner and Homlish presented guiding principles for the repositioning of SAP. The brand would have a clear, relevant promise for

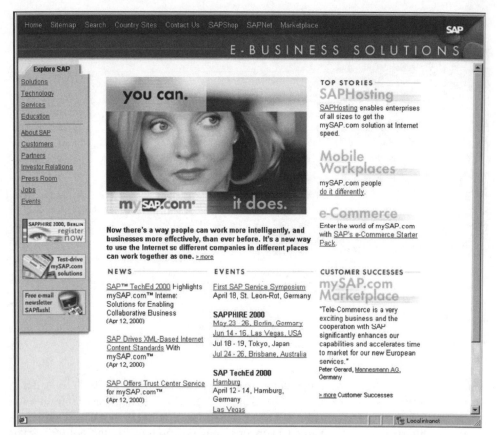

Homlish faced three large challenges in repositioning the brand for a glo
ation: communicating the brand consistently, aligning the organization, an
brand flexible enough to support changing business objectives within a dynan
These three challenges are common to many B2B companies of SAP's size,
manage their corporate brands.

CREATING A GLOBAL BRAND: FIRST STEPS

'The first thing we did was stop everything', said Homlish of his arrival at SAI
further confusion in the market and loss of the SAP brand's equity, all adver
stopped globally until a coherent strategy could be implemented. Almost im
after Homlish's arrival in early 2000, SAP held its annual conference, SAPP
Berlin, Germany for customers, press and analysts. Homlish observed that tl
response was poor.

Homlish's first priority was to send a signal to investors and the press about
North American SAPPHIRE conference was scheduled to be held a few weeks la
Vegas, Nevada, and Homlish believed that this event provided the perfect oppor
establish credibility for the unveiling of the new global messaging. In the planni
ment for the event, Homlish and his team stated a central goal – that attendees sho
thinking: 'SAP gets it'. Homlish and his team got to work transforming the event
the new face of the company, to make it apparent that the former engineerin
company had a new marketing focus and capabilities to match. When the lights
in Las Vegas, SAPPHIRE had focused messaging and a completely new look. It w
tech and cutting-edge – the image visitors would expect to see from a truly cuttin
technology company. The response was powerful. After SAPPHIRE was over, Hc
goal was echoed by analysts, 'SAP gets it. SAP has honed a solid, well structured, at
to understand Internet message for its users and the world' (Bittner, 2000).

Immediately afterwards, Homlish started to assemble the team that would le
branding effort for SAP worldwide. A new group was formed under his leadership
Global Marketing. Many company leaders expected the global operation to be ba
Germany, but Plattner challenged this assumption. He believed SAP had been ope
internationally, but acting like a German company. Now SAP needed to become a
global company, a company that would compete aggressively in worldwide markets,
cially North America. It was decided that SAP Global Marketing would be based
Walldorf, Germany, but in the center of media and marketing activity, New York C

NEW BRAND POSITIONING, LOGO AND TAGLINE

With his team in place, Homlish was ready to create a new brand positioning for SAP.
what would the brand stand for? The answer seemed clear: SAP was passionate about
success of its customers and was dedicated to enabling this success through world-c
technology.

Homlish was worried about moving too fast. Over the past year, SAP's messaging h
shifted radically from that of an enterprise resource planning (ERP) provider to that

Figure 19.4 mySAP.com Website, 2000

customers; the promise would be communicated consistently; it would be delivered not just in advertising but at every customer touchpoint; and the brand promise would have total alignment with the company's business strategy. Research indicated the brand possessed some very positive attributes that were consistent across all audiences – customers, prospects, analysts and employees. More than anything, the new positioning would need to make SAP relevant to its customers and clearly convey the value of SAP's products and services. This new positioning would not manufacture hype, but would tell the truth about SAP.

In 2000, Homlish had a mandate for dramatic change as the new Global Chief Marketing Officer. He knew SAP had the potential for a great brand. 'I saw SAP as a marketer's dream. We already had great products, a strong history of innovation, and a loyal customer base – all we needed to do was transform marketing.' Based on the company's history, it is easy to see how SAP had gone so far on the strength of its products. SAP transformed business, enabling companies across the world to leverage technology to improve efficiency, accountability, visibility, and ultimately, profitability of their businesses. Customers knew the value they received from SAP.

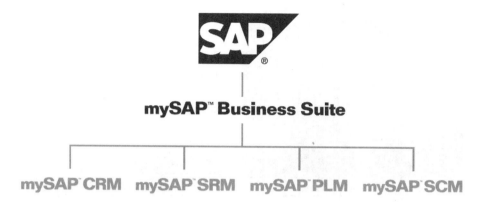

Source: SAP Global Marketing, images provided by the company to the author.

Figure 19.6   SAP brand architecture

Source: SAP Global Marketing, images provided by the company to the author.

Figure 19.7   SAP logo evolution

These changes were introduced when SAP's websites were dramatically consolidated. The original number of web pages was reduced by two-thirds, and various country sites were aligned with the new brand positioning and image. Most of the content now came directly from translations of the global site, www.SAP.com. Going forward, further changes to the global site would trigger automatic updates to the local sites.

NEW GLOBAL CAMPAIGN

With the brand promise, architecture and visual identity in place, Homlish felt the time was right for a global branding campaign. The two overriding aims would be simplicity of message and integration across all communications. To help achieve this goal, SAP hired a single agency, Ogilvy & Mather, to handle all advertising campaigns worldwide.

'At the time we launched this campaign for SAP, the marketplace was filled with hype about the promise of technology and how it would change business as we know it', says Shelly Lazarus, Chairman and CEO of Ogilvy & Mather Worldwide. 'But what we learned about SAP was that this great company was in fact already doing amazing things for its customers. The simple reality that the "best-run businesses run SAP" became the whole expression for the brand – a single, powerful idea that continues to differentiate and provide leadership in this dynamic environment.'

Source: SAP Global Marketing, images provided by the company to the author.

Figure 19.8   *'New, new economy' campaign, 2000–2001*

SAP and Ogilvy & Mather developed a two-part global advertising campaign in 2000. The first part carried a theme that was ahead of its time: 'Welcome to the new, new economy – you know, the profitable one' (see Figure 19.8).

'In the midst of a dot.com economy, traditional paths to profitability were being neglected in favor of "the next big thing"', says Susan Popper, Senior Vice President of Integrated Marketing Communications at SAP. 'SAP's advantage was that we could offer customers bottom-line results and the long-standing credibility of our company. We used our campaign to drive this home.' The stylish black-and-white campaign turned heads for bucking the fads of the day and – months later – for having presaged the bursting of the dot.com bubble in spring 2001. It ran in 41 countries worldwide.

Soon after, the second part of the campaign was launched. According to Popper: 'Where the "new, new economy" ads had presented the brand promise, the "momentum" ads presented the proof: the best-run businesses really do run SAP' (see Figure 19.9).

The ads launched worldwide, leveraging the power of SAP's client base by showcasing simple headlines based on the brand tagline: 'Lufthansa runs SAP.' 'Adidas runs SAP.' 'BMW runs SAP.' Oversized posters in airports heavily trafficked by corporate decision-makers helped to globalize the SAP brand.

The 'momentum' ads were designed to appeal to any company by showing that SAP could help them become a best-run business. Like Nike's 'Just Do It' campaign, the ads gave the customer something to aspire to. In its 2001 article on 'The 100 Top Brands',

Source: SAP Global Marketing, images provided by the company to the author.

Figure 19.9 *'Momentum' campaign, 2001–present*

BusinessWeek announced that 'SAP has delivered on theme: The best-run e-businesses run SAP.'

A NEED FOR ALIGNMENT

In re-branding a large company like SAP, a global advertising campaign can be like the tip of an iceberg. It is the part that is most visible to the outside world. But, achieving consistent communication of the brand requires a much larger infrastructure change below the surface. Where a global advertising campaign requires executive buy-in, driving the brand through communications worldwide requires the involvement of many local field organizations. Aligning the organization was essential if SAP was to truly communicate its brand consistently. Homlish knew there would be many challenges to global integration for SAP. A multitude of languages, different leaderships and conflicting priorities can all hamper efforts.

To integrate all communications with the new brand, SAP Global Marketing developed a series of tools which grew between 2001 and 2005, offering global field offices the promise of automated assistance in their marketing needs, and in doing so, bringing regional marketing into alignment. Regional offices were not forced to adopt standards from SAP Global Marketing. Instead, a range of incentives were used to encourage adoption of Global Marketing's rules and syndicated tools.

'We drove change through alignment,' says Homlish, 'working with stakeholders across SAP. This approach takes more time, vs. strict "command and control", but ultimately, it results in wider acceptance.'

ONE VOICE, ONE LOOK AND FEEL

In a company as large and diverse as SAP, it is not uncommon for differences to exist in the way local business units communicate. The first major tool for aligning the organization was a communications guide called 'One Voice', an online resource, which was available to every employee through SAP's Intranet. It included information on approved names and trademarks, as well as key messages and positioning for each of SAP's solutions and products, all in language that customers understand. Its contents are continually updated by an inter-departmental team in SAP Global Marketing that sets policy, publishes the tool, and edits every piece of global collateral and web content before publication.

In addition, a suite of online tools was developed to begin to align communications at every customer contact point with the brand. Because sales and demand-generation are primarily local activities, local offices would need to be able to adapt these communications. These 'syndication' tools began with a Sales and Marketing Asset Repository Toolset (SMART). The simple vision behind SMART was to deliver sales and marketing content and assets to the field offices in a consistent fashion, helping sales and marketing employees to find the content they needed efficiently. Users could rely on finding finished assets they knew would be relevant and tested, and adaptable to meet local needs.

The capabilities of SMART were further enhanced with the development of the Sales and Marketing Intranet (SMI). SMI included SMART, along with One Voice, branding standards, an image library, customer brochures, industry reports, BlackBerry tools, and online demos for customers. In total, these tools offered a range of resources to help customer-facing employees do their jobs more easily and efficiently; at the same time, they served to align the content, image and branding of extremely diverse communications to customers across a very large global corporation.

A BRANDING CULTURE

Employees worldwide were enlisted as 'brand stewards' to promote the brand both inside and outside the organization. At the January 2001 Field Kick-Off Meetings, Homlish made presentations to the North American and EMEA-based field employees. This was the biggest internal launch of the SAP brand. 'We needed to instill "SAP pride" back into the field organization', says Léo Apotheker, President of Customer Solutions and Operations for SAP, and member of the executive board. 'The brand re-launch reminded all of our employees why we were such a great company. It reinforced our history of excellence and our dedication to our customers. It reiterated that the competition was and should be afraid of us, that SAP stands for all the right things.'

To further build alignment across the company, SAP Global Marketing created 'country champions' to roll out each campaign, as a way of ensuring support from each region. The approach focused on change management through 'doing, not telling'. Both Germany and the US were used as champions in the development of new model marketing programs before they were translated for roll-out worldwide. This key involvement of the local field office as a co-developer alongside SAP Global Marketing helped build compliance around global messaging.

Homlish's goal was to help every employee understand the shared goals of the brand and how to express them to an external audience often unfamiliar with the sophisticated terminology of the industry and products. 'When I arrived at SAP and would ask questions about our company and our products, I would get a lot of jargon', says Homlish. 'I called it SAP-anese.' To address this issue, a pocket-sized 'brand card' was distributed worldwide, offering employees a graspable guide to the core positioning, personality and attributes of the brand. Afterwards, brand workshops were conducted at offices around the globe, and brand ambassadors were selected to champion the brand within their local organization. 'Today, if you ask an SAP employee at a cocktail party, "What does SAP do?", they can tell you – "We help every customer become a best-run business".'

BRANDING THE CUSTOMER EXPERIENCE

To deliver on their brand, companies need not only to communicate it consistently, but also to deliver against the brand's promise at every touchpoint and every interaction of the customer experience. SAP adopted this philosophy, bringing the brand promise to life by demonstrating that the company was a best-run business itself.

A great example of this can be seen in the North American market. 'When I arrived at SAP,' says Bill McDermott, President of SAP America, 'I saw that "best-run businesses" was a very big idea.' McDermott used the brand promise as a focal point in developing a vision for a customer-focused organization. SAP America was reorganized into regional offices to empower those closest to the customer. McDermott formed a new Value Engineering Business Team to leverage SAP's industry knowledge by providing compelling business case studies for new prospects. This group is tasked with telling not only the technology story but also the bottom-line impact of becoming a best-run business with SAP's partnership. The external results of this internal change have been dramatic. Since McDermott's arrival, the company posted 13 consecutive quarters of double-digit growth through 2005, and increased profitability.

Much of this success came from a synergy of brand leadership and local leadership. 'At the same time that Marty Homlish was working to transform the brand into the midmarket, I was working to transform the North American Field Organization towards a push into midmarket', says McDermott. 'Our two groups were in total alignment, and you could see the results we achieved.'

Another key aspect of branding the customer experience is to look not only at SAP's interaction with the customer, but also at the customer's interaction with SAP's products. SAP worked to fine-tune the usability and design of its products to meet the brand promise and demonstrate a focus on the customer experience. A Customer Labs group was developed to improve user interaction with products, and a Design Services Team in the office of the CEO was formed to ensure new product development was driven outside-in, with market insight from customers, competitors and market forecasting.

LEVERAGING THE BRAND FOR CHANGING BUSINESS OBJECTIVES

'The true test of whether SAP has built a strong and flexible brand,' says Henning Kagermann, CEO of SAP, 'is how well it can be leveraged against today's business objectives, as well as in changing market conditions of the future.'

In November 2000, as the first ads of the 'new, new economy' campaign were launched, a meeting of 50 top executives was called for 2001 planning. Over two days, a broad range of business objectives were discussed for SAP's businesses worldwide. But to focus the use of resources spent on the brand, Homlish asked for five top business objectives for the year. 'If everything is a priority, then nothing is a priority', Homlish says. 'SAP has an enormous breadth of products and services. It was critical to identify the key areas of focus.' At the end of the meeting, the top executives signed a paper which summarized what came to be known as 'The Big Five'. As a set of marketing priorities for the company, the Big Five became a strategic driver for annual planning and were used to help focus the entire company, beginning with worldwide executive alignment.

'Business objectives evolve,' says Kagermann, 'and a powerful brand has to be flexible enough to stay constant at its core, while adding value to a changing marketplace and shifting corporate strategy. As our company continues to grow, the SAP brand consistently contributes to our success.'

SAP's rapid growth in 2000–2002 meant the company needed to seek opportunities in new customer segments. By 2003, competitors had begun courting the small and medium enterprise segment (SME) for enterprise software. SAP, traditionally seen as a large enterprise player, put a stake in the ground in this segment with new offerings sold through two primary channels: SAP Business One and mySAP All-in-One.

But SAP was aware of the obstacles it faced among midmarket customers. On the positive side, the brand was already perceived by midmarket prospects as 'the Rolls Royce' of its category. SAP's traditional strengths – reliability, expertise, innovation, ethics and product quality – provided credibility with midmarket customers. However, there were negative perceptions among midmarket customers as well; SAP was seen as too big, too expensive, too complex, and difficult to install.

Since there was little awareness that SAP had an SME offering, SAP started with bold, brand-building ads to announce SAP as a player in this market, with copy such as 'Finally, powerful software for the Fortune 500 000' (see Figure 19.10). The campaign built upon the visual style of the brand campaign, with its signature typeface and yellow color. But the bold graphic approach, and somewhat cheeky headlines, created a separate and more accessible personality for SME prospects.

The challenge was to overcome the prospect's barriers to consideration by showing that midmarket companies didn't have to wait to become best-run businesses – they could do it now. One series of ads directly tackled the negative perceptions of the brand by showing SAP's small and midmarket customers how 'Companies that thought they couldn't afford SAP run SAP'. 'Companies that need it now run SAP.' 'Companies that were just ideas yesterday run SAP.' Select midmarket customers were also incorporated into the ongoing 'momentum' campaign: 'Oakley runs SAP.' 'The North Face runs SAP.' 'Mont Blanc runs SAP.'

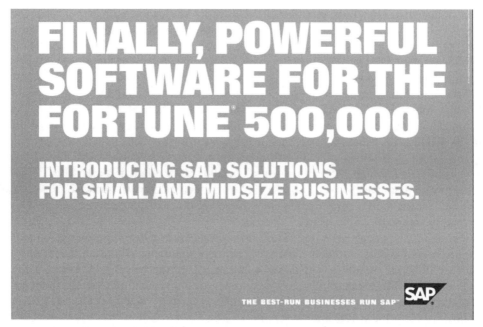

Figure 19.10   SME campaign, 2003

SAP research also showed another opportunity for making the brand relevant: mid-market prospects wanted software providers to have strong knowledge of their particular industry. However, they also wanted to maintain the strengths they viewed as unique to their individual businesses. The branding campaign in 2005 therefore focused on leveraging SAP's extensive experience in diverse industries to show proof of its brand promise: 'We know business fundamentals, and we know what makes each business fundamentally different'. Focusing on 27 vertical industries, the ads show how SAP helps companies become best-run businesses, whether they are in healthcare or high tech, retail or railways.

THE END RESULT

Five years after Homlish's launch of SAP Global Marketing in 2000, SAP's brand has powerful results to show for the company. According to *BusinessWeek*'s annual brand rankings, the value of the brand rose $2.86 billion, or 46 per cent, between 2000 and 2005, and in 2005 was ranked at number 36. That placed SAP above established brands such as Apple, Volkswagen and Starbucks. It was the only software company on the list to gain brand value for five years in a row.

At the same time, financial results for the firm have been impressive across the board. SAP's brand turnaround has paralleled powerful growth. In the first two years of the rebranding, revenue grew 43 per cent (1999–2001); in six years, the company's profit grew 202 per cent (1999–2005).

SAP also maintained its position as market leader worldwide, with 21 per cent global market share in the enterprise application software market. Amongst its peer group, SAP's market share has steadily grown to 62 per cent. In addition, growth in the mid-market segment helped to fuel a 255 per cent growth in software installations worldwide, from 25 000 in 1999 to 88 700 in 2004.

Press and industry observers also took notice of the SAP brand and its success story. In 2004, Marty Homlish was named 'Chief Marketing Officer of the Year' by the CMO Council and *BusinessWeek*, and *BtoB Magazine* named him a 'Top Marketer' in its 'Best of 2004' issue. Advertising and communications awards from 2002 to 2005 have included *Forbes* 'Best of the Web', the Web Marketing Association Web Award, and *Adweek Magazine*'s Technology Marketing Award. In 2001, SAP Global Marketing's office in Greenwich Village received the *BusinessWeek*/Architectural Record Award for design that achieves business objectives, namely fostering a creative collaborative culture in SAP's new global marketing hub.

Perhaps the best news came from SAP's own customers in a 2005 Stratascope Inc. study. An analysis of publicly-available financial results of companies listed on the NASDAQ and NYSE stock exchanges found that companies that run SAP are 32 per cent more profitable than those that don't run SAP, and deliver 28 per cent more return on capital. A powerful illustration of the brand's unique claim: the best-run businesses run SAP (see Figures 19.11 to 19.16 and Tables 19.1 and 19.2).

CONCLUSION

The story of SAP shows that B2B corporate brands create real value for their shareholders. Branding is not something that can be safely forgotten by B2B in favor of an old-fashioned focus on engineering and product quality that relegates the customer to the sideline.

B2B corporate brands require a promise that is relevant and clear to customers. These brands need to be aligned with business strategy, and flexible to change as that strategy changes. They need to be communicated consistently, often across a vast organization – which requires tools and processes for encouraging global alignment.

B2B corporate brands require leadership from the very top, and buy-in from everyone in the organization. Successful B2B brand leadership can produce results that are profitable for the company, meaningful for customers, and inspiring for employees. Clearly, brand management is no longer a key business practice for B2C companies alone.

NOTE

1. This chapter is based in part on the case study 'SAP: Building a global technology brand' by Bernd H. Schmitt and David Rogers.

REFERENCE

Bittnes, Michael (2000), 'SAP gets it', *AMR Research*, 15 June, www.amrrearchpartners.com/Content/View.asp?pmillid=6915.

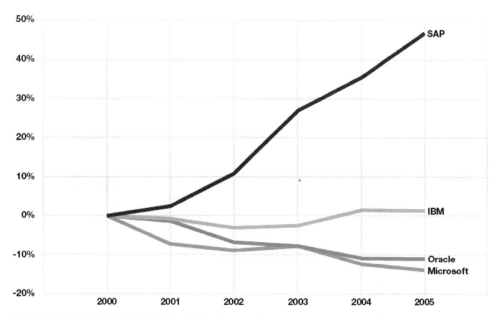

Brand Value $US Million						Overall Change
	2000	2001	2002	2003	2004	2005	2000–2005
Microsoft	70 197	65 068	64 091	65 174	61 372	59 941	(10 256)
IBM	53 184	52 752	51 188	51 767	53 791	53 376	192
Oracle	–	12 224	11 510	11 263	10 935	10 887	(1 337)
SAP	6 136	6 307	6 775	7 714	8 324	9 006	2 870

Source: Business Week 'Top 100 Global Brands' Study.

Figure 19.11   Absolute brand value growth (2000–2005)

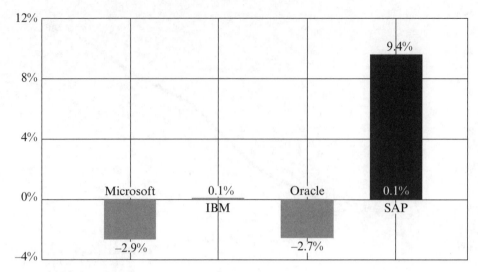

Source: SAP Global Marketing, images provided by the company to the author.

Figure 19.12   Compounded annual growth rate (CAGR)

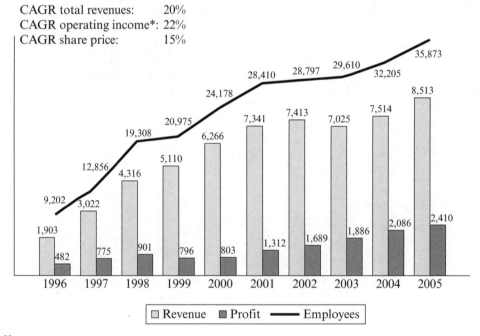

CAGR total revenues: 20%
CAGR operating income*: 22%
CAGR share price: 15%

Notes:
Revenue and profit shown in €M.
* Pro forma.

Source: SAP Analysis.

Figure 19.13   SAP's performance in the last 10 years

Core Enterprise Application Software Market
Rolling 4 Quarters Based on Software Revenue

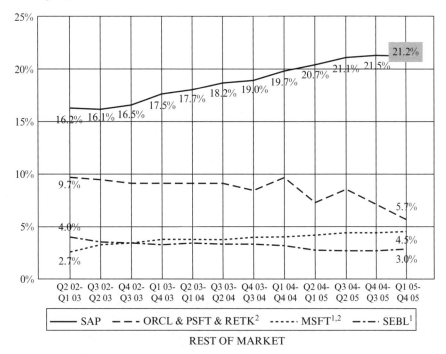

REST OF MARKET

68.7% 67.4% 68.1% 68.0% 66.7% 66.2% 65.6% 65.6% 64.0% 65.5% 65.2% 64.7%

Notes:
1) Forecast by Company Data and Financial Analysts (SEBL, MSFT) and SAP internal estimates.
2) Fiscal year is not calendar year – comparison based on most recent quarter (e.g. SAP Q1 vs. Oracle Q3).

Source: SAP analysis based on company data and financial analysts' estimates.

Figure 19.14   SAP worldwide market share

Rolling 4 Quarters Based on Software Revenue

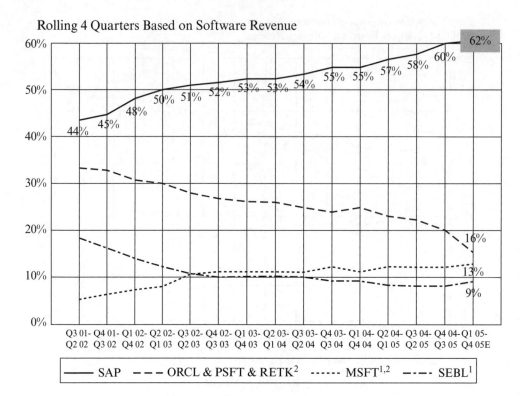

SAP —— ORCL & PSFT & RETK[2] - - -   MSFT[1,2] ······   SEBL[1] -·-·

Notes:
1) Forecast by company data and financial analysts' estimates.
2) Fiscal year is not calendar year – comparison based on most recent quarter (e.g. SAP Q1 vs. Oracle Q3).

Source: SAP analysis based on company data and financial analysts' estimates.

Figure 19.15   Customers and installations

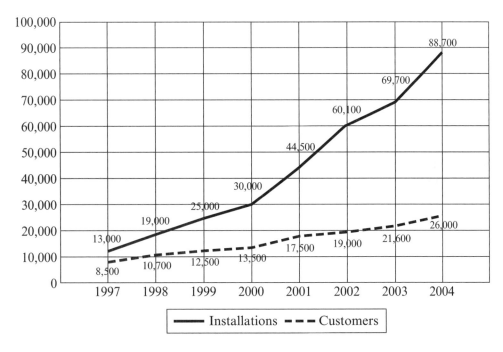

Source: SAP Global Marketing, images provided by the company to the author.

Figure 19.16 SAP worldwide peer group share

Table 19.1 SAP consolidated balance sheets

Balance Sheet Summary (In thousands)	12/31/1999
Fixed assets	€1 523 976
Short-term assets	2 966 945
Deferred Taxes	284 293
Prepaid Expenses & Deferred Charges	51 675
Total Assets	€4 826 889
Shareholders' Equity	€2 559 355
Minority Interests	8 737
Special Reserves for Capital Investment Subsidies & Allowances	166
Reserves and Accrued Liabilities	1 278 149
Other Liabilities	670 498
Deferred Income	309 984
Total Shareholders' Equity & Liabilities	€4 826 889

Source: SAP Annual Report (1999).

Table 19.2   SAP consolidated balance sheets

Balance Sheet Summary (in thousands)	12/31/2005
Fixed Assets	€2 395 000
Current Assets	6 346 000
Deferred Taxes	217 000
Prepaid Expenses & Deferred Charges	87 000
Total Assets	€9 045 000
Shareholders' Equity	€5 783 000
Minority Interest	8 000
Reserves and Accrued Liabilities	2 004 000
Other Liabilities	846 000
Deferred Income	404 000
Total Shareholders' Equity & Liabilities	€9 045 000

Note: Figures are preliminary and unaudited.

Source: Investor Relations, www.SAP.com.

Index

£120.00

175905

UNIVERSITY COLLEGE BIRMINGHAM
COLLEGE LIBRARY, SUMMER ROW
BIRMINGHAM. B3 1JB
Tel: (0121) 243 0055

	DATE OF RETURN	
2/7/10.		

Please remember to return on time or pay the fine

Source: SAP Global Marketing, images provided by the company to the author.

Figure 19.3 *'The City of e' campaign*

constantly shifting, from 'We Can Change Your Business Perspective' (1997) to 'A Better Return on Information' (1997–1998) to 'The City of e' (1999) to 'The Time of New Management' (2000) to 'You Can. It Does.' (2000) (see Figure 19.3). Advertising campaigns in different markets resulted in inconsistent positioning for the company. The company was represented on the Internet by one global website, more than 30 local country sites, and numerous subsidiary company sites – with a total of 9000 web pages with no consistent governance, design or content creation across them (see Figure 19.4). The result was a weak and unclear brand promise. The challenge, as Plattner identified it, was how to transform SAP from a product-driven company into a market-driven company. To rebuild the SAP brand, he would need to change the mindset of the entire organization.

THE GLOBAL MARKETING OFFICE

Plattner began by radically changing the way marketing was led and organized within the company. In picking a leader for the new marketing mission, he broke several taboos: going outside the company, outside the software industry, and outside Germany. He hired an American, Martin Homlish, from Sony, to serve as SAP's new Global Chief Marketing Officer. Many were surprised by the appointment of Homlish, the man who launched the hit Sony Playstation, to lead marketing at a traditional B2B company. But Plattner was looking for a new vision.

   At a board meeting in the Spring of 2000, Plattner and Homlish presented guiding principles for the repositioning of SAP. The brand would have a clear, relevant promise for

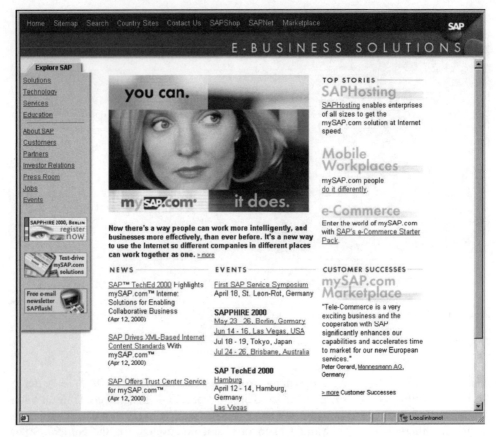

Source: SAP Global Marketing, images provided by the company to the author.

Figure 19.4   mySAP.com Website, 2000

customers; the promise would be communicated consistently; it would be delivered not just in advertising but at every customer touchpoint; and the brand promise would have total alignment with the company's business strategy. Research indicated the brand possessed some very positive attributes that were consistent across all audiences – customers, prospects, analysts and employees. More than anything, the new positioning would need to make SAP relevant to its customers and clearly convey the value of SAP's products and services. This new positioning would not manufacture hype, but would tell the truth about SAP.

In 2000, Homlish had a mandate for dramatic change as the new Global Chief Marketing Officer. He knew SAP had the potential for a great brand. 'I saw SAP as a marketer's dream. We already had great products, a strong history of innovation, and a loyal customer base – all we needed to do was transform marketing.' Based on the company's history, it is easy to see how SAP had gone so far on the strength of its products. SAP transformed business, enabling companies across the world to leverage technology to improve efficiency, accountability, visibility, and ultimately, profitability of their businesses. Customers knew the value they received from SAP.

Homlish faced three large challenges in repositioning the brand for a global organization: communicating the brand consistently, aligning the organization, and creating a brand flexible enough to support changing business objectives within a dynamic industry. These three challenges are common to many B2B companies of SAP's size, seeking to manage their corporate brands.

CREATING A GLOBAL BRAND: FIRST STEPS

'The first thing we did was stop everything', said Homlish of his arrival at SAP. To avoid further confusion in the market and loss of the SAP brand's equity, all advertising was stopped globally until a coherent strategy could be implemented. Almost immediately after Homlish's arrival in early 2000, SAP held its annual conference, SAPPHIRE, in Berlin, Germany for customers, press and analysts. Homlish observed that the overall response was poor.

Homlish's first priority was to send a signal to investors and the press about SAP. The North American SAPPHIRE conference was scheduled to be held a few weeks later in Las Vegas, Nevada, and Homlish believed that this event provided the perfect opportunity to establish credibility for the unveiling of the new global messaging. In the planning document for the event, Homlish and his team stated a central goal – that attendees should leave thinking: 'SAP gets it'. Homlish and his team got to work transforming the event to reflect the new face of the company, to make it apparent that the former engineering-driven company had a new marketing focus and capabilities to match. When the lights came up in Las Vegas, SAPPHIRE had focused messaging and a completely new look. It was high-tech and cutting-edge – the image visitors would expect to see from a truly cutting-edge technology company. The response was powerful. After SAPPHIRE was over, Homlish's goal was echoed by analysts, 'SAP gets it. SAP has honed a solid, well structured, and easy to understand Internet message for its users and the world' (Bittner, 2000).

Immediately afterwards, Homlish started to assemble the team that would lead the branding effort for SAP worldwide. A new group was formed under his leadership – SAP Global Marketing. Many company leaders expected the global operation to be based in Germany, but Plattner challenged this assumption. He believed SAP had been operating internationally, but acting like a German company. Now SAP needed to become a truly global company, a company that would compete aggressively in worldwide markets, especially North America. It was decided that SAP Global Marketing would be based not in Walldorf, Germany, but in the center of media and marketing activity, New York City.

NEW BRAND POSITIONING, LOGO AND TAGLINE

With his team in place, Homlish was ready to create a new brand positioning for SAP. But what would the brand stand for? The answer seemed clear: SAP was passionate about the success of its customers and was dedicated to enabling this success through world-class technology.

Homlish was worried about moving too fast. Over the past year, SAP's messaging had shifted radically from that of an enterprise resource planning (ERP) provider to that of

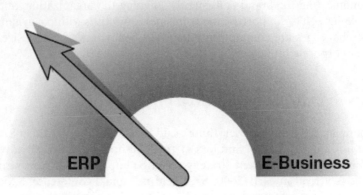

ERP   E-Business

Source: SAP Global Marketing, images provided by the company to the author.

Figure 19.5   The 'SAP-ometer'

an e-business player. 'For the last year, the "SAP-ometer" had been swinging wildly,' said
Homlish, 'from the old image of the enterprise provider, to the new "Internet-friendly"
image of mySAP.com. I didn't want another wild swing in the brand. If we were going to
change the perception, it would need to be evolutionary, not revolutionary. We needed a
credible brand promise' (see Figure 19.5).

Homlish looked to center the SAP brand promise around the company's proven
strengths. These strengths became obvious through customer feedback. 'When I spoke
with customer executives, I saw a common theme,' recalled Homlish. 'SAP was considered
a mission-critical part of almost every great company on the planet.' The brand promise
selected was that SAP turns businesses into best-run businesses. A tagline was needed to
convey this promise. However, given Homlish's concern about sudden changes in the
brand, it was decided that the new tagline would evolve through three distinct stages.

The tagline would begin with a positioning that had much in common with the Internet
image of 1999. The three stages planned for the tagline were:

- The Best-Run e-Businesses Run mySAP.com
- The Best-Run e-Businesses Run SAP
- The Best-Run Businesses Run SAP

This evolutionary approach, which took place over 18 months, enabled the SAP positioning to be relevant over time, evolve as the business changed, and stay true to SAP's
core.

The tagline was just the first of several elements of the brand identity that needed to
change. SAP's brand architecture was redesigned to give the SAP brand its own identity.
The logo for mySAP.com, with its bright multi-colored lettering (more reminiscent of
mass consumer brands such as eBay and Yahoo! than a B2B firm) was pared down to a
simple white 'SAP' on blue backdrop. The new brand architecture clearly placed the SAP
brand as the master brand, with the product sub-brands (mySAP CRM, etc.) sitting
under it (see Figures 19.6 and 19.7).